Texts in Computing

Volume 13

Picturing Programs

An Introduction to Computer Programming

Texts in Computing Series Editor
Ian Mackie   mackie@lix.polytechnique.fr

Picturing Programs
An Introduction to Computer Programming

Stephen Bloch [*]

[*] Math/CS Department, Adelphi University. Supported in part by NSF grant 0618543. Any opinions, findings and conclusions or recommendations expressed in this material are those of the author and do not necessarily reflect the views of the National Science Foundations (NSF).

ISBN 978-1-84890-015-8

College Publications
Scientific Director: Dov Gabbay
Managing Director: Jane Spurr
Department of Computer Science
King's College London, Strand, London WC2R 2LS, UK

http://www.collegepublications.co.uk

Original cover design by Richard Fraser
Cover produced by orchid creative   www.orchidcreative.co.uk
Printed by Lightning Source, Milton Keynes, UK

Dedicated to my wife Deborah, with whom I would have done more fun things in the past year if I hadn't been busy writing a book.

Contents

Chapter 0

Introduction

0.1 Languages and dialects

Computers don't naturally understand human languages such as English. Instead, we invent artificial languages to communicate with them. These artificial languages are typically much simpler than any human language, so it's easier to learn them than for, say, an English speaker to learn Chinese. But it's still hard work. As with any language, you'll need to learn the spelling, punctuation, grammar, vocabulary, and idioms[1] of the new language.

Among the artificial languages people use to communicate with computers (and computers use to communicate with one another) are HTML, XML, SQL, Javascript, Java, C++, Python, Scheme, PHP, Ruby, sh, awk, Racket, and hundreds more. Some of these languages are called *programming* languages because they are used mostly to write programs — that is, to teach a computer new tricks by combining the tricks it already knows.

This is a book about how to write computer programs. Pretty much every such book chooses one particular programming language. I've chosen to use a new language called Racket (which is based on a 30-year-old language named Scheme, which is based on a 50-year-old language named Lisp, which is based on an 80-year-old mathematical theory named lambda-calculus...). But it's not a Racket book; the Racket language is not the *goal*, but only a *means* towards the goal of knowing how to program.

Here's why: throughout the history of computers, the dominant languages have changed every five to ten years. (Fortran, Cobol, BASIC, PL/I, Pascal, C++, Java, Python, ...) No matter which of these languages you learn, it will probably become obsolete in a few years. If you plan to get a job as a computer programmer next month, then by all means study the language(s) used in industry right now. But if you plan to get a job programming several years from now, you'll have to learn a new language then anyway. The current school term will be better spent learning more long-lasting skills, habits, and principles: how to structure a program, what steps to take in developing a program, how to manage your time so you finish the program on time, *etc.* And if you don't plan to be a professional programmer at all, then you don't need to learn this year's "hot" language at all; you need to learn the important principles of programming, in whatever language will "get out of the way" and let you learn them.

---

[1] "Idiom" means the way a particular language is *typically* used by those who use it heavily. For example, if I said "This book is more good than any other programming book," you would know what I meant, but you would also know I wasn't a native English-speaker; a native English speaker would say "This book is *better* than any other programming book." Every language, including computer programming languages, has its own idioms.

In fact, we won't even be using very much of the Racket language. The software we use, a program named DrRacket, provides several *dialects* of Racket, intended for different kinds of users. (By way of analogy, the United States and England use different dialects of English: most of the words are the same, but sometimes the same words mean completely different things in different countries. Furthermore, an elementary school student, an economist, and a sculptor may all use English, but they use it differently, and they may use the same word to mean different things.) The "Beginning Student" dialect, in which we'll start, doesn't allow you to do some things that are technically legal Racket, but which tend to confuse beginning programmers. If you really need to do these things, you can switch to a larger dialect with a few mouse-clicks.

In this book, there will be no "black magic": nothing that you need to memorize on faith that you'll eventually understand it. On the first day, you will see just enough language to do what you need on the first day. By the end of the term, you will see just enough language to do what you need in one term. Any language feature that doesn't help to teach an important programming principle doesn't belong in this book. Most programming languages, frankly, don't allow me to do that: in C++ or Java, for example, the very first program you write requires knowing dozens of language features that won't be fully explained for months. Racket allows me to postpone irrelevant language features, and concentrate on the important stuff.

Racket is also a much simpler, more consistent language than C++, Java, or Python, so it takes much less time to learn. This, too, allows you to concentrate on the important stuff, which is how to write a program.

Again, Racket is only a means to an end. If six months after taking this course you don't remember any Racket at all but can follow the steps of solving a problem, as explained in this book, the course has been a success.

0.2   Problems, programs, and program testing

A computer program that answered only one specific question, like

> add 3 and 4

wouldn't be very useful. Most computer programs are written to be *general*, in that a *single* program can answer any one of *many similar questions*:

- add 3 and 4

- add 19 and -5

- add 102379 and -897250987

etc. Somebody writes the program to add two numbers once and for all; later on, when you *run* the program, you provide specific values like 3 and 4, and the program produces the right answer for those values. Run it again with different values, and it should produce the right answer for the new values instead.

To take a more realistic example, a word processor program is written to handle whatever words you choose to write. When you run the program, you provide specific words — a grocery list, a letter to your grandmother, the next best-selling novel — and the program responds by doing things like formatting them to fit on a page. Likewise, when you run a Web browser, you provide a specific URL for a page you want to look at; the browser program uses the network to retrieve specific words and pictures from that Web page, and then arranges these words and pictures on the screen. If you've done a lot of Web surfing, you've probably found an occasional page that showed up on the screen as nonsense; this probably means the page had some weird information that the browser wasn't written to handle correctly.

For a computer program to be considered "correct", it has to produce the right answer for *all possible* values it might be given to work on — even the weird ones. One of the important steps in writing a computer program is *testing* it to make sure it works correctly. However, since there are usually far too many possible values to test them all, we have to *choose test cases*, being careful to pick not only the easy cases but also the weird ones, so that if there's something our program doesn't handle correctly, we find out as soon as possible so we can fix it.

A program that hasn't been tested convincingly is worthless: nobody will (or should!) trust the answers it produces. Indeed, if you *tell* me you've tested the program, but don't provide me with what I need in order to test it myself, I may not trust either you *or* the program.

So one of the themes of this book will be "how to tell whether your program is correct." We'll discuss how and when to choose good test cases, as well as how to interpret patterns of correct and incorrect test cases to track down the source of the error.

0.3   Using DrRacket

This section doesn't cover any "big ideas", only the details of how to get DrRacket to work the way you need it to in this book. If you've already got DrRacket and the `picturing-programs` library installed, you can skip this section.

0.3.1   Getting DrRacket

If you haven't got the DrRacket program installed on your computer already (it usually has a red-white-and-blue icon, a circle with the Greek letter λ on it), you'll need to get it. You can download it for free, for Windows, Macintosh, and Linux, from `http://www.racket-lang.org`. This textbook assumes you have a version of DrRacket numbered 5.0.1 or higher.

0.3.2   Starting DrRacket

Once you've got DrRacket downloaded and installed, you should be able to run it by double-clicking the icon. It should open a window with a few buttons across the top, and two large panes. In the lower pane (the "Interactions Pane", where we'll be working at first) should be a welcome message like

> Welcome to DrRacket, version 5.1.
> Language: Beginning Student.
> >

(Your version number and language may be different.)

The "> " prompt is where you'll type things.

0.3.3   Choosing languages

DrRacket provides a number of different computer languages, most of which are dialects of Racket. For now, we want to be working in the "Beginning Student" language. If the welcome message says something other than "Beginning Student" (or perhaps "Beginning Student custom") after the word "Language:", do the following:

1. Pull down the "Language" menu and select "Choose Language..."

2. Find the group of languages named "How to Design Programs"

3. If necessary, click the triangle to the left of "How to Design Programs" to show its sub-headings

4. Select "Beginning Student"

5. Click "OK"

6. Quit DrRacket and start it again, and it should now say "Language: Beginning Student".

(You don't *really* have to quit and re-start DrRacket; you can get the same effect by clicking the "Run" button. However, quitting and restarting demonstrates that DrRacket remembers your choice of language from one time you use it to the next.)

0.3.4   Installing libraries

A "library", or "teachpack", is a collection of optional tools that can be added into Dr-Racket. For most of this book, we'll need one named `picturing-programs`.

Skip this section if you have DrRacket version 5.1 or later: `picturing-programs` is already installed on your computer.

If you don't already have the `picturing-programs` library, here's how to get it. You'll only have to do this once on any given computer.

1. Make sure your computer is connected to the Internet.

2. Start DrRacket.

3. From the "Language" menu, "Choose Language", then select "Use the language declared in the source".

4. Click "Run".

5. At the "> " prompt in the bottom half of the screen, type

   `(require (planet sbloch/picturing-programs:2))`

   exactly like that, with the parentheses and the slash and all. It may take a few seconds to a few minutes (most of which is updating the help system to include information on this library), but eventually you should see the message "Wrote file "picturing-programs.ss" to installed-teachpacks directory."

6. From the "Language" menu, "Choose Language", then click on to "How to Design Programs", then select "Beginning Student". Hit "Run" again.

0.3.5 Getting help

If you want to look up reference information about this library (or anything else in the language),

1. from the "Help" menu, choose "Help Desk".

2. find the search box at the top of the screen and type the name of a library or function you want to learn about. Then hit ENTER.

3. If the name is found, you'll get a list of places it appeared in the documentation. Click one of them (probably one that says it's from the "picturing-programs" library).

4. Documentation for that library or function should appear on the screen.

0.4 Textbook web site

In order to keep the cost of this book down, we've put all the illustrations in black and white. You can find colored versions of many of them, as well as corrections, updates, additions, image files, and downloadable versions of worked exercises (so you don't have to type them in by hand), *etc.* at `http://www.picturingprograms.com`.

PART I

Running and writing programs

Chapter 1

Picture this! Drawing pictures in DrRacket

As you probably know, computers are very good at doing arithmetic. But frankly, arithmetic is pretty boring. So to get our first taste of computer programming, we'll work with pictures instead. (Behind the scenes, the computer is *really* using arithmetic to control these pictures, but we don't need to worry about that for now.)

Before trying anything in this chapter, make sure you've installed DrRacket and the `picturing-programs` teachpack, as described in section 0.3.

1.1 Working with pictures

1.1.1 Importing pictures into DrRacket

The easiest ways to get a picture to work with is to copy it from somewhere: a Web page, or a file that's already on your computer. Here's how.

Without quitting DrRacket, open a Web browser and find a Web page that has pictures on it. For example, many of the pictures used in this textbook are on the book Web site at `http://www.picturingprograms.com/pictures/`. And you can find lots of good examples on Google Image Search (`http://images.google.com`); for purposes of this chapter I recommend restricting your search to "small" images.

Right-click (or control-click) on a picture, and choose "Copy image". Now switch back to DrRacket, click in the Interactions pane (the lower half of the window) to the right of the "> " prompt, and paste. You should see the same image in the DrRacket window.

That's fine for pictures on Web pages. If you have picture files (GIF, JPEG, TIFF, etc.) already on the computer you're using, there's another way to get them into DrRacket. Click in the Interactions pane (to the right of the "> " prompt), then pull down the "Insert" menu and select "Insert image...." Find your way to the image file you want and select it; the image will appear in the DrRacket window.

1.1.2 The Interactions and Definitions panes

When you type anything into the Interactions pane and hit RETURN/ENTER, DrRacket shows you the "value" of what you typed. In many cases, that'll be exactly the same thing as you typed in. For example, if you import an image into DrRacket in either of the above ways, and then hit the RETURN or ENTER key on the keyboard, you'll see it again. **Try this.**

When you start *manipulating* pictures in section 1.2, things will get more interesting.

The upper half of the window is called the "Definitions pane". We'll get to it shortly, but for now, especially if you're using large pictures, you may want to hide it. Pull down the "View" menu and select "Hide Definitions"; now the Interactions pane takes up the whole window, and you can see more of your pictures.

1.1.3 Choosing libraries

Once you've installed a library such as `picturing-programs`, you still have to decide whether you need it for a particular problem. For everything in the rest of this chapter, and most of this book, you'll need `picturing-programs` . To tell DrRacket that you want to use that library, type

```
(require picturing-programs)
```

in the Interactions Pane and hit RETURN/ENTER.

(If your DrRacket is older than version 5.1, use

```
(require installed-teachpacks/picturing-programs)
```

instead.)

Any time you re-start DrRacket, or hit the "Run" button at the top of the window, DrRacket will erase everything that was in the Interactions pane, so you'll need to type this `require` line again before you can do anything else with pictures. We'll see a way to avoid repeating this in section 1.6.

1.2 Manipulating pictures

Now we'll learn to do some more interesting things with pictures: move them around, combine them into larger pictures, and so on.

For the examples in this section, I suggest copying a reasonably small, but interesting, picture from the web, such as this "calendar" picture from http://www.picturingprograms.com/pictures .

Click to the right of the "> " prompt and type

```
( flip-vertical
```

then paste or insert an image as above. Then type a right-parenthesis to match the left-parenthesis at the beginning of what you typed, and hit ENTER/RETURN. You should see the image upside-down:

> (flip-vertical   )

Practice Exercise 1.2.1 *Try the same thing, with* `flip-horizontal` *in place of* `flip-vertical`, *and the image will be reflected left-to-right.*

Practice Exercise 1.2.2 *Try* `rotate-cw`, *which rotates clockwise;* `rotate-ccw`, *which rotates counterclockwise; and* `rotate-180`, *which rotates by 180 degrees. See if you can predict (e.g. by drawing a rough sketch on paper) what each result will look like before you hit ENTER/RETURN.*

By the way, at the end of this chapter is a list of the picture-manipulating functions covered in the chapter.

1.2.1 Terminology

All the stuff you've typed (from the left parenthesis through the matching right parenthesis) is called an *expression*.

`rotate-cw`, `rotate-ccw`, and `rotate-180` are all *functions* (also called *operations* or *procedures*) which, given a picture, produce a different picture.

The picture you give them to work on is called an *argument* to the function.

The new picture you see as a result of applying the function to the argument is called the *value* of the expression.

By way of analogy, consider an English sentence like "Eat the banana." It contains a *verb*, "eat", which tells what to do, and an *object*, "the banana", which tells what to do it *to*. In computer programming, we use the words *function* and *argument* instead of *verb* and *object*, but the idea is similar.

A picture by itself, *without* parentheses or a function name, can also be thought of as an expression. It's an extremely simple expression in which there is nothing to "do"; the value of the expression is the expression itself. Such expressions (whose values are themselves) are called *literals*.

1.2.2 Combining pictures

Pick two different images of similar size and shape, both reasonably small. Click to the right of the "> " prompt and type (`above`, then an image, then another image, then a right-parenthesis. Hit ENTER/RETURN, and you should see one image stacked above the other. Try it again with the images in the opposite order. Note that whichever image you put in first ends up above the one you put in second.

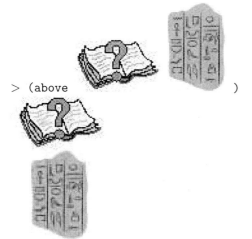

> (above   )

Practice Exercise 1.2.3 *Try the same experiment, but using the same image twice rather than two different images.*

Practice Exercise 1.2.4 *Try the same experiment with* `beside`, *which puts one image next to the other.*

Worked Exercise 1.2.5 *Try the same experiment with* `overlay`, *which draws two images in the same place, the first one overwriting part of the second. (If the first is larger than the second, you may not see any of the second at all.)*

Be sure to try `overlay` *with two different images in both possible orders.*

Solution:

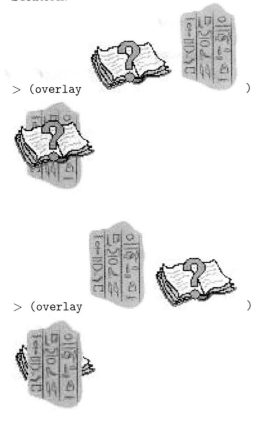

Exercise 1.2.6
Now try the `above`, `beside`, *and* `overlay` *operations with* three *or more pictures. (For* `overlay`, *you'll want to pick a small picture as the first one, then larger and larger pictures, so you can see all of the results.)*

1.2.3   A Syntax Rule, Sorta

We can summarize what we've learned so far as follows:

Syntax Rule 0 *To do something to one or more images, type a left-parenthesis, the name of the operation you want to do, then the image(s) you want to do it to, then a right-parenthesis.*

Note that `beside`, `above`, and `overlay` are functions too, just like `flip-vertical`, `rotate-ccw`, *etc.*, but they work on *two or more* arguments rather than one; they wouldn't make sense applied to only one picture.

1.3 Making mistakes

In the course of typing the examples so far, you've probably made some mistakes. Perhaps you left out a left-parenthesis, or a right-parenthesis, or misspelled one of the operation names. This is nothing to be ashamed of: every programmer in the world makes mistakes like this every day. In fact, being a programmer is largely *about* mistakes: making them, recognizing them, figuring out how to fix them, figuring out how to avoid making the same mistake next time, making a different mistake instead.

In many math classes, you're given a large number of exercises to do, of which the odd-numbered ones have solutions given in the back of the book. What happens if you work out an exercise and your solution doesn't match the one in the back of the book? In many cases, all you can do is go on to the next problem and "hope and pray" that you get *that* one right.

Hope and prayer are not particularly effective in computer programming. Almost *no* computer program is exactly right on the first try. Rather than "hoping and praying" that the program will work, you need to develop the skills of *identifying* and *categorizing* mistakes, so that when you see a similar mistake in the future, you can recognize it as similar to this one, and fix it in the same way.

DrRacket provides a variety of useful *error messages*. Let's look at several of the most likely mistakes you might have made up to this point, make them *on purpose*, and see what message we get. That way, when you make similar mistakes by accident in the future, you'll recognize the messages.

1.3.1 Leaving out the beginning left-parenthesis

Ordinarily, when you type a right-parenthesis, DrRacket helpfully shades everything between it and the matching left-parenthesis.

> (flip-vertical )

Your first sign that you've left out a left-parenthesis is that when you type the right-parenthesis, it'll be highlighted in RED because DrRacket can't *find* "the matching left-parenthesis". To see this, try typing `flip-vertical`, then pasting a picture, and typing a right parenthesis.

> flip-vertical )

If you go ahead and hit RETURN/ENTER anyway, one of several things will happen. Some versions of DrScheme/DrRacket will treat `flip-vertical` and the picture as two separate expressions: you'll see the word `flip-vertical`; then on the next line, the picture you pasted in; and on the next line, the error message

read: unexpected ')'.

In other versions, it just waits for you to type something reasonable. But nothing you can add after the right-parenthesis will make it reasonable. There are several things you can do: you can move (with the arrow keys or the mouse) to where the left parenthesis should have been, put it in, then move to the end and hit ENTER again; or you can hit BACKSPACE or DELETE until the right-parenthesis is gone (at which point you've simply typed two expressions on one line, and it'll give you the values of both).

1.3.2   Leaving out the ending right-parenthesis

Sometimes what you need to type between parentheses is longer than will fit on one typed line, e.g. several large pictures. So DrRacket allows you to hit ENTER/RETURN in the middle, and type or paste the next thing on the next line.

Note also that DrRacket will *automatically indent* the next line to line up nicely with the previous line. This is another clue that DrRacket thinks you're still inside an expression. If you don't want the line indented, you can hit DELETE/BACKSPACE a few times, but that doesn't change the fact that you're still inside an expression.

If you leave out the ending right-parenthesis, DrRacket thinks you've just gone to the next line and still want to type some more, so it'll quietly wait for you to finish. There is no error message, because DrRacket doesn't know that you've done anything wrong.

Fortunately, this is easy to fix, even if you've already hit ENTER/RETURN: just type the missing right-parenthesis, DrRacket will shade back to the left-parenthesis on the previous line, and you can hit ENTER/RETURN again to apply the operation.

1.3.3   Misspelling the operation name

Suppose you mistyped `flip-vertical` as `flip-verticle`. Any human would realize what was wrong, and guess that you actually meant `flip-vertical`. But computers aren't particularly good at "common sense" or guessing what you meant, so instead DrRacket produces the error message

reference to an identifier before its definition: flip-verticle

What does this mean? "Identifier" simply means "name"; all the operations like `flip-vertical`, `above`, `overlay`, etc. are referred to by their names, but the name `flip-verticle` hasn't been defined. However, DrRacket leaves open the possibility that it *might* be defined in the future.

By the way, you might wonder why DrRacket isn't programmed to recognize that `flip-verticle` was probably supposed to be `flip-vertical`. This could be done, but if DrRacket had this "guessing" capability, it would eventually guess *wrong* without even telling you it was making a guess at all, and that kind of mistake is incredibly difficult to track down. The authors of DrRacket decided it was better to be picky than to try to guess what you meant. For the same reason, DrRacket is *case-sensitive*, that is, it doesn't recognize `FLIP-VERTICAL` or `Flip-Vertical`.

Likewise, DrRacket doesn't recognize names that have spaces in the middle, such as `flip - vertical`: it thinks you're calling a function named `flip` with - as its first argument and `vertical` as the second, which doesn't make sense.

1.3.4 Too few or too many arguments

Try typing (`flip-vertical`) and hitting ENTER/RETURN. You'll see the error message

procedure flip-vertical: expects 1 argument, given 0.

This is a more helpful message, telling you precisely what went wrong: the `flip-vertical` operation (or "procedure") expects to work on an image, and you haven't given it one to work on.

Try typing (`flip-vertical`, then pasting in *two* images (or the same one twice), then typing a right-parenthesis. Again, the error message is fairly helpful:

procedure flip-vertical: expects 1 argument, given 2:...

The rest of the error message tells what the arguments *were*, which isn't very helpful for images, but will be very helpful when we start working with numbers, names, etc.

1.3.5 Putting the operation and arguments in the wrong order

Suppose you wanted to put two pictures side by side, but had forgotten that the operation goes *before* the arguments; you might type something like

(beside   )

You would get the error message

function call: expected a defined name or a primitive operation after an open parenthesis, but found something else

Again, this is a fairly specific and helpful message: the only things that can legally come after a left-parenthesis (for now) are function names, and a picture of a calendar is not a function name.

1.3.6   Doing something different from what you meant

All these error messages can get really annoying, but they're really your friends. Another kind of mistake is much harder to figure out and fix because there *is no error message.*

Suppose you wanted a left-to-right reflection of a particular picture, and you typed (`flip-vertical`, then pasted in the picture, and typed a right-parenthesis. You wouldn't get an error message, because what you've typed is perfectly legal. You would, however, get a *wrong answer* because what you've typed isn't what you meant. DrRacket can't read your mind, so it doesn't know what you *meant*; it can only do what you *said*. (This is one of the most frustrating things about computers, so much so that computer science students sometimes joke about a newly-defined function named `dwim`, for "Do What I Mean".) Of course, typing `flip-vertical` when you mean `flip-horizontal` is a fairly simple mistake, but in general these "wrong answer" errors are among the hardest ones to find and fix, because the computer can't give useful error messages to help you.

1.4   Getting Help

You've seen a number of builtin functions above, and you'll see many more in future chapters. Nobody can remember all of these, so (as mentioned in section 0.3.4) DrRacket has a "Help Desk" feature that allows you to look up a function by name. From the Help menu, choose "Help Desk"; it should open a Web browser window with a search box near the top. (By the way, this works even if you don't have a net connection at the moment.) Type the name of a function you want to know about, like `rotate-cw` or `above`, and it'll show you links to all the pages it knows about that function. (If there are more than one, look for one that's "provided from picturing-programs" or "provided from 2htdp/image".)

You can also type `picturing-programs` into the search box, and it'll show you a link to documentation about the whole teachpack.

1.5   More complex manipulations

Worked Exercise 1.5.1 *What would you do if you wanted to see a picture, beside its left-to-right reflection?*

Solution: You know how to get a reflection using `flip-horizontal`, and you know how to put one image next to another using `beside`, but how do you do *both*? You really want to put one image beside another, one of which is a reflection of the other.

Very simply, instead of pasting an image as one of the operands of the `beside` function, type in an expression involving `flip-horizontal`:

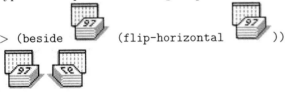

Since (`flip-horizontal`   ) would be a perfectly good expression in its own right, but it's also a *part* of a larger expression, we call it a *sub-expression.*

Exercise 1.5.2

Write an expression which displays a picture beside its top-to-bottom reflection.

Exercise 1.5.3

Write an expression which displays a picture beside its 180-degree rotation.

Exercise 1.5.4

Write an expression which displays four copies of a picture arranged in a two-by-two square.

Hint: There are at least two different ways to do this, using what you've seen so far. Either one is acceptable, as long as you type an expression that uses the smaller picture, and its value is the correct larger picture.

Exercise 1.5.5

Write an expression which displays four copies of a picture in a two-by-two square, each rotated differently: the top-right one should be rotated 90 degrees clockwise, the bottom-left one 90 degrees counter-clockwise, and the bottom-right one 180 degrees.

Hint: This expression will be fairly long and complicated; feel free to break it up over several lines. In particular, if you hit ENTER/RETURN after each right-parenthesis, DrRacket will automatically indent the next line in a way that indicates the structure of the expression: things inside more layers of parentheses are indented farther.

Hint: If you solve this problem the way I expect, it'll work well with square or nearly-square pictures, but won't look so good with long skinny pictures. We'll see how to improve it later.

1.6   Saving Your Work: the Definitions pane

When you type an expression in the Interactions pane and hit RETURN/ENTER, you immediately see the value of that expression. But as soon as you quit DrRacket, all your work is lost. Furthermore, even if you're not quitting DrRacket yet, sometimes you want to write expressions now and see the results later.

If you've hidden the Definitions pane earlier, show it again: pull down the "View" menu and choose "Show Definitions".

Click the mouse in the Definitions pane and type in the line

```
(require picturing-programs)
```

or, if you have an older version of DrRacket,

```
(require installed-teachpacks/picturing-programs)
```

as the first line of the Definitions pane. (Now that it's in the Definitions pane, you won't have to keep typing it again and again in the Interactions pane.) Hit RETURN/ENTER, and nothing will happen (except that the cursor will move to the next line). From now on, almost *every* Definitions Pane should start with that line.

On the next line of the Definitions pane, type in one of the expressions you've already worked with. Hit RETURN/ENTER. Type in another expression, and another. (These don't *have* to be on separate lines, but it's easier to keep track of what you're doing if they are. In fact, if they're long, complicated expressions, you might want to put a blank line or two in between them so you can easily see where one ends and the other begins.)

Now, to see how these expressions work, click the "Run" button just above the Definitions pane. Anything that was in the Interactions pane before will disappear and be replaced by the *values* of the expressions in the Definitions pane, in order. If any of them were illegal (e.g. mismatched parentheses, misspelled function names, etc.) it'll show an error message in the Interactions pane, and won't go on to the next expression.

If you've worked out a big, complicated expression (or several), and want to save it to use again tomorrow,

1. type the expression(s) into the Definitions window,

2. pull down the "File" menu,

3. choose "Save Definitions",

4. navigate to the appropriate folder on your computer,

5. type a suitable filename (I recommend a name ending with ".rkt"), and

6. click "Save" or "OK" or whatever it is on your computer.

Now you can quit DrRacket, double-click the new file, and it should start DrRacket again with those expressions in the Definitions window. Or you can double-click DrRacket, pull down the "File" menu, choose "Open...", and find the desired file to bring it into the Definitions window.

1.7   Working through nested expressions: the Stepper

When you develop a big, complicated expression and it doesn't work the way you expected it to, you need a way to see what it's doing along the way. The Stepper feature of DrRacket allows you to see the values of *sub-expressions*, one at a time, until you get to the whole expression.

For example, suppose you were working on exercise 1.5.2, and your (incorrect) attempt at the answer was

If you type this into Interactions and hit RETURN/ENTER, or type it into Definitions and click the "Run" button, you'll get an answer, but not the *right* answer. To see what's going wrong, type the expression into the Definitions pane and, instead of clicking the "Run" button, click the "Step" button. You should see a new window, showing you the original expression on the left, and a slightly modified version of it on the right. In particular, the

sub-expression (`flip-horizontal` 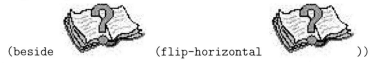) on the left will be highlighted in green, while its *value*, another picture, will be highlighted in purple on the right. Everything else about the two expressions should be identical.

Worked Exercise 1.7.1 *Show the sequence of steps the Stepper would take in evaluating the expression*

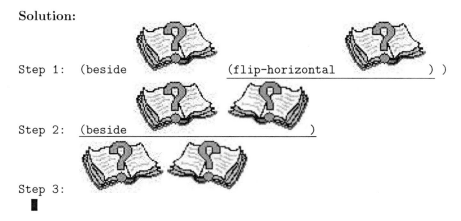

(beside   (flip-horizontal   ))

At each step, underline the sub-expression that's about to be replaced.

Solution:

Step 1:   (beside   <u>(flip-horizontal   )</u>)

Step 2:   <u>(beside   )</u>

Step 3: ▪

Exercise 1.7.2 *Show the sequence of steps the Stepper would take in evaluating the expression*

(beside (rotate-ccw   ) (rotate-cw   ))

1.8 Syntax and box diagrams

Recall rule 0: *To do something to one or more images, type a left-parenthesis, the name of the operation you want to do, then the image(s) you want to do it to, then a right-parenthesis.*

In fact, as we've seen, things are a little more general and flexible than that: instead of putting images inside the parentheses, we can also put *sub-expressions* whose *values* are images. Indeed, these sub-expressions may in turn contain sub-expressions of their own, and so on.

At the same time, we've seen that certain attempts at expressions aren't grammatically legal. Computer scientists often explain both of these issues — how do you perform an operation, and what is or isn't a legal expression — at the same time, by means of *syntax rules*, and we now rephrase things in that style.

Syntax Rule 1 *Any picture is a legal expression; its value is itself.*

Syntax Rule 2 *A left-parenthesis followed by a function name, one or more legal expressions, and a right parenthesis, is a legal expression. Its value is what you get by applying the named function to the values of the smaller expressions inside it.*

Note that we can understand all the expressions we've seen so far by using a combination of these two rules, even the ones with several levels of nested parentheses, because rule 2 allows *any legal expressions* to appear as arguments to the function, even expressions constructed using rule 2 itself.

Let's illustrate this using "box diagrams". We'll start with an expression, then put a box around a sub-expression of it. Over the box we'll write a 1 or a 2 depending on which rule justifies saying that it is an expression.

Worked Exercise 1.8.1 *Draw a box diagram to prove that the picture* *is a legal expression.*

Solution: Rule 1 tells us that any picture is a legal expression, so we put a box around it

with the number 1 over it: ▮

Worked Exercise 1.8.2 *Draw a box diagram to prove that*

(rotate-180 )
is a legal expression.

Solution: We'll start from the inside out. The picture of the calendar is a legal expression

by rule 1, so we have (rotate-180 )

Now that we know that the inner part is a legal expression, we can use Rule 2 (which requires a left-parenthesis, a function name, an expression, and a right-parenthesis) to show that the whole thing is a legal expression:

(rotate-180 ) ▮

Exercise 1.8.3 *Draw a box diagram to prove that*

(rotate-cw 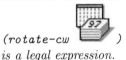)
is a legal expression.

Worked Exercise 1.8.4 *Draw a box diagram to prove that*

(beside )

is a legal expression.

Solution: We need to use rule 1 twice:

(beside )

Once we're convinced that both pictures are legal expressions, we need to use rule 2 to show that the whole thing is a legal expression:

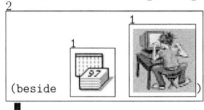

(beside)

Worked Exercise 1.8.5 *Draw a box diagram to prove that*

(beside)

is a legal expression.

Solution: We can use rule 1 twice to convince ourselves that the two pictures are legal expressions:

(beside)

But now we're stuck: there is no rule in which an expression can appear between a left parenthesis and a function name. Since we are unable to prove that this is a legal expression, we conclude that it is *not* a legal expression. Indeed, if you typed it into DrRacket, you would get an error message:

> *function call: expected a defined name or a primitive operation name after an open parenthesis, but found something else.*

Whenever you type a left-parenthesis, Scheme expects the next things to be the name of an operation, and the calendar picture is not the name of an operation. ∎

Exercise 1.8.6 *Draw a box diagram to prove that*

(rotate-cw
is a legal expression.

Hint: This should be impossible; it *isn't* a legal expression. But how far can you get? *Why* is it not a legal expression?

Exercise 1.8.7 *Draw a box diagram to prove that*

(rotate 5   )
is a legal expression.

Hint: This too should be impossible. In fact, it *is* a legal expression, but not using the two rules you've seen so far; we'll add some more syntax rules later.

Worked Exercise 1.8.8 *Draw a box diagram to prove that*

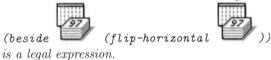

is a legal expression.

Solution: As usual, we'll work from the inside out. Each of the two pictures is obviously a legal expression by rule 1:

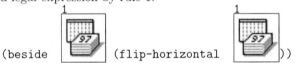

Next, we can apply rule 2 to the part of the expression starting with the inner left-parenthesis:

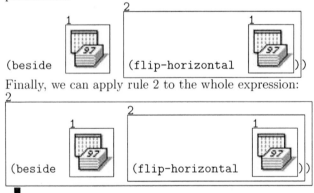

Finally, we can apply rule 2 to the whole expression:

Exercise 1.8.9 *Draw a box diagram to prove that your solution to Exercise 1.5.2 or 1.5.4 is a legal expression.*

At this point you may be wondering how these "box diagrams" are supposed to help you write programs. The box diagram for a really simple expression (as in exercises 1.8.1 or 1.8.2), frankly, isn't very interesting or useful. But as the expressions become more complicated, the box diagrams become more and more valuable in understanding what's going on in your expression. Furthermore, every time you type an expression, DrRacket actually goes through a process (behind the scenes) very similar to these box diagrams, so by understanding them you can better understand DrRacket.

Ultimately, you should be able to avoid most syntax error messages by never typing in any expression that isn't grammatically legal; you'll know which ones are legal because you can draw box diagrams for them yourself.

1.9 Review of important words and concepts

Regardless of which pane you're typing into, you type **expressions** and (immediately or eventually) see their **values**.

A **literal** is an expression whose value is itself; the only examples you've seen so far are pictures copied-and-pasted into DrRacket, but there will be other kinds of literals in later shapters. More complicated expressions are built by applying a **function** or **operation** to one or more **arguments**, as in

(rotate-cw   )

In this example, rotate-cw is the name of a predefined function, and the literal picture is its argument. The parentheses around the whole expression let DrRacket know which function is being applied to which arguments. Note that different functions make sense for different numbers of arguments: rotate-cw only makes sense applied to one argument, while beside only makes sense for two or more. Other expressions can be even more complicated, containing smaller expressions in place of some of the pictures; these smaller expressions are called **sub-expressions**.

DrRacket has many built-in functions, and they each have to be called in a specific way with a specific number of arguments. Nobody memorizes all of them, so DrRacket's "Help Desk" feature allows you to look up a function by name.

1.10 Reference: functions that work on images

We've seen a number of built-in Scheme functions that work with images. These aren't really "important concepts", but here's a list of them that you can refer to later:

- flip-vertical

- flip-horizontal

- rotate-cw

- rotate-ccw

- rotate-180

- above

- beside

- overlay

We've also seen a special function named require, which is used to tell DrRacket that you need a particular library.

Chapter 2

Shorthand for values: variables

2.1 Defining a variable

You've typed a lot of expressions into the computer involving pictures, but every time you need a different picture, you've needed to find it (e.g. in a Web browser) and copy-and-paste it into DrRacket. This is repetitive and a pain. It would be much more convenient if you could give each picture a name and refer to it that way.

To do this, DrRacket provides a built-in function named `define`. To see how it works, type (in the Interactions pane) the line

> (define calendar)

and hit ENTER/RETURN. You won't see any "result", but now you can use the word `calendar` any time you want that picture:

> calendar

> (beside calendar calendar)

> (flip-vertical calendar)

(Note that if you leave out the space between `define` and `calendar`, or between `beside` and `calendar`, or between any two typed words, Racket won't know where one word ends and the next begins, and you'll get an error message like *reference to undefined identifier: definecalendar*.) There's nothing magical about the name `calendar` — you could have named it anything else, like `fred` or `antidisestablishmentarianism`, but since it stands for a picture of a calendar, the name `calendar` is a lot easier to remember.

Practice Exercise 2.1.1 *Define another variable to hold another picture you've found on the Web. Write some expressions using each of the two variables, and some using both.*

You can also define a variable to hold the result of another expression, *e.g.*

```
(define two-calendars (beside calendar calendar))
```

Practice Exercise 2.1.2 *Define a variable* six-calendars *whose value is a six-pack of calendars: two wide and three high. Test your definition by typing the name of the variable, all by itself, in the Interactions pane and hitting ENTER/RETURN; you should see the picture of six calendars. If not, you've done something wrong.*

Hint: This is simpler if you use the already-defined the variable two-calendars.

Practice Exercise 2.1.3 *Choose a reasonably small picture from this book or the Web, and store it in a variable. Then define another variable named* two-copies *whose value is two copies of that picture, side by side, by using the previous variable. Then define a third variable named* six-copies *whose value is a six-pack of the picture, two wide by three high, by using* two-copies.

Practice Exercise 2.1.4 *Construct another interesting picture from pieces in this book or on the Web, and store it in a variable with an appropriate name. Test it as before. If you use a particular piece more than once, you may want to give that piece a name of its own, so you can use its name in constructing the whole picture.*

Common beginner mistakes

Recall from Chapter 1 that a *literal* is a simple expression that doesn't "stand for" anything else; if you type it into the Interactions window, the value you get back is the same thing you typed in. By contrast, a variable *does* "stand for" something else: if you type in the name of a variable, you get back a picture rather than the variable name you typed.

You can only define a variable; you cannot define a literal. Furthermore, (in Beginner DrRacket) you cannot define a variable more than once: once you've decided what value it "stands for", that's its value until the next time you click "Run".

Practice Exercise 2.1.5 ***Type*** *each of the following expressions into a newly-opened interactions pane, one by one. For each one,* predict *what you think it will do, then hit ENTER and see whether you were right.* ***Explain*** *the results. Several of them will produce error messages: in each such case, read and understand the error message.*

-

- *calendar*

- *(define*  *calendar)*

- *(define calendar calendar)*

- *(define calendar*  *)*

-

- *calendar*

- *(define other-pic book)*

- *(define other-pic calendar)*

- *(define calendar* *)*

- *other-pic*

Note that when you type an expression to be evaluated, all variables in it must already be defined, or you get the error message *reference to an identifier before its definition ....* On the other hand, when you define a variable, it must *not* already be defined, or you get the error message *define: cannot redefine name ....*

And of course, when you define a variable, it must be an identifier rather than a literal like

, or you get the error message *define: expected a function name, constant name, or function header for 'define', but found ...*

2.2 Defining variables and the Definitions pane

As its name suggests, the Definitions pane (normally the top half of the DrRacket window) is intended to hold definitions. Try typing several variable definitions into the Definitions pane, then click the "Run" button. Everything you've typed in the Interactions pane will disappear, but the variable definitions are available so you can use them as much as you wish in the Interactions pane. One benefit of this is that, once you've found or constructed several interesting pictures, you can save them all to a file so you can easily work with the same named pictures again the next time you start DrRacket.

Practice Exercise 2.2.1 *Type the (legal) definitions from Section 2.1 into the Definitions pane, save it to a file, quit DrRacket, double-click the file, and hit the "Run" button. Type some expressions involving those variables (calendar, two-calendars, etc.) into the Interactions pane and check that they do what you expect.*

2.3 What's in a name?

We've been using the names of functions for some time already, and now we're making up new names for things. So what qualifies as a "name"? (The technical term in computer science is *identifier*.) The rules differ slightly from one programming language to another, but

*in Racket, an **identifier** can be made up of letters, numerals, and punctuation marks. It may not contain spaces, commas, # signs, parentheses, square brackets, curly braces, quotation marks, apostrophes, or vertical bars.*

An identifier may contain upper- and/or lower-case letters, and it makes a difference which one you use (*e.g.* calendar is different from Calendar or CALENDAR). An identifier may *not* consist entirely of numerals (if you type such a thing, DrRacket treats it as a number instead; we'll learn more about this in Chapter 3.)

For example, `rotate-cw` is a legal identifier, which happens to represent a predefined function. `rotate$cw` would also be a legal identifier, although it doesn't already stand for anything. `rotate cw` contains a space, so DrRacket would treat it as *two* identifiers, not one.

2.4   More syntax rules

Why are these new expressions, involving `define` and defined variables, legal? Based on the grammar rules you've seen so far (Syntax Rules 1 and 2 from Section 1.8), they're not. So we need some more syntax rules (for easy reference, we repeat the first two):

Syntax Rule 1 *Any literal picture is a legal expression; its value is itself.*

Syntax Rule 2 *A left-parenthesis followed by a function name, one or more legal expressions, and a right parenthesis, is a legal expression. Its value is what you get by applying the named function to the values of the smaller expressions inside it.*

Syntax Rule 3 *Any identifier, if already defined, is a legal expression. Its value is what it was defined to stand for.*

Syntax Rule 4 *A left-parenthesis followed by the word* ***define****, a previously-undefined identifier, a legal expression, and a right-parenthesis is a legal expression. Think of it as anything matching the pattern*
*(****define*** *new-identifier expression)*

It has no "value", but the side effect of defining the variable to stand for the value of the expression.

Worked Exercise 2.4.1 *Draw a box diagram to prove that*

(*define calendar* *)*
is a legal expression. Assume that `calendar` *is not already defined.*

Solution: The picture is obviously a legal expression, by rule 1:

(define calendar)

The word `calendar` is a legal identifier. It does not qualify as a legal expression in its own right, since it isn't already defined; however, by rule 4 an undefined identifier can be combined with `define` and the picture to make a legal expression.

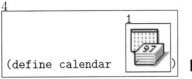

Exercise 2.4.2 *Draw a box diagram to prove that*
(`rotate-cw calendar`)
is a legal expression. Assume that `calendar` *is already defined.*

Exercise 2.4.3 *Draw a box diagram to prove that your solution to Exercise 2.1.2 or 2.1.3 is a legal expression.*

Exercise 2.4.4 *Draw a box diagram for*
(`define snark boojum calendar`)
Assume that `calendar` *is already defined, and* `snark` *and* `boojum` *are not. The whole thing is not a legal expression; why not?*

2.5 Variables and the Stepper

Variable definitions provide another opportunity to see what's going on "behind the scenes" by using the Stepper. Make sure you've got some variable definitions in the Definitions pane, then add some expressions at the end like

(`beside (flip-vertical calendar) calendar`)

Click the "Step" button. It'll skip over all the simple definitions, until you get to an expression involving Syntax Rule 2 (applying a function to something) or 3 (getting the value of a variable). Any variable names in the original expression will be replaced (one by one) with the values of those variables, and then the function (if any) can be applied as usual.

Practice Exercise 2.5.1 *Make up some expressions involving variables, type them into the Definitions window, and step through them. At each step, make sure you understand what's being replaced with what, and why.*

2.6 Review of important words and concepts

A **variable** is a word that "stands for" some other value. An **identifier** is any word; it may contain some punctuation marks, but it cannot contain spaces, parentheses, quotation marks, or commas.

Every variable is an identifier, but not every identifier is a variable. For example, `define`, `rotate-180`, `beside`, etc. are identifiers but not variables: they stand for operations rather than values. A variable can be defined by using Syntax Rule 4 on a previously-undefined identifier. After that, you can use it anywhere that you could use any other expression, according to Syntax Rule 2. By chaining a sequence of variable definitions, you can build complex pictures without getting nearly as confused as you might if you tried to write the whole thing as one big expression.

2.7 Reference: functions for defining variables

The only new function introduced in this chapter is `define`.

Chapter 3

Building more interesting pictures

3.1 Other kinds of arguments

3.1.1 Strings as arguments

You may have noticed that if you put two images of different height beside one another, or two images of different width above one another, their centers are usually lined up:

> (beside 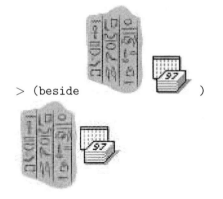)

Now let's try something slightly different. Type each of the following three expressions and observe the results:

(beside/align "top" )

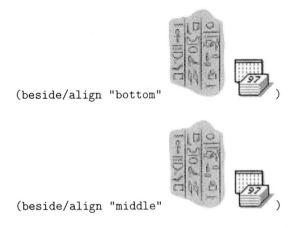

(beside/align "bottom"   )

(beside/align "middle"   )

Try using **above** with two or more pictures of different widths; then try each of the following three expressions.

(above/align "right"   )

(above/align "left"   )

(above/align "middle"   )

You've just seen two new functions, **beside/align** and **above/align**, each of which expects an *extra argument* to indicate how you want things lined up. This extra argument isn't an image, it's a different kind of information called a *string* — a sequence of letters enclosed in double-quote marks. (We'll go into more detail on this in Section 3.4.) If you leave out the quotation marks, *e.g.*

(above/align `right`   )

then DrRacket will think `right` is an undefined variable, and will give you an error message.

There's also an `overlay/align` function with *two* string arguments: it expects the first argument to be either `"left"`, `"right"`, or `"middle"`, and the second to be either `"top"`, `"bottom"`, or `"middle"`. The third, fourth, *etc.* arguments should be images. **Play with these functions.**

3.1.2 Numbers as arguments

Next, try

(rotate 15 )

which rotates the image by 15 degrees instead of 90. **Play with this.**

Now, try

(scale 2 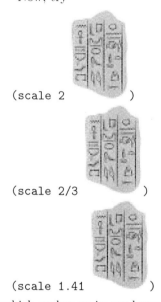)

(scale 2/3)

(scale 1.41)

which makes an image larger or smaller. **Play with this.**

Note that the `rotate` and `scale` functions expect an extra argument that is neither an image nor a string — it's a *number*. Numbers can be written in several ways, as you saw above, but they cannot contain spaces (so, for example,

(scale )

wouldn't work). We'll learn more about numbers in Racket in Chapter 7.

(There's also a `scale/xy` function that allows you to stretch or squash a picture by one factor vertically and a different factor horizontally. Look it up in the Help Desk.)

3.2 More mistakes

Now that we've seen functions that expect different types of arguments, there's a whole new world of things that can go wrong, with a whole new set of error messages to tell you

about them. As before, let's make some of these mistakes *on purpose* so that when we
make them by accident later, we'll recognize what's going on.

Try typing

(beside/align   "top"   )

You would get the error message

> *beside/align: expected <y-place> as first argument, given: ...*

because `beside/align` expects its *first* argument to be the string (specifically, a "y-place",
i.e. one of the strings `"top"`, `"middle"`, or `"bottom"`).

Likewise,

(overlay/align "top" "right"   )

produces an error message because it expects an *x-place* (*i.e.* either `"left"`, `"right"`, or
`"middle"`) as its first argument, and `"top"` is none of those.

3.3   Creating simple shapes

So far, all your pictures have either been copied-and-pasted from other programs, or constructed from copied-and-pasted pictures using `beside`, `rotate-cw`, *etc.* In this section
we'll learn to build simple geometric shapes from scratch. (As in the rest of the book,
we've put the pictures in black and white to save on printing. If some of them don't make
sense, try looking at the textbook Web site, where a lot of this stuff appears in color.)

One of the simplest geometric shapes is a rectangle. But there are lots of different
possible rectangles, of different sizes, shapes, and colors. In addition, DrRacket allows you

to draw both *solid* rectangles 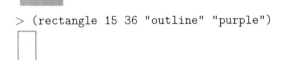 and *outline* rectangles   . When we create
a rectangle, we need to make all these decisions and tell DrRacket exactly what kind of
rectangle we want.

DrRacket has a built-in function named `rectangle` that creates such pictures. It needs
to be told the width and height of the rectangle (in pixels on the screen), whether it's solid
or outline, and what color it should be, in that order:

```
> (rectangle 34 21 "solid" "green")
```

```
> (rectangle 15 36 "outline" "purple")
```

Practice Exercise 3.3.1 *Make up several examples of rectangles by plugging in different values for width, height, solid vs. outline, and color.*

If you try a color DrRacket doesn't recognize, you'll get an error message, but it won't hurt anything. Likewise, if you put anything other than "solid" *or* "outline" *in the third argument position, you'll get an error message, but it won't hurt anything.*

SIDEBAR:

The complete list of known color names is in the Help Desk; look up `color-database<%>`.

Practice Exercise 3.3.2 *What do you think would happen if you left out the color, e.g.* (rectangle 34 21 "solid") *? Type it in and find out whether you were right.*

What happens if you put the color first, e.g. (rectangle "green" 34 21 "solid") *? Try various other mistakes, read the error messages, and make sure you understand them.*

Practice Exercise 3.3.3 *Define a variable named* solid-green-box *whose value is a solid green rectangle, and another named* outline-blue-box *which is what it sounds like. Combine these in various ways using* above, beside, overlay, *etc.*

Another built-in function, `circle`, does exactly what you expect: it creates circles. Circles, like rectangles, can be either solid or outline, and of various colors, but rather than having a separate width and height, they have only a radius: for example, (`circle 10 "solid" "orange"`) produces a solid orange circle of radius 10.

Practice Exercise 3.3.4 *Make up several examples of circles. Use* above, beside, *and* overlay *to compare a circle of radius 10 with a square whose width and height are both 10. How would you build a picture of a solid orange circle just fitting inside a solid blue square,* *?*

Yet another built-in function, `ellipse`, has arguments similar to those of rectangle: width, height, solid or outline, and color. Try it.

Practice Exercise 3.3.5 *Make up several examples of ellipses. Show another way to construct a picture like* *.*

The `triangle` built-in function has arguments similar to those of `circle`: a number representing the length of each edge of the triangle, the word `"outline"` or `"solid"`, and a color name. It builds an equilateral triangle pointing up.

There are lots of other built-in functions like these. Look up the following in the Help Desk:

- `right-triangle`

- `isosceles-triangle`

- `rhombus`

- `regular-polygon`

- `star`

- `star-polygon`

- `line`

- `add-line`

Practice Exercise 3.3.6 *Make up several examples using these functions.*

Of course, nobody actually memorizes all these functions — I certainly haven't! You should know that these functions exist, and how to look them up when you need them.

Exercise 3.3.7 *How would you construct a picture like* *? (Note that the top edge of the triangle matches* exactly *the top edge of the square, and the bottom point of the triangle is* exactly *in the middle of the bottom edge of the square.)*

Hint: It *is* possible to do this, using what you've seen so far, with no math beyond elementary school.

3.4   Data types and contracts

In the previous chapter, you asked Racket to operate on images and produce images. In this chapter we've seen two additional kinds of information, or *data types*: numbers and strings.

You already have a pretty good idea of what numbers are, but strings may be new to you. In Racket (and C, and C++, and Java, and most other programming languages), a *string* is a sequence of letters, numbers, punctuation marks, spaces, etc. surrounded by double quote marks. The rules for what makes a string are similar to, but not quite the same as, those for what makes an identifier: an identifier can't contain spaces, or certain punctuation marks, while *almost any* key you can type on the keyboard can go inside a string. (The main exception is the double-quote mark itself, as this indicates the *end* of the string. If you really want to put a double-quote mark inside a string, there is a way to do it, but we won't go into that here.)

3.4.1   String literals and identifiers

When you type a string, enclosed in quotation marks, it's a *literal* — that is, its value is just itself. By contrast, when you type a word that isn't enclosed in quotation marks, DrRacket thinks of it as an *identifier*: if there's a function or a variable by that name, that's what it "stands for", and if there isn't, it doesn't "stand for" anything.

A variable in Racket may "stand for" *any type* of information — a picture, a number, a string, or other types we'll learn about later.

Practice Exercise 3.4.1 *Type each of the following expressions into a newly-opened interactions pane, one by one. For each one,* predict *what you think it will do, then hit ENTER and see whether you were right.* **Explain** *the results. If you get an error message (as you should for some of them),* read and understand the error message.

- `"hello"`

- `hello`

- `(define "author" "Bloch")`

- `(define author Bloch)`

- `(define author "Bloch")`

- `"author"`

- `author`

- `(define author "Bloch")`

- `(define calendar` `)`

- `(define age 19)`

- `"calendar"`

- `calendar`

- `"age"`

- `age`

- `"Bloch"`

- `Bloch`

- `(beside calendar calendar)`

- `(beside "calendar" "calendar")`

- `(define age 20)`

- `(define 20 age)`

3.4.2   Function contracts

As you've already seen if you tried exercise 3.3.2, each built-in function "knows" how many pieces of information, of what kinds, in what order, it should be given, and will reject other kinds of information. For example, `flip-vertical`, `rotate-cw`, *etc.* all expect to be given a single image, and will produce an error message if you give them *no* image, or *more than one* image, or a *non-image* such as a number or a string. (**Try** each of these mistakes and see what message you get.) This kind of pickiness may sometimes feel as though it's intended to annoy you, but really, what would it *mean* to "rotate" two pictures, or a number? The designers of DrRacket didn't see any obvious answer to these questions, so they simply made it illegal to do those things.

Similarly, `beside`, `above`, and `overlay` each expect to be given two or more images; they produce an error message if you give them too few images, or anything other than an image. The `beside/align` and `above/align` functions each expect a string and two or more images, while `overlay/align` expects two strings and two or more images.

Practice Exercise 3.4.2 *See what happens if you break these rules.*

The `rectangle` and `ellipse` functions expect to be given two numbers and two strings, in that order; furthermore, the first string must be either `"solid"` or `"outline"`, and the second must be a color name. If you give either of these functions the wrong number of things, or the wrong types of things, or the right types in the wrong order, it'll produce an error message.

Practice Exercise 3.4.3 *Try these various mistakes and see what different messages you can get.*

Obviously, you can't properly use any function unless you know how many arguments, of what types, in what order, it expects to be given. You also need to know what type of *result* it produces (so far, all our functions produce images, but that will change soon!). All of this information together is called a *function contract*: think of it as the function making a "promise" that "if you give me two numbers and two strings, in that order, I'll give you back an image." A function contract can be described in words, as in the previous three paragraphs, but we'll have a *lot* of functions to deal with in this course, and that gets tiresome. Instead, we'll adopt a shorter convention for writing function contracts:

```
flip-vertical :  image -> image
beside :  image image ...  -> image
above/align :  string image image ...  -> image
rotate :  number image -> image
```

In this convention, we write the *name* of the function, then a *colon* (:), then the *type(s)* of the arguments, then an *arrow* (I usually use a minus sign and a greater-than sign, which together look sorta like an arrow), then the *type* of the result. We use ellipses (...) to indicate that there may be an indefinite number of additional arguments.

When a function takes several arguments of the same type, it often helps to say something about what each one means, so you remember to use them in the right order. I do this with parentheses:

```
rectangle:  number(width) number(height)
            string("outline" or "solid") string(color) -> image
```

By reading this one contract, you can immediately tell that to create, say, an outlined blue rectangle 30 wide by 17 high, you should type (`rectangle 30 17 "outline" "blue"`)

Practice Exercise 3.4.4 *Write the function contracts for* `ellipse`, `circle`, `triangle`, *and* `star-polygon`, *using the standard convention.*

There's nothing magical about this convention for writing function contracts, but following a common convention makes it easier for programmers to understand one another.

3.4.3 Comments

If you try to type function contracts into the DrRacket window, you'll get an error message because they're not legal expressions (according to rules 1-4). However, people frequently want to include function contracts in a Racket program, so they use *comments* to indicate something intended for the human reader, not for Racket.

Different programming languages specify comments in different ways, but every programming language I know of has *some* way to write comments. Here are three common ways it's done in Racket:

End-of-line comments

The most common way of making something a comment in Racket is to put a semicolon at the beginning of the line; everything else on that line will be *ignored completely*. You can write anything in a comment, including a letter to your grandmother:

```
( define calendar            )
; Dear Grandma,
; I am learning to program, using the Racket language.  So far
; I've learned to rotate and scale pictures, put pictures
; together in various ways, and make rectangles, circles,
; ellipses, triangles, and stars, and I can keep these pictures
; in variables to use later.  However, this letter is in
; English, not in Racket, so I've "commented it out" to keep
; DrRacket from complaining about it.  That's all for now!
; Love,
;                      Joe Student
(beside calendar calendar)
```

Of course, that's not a realistic use of DrRacket: there are much better programs around for writing letters to your grandmother! More likely, if you were using several built-in functions, you would write down their contracts in comments for easy reference:

```
; beside :  image image ...-> image
; rectangle :  number (width) number (height)
;     string ("outline" or "solid") string (color) -> image
; rotate-cw :  image -> image
```

Multi-line comments

If you want to write several lines of comments in a row, it may be more convenient to use another kind of comment: type `#|` (the number sign and the vertical bar), and everything after that (even onto later lines) will be ignored, until you type `|#`.

```
( define calendar          )
#|
Here are several lines of commented-out contracts.
beside :  image image ...-> image
rectangle :  number (width) number (height)
     string ("outline" or "solid") string (color) -> image
rotate-cw :  image -> image
|#
(beside calendar calendar)
```

Practice Exercise 3.4.5 *Write six different expressions on separate lines of the Defini-tions pane. "Comment out" the second one with a semicolon, and the fourth and fifth with #|...|#. Hit "Check Syntax", and the commented parts should turn brown. Hit "Run", and you should see the results of the first, third, and sixth expressions.*

Expression comments

Yet a third kind of comment allows you to "comment out" exactly one expression, regardless of whether it's a single line, part of a line, or multiple lines.

Practice Exercise 3.4.6 *Type the following lines into the Definitions pane (assuming you've already got definitions of the variables* calendar, hacker, *and* solid-green-box*):*

```
#; calendar hacker
#; (beside calendar hacker)
#; (beside
  hacker
  calendar
  ) solid-green-box
(beside calendar #; hacker solid-green-box)
```

On the first line, calendar *is ignored, but* hacker *isn't, so you get a picture of a hacker. The entire next line is ignored. Of the next four lines,* (beside hacker calendar) *is ignored, but the* solid-green-box *is not. And on the last line, the* hacker *is ignored and you get a picture of a calendar next to a solid green box.*

Regardless of which kind of comment you use, DrRacket will automatically color it brown to show what parts it is ignoring.

3.4.4   Comments in Practice

There are two especially common reasons that we'll use comments: to write down function contracts, and to temporarily "hide" part of a program while working on another part. For example,

```
; beside :  image image ... -> image
; flip-vertical :  image -> image
; image-width :  image -> number
; rotate-180 :  image -> image

(define calendar
```

```
                                )
; (define two-cals (beside calendar calendar))
; (above two-cals (rotate-180 two-cals))
(above calendar (flip-vertical (scale/xy 1 1/2 calendar)))
```

The first four lines specify the contracts of functions we may be using. The next defines a variable. The next two are "commented out": presumably either they already work, and we don't want to be bothered with them while working on something else, or they *don't* work as desired yet, and we'll come back to them later.

SIDEBAR:

If you have a large section of program that you want to comment out temporarily, select all the relevant lines and use the "Comment Out with Semicolons" command on the Racket menu, and it'll put a semicolon in front of each line. Likewise, the "Uncomment" menu command allows you to remove the semicolons from a whole bunch of lines at once.

3.5 More functions on pictures

3.5.1 Cutting up pictures

So you know how to get a picture of a circle:

```
(circle 30 "solid" "green")
```

How would you get a picture of the *upper half* of this circle? The `picturing-programs` library includes a function named `crop-bottom` which helps with this kind of problem. Its contract is

```
crop-bottom :  image number -> image
```

It cuts off (or "crops") the specified number of pixels from the bottom of a picture.

Worked Exercise 3.5.1 ***Write an expression*** *which produces the upper half of a solid green semicircle of radius 30.*

Solution: We already know that `(circle 30 "solid" "green")` produces the whole circle. How many pixels do we want to cut off the bottom? Well, the *radius* of a circle is the distance from the center to any edge of the circle, in particular the bottom edge. So if the radius is 30, then we want to cut off 30 pixels:

```
(crop-bottom (circle 30 "solid" "green") 30)
```

∎

Exercise 3.5.2 *Here's a picture of me.*
Write an expression *that chops the bottom 25 pixels off this picture.*

The `picturing-programs` library also contains functions named `crop-top`, `crop-left`, and `crop-right`, which behave the same way but crop the top, left, or right edges respectively. There's also a `crop` function which allows you to pick *any* rectangular region from a picture. As usual, in exchange for more power, it's a bit harder to use. Look it up in the Help Desk.

Practice Exercise 3.5.3 *Play with these.*

SIDEBAR:

Actually, you don't need all four of these: any one would be enough, combined with things you already know. Try writing an expression that chops the *leftmost* 25 pixels off the picture of me, using `crop-bottom` but none of the other cropping functions.

The technique you probably used to do this is something mathematicians call *conjugation.* It's not difficult, and it's worth knowing for future purposes, but for the sake of convenience, we've given you all four cropping functions.

Exercise 3.5.4 **Write an expression** *which produces the bottom 45 pixels of an outlined*

circle of radius 30.

Exercise 3.5.5 **Write an expression** *which produces the top-right quarter of a solid*

ellipse 50 wide by 30 high.

Exercise 3.5.6 **Invent** *some other interesting pictures, using cropping together with the other functions you've already seen. Go wild.*

3.5.2   Measuring pictures

In order to know how many pixels to crop, it might be helpful to know how many pixels there *are.* The library provides two functions to help with this:

```
; image-width  :  image -> number
; image-height :  image -> number
```

Notice that these are the first functions we've seen yet that return a *number* as their result, rather than an *image.* This will become more useful once we study arithmetic in Chapter 7.

Practice Exercise 3.5.7 *Find the widths and heights of some of your favorite pictures. Then **write an expression** to cut off the left one-third of a particular picture.*

Note that numeric results appear in the Interactions window just as image results have been appearing.

3.5.3 Placing images precisely

Here's a picture of me.
Suppose you wanted to take revenge on me for writing this book by blotting out my eyes:

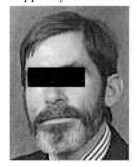

How would you do this? Obviously, you need a black rectangle, and after some trial and error you might conclude that (`rectangle 45 15 "solid" "black"`) is the right size and shape.

But when you try to overlay it on the picture, you get this picture instead: the blot is exactly centered in the picture, and my eyes aren't. You could make the blot bigger, but then it would blot out more of my nose and eyebrows. You could move the blot all the way to the top, or the bottom, or the left, or the right, using `overlay/align`, but none of those puts it exactly where you want it. To deal with this sort of situation, DrRacket provides a function named `place-image` that superimposes one picture at a *specified location* on another. Its contract is

```
place-image :  image (foreground)
               number (horizontal offset) number (vertical offset)
               image (background) -> image
```

As with `overlay`, the second image is the "background", and the first is superimposed "on top" of it. Unlike `overlay`, it only accepts *exactly two* images. It places the *center* of the foreground image *horizontal-offset* pixels from the left, and *vertical-offset* pixels down from the top, of the background image.

Experiment by plugging in various horizontal and vertical offsets, both positive and negative, to see what happens. What horizontal and vertical offsets do you need in order to blot out my eyes as in the picture above?

Exercise 3.5.8 *Write a Racket expression, using* `place-image`, *to produce a solid blue rectangle 80x50 with a solid orange rectangle 30x20 whose bottom-left corner is at the*

center of the blue box:

Recall that the `place-image` function places the *center* of the foreground image. Sometimes it's more natural to place the top-left corner, or the bottom-right corner, *etc.* **Look up** the `place-image/align` function in the Help Desk.

In experimenting with `place-image`, you may have noticed that the result is always the same size and shape as the background image. Even if the foreground image laps over the edges of the background, the excess is cut off. This is often what you want, but not always. **Look up** the `overlay/xy` function in the Help Desk, and **play with it**.

3.5.4   Text

Suppose you wanted to draw a picture with words in it. In theory, you could build letters from tiny rectangles, circles, ellipses, lines, etc. and place them where you wanted them with `place-image`, but that would be a Royal Pain. Instead, DrRacket provides a function named `text` to do exactly this job. Its contract is

```
text :  string (text to draw) number (font size)
        string (color) -> image
```

For example, try `(text "hello there" 12 "forest green")` . **Experiment** with different font sizes and colors.

Exercise 3.5.9 *Write a Racket expression that produces my picture with the caption "Wanted!" in red near the bottom:*

(I've put the word "Wanted!" in black in this picture so it shows up in a black-and-white

printing. On your computer, it'll probably show up better if you use red or yellow or something like that.)

Exercise 3.5.10 *Write a Racket expression placing a word (in blue) on a yellow back-*

ground inside a purple border:

Exercise 3.5.11 *Write a Racket expression for an interesting picture involving text, positioning, geometric shapes, rotation, scaling, etc. Go wild.*

3.5.5 For further reading...

If you want to learn about other ways to manipulate pictures, go to the "Help" menu in DrRacket, select "Help Desk", search for "2htdp/image", and read the documentation. It'll tell you about a number of other functions:

- `square`

- `add-curve`

- `text/font`

- `underlay`

- `underlay/align`

- `underlay/xy`

- `empty-scene`

- `scene+line`

- `scene+curve`

- `scale/xy`

- `crop`

- `frame`

Some of these may involve concepts — `define-struct`, Booleans, posns, and lists — that you haven't seen yet, so don't worry about them. As for the rest, play with them and have fun. Don't worry about memorizing them all; just get a general idea of what's there, so you can look it up when you need it.

3.5.6 Playing with colors

We've built a lot of images using color names like `"purple"`, `"yellow"`, *etc..* This is great as long as the color you want happens to be one of the ones whose name DrRacket recognizes. But what if you want just a *little* bit more blue in your purple, or a *slightly darker* turquoise than `"turquoise"`?

The `picturing-programs` library, like most computer graphics systems, represents colors as combinations of red, green, and blue, each of which (for historical reasons) can be any whole number from 0 to 255. For example, black is made from 0 red, 0 green, and 0 blue; white is 255 red, 255 green and 255 blue; pure blue is 0 red, 0 green, and 255 blue;

yellow is 255 red, 255 green, and 0 blue; and so on. You can mix your own colors by using the `make-color` function, and passing the result into a function like `rectangle`, `triangle`, *etc.*in place of the color name:

```
> (rectangle 50 30 "solid"
              (make-color 180 100 150))
```

```
> (circle 20 "solid" (make-color 20 250 200))
```

This means the contracts for those functions are actually something like

```
; circle :  number string("solid" or "outline") string-or-color -> image
```

Practice Exercise 3.5.12 *Play with this. Make up a bunch of shapes in various colors that you've mixed yourself, and compare them with shapes in predefined colors.*

If you want to see the numeric value of one of the standard named colors, use

```
; name->color :  string -> color or false
; returns false if color name isn't recognized
```

For example,

```
> (name->color "white")
(make-color 255 255 255 255)
> (name->color "forest green")
(make-color 34 139 34 255)
```

Note that this returns a color with *four* parts, not three. The fourth is called "alpha", and it controls transparency: a color with an alpha of 255 is completely opaque, covering whatever was behind it, while a color with an alpha of 0 is completely transparent. If you call `make-color` with three arguments, it assumes you want the color to be opaque, so it fills in 255 for the fourth argument automatically, but if you wish you can make shapes that are "semi-transparent".

Practice Exercise 3.5.13 *Play with this. Make a shape whose color has an alpha component of 120, and see what happens when you overlay or underlay it on another shape.*

We'll learn more about the "color" data type in Chapter 20.

3.6   Specifying results and checking your work

When you try to do one of these exercises, the odds are that your first attempt won't exactly work. How do you know? Well, you type the expression into the Interactions pane, hit RETURN/ENTER, and you get either an error message or a picture that isn't what you were trying for. It may be interesting, it may be pretty, and often that's how creative work starts — as an unsuccessful attempt to do something else — but it doesn't fulfill the assignment. So you figure out what you did wrong, come up with something that addresses the problem, and try that to see if it actually works.

What about the "near misses", in which the picture is *almost* what you wanted? In these cases, your mind may play tricks on you and pretend that what you got really is what you wanted all along. (The first attempt at blotting out my eyes, in section 4.4, *almost* does the job, and you could convince yourself that it was OK, but in your heart you would know it wasn't quite right.) To prevent these mind tricks and make sure you come up with an expression that produces what you *really* wanted, I recommend **describing precisely, in writing** what the result should look like, before you try anything to get that result. This way if the result isn't correct, it's harder for your mind to fool itself into accepting it as correct.

For example, consider exercise 3.5.9 above. It's a reasonably precise description of what the result should be, but it still has some ambiguity. I didn't say specifically that the word "Wanted!" had to be superimposed on the picture; it could have been below the bottom of the picture. And I didn't say exactly what font size the word should be. To make this more precise, one might have written:

> The word "Wanted!", in black, should be superimposed on the picture so there is little or no space between the bottoms of the letters and the bottom of the picture. The word should not lap outside either side of the picture, nor cover any part of Dr. Bloch's mouth (not to mention nose, eyes, etc.); however, it should be large enough to read easily.

Or one could go even farther and specify the font size of the word, the exact number of pixels between it and the bottom of the picture, etc. This sort of precise description of desired outcomes is easier when the result is a number, a string, or some other type that we'll see later in the course, but you can start developing the habit now.

3.7 Reading and writing images

If you've built a really cool picture, you may want to save it so you can use it outside DrRacket (*e.g.* on a Web page, or in a slide presentation or word-processing document). This is easy, using the `save-image` function, which takes in an image and a string, and stores the image in the file with that name. It uses the PNG image format, so it's a really good idea to choose a filename that ends in ".png". For example,

```
(save-image (triangle 40 "solid" "purple") "purple-triangle.png")
```

If you already have an image file, you can get it into DrRacket in any of several ways:

- As you already know, you can open it in a Web browser or other program, copy it, and paste into DrRacket.

- As you may also already know, you can use the "Insert Image" command (on the "Insert" menu of DrRacket).

- You can use the `bitmap` function, which takes in a string filename and returns the image. If the file doesn't exist, it'll return an image of 0 width and 0 height. For example,

  ```
  (rotate-cw (bitmap "purple-triangle.png"))
  ```

By the way, although `save-image` always saves things in PNG format, `bitmap` can read things in a variety of formats, including PNG, GIF, JPG, *etc.*

3.8   Expanding the syntax rules

Based on the syntax rules you've seen in Section 2.4, most of the examples in this chapter aren't legal Racket expressions, because Syntax Rule 1 allows pictures, but not strings or numbers. A more accurate and inclusive version would say

Syntax Rule 1 *Any picture, number, or string literal is a legal expression; its value is itself.*

Worked Exercise 3.8.1 *Draw a box diagram to prove that*

```
(circle 10 "solid" "green")
```

is a legal expression.

Solution: With the new and improved Rule 1, we can recognize 10, `"solid"`, and `"green"` each as legal expressions:

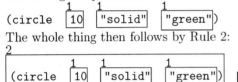

The whole thing then follows by Rule 2:

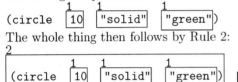

Exercise 3.8.2 *Draw a box diagram to prove that*

```
(define tri (triangle 15 "solid" "orange"))
```

is a legal expression (assuming `tri` *isn't already defined).*

Exercise 3.8.3 *Draw box diagrams to prove that*
`(rectangle 40 26 "solid" "dark blue")`
and
`(rotate-180 (scale 2 (rectangle 20 13 "solid" "dark blue")))`
are both legal expressions.

    Are they the same *expression? Type each of them into the Definitions pane and click "Run". Now click "Step" instead. What does "the same expression" mean?*

3.9   Review of important words and concepts

In this chapter, we've seen how to use additional built-in functions to create pictures "from scratch", rather than copying and pasting them from the Web or other files. To tell these functions what we want them to do, we need to provide different kinds of information, *e.g. numbers* and *strings*. The categories "number", "string", "image", and many others that we'll see in later chapters are all called *data types*.

    Each function "knows" how many arguments, of what types, in what order, it should be given, and what type of information it will produce. We typically write down this informa- tion, the *function contract*, in a standard format: the function name, a colon, the types of its arguments, an arrow, and the type of its result. Where there are multiple arguments of the same type, we may provide additional information about them in parentheses to keep track of which does what. However, this format is not Racket; it's only a convention among human programmers, so if you want to put function contracts into a DrRacket window, you need to "*comment* them out" with one of the several kinds of Racket comments.

Since many of the functions in this chapter take in numbers or strings, we need to modify our syntax rules so that literal numbers and strings, as well as literal pictures, are treated as legal expressions, from which more complex expressions can be built. Henceforth we'll use the expanded version of Syntax Rule 1, allowing not only images but numbers and strings.

3.10 Reference: Built-in functions for images

In this chapter, we discussed the following functions:

- above/align
- beside/align
- overlay/align
- rotate
- scale
- rectangle
- circle
- ellipse
- triangle
- star
- crop-bottom
- crop-top
- crop-left
- crop-right
- place-image
- text
- image-width
- image-height
- `make-color`
- `name->color`
- save-image
- bitmap

and mentioned the following, which you are invited to look up in the built-in DrRacket Help Desk:

- `place-image/align`

- overlay/xy

- right-triangle

- isosceles-triangle

- square

- rhombus

- regular-polygon

- star-polygon

- line

- add-line

- add-curve

- text/font

- underlay

- underlay/align

- underlay/xy

- empty-scene

- scene+line

- scene+curve

- scale/xy

- crop

- frame

Chapter 4

Shorthand for operations: writing your own functions

As a general rule in computer science, *if you write almost the exact same thing over and over, you're doing something wrong.* For example, we've already seen how to *define a variable* so we don't have to keep finding or building the exact same image over and over. In this chapter, we'll learn to write *programs* as a way to avoid writing similar expressions over and over.

4.1 Defining your own functions

Worked Exercise 4.1.1 *Write a Racket expression that produces a picture of a textbook, side by side with its right-to-left reflection:*

And then a picture of a calendar, side by side with its right-to-left reflection:

And then a picture of me, side by side with my right-to-left reflection:

Solution: Each of these should be routine by now: you can get the results by typing

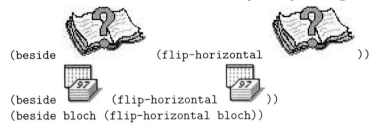

(beside $\qquad$ (flip-horizontal $\qquad$))

(beside ▦ (flip-horizontal ▦))
(beside bloch (flip-horizontal bloch))

(the last one assumes that you've defined a variable `bloch` to hold a picture of me). ∎

Obviously, these are all very similar expressions: they all match the pattern

(beside *something* (flip-horizontal *something*))

with various different pictures plugged in as *something*. Now imagine you were working on a project in which you needed a *lot* of different pictures, *each* side by side with its right-to-left reflection. You could type basically this same expression over and over again, but it would be tedious, repetitive, and error-prone. Frankly, human beings don't do tedious, repetitive jobs very well without making mistakes. *But computers do!* It makes sense, therefore, to use the computer to *automate* this tedious, repetitive process, so we can concentrate our human abilities on more interesting tasks like picking the right pictures for our project.

The task can be broken down into two parts: the part that's the same every time, *i.e.*

(beside *something* (flip-horizontal *something*))

and the part that's different every time, *i.e.* what specific picture is plugged in as *something*. We'll teach the computer that repeated pattern, and whenever we want to use it, we'll simply provide the right picture to plug in for *something*.

We need to provide a *name* for our new pattern, so we can refer to it by name and the computer will know which pattern we're talking about. Let's use the name `mirror-image`. Type the following in the Definitions pane (after the usual (`require installed-teachpacks/picturing-programs`)):

(define (mirror-image something)
   (beside something (flip-horizontal something)))

and click the "Run" button.

Now to get a mirror-image effect on various pictures, we can just type

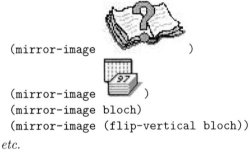

(mirror-image $\qquad$)

(mirror-image ▦)
(mirror-image bloch)
(mirror-image (flip-vertical bloch))

etc.

We've *defined a new function* named `mirror-image`, and taught the computer that whenever you call that function on an image, it should match up the image you provided with the "place-holder"' word *something*, and act as though you had typed (`beside`, the image, (`flip-horizontal`, the same image again, and two right-parentheses. From now until you quit DrRacket, it will remember this pattern and use it whenever you call the `mirror-image` function. Now that the computer "knows" how to do this, we never have to worry about it again ourselves. We've taught the computer a new trick by combining things it already "knows" how to do; in other words, we've *written a program*.

By the way, there's nothing magical about the name `something`; we could equally well have said `x`, or `picture`, or `horse-chestnut`, as long as we spell the name the exact same way in all three places it appears. The name is just a "place-holder" (the technical word is *parameter*), to be matched up with whatever specific picture is provided when a user calls the function. The most sensible of these names would be *picture*, as that's what it's supposed to represent, so a better definition would be

```
(define (mirror-image picture)
  (beside picture (flip-horizontal picture)))
```

Practice Exercise 4.1.2 *Type the above definition (the version with the parameter name* **picture***) into the Definitions pane of DrRacket, along with definitions of the variables* **book***,* **calendar***, and* **bloch***. Click "Run", then type the examples*

```
(mirror-image book)
(mirror-image calendar)
(mirror-image bloch)
(mirror-image (flip-vertical bloch))
```

into the Interactions pane. After each one, hit ENTER/RETURN and you should see the correct result.

4.2 What's in a definition?

4.2.1 Terminology

The definition above is actually made up of several parts. The

```
(define (mirror-image picture)
```

part, which I've put on the first line, is called the *function header*, while the

```
(beside picture (flip-horizontal picture)))
```

part, which I've put on the second line, is called the *function body*.

The function header is always made up of a left-parenthesis, the word `define`, a left-parenthesis, a function name (which must be an identifier that's not already defined, just like when you define a variable), one or more parameter names (identifiers), and a right-parenthesis.

The function body is simply an expression (plus a right-parenthesis at the end to match the one at the beginning of the header), in which the parameter names may appear as though they were defined variables. Indeed, if you have a parameter name in the header that doesn't appear inside the function body, you're probably doing something wrong.

4.2.2 Lines and white space

In each of the above examples, I've written the definition over two lines. You could write it all on one line:

```
(define(mirror-image picture)(beside picture(flip-horizontal picture)))
```

Or you could break it up over many lines, with as many extra blanks as you wish:

```
(
 define                         (
      mirror-image


    picture
                  )                ( beside
      picture        (
          flip-horizontal
              picture    )
  )
       )
```

Racket doesn't care: both of these will work equally well. However, neither of them is particularly easy for a human being to read. For the sake of human readers, most Racket programmers put the function header on one line, then hit ENTER/RETURN and put the function body on one more subsequent lines, depending on how long and complicated it is:

```
(define (mirror-image picture)
  (beside picture (flip-horizontal picture)))
```
or
```
(define (mirror-image picture)
  (beside picture
          (flip-horizontal picture)))
```

Also notice that if you write a definition over more than one line, DrRacket will *automatically indent* each line depending on how many parentheses it's inside; this makes it easier for the human reader to understand what's going on. If you have a badly-indented definition (like the one above for mirror-image spread over eleven lines!), you can select it all with your mouse, then choose "Reindent All" from the Racket menu in DrRacket, and DrRacket will clean up the indentation (but not the line breaks or the extra spaces in the middles of lines).

Exercise 4.2.1 *Define a function named* vert-mirror-image *which, given an image, produces that image above its top-to-bottom reflection. As before, type your definition into the Definitions pane, after the definitions already there. Put the function header on one line, and the function body on the next line or two.*

Click "Run", then **test** *your function by trying it on various images, such as* book, calendar, *and* bloch, *and checking that the results are what you expected.*

Exercise 4.2.2 *Define a function named* four-square *which, given an image, produces*

a two-by-two square of copies of it, e.g. . *Put the function header on one line, and the function body on the next line or two.* **Test** *your function by trying it on various images and checking that the results are what you expected.*

Worked Exercise 4.2.3 *Define a function named* `counterchange` *which, given two images, produces a two-by-two square with the first image in top-left and bottom-right positions, and the second image in top-right and bottom-left positions, e.g.*

Solution: The only new feature of this problem is that the function takes in *two* images rather than one. To keep them straight, we need to have two different parameter names, *e.g.* `image1` and `image2`. The definition then looks like

```
(define (counterchange image1 image2)
  (above (beside image1 image2)
         (beside image2 image1)))
```

Note that as usual, we've put the function header on one line and the function body on another — except that this function body is long enough and complicated enough that we split it across two lines. DrRacket's automatic indentation lines up the two calls to `beside` so the reader can easily see that they are both used as arguments to `above`.

Now we need to test the function. With the above definition in the Definitions pane, we hit the "Run" button, then type (in the Interactions pane)

(counterchange )

and get the result above. For another example, try

(counterchange ))

Is the result what you expected? ∎

Exercise 4.2.4 *Define a function named* `surround` *which, given two images, produces a picture with the second, first, and second side by side, i.e. the first image is "surrounded" on left and right by the second image. Follow the usual convention for code layout, and test your function on at least two different examples.*

4.3 Parameters and arguments

Some people use the words *argument* and *parameter* interchangeably. But there is a subtle, yet important, difference. An *argument* is a specific value in a function call, while a *parameter* is a "place-holder" introduced in the header part of a function definition. An argument may look like a number, string, image, variable, or more complex expression, while a parameter always looks like just a variable. For example,

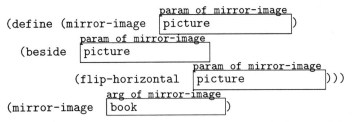

The name `picture` is introduced in the "header" part of the definition of `mirror-image`, so it is a *parameter* of `mirror-image`. That same parameter is used two other times in the definition of `mirror-image`. The name `book` is used as an *argument* in a call of `mirror-image`.

For that matter, `mirror-image` is defined by calling two other functions, which have arguments of their own:

(define (mirror-image picture)

  (beside picture

    (flip-horizontal picture)))

(mirror-image book)

Note that inside the function definition, the word `picture` can be thought of both as a parameter to `mirror-image` (because it appeared in the header of `mirror-image`'s definition), and also as an argument to `beside` and `flip-horizontal` (because it appears in calls to those functions).

To put it another way, an "argument" and a "parameter" both represent information passed into a function from its caller, but the "argument" is that information as seen from the caller's point of view, and the "parameter" is the information as seen by the function being called.

Exercise 4.3.1 *Consider the following Racket code:*

```
( define ( mystery x y )

   ( above ( flip-horizontal x ) y ) )

( mystery calendar book )

( mystery book calendar )
```

What words are used as parameters to which functions? What words are used as arguments to which functions?

Exercise 4.3.2 *Consider your solution and test cases for Exercise 4.2.1, 4.2.2, or 4.2.4. What words are used as parameters to which functions? What words (and expressions) are used as arguments to which functions?*

4.4   Parameters, arguments, and the Stepper

To get a clearer picture of what's going on, type the definitions of `bloch` and `mirror-image`, along with several examples of the latter, into the Definitions pane:

```
(define bloch            )
(define (mirror-image picture)
  (beside picture (flip-horizontal picture)))
```

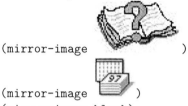

```
(mirror-image            )
```

```
(mirror-image            )
(mirror-image bloch)
(mirror-image (flip-vertical bloch))
```

Now, instead of clicking "Run", click the "Step" button. It'll skip through the definitions, and start stepping at the expression

```
(mirror-image            )
```

which expands to

```
(beside            (flip-horizontal            ))
```

This is because Racket matched up the argument  with the parameter `picture`, and everywhere inside the function definition that the parameter `picture` appeared, replaced it with that specific picture. The next few steps in the Stepper will behave exactly as you expect them to: the innermost expression

```
(flip-horizontal            )
```

is replaced by , and then the `beside` function combines this with the

original picture to produce the result .

Step through the remaining examples, and make sure you understand what is being replaced with what, and why, at each step.

Practice Exercise 4.4.1 *Consider the Racket code from Exercise 4.3.1:*

```
(define (mystery x y)
  (above (flip-horizontal x) y))
(mystery calendar book)
(mystery book calendar)
```

In each of the two calls to mystery, **tell** *which argument is matched with which parameter, and* **write down** *(without using DrRacket) the sequence of steps of expansion that the Stepper would do. Type this code into DrRacket's Definitions pane, hit "Step" several times, and see whether you were right.*

Practice Exercise 4.4.2 *Repeat the previous exercise, replacing the mystery function with your solution to Exercise 4.2.1, 4.2.2, or 4.2.4.*

4.5   Testing a Function Definition

As this course goes on, you'll need to define hundreds of functions; defining a new function is one of the most common tasks for a programmer. But as you may have already found out, it's easy to make a mistake in defining a function. Before we can consider our task finished, we need to *test* the function for correctness.

Program testing can be an unpleasant job, as it often gives you the bad news that your program doesn't work. But it's much better for *you* to discover that your program doesn't work, than for your teacher or customer to make the discovery and penalize you for it. The worst thing that can happen is that we *think* our program is correct, but fail to spot an error that leads to somebody else getting wrong answers, which (in the real world) can cause airplanes or spaceships to crash, bridges to fall down, medical equipment to kill patients, *etc.*

So we owe it to ourselves to *try to break our own programs.* The harder we've tried without managing to break a program, the more confidence we have in turning it over to a teacher or customer. The more devious and malicious we are towards our own programs before releasing them, the less likely they are to be released with errors.

Recall from Chapter 1 that a function is considered correct only if it produces correct answers *for all possible inputs.* However, for a function like `mirror-image`, there are infinitely many possible pictures we could call it on; we can't possibly test it on every one. Fortunately, the function is simple enough that picking two or three different pictures is probably enough: it's unlikely to get those right without also getting everything else right.

4.5.1   Testing with string descriptions

One way I often test a program is by writing several calls to the function in the Definitions pane, after the function definition itself. Each call is followed by a description, in quotation marks, of what the answer should have been. This way, when I hit "Run", DrRacket not only learns the function definition but shows the results of each call, followed by what it should have been. For example, the Definitions pane might look like (in part)

```
(define (mirror-image picture)
  (beside picture (flip-horizontal picture)))
(mirror-image book)
"should be two mirror-image books side by side, the left one with
a question mark, the right one with a backwards question mark"
(mirror-image bloch)
"should be two mirror-image pictures of me side by side,
faces turned slightly away from one another"
```

Hit "Run", and you'll get an Interactions pane looking like

```
"should be two mirror-image books side by side, the left one with
a question mark, the right one with a backwards question mark"
```

```
"should be two mirror-image pictures of me side by side,
faces turned slightly away from one another"
```

Since both actual answers match the descriptions of what they should be, we would tentatively conclude that the program works correctly.

Note that we've used strings to describe the "right answers". This works because when you type a quoted string by itself (not as an argument to a function), the value of that expression is simply the string itself.

Now suppose we had written a program incorrectly, for example

```
(define (vert-mirror-image picture)
  (above picture (flip-horizontal picture)))
(vert-mirror-image book)
"should be two books, one right side up with a question mark,
above another one upside down with an upside-down question mark"
```

Hit "Run", and the result will be

```
"should be two books, one right side up with a question mark,
above another one upside down with an upside-down question mark"
```

The answer the function *actually* produced doesn't match what we *said* it should produce, so something is wrong. Looking through the function definition (possibly with the aid of the Stepper), we would soon realize that the picture was being reflected horizontally, rather than vertically. We would correct this, hit "Run" again, and get

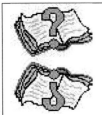

```
"should be two books, one right side up with a question mark,
above another one upside down with an upside-down question mark"
```

This time the actual answer *does* match the "right" answer, so things look good. One test case, however, is almost never enough to build real confidence in a function; **choose at least two or three test cases**.

Not all test cases are created equal. For example, if instead of using the picture of a book, we had written

```
(vert-mirror-image (rectangle 30 20 "solid" "blue"))
"should be a 30x20 solid blue rectangle, above another one upside down"
```

and then clicked "Run", the actual answer would have looked correct, even *without* finding and fixing the error, because a rectangle flipped upside down looks just like a rectangle flipped left-to-right (or not flipped at all). In other words, there would be an error in the program, but we wouldn't know about it because we weren't nasty enough to our program. **Choose test cases that are likely to reveal errors**.

Occasionally, you'll get an actual result that doesn't match what it "should be", and the function is actually right; your "should be" answer was wrong. For example, suppose you had defined `vert-mirror-image` correctly but written the test case

```
(vert-mirror-image calendar)
"should be a calendar, above another calendar flipped left-to-right"
```

When you hit "Run", you'll get an image that doesn't match the description of what it "should be", but this time it's because your "right answer" was wrong. That doesn't mean everything is OK: a correct program which looks wrong is almost as bad as an incorrect program which looks right. But this situation is at least easy to fix: once you're sure the program is right, just correct the "right answer". **This doesn't happen often**: when the actual answer doesn't match your "right answer", it's much more likely that the program is wrong. But keep this other possibility in mind.

4.5.2   Common beginner mistakes

I've frequently had students write "test cases" like the following (I've highlighted them for visibility):

```
(define (mirror-image picture)
  (beside picture (flip-horizontal picture)))
book
"should be two mirror-image books side by side,
the left one with a question mark, the right one
with a backwards question mark"
bloch
"should be two mirror-image pictures of me side by side,
faces turned slightly away from one another"
```

What's wrong with this? Well, when you type **book** or **bloch** by itself, DrRacket has no idea what you want to *do* with that picture. DrRacket certainly can't guess that you want to look at its mirror image (as opposed to rotating it clockwise, or putting it above itself, or thousands of other things DrRacket might be able to do with it). The fact that you've recently defined the **mirror-image** function does not mean that the **mirror-image** function will be called automatically; if you want to use a particular function, you have to call it by name. Just saying **book** will give you a picture of a book, no matter what functions you've defined.

Another common mistake in writing test cases:

```
(define (mirror-image picture)
  (beside picture (flip-horizontal picture)))
  (beside book (flip-horizontal book))
"should be two mirror-image books side by side,
the left one with a question mark, the right one
with a backwards question mark"
  (beside bloch (flip-horizontal bloch))
"should be two mirror-image pictures of me side by side,
faces turned slightly away from one another"
```

There are two things wrong with this. First, it misses the point of defining a new function: once you've defined a function, you shouldn't have to think about (or repeat) its body ever again. Second and more seriously, it *doesn't test the function* you defined. These examples test whether **beside** and **flip-horizontal** work correctly, but since they never actually use **mirror-image** itself, they don't tell whether or not *it* works correctly. If the **mirror-image** function had been written incorrectly (*e.g.* using **above** rather than **beside**), these test cases wouldn't show us that anything was wrong.

Many of my students in the past have balked at describing "what the right answer should be"; they would rather type in the test case, run it, see what the answer *is*, then (since the mean old professor insists on test cases) describe this answer and say that's what it "should be". **Don't do this!** These students will *never* discover any errors in their programs, because they're assuming the program is correct. They have completely missed the point of testing (and lost a lot of points on their homework grades, to boot!)

4.5.3 The **check-expect** function

If you've got a lot of test cases for a particular function, or if you have a lot of functions in the Definitions pane, it can be a lot of work to look through all the answers and compare them with their descriptions. DrRacket comes with a function named **check-expect** that automates this process: no matter how many test cases you have in the Definitions pane, it tells you instantly how many of the actual answers matched what you said they "should be", and which of them didn't.

Unfortunately, `check-expect` isn't smart enough to understand an English-language description of the right answer, so to take advantage of it, you have to build the *exact* right answer for each specific test case.

For example, consider the `vert-mirror-image` function from before. To test it using check-expect, we would replace the test case

```
(vert-mirror-image book)
"should be two books, one right side up with a question mark,
 above one upside down with an upside-down question mark"
```

with

```
(check-expect (vert-mirror-image book)
              (above book (flip-vertical book)))
```

In addition, let's use the "bad test case" from section 4.5.1:

```
(check-expect
    (vert-mirror-image (rectangle 30 20 "solid" "blue"))
    (above (rectangle 30 20 "solid" "blue")
           (flip-vertical (rectangle 30 20 "solid" "blue"))))
```

Practice Exercise 4.5.1 *Type a correct definition of* `vert-mirror-image` *into the Dr-Racket definitions pane, followed by the above* `check-expect` *lines. Click "Run" and see what happens.*

Now change the definition to be incorrect *— for example, use* `flip-horizontal` *instead of* `flip-vertical` *— but leave the* `check-expect` *the same. Click "Run" and see what happens.*

By the way, `check-expect` *is* "smart" in another way: you can put test cases using check-expect *ahead* of the definition and DrRacket won't complain that the function isn't defined yet. This doesn't work with "should be"-style test cases.

4.6   A new syntax rule

Why is something like

```
(define (mirror-image picture)
  (beside picture (flip-horizontal picture)))
```

legal Racket? Well, based on the syntax rules you've seen so far, it isn't: there is no way to draw a box diagram for it, justifying each box with one of the rules

Syntax Rule 1 *Any picture, number, or string is a legal expression; its value is itself.*

Syntax Rule 2 *A left-parenthesis followed by a function name, one or more legal expressions, and a right parenthesis, is a legal expression; its value is what you get by applying the named function to the values of the smaller expressions inside it.*

Syntax Rule 3 *Any identifier, if already defined, is a legal expression.*

Syntax Rule 4 *A left-parenthesis followed by the word* **define**, *a previously-undefined identifier, a legal expression, and a right-parenthesis is a legal expression. It has no "value", but the side effect of defining the variable to stand for the value of the expression.*

To define new functions, as we've just done, we need a new syntax rule:

Syntax Rule 5 *A left parenthesis followed by the word* `define`*, a left parenthesis, a previously-undefined identifier, one or more identifiers, a right parenthesis, a legal expression, and another right parenthesis is a legal expression. Think of it as anything matching the pattern*

```
(define ( new-identifier identifier ...)  expression )
```

This sort of expression has no "value", but the side effect of defining a new function whose name is the new-*identifier. Note that the parameter names from the function header can appear inside the function body as though they were defined variables.*

Notice the difference between Syntax Rules 4 and 5: a variable definition looks like

```
(define variable-name ...)
```

whereas a function definition looks like

```
(define (function-name parameter-names) ...)
```

Racket can tell which one you mean by whether there's a left parenthesis after the `define`.

Worked Exercise 4.6.1 *Draw a box diagram to prove that*

```
( define ( two-copies picture )
    ( beside picture picture ))
```

is a legal expression. Assume that `two-copies` *is not already defined.*

Solution: Since `picture` is one of the identifiers in the function header, it can appear inside the function body as if it were a defined variable. So the last two occurrences of the word picture are legal expressions, by Rule 3:

```
(define (two-copies picture)
          3          3
  (beside │picture│ │picture│))
```

Then the whole call to `beside` is a legal expression, by Rule 2:

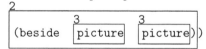

Finally, by Rule 5, we can recognize the whole thing as a legal expression defining a new function:

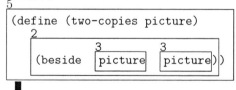

Exercise 4.6.2 *Draw a box diagram to prove that*

```
(define (mirror-image picture)
    (beside picture (flip-horizontal picture)))
```

is a legal expression. Assume that `mirror-image` *is not already defined.*

Exercise 4.6.3 *Draw a box diagram to prove that your solution to Exercise 4.2.1, 4.2.2, or 4.2.4 is a legal expression.*

4.7   Scope and visibility

You may have already noticed (perhaps by accident) that two different functions can have parameters with the same name (which I've highlighted), *e.g.*

```
(define (horiz-mirror-image pic )
  (beside pic (flip-horizontal pic )))
(define (vert-mirror-image pic )
  (above pic (flip-vertical pic )))
```

In fact, there could even be a global variable by the same name:

```
(define pic            )
```

```
(define (horiz-mirror-image pic )
  (beside pic (flip-horizontal pic )))
(define (vert-mirror-image pic )
  (above pic (flip-vertical pic )))
```

```
(rotate-cw pic )
(horiz-mirror-image pic )
(horiz-mirror-image (rotate-cw pic ))
```

There's nothing wrong with this: when a parameter name appears in a function header, it "hides" any other definition of that name that might already exist, until the end of the function definition.

By way of analogy, when I'm at home, the name "Deborah" always refers to my wife, even though there are lots of other Deborahs in the world. If I meant one of the other Deborahs, I'd have to specify a last name, *e.g.* the author Deborah Tannen; the name "Deborah" by itself still means my wife. Similarly, inside the body of `vert-mirror-image`, the word `pic` always refers to the parameter `pic` introduced in its header, regardless of whether there are other things named `pic` defined elsewhere.

Furthermore, there is *no way whatsoever* to refer to that parameter from outside the function; the parameter simply doesn't exist outside the function. (I suppose the best analogy to this would be if my wife never left the house, and I kept her existence a secret from the rest of the world....) The world outside the definition of `horiz-mirror-image` neither knows nor cares what parameter name it uses internally. Another result of this is that you can call `horiz-mirror-image` with an argument that happens to be named `pic`, or with some other argument; it makes no difference whatsoever.

Of course, if you *prefer* to use different parameter names in each function, there's nothing wrong with that either:

```
(define pic          )

(define (horiz-mirror-image pic2 )
  (beside pic2 (flip-horizontal pic2 )))
(define (vert-mirror-image pic3 )
  (above pic3 (flip-vertical pic3 )))

(rotate-cw pic )
(horiz-mirror-image pic )
(horiz-mirror-image (rotate-cw pic ))
```

but it's an unnecessary complication. When choosing parameter names, I choose whatever makes the most sense inside this function, without worrying about whether there's something else with the same name somewhere else.

Computer scientists refer to the part of the program in which a variable is visible as that variable's *scope*. In the above example, the global variable `pic`'s scope is "everywhere, until you quit DrRacket"; the parameter `pic2`'s scope is "inside the definition of `horiz-mirror-image`", and the parameter `pic3`'s scope is "inside the definition of `vert-mirror-image`".

4.8 An analogy from English

We've encountered a number of new concepts in the past few chapters: *expression, function, argument, variable, data type, etc.* Some people may have an easier time understanding these terms by analogy to English.

4.8.1 Proper nouns and literals

In English (and most other natural languages), one can name an individual person, place, or thing with a *proper noun*, e.g. "Joe Smith", "New York", "Harvard University", "Rover", *etc.* The analogous concept in Racket (and most other programming languages) is a *literal*,

e.g. a picture like , a number like 7, or a string like `"hello there"`. All of these represent specific pieces of information, which you can tell simply by looking at them.

4.8.2 Pronouns and variables

English also has pronouns like "he", "she", "it", *etc.*: words that represent an individual person, place, or thing, but only in context. If I say "He is very tall," you know that I'm talking about a person, but you don't know *which* person unless you've heard the previous sentence or two.

Analogously, in Racket and other programming languages, we have *variables* that represent an individual piece of information, but just by looking at the variable in isolation you can't tell *which* piece of information; you need to see the variable's definition. For example, if I said (`beside image1 image2`), you could tell that I was putting two images side by side, but without seeing the definitions of the variables `image1` and `image2`, you would have no idea *what* images I was putting beside one another. Parameters inside a function definition are just like variables in this sense.

4.8.3 Improper nouns and data types

English also has *improper nouns*: words describing a *category* of things rather than an *individual* thing, like "person", "state", "school", and "dog". The analogous concept in Racket and other programming languages is *data type*: the three data types we've seen so far are "image", "number", and "string".

4.8.4 Verbs and functions

English also has *verbs*: words that represent *actions* that take place, at a particular time, often to one or more particular objects. For example, "Sam kissed Angela last night" includes the verb "kissed", involving the two objects "Sam" and "Angela" (both of which are proper nouns, as discussed above), and the action took place at a particular time (last night).

The closest analogue to verbs in Racket and other programming languages is *functions*: when you call a function on particular arguments, it performs an action on those arguments. (By contrast, literals, variables, and data types aren't so bound to time: they just *are*, rather than doing anything at a particular time.) For example, when you type the expression

(above   )

into the Interactions pane (or type it into Definitions and hit "Run"), the function `above` operates on the two specified pictures at that particular time and creates a new picture including both of them.

4.8.5 Noun phrases and expressions

In English, one can often string several words together into a *noun phrase*, like "my best friend's aunt's house," which represents a specific thing, like a proper noun or a pronoun but which requires a little more work to identify. In this case, it takes three steps: Who is my best friend? Who is that person's aunt? Where is that person's house?

The analogous concept in Racket and other programming languages is the *expression*, which represents a specific piece of information that may be the result of calculation, *e.g.*

```
(beside (flip-vertical bloch) (circle 10 "solid" "green"))
```

whose evaluation requires four steps: What does the variable `bloch` refer to? What do I get when I reflect that picture vertically? What does a solid green circle of radius 10 look like? What do I get when I combine those two images side by side?

We summarize this section in table 4.1.

4.9 Review of important words and concepts

Instead of typing in a bunch of very similar expressions ourselves, we can use the computer to automate the process by *defining a function*. This requires identifying which parts of the expressions are always the same (these become the function body), and which parts

Table 4.1: Analogy between English parts of speech and Racket

English term	English examples	Racket term	Racket examples	What it represents
Proper noun	Joe, Harvard, Rover, Chicago	Literal	, 7, "hello"	A single object, which you can tell just by looking at it
Pronoun	Him, her, it	Variable, parameter	calendar, picture, image1	A single object, but needs *context* to tell which one
Improper noun	Person, school, dog, city	Data type	image, number, string	A *category* of objects
Verb	Eat, kiss, study	Function	flip-vertical, mirror-image, counterchange, define	An action applied to specific objects at a specific time
Noun phrase	"Jeff's house", "the tallest boy in the class"	Expression	(flip-vertical book), (above bloch (circle 10 "solid" "red"))	A single object, maybe the result of computation

are different (which are referred to inside the function body as *parameters*, and which are replaced with specific *arguments* when the function is called).

A function definition can be divided into a *function header* (specifying the name of the function and of its parameters) and a *function body* (an expression that uses the parameters as though they were defined variables). Ordinarily, the function header is written on one line and the function body on the next one (or more, if it's long and complicated). Racket doesn't actually care whether you define a function on one line or a hundred, nor how you indent the various lines, but human readers (including you!) will find it much easier to read and understand your programs if you follow standard conventions for line breaks and indentation. DrRacket helps with the indentation: every time you hit RETURN/ENTER, it automatically indents the next line as appropriate.

You can see what DrRacket is doing "behind the scenes" by using the *Stepper*: it sho how the arguments in a function call are matched up with the parameters in the function's definition, and how the function call is then replaced by the function body, with parameters replaced by the corresponding arguments.

Before a program can be turned over to a teacher or a customer, it must be carefully tested. If there are errors in a program, it's much better for *us* to discover them than for the teacher or customer to discover them, so try to come up with weird, malicious *test cases* that are likely to uncover errors.

One way to write test cases in DrRacket is to put them in the Definitions pane, after the definition itself, each test case followed by a description in quotation marks of what the right answer should be.

Another way is a little more work to write, but easier to use in the long run: the check-expect function, which compares the actual answer with what you said it should be, and gives you a report on how many and which of your test cases failed.

The act of defining a function requires a new syntax rule, Rule 5:

(`define` (*new-identifier identifier* ...) *expression*)

The parameter names introduced in the function header can be used inside the function body, but are not visible outside the definition.

Many of the new concepts introduced in the programming-language setting so far correspond to familiar notions from English grammar: literals are proper nouns, variables are pronouns, data types are improper nouns, functions are verbs, and expressions are noun phrases.

4.10   Reference: Built-in functions for defining and testing functions

The only new built-in functions introduced in this chapter are `define` (used to define a *function* rather than a *variable*) and `check-expect`.

Chapter 5

A recipe for defining functions

5.1 Step-by-step recipes

I will now give you a simple recipe to accomplish *anything* in the world. Ready?

Design recipe for anything, version 0

1. Decide what you want to do.

2. Do it.

3. Check that you did it right.

4. Keep doing it.

Okay, I admit that's a little vague; you'd need to fill in a lot of details. But it's basically right. In fact, many of the bad inventions, bad laws, bad wars, bad teaching, and bad computer programs in the world can be blamed on somebody skipping either step 1 or step 3 (or both).

Skipping step 3 is understandable, since after you've done your great creative work, *checking* it is boring and unrewarding. But, you may ask, how could anybody skip step 1? In practice, people often charge into "doing it" before they've decided *clearly, unambiguously, and in detail* what they want to do and how they'll know when they've done it. Since they have only a vague mental picture of what they want to accomplish, what actually gets done is a hodgepodge of different goals. (This is especially bad when the task is undertaken by a *group* of people, each of whom has a slightly different idea of what they're trying to do!)

5.2 A more detailed recipe

Here's a version that's more useful for actual programming.

Design recipe for functions, version 1

1. Write a *function contract* (and possibly a *purpose statement*) for the function you want to write.

2. Write several *examples* of how the function will be used, with their correct answers.

3. Write a *skeleton* of the function you want to write.

4. Add to the skeleton an *inventory* of what you have available to work with.

5. Add the *body* of the function definition.

6. *Test* your program on the examples you chose in step 2.

7. *Use* your program to solve other problems.

Steps 1 and 2 correspond to "decide what you want to do"; steps 3–5 to "do it"; and step 6, obviously, to "check that you did it right." Step 7 corresponds roughly to "keep doing it": in the real world, programs aren't a goal in themselves, but are written in order to get answers to questions. We'll look at all these steps in more detail in a moment.

But first, why do we *need* a recipe like this? For very simple functions, frankly, we don't. But we won't always be writing "very simple functions". I want you to get into the habit of following these steps now, so that by the time you really need them, they'll be second nature. So how does it help?

- Each step is small and manageable. Even if you have no idea how to solve the whole problem, you can do one step of it and have a small feeling of accomplishment.

- You always know what to work on next, and what questions to ask yourself.

- The contract, purpose, and examples help you understand the question before you start trying to solve it.

- In my class, you get partial credit for each step you solve correctly.

- In my class, the teacher stubbornly refuses to give you any help with a later step until you've finished all the previous ones.

Now let's look at the individual steps and see how to do them.

5.3   Function contracts and purpose statements

Before you can solve any programming problem, you have to understand the problem. Sounds obvious, but I've had a lot of students over the years charge into writing the program before they had finished reading the assignment. (They ended up writing the wrong program and getting lousy grades.) In particular, you need to be able to write a *function contract* (remember Section 4.2?) for the function you're about to define.

What's in a function contract? Three essential pieces of information: the *name* of the function, the *type(s)* of the input(s), and the *type* of the result. (So far, the type of the result has always been "image", but that will change soon.) Once you've written this down (in a comment, in the usual notation from Section 4.2), both you and any other programmer who reads the contract will know how to use your function.

Sometimes, if the program's purpose isn't obvious from its name, it's useful to also write a "purpose statement": a brief sentence or two, also in Racket comments, explaining what the program does. This does *not substitute* for a contract, but *expands* on the contract.

Worked Exercise 5.3.1 *Write a contract and purpose for the* `counterchange` *function of Exercise 4.2.3.*

To remind you what Exercise 4.2.3 was, I'll repeat it here:
Define a function named `counterchange` which, given two images, produces a two-by-two square with the first image in top-left and bottom-right positions, and the second image

in top-right and bottom-left positions. The result should look like  .
Solution: The function name is obviously `counterchange`. The assignment says it is to be "given two images", which tells us that it takes two parameters of type "image". It "produces a two-by-two square", which must be an image. So we could write (in the Definitions window) something like

```
; counterchange :   image image -> image
```

This technically answers all the questions, but it doesn't really give a user all the necessary information to use the function. Which of the two images is which? So a better contract would be

```
; counterchange :   image (top-left) image (top-right) -> image
```

If we think it's necessary to add a purpose statement, we might write

```
; counterchange :   image (top-left) image (top-right) -> image
; Produces a square arrangement with the top-left image also
; in the bottom right, and the top-right image also in the
; bottom left.
```

∎

Exercise 5.3.2 *Write a contract and purpose statement for a function named* `copies-beside` *that takes in a number and an image, and produces that many copies of the image side by side.*

Exercise 5.3.3 *Write a contract and purpose statement for a function named* `pinwheel` *that takes in a picture and produces four copies of it in a square, differently rotated: the original picture in the top left, rotated 90° clockwise in the top right, rotated 180° in the bottom right, and rotated 90° counterclockwise in the bottom left. The result should look*

like .

Worked Exercise 5.3.4 *Write a contract and purpose statement for a function named* `checkerboard2` *that produces a 2x2 square checkerboard in specified colors. Each square should be 20 pixels on a side.*

Solution: The function name is obviously `checkerboard2`. The result is an image. As for the input, the assignment refers to "specified colors", but doesn't say what they are, which implies that they can vary from one function call to the next — in other words, they are inputs to the function. The only way we know to specify colors so far is by their names, which are strings in Racket. There are two colors, and the assignment doesn't say which is which, so let's decide arbitrarily that the first one will be in the top-left corner of the checkerboard, and the second in the top-right corner. The "2x2" and "20 pixels on a side" don't concern us yet. Furthermore, it doesn't make sense to call the function with strings that aren't color-names, *e.g.* `"screwdriver"`. So we might write (in the Definitions window)

```
; checkerboard2 :  string (top-left-color)
;                  string (top-right-color) -> image
; Assumes that both strings are color names.
; Produces a 2x2 checkerboard, with each small square 20
; pixels on a side, with the top-left color in the top-left
; and bottom-right positions, and the top-right color in
; the other two positions.
```

∎

Exercise 5.3.5 *Write a contract and purpose statement for the following problem: Design a program named* `bullseye` *which produces a "bull's eye" style target with two rings. It takes in two numbers indicating the radii of the outer ring and the inner disk, and two strings representing the colors of the outer ring and the color of the inner disk.*

Exercise 5.3.6 *Write a contract and purpose statement for the following problem: Design a program named* `dot-grid` *which expects two numbers (the width and height of the grid, respectively) and produces a rectangular grid of radius-5 circular blue dots .*

> (dot-grid 5 3)

Exercise 5.3.7 *Write a contract and purpose statement for the following problem: Design a program named* `lollipop` *which produces a picture of a lollipop. It takes in two numbers — the radius of the lollipop "head" and the length of the "stick" — and a string,*

indicating the color of the lollipop. For the stick, use a rectangle of width 1.

5.4 Examples (also known as Test Cases)

A function contract and purpose statement are big steps towards understanding what the program needs to do, but they're not specific enough. So for the next step, we'll write down several *examples* of how we would use the program if it were already written. Next to each example, we'll write down, as precisely as we can, the *right answer* to that example (as in Chapter 4).

Why? Several reasons. Most obviously, it provides you with test cases that you can use later in testing. Since testing can be the most frustrating part of programming, your mind will take any excuse it can find to avoid testing. (After all, how often do you do something for which the whole point is to get bad news? Do you look forward to doing such things?) And since testing is also the *last* thing you do before turning in the program, it tends to get skipped when you're running behind schedule. Writing the test cases in advance — before you write the program itself — means you have one less excuse for not testing.

Your mind will try to trick you in another way, too: you'll look at the results of a test run and say to yourself "yes, that's right; that's what I expected," when you really had only a vague idea what to expect. This is why you *must write down right answers* next to each test case: it's much harder to fool yourself into thinking everything is fine when a picture of a blue box is next to the words `"should be a green circle"`. If you use `check-expect`, it becomes even harder to fool yourself.

Another benefit: it makes you specify *very precisely* what the program is supposed to produce. No room for vagueness here. Of course, we'll have to be precise when we write the program; this gives us a chance to "warm up" our precision muscles, and come up with suitably nasty "special cases" that might possibly throw the program off, without having to think about Racket syntax at the same time.

By the way, if you have friends who are professional programmers, you can tell them you're learning "test-driven development". (There's more to test-driven development than this, but its most important feature is writing test cases before you write the program.)

Worked Exercise 5.4.1 *Write several test cases* for the `counterchange` function of Exercise 5.3.1.

Solution: We've already identified the contract for this function, so we should be able to call it with any two images. By Syntax Rules 1 and 2, an example would be

(counterchange   )

What should this produce? Since the contract tells us the first parameter will go into the top-left position and the second into the top-right, we could write

```
"should be a picture with a calendar in the top-left
 and bottom-right corners, and a hacker in the top-right
 and bottom-left"
```

If we wanted to give a more precise "right answer", we could come up with an expression that actually builds the right picture, *e.g.*

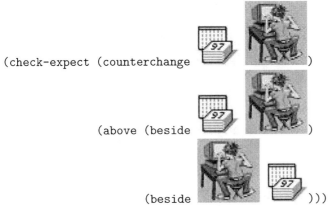

This is, of course, more work, but it also brings two extra benefits: when we get to writing the body, this example will help us do it, and "check-expect" style test cases are much easier to check.

So far we've given only one test case, and it's possible that the function might get that case right even though it's wrong in general. So let's try another:

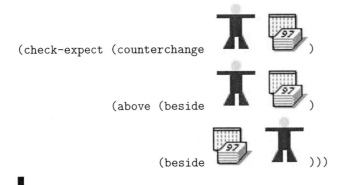

Exercise 5.4.2 *Write several test cases* for the `copies-beside` function described in Exercise 5.3.2.

Hint: the function takes in a "number", but in fact it wouldn't make sense to call this function on a fraction, a negative number, or an irrational number. The only numbers that make sense are *whole numbers*, also known as *counting numbers*: 0, 1, 2, 3, ... In trying to break the program, think about whole numbers that might be considered "special cases". We'll revisit whole numbers in Chapter 24.

Exercise 5.4.3 *Write several test cases* for the `pinwheel` function of Exercise 5.3.3.

Exercise 5.4.4 *Write several test cases* for the `checkerboard2` function of Exercise 5.3.4.

Hint: Technically, any two strings would satisfy the contract, but since the purpose statement adds "Assumes that both strings are color names", you don't need to test it on strings that aren't color names. Ideally, a program to be used by human beings should be able to handle a wide variety of incorrect inputs, and we'll learn techniques for handling such situations in Chapter 19.

Exercise 5.4.5 *Write several test cases for the* `bullseye` *function of Exercise 5.3.5.*

Exercise 5.4.6 *Write several test cases for the* `dot-grid` *function of Exercise 5.3.6.*

Exercise 5.4.7 *Write several test cases for the* `lollipop` *function of Exercise 5.3.7.*

5.5 The function skeleton

A *function skeleton* is a "first draft" of the function definition, based only on Syntax Rule 5 and the information in the contract (not what specific problem the function is supposed to solve). As you recall from Chapter 4, every function definition follows a simple pattern:

(define (*function-name param-name param-name* ...)
   ...)

Once you've written the contract, you already know the function name as well as the number, types, order, and meanings of all the parameters. So it's easy to write the header; the only faintly creative part is choosing good, meaningful names for the parameters. We'll come back to this in a moment.

Worked Exercise 5.5.1 *Write a function skeleton for the* `counterchange` *function of Exercise 5.3.1.*

Solution: Recall that the function takes in two images, which we referred to in the contract as `top-left` and `top-right`. These are probably good choices for parameter names: they make clear what each parameter is supposed to represent. Following Syntax Rule 5, the function definition must look like

(define (counterchange top-left top-right)
   ...)

∎

5.6 Common beginner mistakes

Here are some of the things I've seen a lot of students do wrong in writing examples and skeletons.

Not calling the function by name
A student working on `counterchange` writes the example

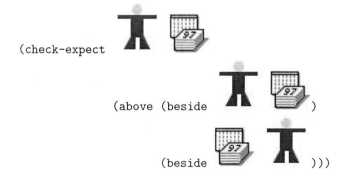

This "example" never actually mentions the `counterchange` function, so DrRacket doesn't know what to do with the two pictures. See Section 4.5.2.

The contract, examples, and skeleton must agree on the number, type, and order of parameters.

For example, suppose I were writing a function that took in a string and two numbers, and returned an image:

```
; do-it :  string number number -> image
```

A student writes the example `(check-expect (do-it "boojum") "fnord")`. This example violates the contract in at least two ways: it gives the function only a string rather than a string and two numbers, and it expects the answer to be a string rather than an image. A *correct* test case would have to call `do-it` on a string and two numbers, and have an image as the "right answer":

```
(check-expect (do-it "boojum" 0 3.14)
              (circle 10 "outline" "green"))
```

```
(check-expect (do-it "blah" 7 32)          )
(check-expect (do-it "fnord" 5/3 -6)
              (triangle 10 "solid" "blue"))
```

Another student writes the example

`(check-expect (do-it 3 4 "boojum")          )`. This has the right number of parameters, and the right return type, but the parameters are in a different order from what the contract said: the string is third rather than first.

Next, a student writes the skeleton `(define (do-it word) ...)`. Again, this violates the contract because `do-it` takes in *three* parameters, and this skeleton has only one. A *correct* skeleton for this function would have to have three parameter names, the first standing for a string and the second and third standing for numbers, for example

```
(define (do-it word num1 num2)
  ...)
```

Notice how the contract, examples, and skeleton *must* "match up":

;	do-it:	string	number	number	→	image
(check-expect (	do-it	"blah"	7	32	)	)
(define (	do-it	word	num1	num2	)	...)

The function name is the same in all three places. The number and order of parameters in the contract are the same as the number and order of arguments in each test case, which are the same as the number and order of parameters in the skeleton. The return type in the contract is the same as the type of the "right answer" in each test case, which is the same type as the "body" expression which will eventually replace the "..." in the skeleton.

Misleading parameter names

In the above example skeleton, the parameter names `word`, `num1`, and `num2` were chosen to suggest to the reader that the first is a string and the other two are numbers. There's actually quite a bit of art to choosing good parameter names.

Remember that a parameter name is a *place-holder*; you can't assume that a particular parameter will always be a picture of a book, or will always be the string `"yellow"`, or will always be the number 7. If the contract says that the first parameter is a picture, you can assume that it's a picture, but not *what* picture. I've seen students write a perfectly-good example like

(counterchange )

but then write a function skeleton like
`(define (counterchange calendar hacker) ...)`

What's wrong with this? It's technically legal, but misleading: the parameter-name `calendar` will stand for whatever first argument is provided when the function is called (which may or may not be a calendar), and the parameter-name `hacker` will likewise stand for the second argument (which may not be a hacker). For example, when you try the second test case

(counterchange )

the parameter name `calendar` will stand for a stick figure, and the name `hacker` will stand for a picture of a calendar! Remember that a function has to work on *all possible inputs*, not only the ones you had in mind.

Duplicate parameter names

Another bad attempt at a skeleton for this function is
`(define (counterchange picture picture) ...)`

"picture" is a perfectly reasonable parameter name, but this student has used it *twice in the same function header*. The purpose of parameter names is to allow you to refer to them in the body of the function; if they both have the same name, how will Racket know which one you mean? This is illegal in Racket, and it'll produce an error message. (Try it.)

Literals as parameter names

Yet another incorrect skeleton is   (define (counterchange ) ...)

This one is also illegal: the parameters in a function header must be variable names, not literals. DrRacket will give you an error message. (Try it.)

More generally, this kind of mistake points to a common beginner confusion between *calling* a function (on specific arguments, *e.g.* pictures or variables already defined to stand for pictures) and *defining* a function (in which you specify place-holder parameter names).

Remember, the parameter names in a function skeleton should indicate what the parameter "means" in general (*e.g.* `top-left` and `top-right`), and/or what *type* it is (*e.g.* `picture`), but should *not* assume anything about what *specific value* it is.

5.7   Checking syntax

Once you've written a contract, examples, and a function skeleton (with "..." where the function body will eventually be), DrRacket will help you check whether you're on the right track. Obviously, since you haven't written the function body yet, it won't produce correct answers, but at least you can check whether you're following all the syntax rules and calling the function with the right number of arguments, thus catching many common beginner mistakes. Click the "Check Syntax" button near the top of the screen. If your examples use the function with the wrong number of arguments, DrRacket will tell you so.

For example, if you made the first of the "common beginner mistakes" above,

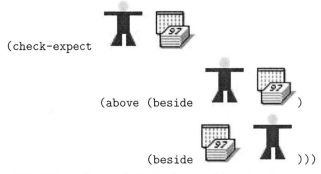

and hit "Check Syntax", DrRacket would notice that you were calling `check-expect` with three arguments rather than two, and tell you so. On the other hand, if you provided just a picture and an answer:

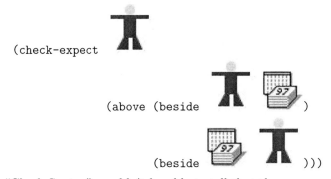

"Check Syntax" wouldn't be able to tell that there was anything wrong, because all your function calls are with the right number of arguments.

The second of the "common beginner mistakes" above is calling a function with the wrong number of arguments, or arguments in the wrong order. "Check Syntax" will complain if you define a function with two parameters but call it with one or three; it can't tell if you call it with two parameters in the wrong order.

The third of the "common beginner mistakes" above, misleading parameter names, is beyond "Check Syntax"'s ability to catch: all your function calls are legal.

However, it can easily catch the fourth and fifth:

```
(define (counterchange picture picture) ...)
```

```
(define (counterchange          ) ...)
```

In both of these cases, the function definition doesn't fit Syntax Rule 5, and "Check Syntax" will tell you so.

5.8 Exercises on writing skeletons

In doing the following exercises, use "Check Syntax to see whether your examples and skeletons match up properly.

Exercise 5.8.1 *Write a function skeleton for the* `copies-beside` *function of Exercise 5.3.2.*

Exercise 5.8.2 *Write a function skeleton for the* `pinwheel` *function of Exercise 5.3.3.*

Exercise 5.8.3 *Write a function skeleton for the* `checkerboard2` *function of Exercise 5.3.4.*

Exercise 5.8.4 *Write a function skeleton for the* `bullseye` *function of Exercise 5.3.5.*

Exercise 5.8.5 *Write a function skeleton for the* `dot-grid` *function of Exercise 5.3.6.*

Exercise 5.8.6 *Write a function skeleton for the* `lollipop` *function of Exercise 5.3.7.*

5.9 The inventory

Imagine that you're trying to bake cookies. A smart cook will get all the ingredients (eggs, milk, butter, sugar, chocolate chips, etc.) out and put them on the counter before mixing anything together: that way you can see whether you have enough of everything. We'll do something similar: list everything that's available for you to use in defining the function, before starting to put things together. At this stage, that basically means the parameters (it will get more interesting later).

You should also recall from Chapter 4 that the parameter names that appear in the function header must exactly match those that appear in the function body — same spelling, same capitalization, etc. You may have no idea how the function body is going to work, but you can be pretty sure that the parameter names you put in the header will be used in it. At this stage, I recommend writing the names of all the parameters, one on each line, commented out, in between the function header and the "..." where its body will eventually be. It's often helpful to also write down, next to each parameter, what *data type* it is; this determines what you can reasonably do with it.

There may also be particular pieces of information that are always the same, regardless of the arguments passed into the function. For example, a function that is supposed to always draw in blue will presumably use the word `"blue"` at least once in its body.

I generally ask students to write a *skeleton*, as above, and then *insert* the inventory information before the "...".

Worked Exercise 5.9.1 *Add an inventory to the skeleton* for the `counterchange` *function of Exercise 5.5.1.*

Solution: We've already written the skeleton:

```
(define (counterchange top-left top-right)
  ...)
```

We don't know yet how the function body will work, but we're pretty sure it will involve the variable names `top-left` and `top-right`. So we list these, one on each line, commented out, along with their types. The complete function skeleton, with inventory then reads

```
(define (counterchange top-left top-right)
  ; top-left  image
  ; top-right image
  ...)
```

Together with the contract and examples we wrote before, the Definitions window should now look like Figure 5.1.

SIDEBAR:

Later in the book, we'll talk about something analogous called an "outventory". Where an inventory answers the question "what am I given, and what can I do with it?", an outventory answers the question "what do I need to produce, and how can I produce it?". If the inventory is like collecting the raw ingredients for cookies, the outventory is like observing that the *last* step in the recipe is baking, and concluding that you'd better preheat the oven and make sure you have a cookie sheet.

We'll come back to this concept when we have problems to solve that need it. For now, inventories will do just fine.

Exercise 5.9.2 *Add an inventory to the skeleton* for the `copies-beside` *function of Exercise 5.8.1.*

Exercise 5.9.3 *Add an inventory* to the `pinwheel` *function of Exercise 5.8.2.*

Exercise 5.9.4 *Add an inventory* to the `checkerboard2` *function of Exercise 5.8.3.*

Hint: In addition to the parameters, this function will almost certainly need to use the number 20 (the size of each small square), so you can include another line with 20 on it. Its type, obviously, is *number.*

Exercise 5.9.5 *Add an inventory* to the `bullseye` *function of Exercise 5.8.4.*

Hint: This function will need to make some solid circles, so it'll need the string `"solid"`. Include this fixed value, on a line by itself, along with the parameters.

Worked Exercise 5.9.6 *Add an inventory* to the `dot-grid` *function of Exercise 5.8.5.*

Figure 5.1: Skeleton and inventory of counterchange

```
; counterchange :  image (top-left)
;                  image (top-right) -> image
; Produces a square arrangement with the top-left image also
; in the bottom right, and the top-right image also in the
; bottom left.




(check-expect (counterchange                                    )



              (above (beside                                    )




                     (beside                                 )))




(check-expect (counterchange                          )




              (above (beside                          )




                     (beside                          )))

(define (counterchange top-left top-right)
  ; top-left  image
  ; top-right image
  ...)
```

Solution: You should already have a skeleton, so we'll discuss only what to add to it. Suppose your parameter names are `width` and `height`. Obviously, you'll need them inside the body:

```
; width          a number
; height         a number
```

In addition, you know that the function will need radius-5 circular blue dots . To produce these, we can be fairly certain that we'll need the expression (`circle 5 "solid" "blue"`). This too can be added to the inventory. The skeleton with inventory now looks like

```
(define (dot-grid width height)
  ; width                     a number
  ; height                    a number
  ; (circle 5 "solid" "blue") an image
  ...)
```

∎

Exercise 5.9.7 *Add an inventory* to the `lollipop` *function of Exercise 5.8.6.*

5.10   Inventories with values

Sometimes listing the available expressions and their types is enough for you to figure out the body expression. But what if you do all that, and don't have any flashes of inspiration? A technique that has helped many of my students is writing an *inventory with values*.

Here's how it works. After you've written down all the "available expressions" and their types, *choose one of your test cases* (preferably one that's not too simple), and for each of the expressions in the inventory, *write down its value for that test case*. Then add another line to the inventory, labelled

```
; right answer
```

and write down the right answer for that test case. Finally, look at the value of the right answer and the values of the available expressions, trying to find a way to get the right answer from the available expressions.

Worked Exercise 5.10.1 *Add values to the inventory* of the `counterchange` *function of Exercise 5.5.1.*

Solution: We already have a skeleton and test cases in Figure 5.1.

We'll pick the second of our test cases, the one involving  and   , and add the values of each inventory item to the inventory:

```
(define (counterchange top-left top-right)
```

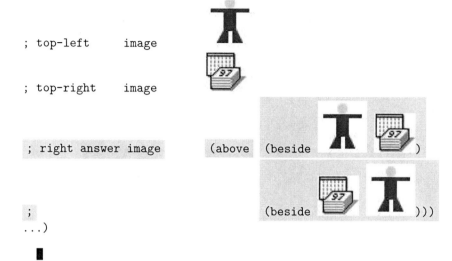

```
  ; top-left      image

  ; top-right     image

  ; right answer image          (above  (beside                    )


  ;                             (beside                      )))
  ...)
```

Note that we're *not* saying that `top-left` will *always* be a stick-figure, or `top-right` will *always* be a calendar, only that we're using those values as an example to see more concretely what the inventory means. We still have to write the function in such a way that it works on *any* values we give it.

5.11 The function body

Now it's time to put some meat on the bones. This, frankly, is the hardest part of programming: coming up with an expression which, no matter what arguments the function is applied to, will *always* produce the right answer. We've done as much of the work ahead of time as possible: we know what types the function is taking in and returning, we've written a couple of specific examples, we have the basic syntax of a function definition, we know what parameters and values are available for us to use, and we have a specific example of them to compare with a specific right answer. Now we have to think about *how we would solve the problem if we were the computer*. In doing this, you will find function contracts (both for predefined functions and for your own functions) extremely useful: for example, if you have a string that you know is supposed to be the name of a color, you can be pretty sure it'll appear as the last parameter to the `circle`, `rectangle`, `ellipse`, or `triangle` function; which one depends on what the function is supposed to draw.

Just as we added the inventory into the skeleton, we'll add the function body just after the commented-out "ingredients" from the inventory stage, still inside the parentheses, in place of the "...", so the whole thing becomes a legal function definition that happens to have a commented inventory in the middle.

Worked Exercise 5.11.1 *Add a body to the skeleton and inventory for the* `counterchange` *function of Exercise 5.9.1.*

Solution: Of course, we've already done this in Exercise 4.2.3. But if we hadn't, here is how we would figure it out. We already have the skeleton and inventory:

```
(define (counterchange top-left top-right)
```

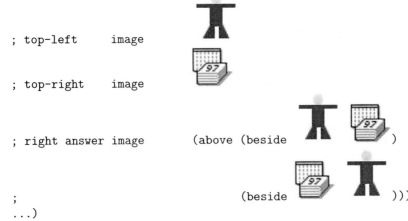

```
  ; top-left      image

  ; top-right     image

  ; right answer image    (above (beside

  ;                       (beside                    )))
  ...)
```

We know that the body will (almost certainly) use the names `top-left` and `top-right` (at least once each). If you immediately see how to put them together to get the right results, great. If not, look at the examples, both of which fit the pattern

```
(above (beside something something-else)
       (beside something-else something))
```

They differ only in what pictures are used as *something* and *something-else*, both of which must be images. Do we have any images available to work with? Yes: according to the inventory, `top-left` and `top-right` are images, so the obvious thing to try is to use those as *something* and *something-else*. But which one is which? In the "inventory with values", the image that was the value of `top-left` was the first argument to the first `beside` and the second argument to the second, while the image that was the value of `top-right` was the second argument to the first `beside` and the first argument to the second. This suggests

```
(above (beside top-left top-right)
       (beside top-right top-left))
```

as the body, and we'll type this in between the inventory and the closing parenthesis of the skeleton. We should now have a Definitions window that looks like Figure 5.2. ∎

Together with the contract and examples we wrote before, the Definitions window should now look like Figure 5.2.

Unfortunately, I haven't yet told you everything you need to write the bodies of `copies-beside` or `dot-grid`. (We'll get to these in Chapter 24.) However, you should be able to do the following four, especially if you've done all the steps up until now for them.

Exercise 5.11.2 *Add a body to the* `pinwheel` *function of Exercise 5.9.3.*

Exercise 5.11.3 *Add a body to the* `checkerboard2` *function of Exercise 5.9.4.*

Hint: You can write this function directly, using `beside` and `above`, or you can write it shorter and simpler by re-using another function we've already written. Shorter and simpler is good!

Exercise 5.11.4 *Add a body to the* `bullseye` *function of Exercise 5.9.5.*

Exercise 5.11.5 *Add a body to the* `lollipop` *function of Exercise 5.9.7.*

Figure 5.2: Complete definition of counterchange

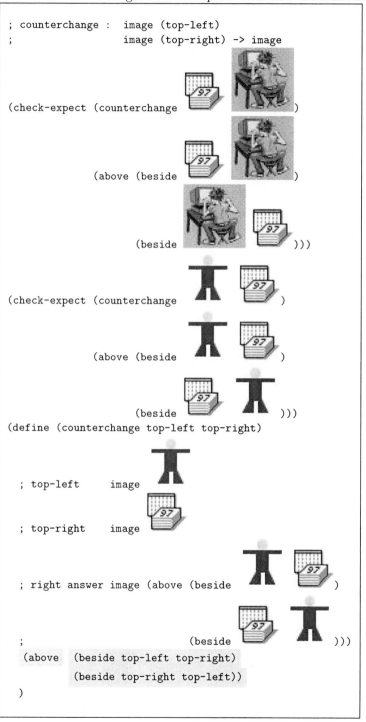

5.12   Testing

Now it's the moment of truth: the time to find out whether your function definition *works*. If you've typed everything into the Definitions window correctly, just click the "Run" button. If you're using "should be" for test cases, you'll see the results in the Interactions window, each followed by the words "should be" and the right answer. Check that each of the actual answers matches what you said it "should be": if any of them don't match, figure out what's wrong and fix it. If, on the other hand, you're using check-expect, you should see a report telling you exactly how many and which of your test cases failed.

If you get an error message like *reference to an identifier before its definition*, it means that you tried to *use* the new function before *defining* it — for example, if you have "should be"-style examples appearing ahead of the definition. (Examples using check-expect *are* allowed to appear ahead of the definition.) A slightly different error message, *name is not defined, not an argument, and not a primitive name*, means that the name of the function in the examples doesn't exactly match the name of the function in the definition (in spelling, or capitalization, or something like that).

If you get an error message like *this procedure expects 2 arguments, here it is provided 1 argument*, it means your contract, examples, and skeleton disagree on how many arguments the function is supposed to take in. An error message like *expects type <number> as 1st argument, given "hello"* likewise indicates a disagreement among contract, examples, and skeleton on either the types or the order of the arguments.

Exercise 5.12.1 *Test each of the functions whose definitions you wrote in Section 5.11. If any of them produce wrong answers, fix them and test again until they produce correct answers for every test case.*

5.13   Using the function

Now that you've tested the function on problems for which you know the right answer, you have confidence that it works correctly. So you can use it on problems for which you *don't* know the right answer, and be reasonably confident that the answers it produces are right.

Just as important, you can now use your new function in writing other functions, knowing that if something is wrong with the new function, it's not the old function's fault. When a new piece of commercial software is written, it may rely on hundreds or thousands of previously-written functions; if a programmer had to re-examine every one of them to fix a bug in the new program, nothing would ever get done.

5.14   Putting it all together

In reality, you would seldom want to write just the contract, or just the examples, of a function. Much more common is to go through all the steps for a single function, then go through all the steps for another function. In this section are several more function-definition exercises: for each one, go through all the steps of the design recipe.

Exercise 5.14.1 *Develop a function* named diamond *that takes in a string (the color of the diamond) and a number (the length of one of its sides) and produces a diamond shape, i.e. two triangles connected along one side.*

```
> (diamond "blue" 20)
```

```
> (diamond "green" 30)
```

Exercise 5.14.2 *Develop a function* named `text-box` *that takes in two strings, of which the second should be a color-name, and two numbers (width and height), and produces a picture of the first string, in 18-point black type, on a background rectangle of the specified color, width, and height.*

Exercise 5.14.3 *(Thanks to Leon LaSpina for this problem)*

Develop a function named `two-eyes` *that, given a number and a color name, produces a picture of two circular "eyes", 100 pixels apart horizontally. Each one should have a black "pupil" of radius 10, surrounded by an "iris" of the specified color and radius (which you may assume is more than 10). The 100-pixel separation is measured from edge to edge, not center to center.*

Exercise 5.14.4 *(Thanks to Leon LaSpina for this problem)*

Develop a function named `circle-in-square` *that takes in a number (the length of a side of a square) and two strings (the colors of a square and a circle), and produces a picture of a square of one color, with a circle of the other color inscribed inside it. The diameter of the circle should be the same as the side of the square, so the circle just barely touches the edge of the square at the middle of each side.*

Hint: If you've already read Chapter 7, you'll be tempted to do this using arithmetic. But it can be done without arithmetic, using only what you've seen so far.

Exercise 5.14.5 *Develop a function* named `caption-below` *that takes in an image and a string, and produces a copy of the same image with a caption underneath it:*

```
> (caption-below pic:bloch "Dr. Bloch")
```

5.15   Review of important words and concepts

Projects (such as writing a computer program) are more likely to be finished successfully if you follow a **recipe**. In particular, you need to have a very clear, precise idea of what a program is supposed to do before you start writing it. To design a Racket function, follow the following seven steps:

1. Write a *function contract* (and possibly a *purpose statement*) for the function you want to write. Include the *function name*, the *numbers, types, and order of inputs*, and the *type of the result* (which so far is always "image").

2. Write several *examples* of how the function will be used, with their correct answers. Include special cases and anything else "weird" (but legal, within the contract) that might help you uncover errors in your program.

3. Write a *skeleton* of the function you want to write, by combining Syntax Rule 5 with the decisions you've already made about number, type, and order of parameters in step 1. At this point you can use "Check Syntax" to confirm that your examples and skeleton match one another.

4. Add an *inventory* to the skeleton, showing the names and types of all the parameters, and any "fixed data" that you know will be needed no matter what arguments are plugged in. If there are more complex expressions that you're confident you'll need, you can write those at this point too. It's often a good idea to *choose a specific test case* and *write down the values* of all the inventory items for this test case, as well as what the right answer should be for this test case.

5. Fill in the *body* of the function definition. This will be based on the skeleton, with the help of any patterns you notice from the "right answers" of your examples. At this point you can use "Check Syntax" again to confirm that all the parentheses are matched correctly, you're calling functions with the right number of arguments, and so on.

6. *Test* your program on the examples you chose in step 2. If the actual answers don't match what you said they "should be", figure out what's wrong, fix it, and test again.

7. *Use* your program to answer questions for which you don't already know the right answer, or to build other, more complex functions, secure in the knowledge that *this* one works.

Although this chapter didn't introduce a lot of new Racket constructs, it is probably the most important chapter in the book. If, a year after completing this course, you've forgotten all your Racket but you remember the design recipe, I'll be happy, and you'll be well on your way to being a good programmer.

5.16   Reference

No new functions or syntax rules were introduced in this chapter.

Chapter 6

Animations in DrRacket

6.1 Preliminaries

Up to this point we've been working with static pictures. But it's much more fun and interesting to deal with pictures that change over time and interact with the user.

We think of an animation as showing, at all times, a simulated "world".[1] The world changes over time, and we watch it through the animation window. Our animations will use a built-in function (defined in the teachpack) named big-bang (because it "starts the world"). Here's its contract:

```
; big-bang :  image(start) event-handler ...  -> image
```

What does all this mean? The big-bang function takes in one or more parameters: the first parameter is the first image the animation should show, and any remaining parameters are "event handlers". An event handler is a kind of function, and since there are several different kinds of events to be handled, we need to specify which one goes with which kind of event. When the animation ends, the function returns the last image it showed. (Again, this is slightly simplified; we'll see more details in Chapters 8 and 10.)

An event handler is a function for the animation to call whenever a certain "event" happens. There are several kinds of "events": draw the screen, clock tick, mouse activity, keyboard activity, *etc.* but for our first example, the only one we need is called a "draw handler", whose job is to decide what to show on the screen at each step. For now, we'll use a built-in function named show-it, which takes in an image and returns it unchanged, as our draw handler. To tell DrRacket to use show-it as a draw handler, we put (on-draw show-it) as one of the "event handler" arguments to big-bang. This means that whenever DrRacket needs to redraw the screen, it will show the current image.

Worked Exercise 6.1.1 *Develop an animation* that displays an unchanging green circle of radius 20.

Solution: The starting image needs to be a green circle of radius 20; we know how to create such a thing with (circle 20 "solid" "green"). And since what we want to show

---

[1]There's also something called a "universe", which is several worlds running at the same time, either on the same computer or on different computers communicating over a network. We won't get to that in this book, but the picturing-programs library provides everything you need. If you want to learn to write such programs, first get through Chapter 10, then open DrRacket's Help Desk and search for "multiple worlds".

in the animation window is exactly this picture, we'll use `show-it` as our draw handler. The result is

```
(big-bang (circle 20 "solid" "green") (on-draw show-it))
```

Try this, either by typing it into the Interactions pane and hitting ENTER, or by typing it into the Definitions pane and clicking "Run". It should bring up a separate window with a green dot in it; when you click the "close" box of this window, the window goes away and `big-bang` returns the picture of the green dot. ∎

Practice Exercise 6.1.2 *Try some different pictures.*

Exercise 6.1.3 Develop an animation *that displays an unchanging green circle of radius 20 in the center of a square white window 100 pixels on a side.*

Hint: Use either `place-image` or `overlay` to put the circle onto a background built using `rectangle`.

Specifying window size

In several of our animations so far, we've used `overlay` or `place-image` to place a picture onto a background, which is usually built by `rectangle`. If all you want is to have a larger animation window, there's a simpler way: specify the width and height of the window as additional arguments to `on-draw`.

```
(big-bang            (on-draw show-it 300 200))
```

and see what happens. It should create an animation window, 300 pixels wide by 200 high, with a calendar in the top-left corner.

Of course, as you've already seen, these extra arguments to `on-draw` aren't required; if you leave them out, the animation window will be just big enough to hold your starting picture.

Practice Exercise 6.1.4 *Make up several examples like the above with pictures of various sizes and animation windows of various sizes. See how they behave.*

6.2   Tick handlers

Of course, these "animations" aren't very interesting. To get one to change over time, we need another *event handler*: specifically a *tick handler* , *i.e.* a handler which will be called "every time the clock ticks". You tell `big-bang` that you're giving it a tick-handler by saying (`on-tick` *function-name interval*) as one of the arguments to `big-bang`. The *interval* parameter is how many seconds there should be between one "tick" and the next; if you leave it out, the animation will run as fast as it can. The *function-name* parameter is the name of any function that takes in an old image and returns a new one. Ordinarily, you'll write a function yourself to do this job, but for this example, we'll use one that's already built in.

Worked Exercise 6.2.1 Develop an animation *of a calendar that rotates 90° clockwise every half second in the center of a 100x100 window.*

Solution: The starting picture is our calendar picture, `overlay`-ed into the middle of an empty 100x100 box. The interval is half a second. For the tick handler, we need a function that takes in an image and returns that image rotated clockwise 90°. Conveniently enough, `rotate-cw` does exactly this, so our handler will be (`on-tick rotate-cw 1/2`) and the whole animation becomes

```
(big-bang (overlay          (rectangle 100 100 "solid" "white"))
          (on-draw show-it)
          (on-tick rotate-cw 1/2))
```

Try this.

By the way, you could also have said

```
(big-bang (overlay          (rectangle 100 100 "solid" "white"))
          (on-tick rotate-cw 1/2)
          (on-draw show-it))
```

and this would work too: the various handlers can be specified in *any order*, as long as the starting picture comes first.

∎

Practice Exercise 6.2.2 *What would happen in Exercise 6.2.1 if you skipped the* `overlay` *and the 100x100 rectangle, and simply used the additional arguments to* `on-draw` *to make the window 100x100?* **Try it.** *Do you understand why it did what it did?*

Exercise 6.2.3 Develop an animation *of a picture of your choice that flips upside down every 1.5 seconds in the center of the window.*

Practice Exercise 6.2.4 Make up *some other variations: different time intervals, different pictures, different functions in place of* `rotate-cw`. *(Note that the only functions that make sense here are functions that take in one image and return another — for example,* `rotate-cw` *and* `flip-vertical` *but not* `beside` *or* `overlay/xy`.)

What happens if you change the solution to Exercise 6.2.1 to use a colored background? What if the background isn't a square (say, it's wider than it is high)? What if the calendar isn't in the center? If you don't like the results of some of these, we'll see later how to fix them.

SIDEBAR:

Technically, `on-tick` and `on-draw` aren't functions, but rather something called *special forms*. What this means in practice is that you can't use them anywhere except as an argument to `big-bang`.

6.3 Common beginner mistakes

Leaving out the draw handler

If you write an animation with no `on-draw` clause, like

```
(big-bang calendar (on-tick rotate-cw 1/2))
```

then DrRacket doesn't know how you want to show the animation window, so it doesn't. The animation will actually run, but there will be no animation window, and you'll have to hit the "Stop" button in the top-right corner of the DrRacket window.

There actually are times when you want to run an animation without displaying it — *e.g.* when it's communicating over the network with other computers, and *they're* displaying it — but we won't get to that in this book.

Testing big-bang **with** check-expect

A student wrote the following:

```
; rotating :  image -> image
(check-expect (rotating calendar)
  (big-bang (overlay calendar
                     (rectangle 200 200 "solid" "white"))
            (on-draw show-it)
            (on-tick rotate-cw 1/2)))
(define (rotating pic)
  (big-bang (overlay pic
                     (rectangle 200 200 "solid" "white"))
            (on-draw show-it)
            (on-tick rotate-cw 1/2)))
```

This is all legal. It passes a syntax check, it runs, and it shows a rotating calendar on the screen. In fact, after I close the animation window, it shows *another* rotating calendar on the screen. After I close the *second* animation window, it tells me that the program failed its one test case. What's going on here?

The above code calls `rotating-calendar`, which calls `big-bang`, which starts an animation. When a user closes this animation window, it returns from `rotating-calendar`, and `check-expect` calls `big-bang` again to construct the "right answer"; this starts *another animation*. When the user closes *this* animation window, `check-expect` compares the result of the first `big-bang` with the result of the second.

Recall from Section 6.1 that the result of `big-bang` is the last image it showed in the animation window. So unless both animations happen to end with the calendar pointing the same direction, the results won't match and `check-expect` will say the test failed. In general, `check-expect` **is not useful on the results of** `big-bang`.

This student has made things much more complicated than they need to be. I seldom call `big-bang` inside a function definition at all; instead, I **call** `big-bang` **directly in the Definitions or Interactions window,** *not* **inside a function definition.** So instead of the eleven lines the student wrote above, I would write the two lines

```
(big-bang (overlay calendar (rectangle 200 200 "solid" "white"))
          (on-tick rotate-cw 1/2))
```

If you *really* want to define a function that runs a particular animation, so you have a shorter name for it, the above definition is a good one: it takes in an image, and puts that image rotating every half second in the middle of a 200x200 animation window. But don't bother writing test cases for it, since we're interested in the function for the animation it runs, not for the result it returns.

6.4   Writing tick handlers

In most cases, you want to do something more complicated when the clock ticks, something for which there isn't already a built-in function like `rotate-cw`. So we *write one.*

Worked Exercise 6.4.1 *Develop an animation of a calendar that starts in the top-left corner of a window and moves 10 pixels to the right every second.*

Solution: Obviously, we'll need a tick handler with an interval of 1 second. It'll be convenient to specify the size of the window with something like

```
(on-draw show-it 500 100)
```

(note that we've left lots of width so there's room for the calendar to move right). The starting picture can be just `calendar`. What's not so obvious is how to move a picture to the right by 10 pixels; there isn't already a built-in function that does that. So we'll write one.

Following the usual design recipe, we'll start with the **contract**. Let's name our function `move-right-10`. In order to work as a tick handler, it must take in an image and return an image, so the contract is

```
; move-right-10 :  image -> image
```

The purpose is obvious from the function name, so we'll skip the purpose statement.

Next we need some **examples**. Any image should work, e.g.

(move-right-10)

But what should the right answer be? We could move the calendar right 10 pixels by putting it to the right of something 10 pixels wide with `beside`. What should we put it beside? A rectangle 10 pixels wide should do the job... but how high? We don't actually want to *see* a rectangle there, so let's make it 0 pixels tall (which makes it invisible; it really doesn't matter whether it's outlined or solid, or what color it is.)

```
(check-expect (move-right-10         )
```
```
              (beside (rectangle 10 0 "solid" "white")         ))
(check-expect (move-right-10 (circle 3 "solid" "green"))
              (beside (rectangle 10 0 "solid" "white")
                      (circle 3 "solid" "green")))
```

The next step in the design recipe is a **function skeleton**. We know that the function will be named `move-right-10`, and it'll take one parameter that's a picture; in fact, let's name the parameter "picture". So our function skeleton looks like

```
(define (move-right-10 picture)
  ...)
```

Next, we need to add an **inventory**. We only have one parameter, so we'll write down its name and datatype:

```
(define (move-right-10 picture)
  ; picture        image
  ...)
```

The next step in the design recipe is filling in the **function body**. We know that the function body will use the parameter name `picture`, and from our examples we see that the right answer tends to look like

```
(beside (rectangle 10 0 "solid" "white") something)
```

where *something* is whatever picture you want to move to the right.

So our function definition becomes

```
(define (move-right-10 picture)
  ; picture      image
  (beside (rectangle 10 0 "solid" "white")
          picture)
)
```

The complete definition window should now look like Figure 6.1.

Figure 6.1: Complete definition of move-right-10

```
(require installed-teachpacks/picturing-programs)
; move-right-10 :   image -> image



(check-expect (move-right-10            )



              (beside (rectangle 10 0 "solid" "white")            ))
(check-expect (move-right-10 (circle 3 "solid" "green"))
              (beside (rectangle 10 0 "solid" "white")
                      (circle 3 "solid" "green")))

(define (move-right-10 picture)
  ; picture      image
  (beside (rectangle 10 0 "solid" "white") picture)
  )
```

Now we can **test** the function by clicking the "Run" button.

Everything we just went through to define `move-right-10` was so that we could *use* the `move-right-10` function in an animation. The animation itself is now pretty simple:

```
(big-bang
          (on-draw show-it 500 100)
          (on-tick move-right-10 1))
```

Type this into the Interactions pane and see whether it works. ∎

Exercise 6.4.2 *Develop an animation* which moves a picture of your choice down 5 pixels every half second, starting at the top-left corner of the window.

Exercise 6.4.3 *Develop an animation* which moves a picture of your choice to the left by 3 pixels every half second, starting at the top-left corner (so the picture seems to fall off the left edge of the window).

Hint: You can get the effect of moving to the left by cutting off the left-hand few pixels of the image. You'll want to start with either a fairly large picture, or one that's `place-image`d away from the left edge.

Exercise 6.4.4 *Develop an animation* which starts with a small red dot at the top-left corner of the window, then replaces it with two red dots side by side, then with a row of four, then a row of eight, then a row of sixteen ... doubling every three seconds.

6.5 Writing draw handlers

You can get more flexibility in your animations by writing your own draw handlers rather than relying on the default `show-it`.

A draw handler can be any function with contract `image -> image`. You can write such a function, then use it (rather than `show-it`) as an argument to `on-draw`.

Worked Exercise 6.5.1 *Develop an animation of a calendar that sits at coordinates (100, 40) of a 150x200 pink window and rotates clockwise every 1/2 second.*

Solution: Using what we've already seen, we could set the starting image to be just a calendar, which would make it easy to rotate using (`on-tick rotate-cw 1/2`) ... but then it'll appear at the top-left corner of a white window rather than where we want it in a pink window. (Try it!)

Or we could set the starting image to be (`place-image calendar 100 40 (rectangle 150 200 "solid" "pink")`) ... but when we rotated it, it would rotate the *whole window* rather than rotating just the calendar in place. (Try it!)

So we'll solve both of these problems by writing our own draw handler. Let's name it `place-on-pink`. It's pretty straightforward:

Contract:

```
; place-on-pink :  image -> image
```

Examples:

```
(check-expect (place-on-pink calendar)
              (place-image calendar
                           100 40
                           (rectangle 150 200 "solid" "pink")))
(check-expect (place-on-pink (triangle 30 "solid" "blue"))
              (place-image (triangle 30 "solid" "blue")
                           100 40
                           (rectangle 150 200 "solid" "pink")))
```

Skeleton and Inventory:
```
(define (place-on-pink picture)
  ; picture       image
  ...
  )
```

Body:
```
(define (place-on-pink picture)
  ; picture       image
  (place-image  picture
                100 40
                (rectangle 150 200 "solid" "pink"))
  )
```

Once we've tested this, we can *use* it in an animation:
```
(big-bang calendar
          (on-tick rotate-cw 1/2)
          (on-draw place-on-pink))
```
Note that we didn't need to specify the window size, because `place-on-pink` always returns a rectangle of the right size. ▮

Exercise 6.5.2 *Find an outdoor scene on the Web. Develop an animation in which*

a *stick-figure* *is positioned somewhere appropriate in the scene, and flips upside-down every second, staying in the same place; the background scene should* not *flip upside-down!*

Exercise 6.5.3 *Modify your solution to Exercise 6.4.4 so the row of dots is always centered in the window.*

Exercise 6.5.4 *Develop an animation which shows a picture of your choice at the center of the animation window, rotating smoothly (say, 5 degrees every 1/10 second).*

Hint: If you do this the obvious way, the picture may wander around a bit. This is because `overlay` lines up the center of the picture with the center of the background. But the "center" is defined as "halfway between the leftmost and rightmost points, halfway between the top and bottom points", and when the picture is rotated, this can refer to different parts of the picture than before. One way around this is to first overlay the picture on an invisible (*i.e.* the same color as the background) circle that completely contains it, so whatever point on your picture is at the center of the circle will stay put.

6.6 Other kinds of event handlers

As mentioned earlier, "tick handlers" are the simplest kind, but one can also provide handlers to respond whenever somebody types a key on the keyboard, or whenever somebody moves or clicks the mouse. The details are in Figure 6.2. (There's another kind of handler which we use to *stop* an animation; we'll discuss it in Chapter 14.)

Here's a simple example of a mouse handler:

Worked Exercise 6.6.1 *Develop an animation of a picture of your choice, moving right 10 pixels whenever the mouse is moved or clicked.*

Solution: Again, we'll use the calendar picture, with the same width and height as before. We need to install a handler using **on-mouse**, but (according to the contract in Figure 6.2) the function we give to **on-mouse** must take in a picture, two numbers, and a mouse-event, even though we're not interested in most of these things (and don't even know what a "mouse-event" is!). So we'll write a function similar to **move-right-10**, but taking in this extra information and ignoring it.

Contract:
```
; move-right-10-on-mouse :
;      image number number mouse-event -> image
```

Purpose statement:
```
; Just like move-right-10, but takes in three extra
; parameters and ignores them.
```

Examples: We've already come up with examples for **move-right-10**, so these should be similar, only with some extra arguments plugged in. Since we're writing the function and we know it will ignore the "mouse-event" parameter, it doesn't matter what we plug in there; we'll use strings.

```
(check-expect

   (move-right-10-on-mouse 📅  318 27 "whatever")

   (beside (rectangle 10 0 "solid" "white") 📅  ))
(check-expect
   (move-right-10-on-mouse (circle 3 "solid" "green") -3784 3.7 "blah")
   (beside (rectangle 10 0 "solid" "white")
           (circle 3 "solid" "green")))
```

Function skeleton:
```
(define (move-right-10-on-mouse picture x y mouse-event)
   ...)
```

Fill in the inventory:
```
(define (move-right-10-on-mouse picture x y mouse-event)
   ; picture        image
   ; x              number
   ; y              number
   ; mouse-event    whatever this is
   ...)
```

Figure 6.2: big-bang and event handlers

The big-bang function has the contract

```
; big-bang :  image(start) handler ... -> image
```

tick handlers must have the contract

```
; function-name :  image (old) -> image (new)
```

They are installed by using (on-tick *function-name interval*) as an argument to big-bang. The *interval* is the length of time (in seconds) between clock ticks; if you leave it out, the animation will run as fast as it can.

key handlers must have the contract

```
; function-name :  image (old) key -> image (new)
```

The "key" parameter indicates what key was pressed; we'll see how to use it in Chapter 18.

They are installed with (on-key *function-name*).

mouse handlers must have the contract

```
; function-name :  image (old)
;                   number (mouse-x) number (mouse-y)
;                   event
;                   -> image (new)
```

The first parameter is the old picture; the second represents the *x coordinate*, indicating how many pixels from the left the mouse is; the third represents the *y coordinate*, indicating how many pixels down from the top the mouse is; and the "event" tells what happened (the mouse was moved, the button was pressed or released, *etc.*); we'll see in Chapter 18 how to use this.

Mouse handlers are installed with (on-mouse *function-name*).

draw handlers must have the contract

```
; function-name :  image (current) -> image
```

and are installed with (on-draw *function-name width height*). If you leave out the *width* and *height*, the animation window will be the size and shape of the result the first time the draw handler is called.

An especially simple draw handler, show-it, is predefined: it simply returns the same image it was given, and it's useful if what you want to display in the animation window is simply the current image.

Fill in the body: We already know how to use `picture` to get the desired answer. The other three parameters are of no interest to us, so we just won't use them. Thus we can write

```
(define (move-right-10-on-mouse picture x y mouse-event)
  ; picture        image
  ; x              number
  ; y              number
  ; mouse-event    whatever this is
  (beside (rectangle 10 0 "solid" "white") picture)
)
```

Notice that the function body is the same as in `move-right-10`. Most computer scientists would consider this inelegant: if you already wrote it once, the computer knows it, so why should you have to write it again? A briefer and more elegant way to do it is to *re-use* the `move-right-10` function (assuming the definition of `move-right-10` is still in the definitions window, somewhere up above):

```
(define (move-right-10-on-mouse picture x y mouse-event)
  ; picture        image
  ; x              number
  ; y              number
  ; mouse-event    whatever this is
  (move-right-10 picture)
)
```

The entire definitions window (including both definitions) should now look as in Figure 6.3.

Now that we have the `move-right-10-on-mouse` function, we can *use* it in an animation:

```
(big-bang calendar
          (on-draw show-it 500 100)
          (on-mouse move-right-10-on-mouse))
```

■

SIDEBAR:

Notice that the animation only pays attention to mouse motion when the mouse is *inside the animation window*; in the above example, you can move around the rest of the screen without the calendar moving.

Exercise 6.6.2 *Develop an animation* of a picture of your choice that moves right 10 pixels whenever a key is pressed on the keyboard.

Hint: Obviously, you need a key handler. Just ignore the "key" parameter for now; we'll see how to use it in Chapter 18.

A more realistic example of using a mouse handler is the following:

Worked Exercise 6.6.3 *Develop an animation* of a picture of your choice that moves with the mouse on a 500x300 background.

Figure 6.3: move-right-10 and move-right-10-on-mouse

```
(require installed-teachpacks/picturing-programs)

; move-right-10 :   image -> image


(check-expect (move-right-10           )


            (beside (rectangle 10 0 "solid" "white")           ))
(check-expect (move-right-10 (circle 3 "solid" "green"))
            (beside (rectangle 10 0 "solid" "white")
                    (circle 3 "solid" "green")))

(define (move-right-10 picture)
  ; picture   image
  (beside (rectangle 10 0 "solid" "white") picture)
  )


; move-right-10-on-mouse :
;     image number number mouse-event -> image
; Just like move-right-10, but takes in three
; extra parameters and ignores them.

(check-expect


  (move-right-10-on-mouse           318 27 "whatever")



  (beside (rectangle 10 0 "solid" "white")           ))
(check-expect
  (move-right-10-on-mouse (circle 3 "solid" "green") -3784 3.7 "blah")
  (beside (rectangle 10 0 "solid" "white")
(define (move-right-10-on-mouse picture x y mouse-event)
  ; picture       image
  ; x             number
  ; y             number
  ; mouse-event   whatever this is
  (move-right-10 picture)
  )
```

Solution: This animation doesn't do anything on a regular schedule, so it doesn't need a tick handler. It obviously needs a mouse handler, whose job is to place the picture at the right place. Do we need a draw handler? The main reason we've written draw handlers in the past is to put a picture at a specific location, and the mouse handler is taking care of that, so let's try doing without a draw handler.

The trick will be writing a mouse-handler function that puts the picture in the specified location. Let's use the calendar picture again, and name our function `calendar-at-mouse`.

Contract: We've already chosen the name, and the fact that it's a mouse handler forces the rest of the contract to be

```
; calendar-at-mouse :  image(old-picture)
                       num(x) num(y) mouse-event -> image
```

Purpose statement: Recall from above that mouse coordinates are measured in pixels from the left, and pixels from the top. In practice, the coordinates of the mouse will always be positive integers, so let's make that assumption explicit. The function's purpose can be stated as

```
; Produces a picture of a calendar, with its top-left corner
; x pixels from the left and y pixels down from the top of a
; 500x300 white rectangle.
; Assumes x and y are both positive integers.
```

Examples: The function will always draw a calendar on a blank background, regardless of the old picture, so we can ignore the old picture. And we don't even know what a mouse-event is yet, so we'll ignore that too. Thus for our examples, it shouldn't matter much what arguments are plugged in for these. As for x and y, we should be able to plug in any positive integers and get something reasonable.

```
(check-expect (calendar-at-mouse        34 26 "huh?") ...)
```

But what "should" the answer "be"? Ignoring the "old picture" and the "mouse-event", the result should clearly be a calendar that's 34 pixels over from the left and 26 pixels down. The easiest way to put it there is with `place-image`:

```
(check-expect

   (calendar-at-mouse        34 26 "huh?")
   (place-image calendar
                34 26
                (rectangle 500 300 "solid" "white")))
```

The reader is encouraged to come up with another example.

By the way, we're going to be using this 500x300 solid white rectangle a lot, so it makes sense to give it a name:

```
(define white-background (rectangle 500 300 "solid" "white"))
```

The example can then become

```
(check-expect
```

```
  (calendar-at-mouse          34 26 "huh?")
  (place-image calendar 34 26 white-background))
```

Function skeleton: This is pretty straightforward from the contract:

```
(define (calendar-at-mouse old-picture x y mouse-event)
  ...)
```

Inventory: This too is pretty straightforward from the contract:

```
(define (calendar-at-mouse old-picture x y mouse-event)
  ; old-picture       image (ignored)
  ; x                 positive integer
  ; y                 positive integer
  ; mouse-event       whatever this is (ignored)
  ; calendar          a picture we'll need
  ; white-background  a picture we'll need
  ...)
```

Body: We've already decided to ignore old-picture and mouse-event, so we need only figure out how to use x and y. From the code in the "right answer", it seems that x and y should be the second and third arguments to place-image; thus

```
(define (calendar-at-mouse old-picture x y mouse-event)
  ; old-picture       image (ignored)
  ; x                 positive integer
  ; y                 positive integer
  ; mouse-event       whatever this is (ignored)
  ; calendar          a picture we'll need
  ; white-background  a picture we'll need
  (place-image calendar x y white-background) )
```

The whole definition pane should now look like Figure 6.4.

You can now **test** this definition by hitting "Run". Once we know that it works, we can **use** it in an animation. To make sure there's enough room, we need to either provide a 500x300 starting picture (*e.g.* white-background) or specify a draw handler with dimensions of 500x300. Either one will work:

```
(big-bang white-background
          (on-draw show-it)
          (on-mouse calendar-at-mouse))
```
  or
```
(big-bang (empty-scene 1 1)
          (on-draw show-it 500 300)
          (on-mouse calendar-at-mouse))
```

If everything works properly, whenever you move the mouse around within the animation window, a picture of a calendar will move with it. ∎

Figure 6.4: Complete definition of calendar-at-mouse

```
; calendar-at-mouse :   image(old-picture)
;                        num(x) num(y) mouse-event -> image
; Produces a picture of a calendar, with its top-left corner
; x pixels from the left and y pixels down from the top.
; Assumes x and y are both positive integers.


(define calendar            )
(define white-background (rectangle 500 300 "solid" "white"))
(check-expect


  (calendar-at-mouse          34 26 "huh?")
  (place-image calendar 34 26 white-background))
; whatever other examples you've come up with

(define (calendar-at-mouse old-picture x y mouse-event)
  ; old-picture   image (ignored)
  ; x             positive integer
  ; y             positive integer
  ; mouse-event   whatever this is (ignored)
  (place-image calendar x y white-background)
  )
```

6.7   Design recipe for an animation, first version

We've written a number of animations by now. What do they all have in common? I've listed the steps as a "design recipe for animations" in Figure 6.5.

Figure 6.5: Recipe for an animation, version 1

1. **Identify what handlers you'll need** (draw, tick, mouse, and/or key).

   - If your animation needs to change at regular intervals, you'll need a tick handler.

   - If your animation needs to respond to mouse movements and clicks, you'll need a mouse handler.

   - If your animation needs to respond to keyboard typing, you'll need a key handler.

   - You *always* need a draw handler, but in many cases you can get away with using `show-it`. If what should appear in the animation window isn't exactly the picture you're working with (*e.g.* you want to place the picture in a particular place on a background), you need to write your own draw handler.

2. **Write down their contracts** (using Figure 6.2). You can name these functions whatever you want but their contracts *must* be as in Figure 6.2.

3. **Develop each of these functions**, following the usual design recipe for each one. Don't go on to the next one until the previous one passes all of its test cases.

4. **Decide on the starting picture** the animation should start with.

5. **Decide on the width and height** (if they're not the same as those of the picture).

6. **Decide on the time interval between "ticks"** (if you have a tick handler).

7. **Call** `big-bang` with the starting picture and handlers (specified using `on-draw`, `on-tick`, `on-mouse`, and `on-key`). See whether it works.

   Use this recipe to work the following exercises, each of which requires more than one handler.

Exercise 6.7.1 *Modify the animation of Exercise 6.6.3 so the picture slides left and right with the mouse, but stays at the same vertical position — say, halfway down the window — regardless of the mouse's vertical position.*

Exercise 6.7.2 *Develop an animation of a picture of your choice that moves to the right every second, and moves down whenever somebody types on the keyboard.*

Exercise 6.7.3 *Develop an animation of a picture of your choice that moves to the right every second, moves down whenever the mouse moves, and resets to its starting position whenever somebody types on the keyboard.*

6.8 A note on syntax

According to the syntax rules we've seen so far, the only place a function name can appear is just after a left parenthesis, as in (above calendar (flip-vertical calendar)). But we've been using the on-tick, on-key, and on-mouse functions in a strange way: we've been giving them the *names* of functions *as arguments*. It turns out that this is legal, because function names are really *identifiers*, just like variable names, so an expression like

```
(big-bang (circle 5 "solid" "red")
          (on-draw show-it 500 50)
          (on-tick twin-beside))
```

can be justified with a box diagram as follows:

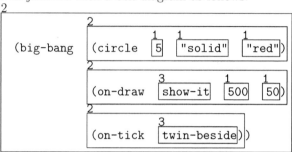

Which raises the question: what is the contract for a function like on-tick? Its argument is supposed to be not an image, or a number, or a string, but a *function*, and its result is an "event handler" (let's not worry about what this is for now). So to oversimplify slightly, the contracts of these functions can be written

```
; on-draw :  function -> handler
; on-tick :  function -> handler
; on-key :   function -> handler
; on-mouse : function -> handler
```

In other words, "function" and "handler" are data types, like "image", "number", "string", *etc.*

However, on-draw, on-tick, *etc.* don't actually work on *any* function; they only work on functions with the right contract. In order for a function to be used as a draw or tick handler, it must take in an image and return an image; to be used as a key handler, it must take in an image and a key and return an image; and to be used as a mouse handler, it must take in an image, two numbers, and a mouse-event, and return an image. Or in short:

```
; on-draw :  (image -> image) -> handler
; on-tick :  (image -> image) -> handler
; on-key :   (image key -> image) -> handler
; on-mouse : (image number number mouse-event -> image) -> handler
```

We'll investigate this in more detail, and learn to write functions that work on other functions, in Chapter 28.

Exercise 6.8.1 *Draw a box diagram for the big-bang call of one of the animations you've written in this chapter.*

Exercise 6.8.2 *Draw a box diagram for one of the function definitions you've written in this chapter.*

6.9   Review of important words and concepts

You can create open-ended, animated pictures in DrRacket, providing *event handlers* or *callback functions* for the animation to "call back" whenever an interesting "event" (such as a clock tick, keyboard or mouse activity, *etc.*) occurs. To install a handler, you use a *function that takes in another function*; this is a powerful programming technique, about which which we'll learn more later.

Many of the details in this section are specific to DrRacket, and to this particular animation package, but the ideas of event-driven programming and callback functions are common to almost all graphics systems and almost all programming languages. For example, the Java language has `ActionListeners`, `MouseListeners`, `KeyListeners`, *etc.* corresponding roughly to the various kinds of event handlers we've used in this chapter. So once you know how to design an animation in DrRacket, most of the ideas will work the same way in other languages; only the language syntax will be different.

6.10   Reference: Built-in functions for animation

In this chapter, we've introduced six new built-in functions:

- `big-bang`

- `on-tick`

- `on-draw`

- `on-mouse`

- `on-key`

- `show-it`

Chapter 7

Working with numbers

7.1 Fitting arithmetic into Racket syntax

The syntax rule we've used most heavily thus far is Rule 2: to use a function, type

```
( function-name argument ...)
```

Racket's built-in arithmetic operations use the exact same rule, which may make arithmetic expressions in Racket look a little unfamiliar, but has the advantage that all functions, whether they involve pictures, numbers, strings, etc. use the same syntax rule.

Most of Racket's built-in arithmetic and mathematical functions have exactly the name you would expect: + for addition, − for subtraction, ∗ for multiplication, / for division, sin for sine, *etc.*.

Worked Exercise 7.1.1 *Write a Racket expression* to represent the standard arithmetic expression $3 + 4$.

Solution: The operation we need to perform is +, so (as always in Racket) it goes after a left-parenthesis, *before* the things it's supposed to operate on:

```
(+ 3 4)
```

Of course, we know the answer should be 7, so we might even write

```
(+ 3 4) "should be 7"
```

or

```
(check-expect (+ 3 4) 7)
```

Test this (*e.g.* by typing it into the Interactions pane and hitting ENTER) and confirm that the answer actually is 7. ∎

Exercise 7.1.2 *Write a Racket expression* to represent the standard arithmetic expression $5 \cdot 3$. *As always,* **test** *to make sure the answer is what you expect.*

Hint: Racket, like most programming languages, uses an asterisk (∗) to represent multiplication.

Exercise 7.1.3 *Write a Racket expression* to represent the standard arithmetic expression $7 − 4$.

(Did you get the arguments in the right order? The value should be 3, not -3.)

Exercise 7.1.4 *Write a Racket expression to represent the standard arithmetic expression* $3 + (5 \cdot 2)$.

Hint: Remember that *both* operations have to follow Syntax Rule 2: they each go after a left-parenthesis, *before* whatever they're supposed to work on. If you get wrong answers, use the Stepper to watch what's going on inside the expression, step by step.

Exercise 7.1.5 *Write a Racket expression to represent the standard arithmetic expression* $(1 + 2) \cdot (3 + 4)$.

Exercise 7.1.6 *Write a Racket expression to represent the standard arithmetic expression* $\sqrt{4 + 5}$.

Hint: Since you can't type the $\sqrt{}$ symbol into DrRacket, the square-root function is spelled `sqrt`.

The operations of "adding one" and "subtracting one" are so common in programming that Racket provides built-in functions `add1` and `sub1` for them.

Practice Exercise 7.1.7 *Write some expressions using* `add1` *and* `sub1`. *Write equivalent expressions using* $+$, $-$, *and* 1.

Exercise 7.1.8 *Make up some more arithmetic expressions and convert them to Racket. Figure out the right answers, type the expressions into DrRacket, and see whether DrRacket agrees. If not, use the Stepper to figure out what went wrong.*

7.2   Variables and numbers

You already know how to define a variable to hold a picture, using Syntax Rule 4, and refer to variables using Syntax Rule 3. You can define variables to hold numbers, and use them in subsequent expressions, in exactly the same way:

```
(define age 20)
(define eggs-per-carton 12)
(check-expect (+ age 1) 21)
(check-expect (* 3 eggs-per-carton) 36)
```

Worked Exercise 7.2.1 *Define a variable named* `bignum` *with the value 1234567890. Compute the value of* $bignum^2$.

Solution: The definition is simply

```
(define bignum 1234657890)
```

The expression $bignum^2$ really means two copies of `bignum` multiplied together, so we would write

```
(* bignum bignum)
```

Note that these can both be in the Definitions pane, with the definition first, or both can be in the Interactions pane, with the definition first, or the definition can be in the Definitions pane and the formula in the Interactions pane. **Try each of these possibilities.** ∎

Exercise 7.2.2 *Define (in the Definitions pane) a variable named x with the value 4. Then **write an expression** (in the Definitions pane) to represent the "standard" algebraic expression*

$$3x + 2$$

*What "should" the answer be? **Try** it and see whether it worked as you expect.*

*   **Change** the value of x to 5 in the Definitions pane and predict what the answer should be now. **Try** it and see whether you were right.*

Hint: Remember that $3x$ in "standard" arithmetic really means 3 *times* x.

Exercise 7.2.3 ***Write an expression** in the definitions pane to represent the "standard" algebraic expression*

$$fnord + snark/boojum$$

***Test** your expression by defining the variable **fnord** to be 5, **snark** to be 12, and **boojum** to be -4. What should the right answer be?*
***Test** your expression again by defining the variables with different values, and predicting what the right answer should be.*

Exercise 7.2.4 *Define (in the Definitions pane) two variables **distance** and **time** to represent how long you spent on a trip, and how far you travelled. Then **write an expression** (again in the Definitions pane) for your average speed (i.e. distance divided by time); hit "Run" and make sure the answer comes out the way you expected.*

*   **Change** the values of **time** and **distance**, but don't change the expression. Hit "Run" and make sure the answer is correct for the new time and distance.*

SIDEBAR:

Time and distance, of course, are measured in *units, e.g.* hours and kilometers respectively. But a Racket numeric variable holds *only a number*; you have to remember what unit is associated with which variable.

Exercise 7.2.5 *Make up some more algebraic expressions and convert them to Racket. Figure out the right answers, type them into DrRacket, and see whether DrRacket agrees.*

If you're comfortable with all of those, here's a trickier one:

Exercise 7.2.6 ***Write an expression** in the definitions pane to represent the "standard" algebraic expression*

$$\frac{(-b) + \sqrt{(b^2) - 4ac}}{2a}$$

***Test** your expression by defining a to be 1, b to be -2, and c to be -3; the answer should be 3.*
***Test** your expression again by defining the variables with different values, and predicting what the right answer should be.*

Exercise 7.2.7 *Develop a function named **simpler-bullseye** [1] that's like the **bullseye** program of exercise 5.3.5, but taking in only* one *number, representing the radius of the outer ring. The radius of the inner disk should be half as large.*

Hint: The only new challenge is computing "half the radius", which you didn't know how to do before.

---
[1] This function is named `simpler-bullseye` because it's simpler to *use* — not necessarily simpler to *write*. There's often a trade-off between those two goals!

7.3   Why prefix notation is your friend

Racket's convention, putting the operation always *before* whatever it works on, is called *prefix notation*[2]. By contrast, the arithmetic notation you learned in grade school has a *few* "prefix operators" (*e.g.* negation, sin, cos, $\sqrt{\ldots}$) that go before their arguments, together with "infix operators" (*e.g.* $+, -, \cdot, /$) that go between their arguments.

An advantage of Racket's notation (aside from consistency) is that operations like $+$, $*$, *etc.* can easily take *more than two* parameters. For example, consider the infix expression

```
1 + 2 + 3 + 4 + 5
```

We *could* convert this to Racket as

```
(+ 1 (+ 2 ( + 3 (+ 4 5))))
```

or

```
(+ (+ (+ (+ 1 2) 3) 4) 5)
```

or various other ways, but since $+$ can take more than two parameters, we could write it more simply as

```
(+ 1 2 3 4 5)
```

which is actually shorter than its infix form because we don't have to keep repeating the $+$ sign.

Exercise 7.3.1 *Write a Racket expression, as simple as possible,* to represent the standard arithmetic expression $3 \cdot 5 \cdot 2$

Exercise 7.3.2 *Write a Racket expression, as simple as possible,* to represent the standard arithmetic expression $(2 \cdot 3 \cdot 4) + 5 + (7 - 4)$

Worked Exercise 7.3.3 *Write a Racket expression* to represent the standard arithmetic expression $3 + 4 \cdot 5$.

Solution: To solve this, you first need to be sure what the "standard" arithmetic expression means. There are actually two possible ways to read this: "add 3 and 4, then multiply by 5," or "add 3 to the result of multiplying 4 by 5," and these two interpretations lead to different answers: 35 and 23 respectively. This is called an *ambiguous expression*. Which interpretation is right?

By convention, "standard" arithmetic uses *precedence rules* (or "order of operations" rules) to resolve this: parentheses, exponentiation, multiplication and division, addition and subtraction (PEMDAS; you may have heard the mnemonic "Please Excuse My Dear Aunt Sally"). According to these rules, multiplication happens before addition, so the second reading is correct, and the right answer should be 23, not 35.

Now that we've agreed that the original expression means $3 + (4 * 5)$, or (in English) "add 3 to the result of multiplying 4 by 5," writing it in Racket is straightforward:

```
(+ 3 (* 4 5))
```

∎

But what if we had meant the other interpretation, *e.g.* if the original expression had been $(3 + 4) \cdot 5$? The Racket expression would be

---

[2]or sometimes *Polish notation*, because it was invented by a Polish mathematician named Jan Łukasiewicz.

```
(* (+ 3 4) 5)
```

Notice that this expression looks *completely different*; it cannot possibly be confused with `(+ 3 (* 4 5))` ! An arithmetic expression in prefix notation doesn't need precedence rules; it has no ambiguity, hence no need to resolve the ambiguity.

In other words, if you had learned Racket in elementary school instead of "standard" arithmetic notation, you would never have heard of My Dear Aunt Sally.

Worked Exercise 7.3.4 *Write a Racket expression to represent the standard arithmetic expression* $3 \cdot -4$.

Solution: The "negation" operator follows the same syntax rule as everything else in Racket: it goes after a left parenthesis, before whatever it applies to. So we could write

```
(* 3 (- 4))
```

However, negative numbers are so common that Racket allows you to type them directly: if you put the $-$ sign *immediately* before the number (with no space in between), the number is treated as negative. So a shorter way of writing the expression would be

```
(* 3 -4)
```

7.4 A recipe for converting from infix to prefix

If you did the problems in the previous sections with no difficulty, you can probably skip this section. If not, here's a step-by-step technique that may help in translating an expression in "standard" infix algebraic notation into Racket's prefix notation:

1. Expand all the abbreviations and special mathematical symbols. For example, $3x$ really stands for `3 * x`; x^2 really stands for `x * x`; and $\sqrt{3x}$ uses a symbol that we don't have on the computer keyboard, so we'll write it as `sqrt(3 * x)`.

2. Fully parenthesize everything, using the usual order-of-operations rules (PEMDAS: parentheses, exponents, multiplication, division, addition, subtraction). By the end of this step, the number of operators, the number of left parentheses, and the number of right parentheses should all be the same. Furthermore, each pair of parentheses should be associated with *exactly one* operator and its operands; if I point at any operator, you can point to its left-parenthesis and its right-parenthesis.

3. Move each operator to just after its left-parenthesis, leaving everything else in the same order it was in before.

This may be clearer with some examples:

Worked Exercise 7.4.1 *Write a Racket expression to represent the standard arithmetic expression* $3 + x$.

Solution: There's nothing to do in Step 1.

Step 2 adds parentheses to get $(3 + x)$.

In Step 3, the $+$ sign moves to just after its left-parenthesis:

after which we can just read off the answer `(+ 3 x)`. ∎

Worked Exercise 7.4.2 *Write a Racket expression* to represent the standard arithmetic expression $3 \cdot 4 + 5$.

Solution: In step 1, we replace the $\cdot$ with $*$.

Step 2 tells us to "fully parenthesize, using order of operations"; since multiplication comes before addition, we rewrite the expression as (3 + (4 * 5)). Note that there are two operators (+ and *), two left parentheses, and two right parentheses; the + is directly inside the outer pair of parentheses, while the * is directly inside the pair enclosing 4 and 5.

In step 3, we move each operator to just after its own left parenthesis:

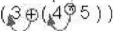

The left parenthesis belonging to + is the one at the beginning, so and the left parenthesis belonging to * is the one before 4, so we get (+ 3 (* 4 5)), which is a correct Racket expression. ∎

Worked Exercise 7.4.3 *Write a Racket expression* to represent the standard arithmetic expression $5 - 6 - 2$.

Solution: In Step 1, there's nothing to do.

In Step 2, we could parenthesize it as $((5 - 6) - 2$, or as $(5 - (6 - 2))$. These two interpretations give different answers: the first produces -3, while the second produces 1. In other words, this expression too is ambiguous. By convention, "standard" arithmetic says that the $-$ operator is applied from left to right, as though it were parenthesized as $((5 - 6) - 2)$. Note that the first $-$ sign is associated with the inner pair of parentheses, and the second is associated with the outer pair.

Step 3 then moves each $-$ sign to just after its own left parenthesis:

(- (- 5 6) 2)

This is a perfectly good, correct expression, but as we've already seen, Racket allows arithmetic operators to work on more than one operand, so we could rewrite it shorter as

(- 5 6 2)

∎

Worked Exercise 7.4.4 *Write a Racket expression* to represent the standard arithmetic expression $\sin x$.

Solution: There's nothing to do in step 1. As for step 2, in "standard" algebraic notation, named functions like sin are customarily placed in front of their arguments, often with the arguments surrounded by parentheses. So the "standard" way to write this, completing step 2, would be sin(x).

In step 3, we move the sin to just after its left parenthesis (which it is currently *outside*):
(sin x). ∎

Exercise 7.4.5 *Write a Racket expression* to represent the standard arithmetic expression $\sqrt{3x}$.

Worked Exercise 7.4.6 *Write a Racket expression* to represent the standard arithmetic expression $7x - \frac{3+x}{y+2}$.

Solution: Step 1 expands the $7x$ to $7*x$.

Step 2 adds parentheses around $3+x$, and around $y+2$, and around the whole fraction, and around $7*x$, and around the whole expression, to get

$$((7*x) - ((3+x)/(y+2)))$$

Step 3 moves each of the five operators to just after its own left parenthesis:

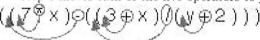

Finally, we can just read this from left to right and get
(- (* 7 x) (/ (+ 3 x) (+ y 2))). ∎

Now try the exercises from the previous sections again, using this technique.

7.5 Kinds of numbers

7.5.1 Integers

All the examples so far deal with *integers*: the counting numbers 0, 1, 2, 3, ... and their negatives. Racket is very good at dealing with integers: consider

(* 1234567890 1234567890 1234567890)

which should come out 1881676371789154860897069000.

SIDEBAR:

If you multiplied three copies of 1234567890 in Java, you would get a negative number! This is because Java, C, C++, and most other programming languages use *limited-range* integers, and once the answers get much beyond two billion, they are no longer guaranteed to be correct. In fact, if you tried it in C or C++, you could get different answers on different computers! In Racket, if you do a computation resulting in a 500-digit integer, every one of those digits will be correct. On the other hand, we pay a price for correctness: arithmetic in Racket is slightly slower than in Java, C, or C++.

7.5.2 Fractions

But many calculations in the real world go beyond the integers, using fractions, irrational numbers, complex numbers, *etc.*. Consider the expression (/ 4 11). In Racket, the answer will print out either in fractional form 4/11 or as a repeating decimal $0.\overline{36}$ depending on how DrRacket is set up. (If you'd like to experiment with this, go to "Language", "Choose Language", "Show Details", and find the radio buttons labelled "Mixed fractions" and "Repeating decimals".)

Racket does arithmetic on fractions the way you learned in grade-school, complete with reduction to lowest terms: for example, (+ (/ 2 3) (/ 1 4)) comes out as 11/12 or $0.91\overline{6}$, and (- (/ 2 3) (/ 1 6)) comes out as 1/2 or 0.5.

Again, fractions are so common that Racket allows you to type them directly, without the parentheses: if you type two integers separated by a "/", *with no spaces in between,* it will treat the whole thing as one fraction; thus the two preceding examples could be written more briefly as (+ 2/3 1/4) and (- 2/3 1/6) respectively.

7.5.3 Inexact numbers

Some numbers cannot be represented even by fractions, *e.g.* $\sqrt{2}$. Try the expression (sqrt 2) and you'll get the answer #i1.4142135623730951. The "#i" at the beginning tells you that this is an "inexact" number, only an approximation to the true square root of 2. You can see this first-hand by multiplying (sqrt 2) by itself; you should get something very close, but not quite equal, to 2. Likewise, most expressions involving trigonometric functions (sin, cos, tan, *etc.*) produce inexact answers.

This poses a problem for writing test cases. The check-expect function expects the answer to be *exactly* what you said it would be, so

(check-expect (* (sqrt 2) (sqrt 2)) 2)

will fail. When we're working with inexact numbers, we instead use a built-in function named check-within, which takes in *three* numbers: the actual answer, the right answer, and "how close" the answer needs to be in order to pass the test. Thus

(check-within (* (sqrt 2) (sqrt 2)) 2 0.0001)

tests whether (* (sqrt 2) (sqrt 2)) is within 0.0001 of the "right answer", 2, and it should pass.

SIDEBAR:

In most programming languages, division on integers does one of two peculiar things. Either it produces an inexact number, so for example $49 * (1/49)$ is almost but not quite equal to 1, or it does "integer division", rounding down to make the answer an integer, so 5/3 is 1 "with a remainder of 2", and $3 * (5/3)$ is 3 rather than 5. The latter can be useful sometimes, and Racket allows you to do it using the quotient and remainder functions, but the plain-old division operator produces fractions which are exactly correct if its arguments were exactly correct.

Exercise 7.5.1 *Write a Racket expression* to represent the standard arithmetic expression $\sqrt{4 + (2 \cdot 3)}$. *Be sure to write a test case!*

Hint: The answer should come out close to 3.162.

SIDEBAR:

Mathematicians also talk about something called *complex numbers*, a system in which negative numbers *do* have square roots. Racket supports complex numbers, which are written like 3+4i, again with no spaces in between. However, we won't need complex numbers in this book.

7.6 Contracts for built-in arithmetic functions

We've seen that to really know how to use a function, you need to know its contract, *i.e.* how many arguments of what types in what order it accepts, and what type of answer it returns.

Worked Exercise 7.6.1 *Write the contract* for the built-in + operator.

Solution: It works on two or more numbers and returns a number, so we can write

```
; + :  number number ...-> number
```

∎

Exercise 7.6.2 *Write the contracts for the built-in* −*,* ∗*,* /*, and* sqrt *functions.*

7.7 Writing numeric functions

You can define functions to do numeric computations in the same way that you defined functions producing pictures in Chapter 4. As always, you should still use the design recipe of Chapter 5. In fact, it'll be a bit easier because for the "right answers", you can just compute the right answer in your head or on a calculator and type in the number, rather than coming up with a Racket expression that builds the correct picture.

Worked Exercise 7.7.1 *Develop a function that takes in a number and returns its cube,* i.e. *three copies of it multiplied together.*

Solution: Contract: The obvious name for the function is cube. It takes in a number and returns a number, so the contract looks like

```
; cube :  number -> number
```

The function's purpose is obvious from its name, so we'll skip the purpose statement.

Examples: Any number should work. Let's start with really easy numbers, for which we know the right answers, and work up to harder ones for which we may only be able to *estimate* the right answers. For example, $20^3 = 8000$, so 19^3 must be a little less.

```
(check-expect (cube 0) 0)
(check-expect (cube 2) 8)
(check-expect (cube -3) -27)
(check-expect (cube 2/3) 8/27)
(check-within (cube (sqrt 2)) 2.828 0.01)
(cube 19) "should be a little under 8000"
(cube bignum) "should be 28-29 digits long"
; assuming bignum is defined to be 1234657890
```

Note that we've picked several things that might be "special cases": 0, both positive and negative numbers, a fraction, *etc.* If the function works correctly on all of these, we can reasonably expect it to work on *all* inputs.

Note also that we've used check-expect where we know the *exact* right answer, check-within where the answer is inexact but we know a good approximation to it, and "should be" where we only know a rough criterion for "is this a reasonable answer?"

Skeleton: The contract gives us much of the information, but we still need to choose a name for the parameter. It's a number, and doesn't necessarily "mean" anything more specific, so I'll choose num. The skeleton then looks like

```
(define (cube num)
  ...)
```

Inventory: We have only one parameter, so we'll add it in a comment:

```
(define (cube num)
  ; num        number
  ...)
```

Body: We know that the body will be an expression involving **num**. To get its cube, we simply need to multiply together three copies of **num**:

```
(define (cube num)
  ; num      number
  (* num num num)
  )
```

Was it obvious to you that the right expression was (* num num num)? Perhaps, but not all functions are this simple; we can't rely on "seeing" what the right expression must be. So what would we do if we got to this point and *didn't* "see" the answer? Remember the **Inventory with Values** technique in Chapter 5: add a line to the inventory labelled "should be", pick a not-too-simple example, and write down next to each inventory item its value for this example. Let's suppose we picked the fourth example, (cube 2/3). Our inventory-with-values would look like

```
(define (cube num)
  ; num            number    2/3
  ; should be      number    8/27
  ...)
```

Now, look at the "should be" value and try to figure out how to get it from the values above. The simplest way to get 8/27 from 2/3 is to multiply together three copies of 2/3, which is the value of the variable **num**, so we would come up with the body expression (* num num num), exactly as before.

The Definitions pane should now look like Figure 7.1.

Figure 7.1: Definition of the cube function

```
(define bignum 1234567890)

; cube :  number -> number

(check-expect (cube 0) 0)
(check-expect (cube 2) 8)
(check-expect (cube -3) -27)
(check-expect (cube 2/3) 8/27)
(check-within (cube (sqrt 2)) 2.828 0.01)

(define (cube num)
  ; num            number    2/3
  ; should be      number    8/27
  (* num num num)
  )

(cube 19) "should be a little under 8000"
(cube bignum) "should be 28-29 digits long"
```

Note that the check-expect and check-within test cases can appear either before the function definition or after it; "should be"-style test cases must appear *after* the definition, or DrRacket will complain that you're calling a function you haven't defined yet.

Testing: Hit "Run" and look at the results. If any of the actual results doesn't match what they "should be", something is wrong. ▮

Exercise 7.7.2 *Develop a function* named `rect-perimeter` *that takes in the width and height of a rectangle, and returns its perimeter.*

Exercise 7.7.3 *Develop a function* named `circle-perimeter` *that takes in the radius of a circle, and returns its perimeter.*

Hint: The formula for the perimeter of a circle is approximately $3.14 \cdot 2 \cdot r$, where r is the radius. Since the 3.14 and 2 are "always the same", they shouldn't be parameters to the function.

Exercise 7.7.4 *Develop a function* named `area-of-circle` *that takes in the radius of a circle and computes its area.*

Hint: The formula for the area of a circle is approximately $3.14 \cdot r^2$, where r is the radius.

Worked Exercise 7.7.5 *Consider the colored rings*

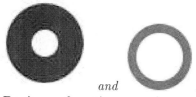

and .
Design a function named `area-of-ring` *which computes the area of such a ring.*

Solution:
Contract: The assignment doesn't actually say what the function should take in, so we need to figure that out. The area clearly doesn't depend on the color or location of the ring, but *does* depend on the size of both the inner and outer circles. How do we usually specify the size of a circle? Most often with its *radius*. So this function needs to take in *two* numbers: the inner radius and the outer radius. It doesn't make sense for the inner radius to be larger than the outer radius, so let's point that out.

```
; area-of-ring :  number (inner-radius)
;                 number (outer-radius) -> number
; assumes inner-radius ≤ outer-radius
```

Examples: As usual, we'll start with really easy ones that we can solve in our heads, then build up to more complicated ones. We'll also throw in some "special cases": one or both of the radii are zero, the two radii are equal, *etc.*

Before we can write down what the answers "should be", we need to know how to find the right answers ourselves. So let's imagine we were cutting out a "ring" in paper. We would probably start by cutting a circle with the outer radius, then marking another circle with the inner radius and the same center, cutting that out, and throwing away the inner part. So the area of what we have left is the area of a circle with the outer radius, *minus* the area of a circle with the inner radius.

```
(check-expect (area-of-ring 0 0) 0)
(check-expect (area-of-ring 2 2) 0)
(check-within (area-of-ring 0 1) 3.14 0.01)
(check-within (area-of-ring 0 2) 12.56 0.01)
(check-within (area-of-ring 1 2) 9.42 0.01)
; 4*3.14 for the outer circle, minus 3.14 for the inner circle
(check-within (area-of-ring 2 5) 65.94 0.01)
; 25*3.14 for the outer circle, minus 4*3.14 for the inner circle
```

Skeleton: The contract already tells us the name of the function and of its two parameters, so we can immediately write

```
(define (area-of-ring inner-radius outer-radius)
  ...)
```

Inventory: There are two parameters, both of type *number*, and we know the "magic number" 3.14 is involved, so...

```
(define (area-of-ring inner-radius outer-radius)
  ; inner-radius     number
  ; outer-radius     number
  ; 3.14             magic number
  ...)
```

Body: If you already see what to do next, great. But for practice (or if you *don't* already see what to do next), let's add a "should be" line and some values to this inventory. We need a "not too simple" example, which rules out those with a zero in them, and those with inner and outer radius the same. Let's try the example (area-of-ring 1 2).

```
(define (area-of-ring inner-radius outer-radius)
  ; inner-radius     number          1
  ; outer-radius     number          2
  ; 3.14             magic number    3.14
  ; should be        number          9.42
  ...)
```

Now how could you get the "right answer" 9.42 from the values above it? Obviously, the value that most resembles it is 3.14; the right answer in this case is exactly $3 \cdot 3.14$. Where did the 3 come from? The most obvious way is from $1 + 2$, so we might guess that the expression is (* 3.14 (+ inner-radius outer-radius)). This seems a bit too simple, since it doesn't use the area formula from before. Still, we can type this in and test it, and find that although it works for this test case, it **fails** two of the six test cases.

We've been led astray by picking *too simple* a test case. If we had picked (area-of-ring 2 5) instead, we would have had a "right answer" of 65.94, which is 21 times 3.14. It may not be obvious where the 21 came from, but it's certainly not (+ inner-radius outer-radius)! And we could reasonably figure out that the 21 comes from $5^2 - 2^2 = 25 - 4$, which would lead us to the correct formula

```
(* 3.14 (- (* outer-radius outer-radius) (* inner-radius inner-radius)))
```

If we type this in as the function body, it passes all the tests.

Another way to approach the problem would be to remember that the area of the ring is the area of the larger circle minus the area of the smaller circle; we can use the formula for the area of a circle twice to get

```
(- (* 3.14 outer-radius outer-radius) (* 3.14 inner-radius inner-radius))
```
which is equivalent to the answer above.

But once we've recognized that we need to compute the areas of circles, why not *re-use* the `area-of-circle` function we already wrote to do this job?

```
(define (area-of-ring inner-radius outer-radius)
  ; inner-radius    number
  ; outer-radius    number
  (-  (area-of-circle outer-radius)
      (area-of-circle inner-radius))
)
```

This is much shorter and clearer.

Testing: Assuming you've typed all of this into the Definitions pane, you should be able to hit "Run" and check the results. ∎

Improving the program: In fact, a more accurate formula for the area of a circle is $\pi \cdot r^2$, where π is a special number, approximately 3.141592653589793. In fact, π is so special that it comes predefined in Racket: there's a variable named `pi` with this value. We can use this to make `area-of-circle` more accurate, by replacing the 3.14 in its body with `pi`. This built-in variable `pi` is inexact, so you'll need to write your test cases using `check-within`.

Practice Exercise 7.7.6 *Replace the 3.14 in* `area-of-circle` *with* `pi`, *and change the test cases for both* `area-of-circle` *and* `area-of-ring` *appropriately. Make sure both functions still pass all their test cases.*

Recall that we defined `area-of-ring` by *re-using* `area-of-circle`. Since we've just made `area-of-circle` more accurate, `area-of-ring` is now *automatically* more accurate too, *without changing anything in its definition!* This is one of the powerful benefits of re-using one function in writing another.

Exercise 7.7.7 *Develop a function named* `hours->minutes` *that takes in a number of hours, and returns how many minutes are in that many hours.*

Hint: You can name the parameter anything you wish, but it's best to give it a name that tells what it means. In this case, the input represents a number of hours, so `hours` would be a good name.

Exercise 7.7.8 *Develop a function named* `days->hours` *that takes in a number of days, and returns how many hours are in that many days.*

Exercise 7.7.9 *Develop a function named* `days->minutes` *that takes in a number of days, and returns how many minutes are in that many hours.*

Hint: By re-using previously-written functions, you should be able to write this function with *no numbers in the definition* (although you'll need numbers in the examples).

Exercise 7.7.10 *Develop a function named* `dhm->minutes` *that takes in* three *numbers: how many days, how many hours, and how many minutes, in that order, and returns the total number of minutes.*

Hint: Again, you should be able to write this with no numbers in the definition.

Exercise 7.7.11 *Develop a function named `feet->inches` that takes in a number of feet, and returns the number of inches in that many feet.*

Exercise 7.7.12 *Develop a function named `total-inches` that takes in a length in feet and inches (e.g. 5 feet, 2 inches) and returns the number of inches in that length (in this example, 62).*

Hint: Look for opportunities to *re-use* functions you've already written.

Practice Exercise 7.7.13 *Try the `sin` function on various values, including 0, 1, pi, (/ pi 2), (/ pi 3), (/ pi 6), etc.*
***Compare** the results of*
`(sin (sqrt something))`
with
`(sqrt (sin something))`
by plugging in various numbers for something.

Exercise 7.7.14 *Develop a function `at-most-10` that takes in a number and returns either that number or 10, whichever is less.*

Hint: Use the built-in function `min` (read about it in the Help Desk). While you're at it, also look up the `max` and `abs` functions.

Exercise 7.7.15 *Develop a function named `celsius->kelvin` that takes in a temperature measurement in Celsius, and returns the corresponding temperature in Kelvin.*

Hint: A degree Kelvin is the same size as a degree Celsius, but $0°K$ is approximately $-273.15°C$. This gives you at least one example:

  `(check-within (celsius->kelvin -273.15) 0 0.01)`

Come up with at least two more examples of your own, and use the "inventory with values" technique to figure out the right algebraic expression.

Exercise 7.7.16 *Develop a function named `fahrenheit->celsius` that takes in a temperature measurement in Fahrenheit, and returns the corresponding temperature in Celsius.*

Hint: The conversion formula is $C = (F - 32) \cdot 5/9$.

Exercise 7.7.17 *Develop a function named `fahrenheit->kelvin` that takes in a temperature measurement in Fahrenheit, and returns the corresponding temperature in Kelvin.*

Hint: You should be able to write this with *no numbers or arithmetic operators* in the body of the function, by re-using previously-written functions.

Exercise 7.7.18 *Develop a function named `convert-3-digits` that takes in the "hundreds", "tens", and "ones" digits of a number, in that order, and returns the number itself. For example,*

  `(convert-3-digits 5 2 8)` `"should be"` `528`

Exercise 7.7.19 *Develop a function* named `convert-3-reversed` *that takes in the "ones", "tens", and "hundreds" digits of a number, in that order, and returns the number itself. For example,*

```
(convert-3-reversed 7 0 1) "should be" 107
```

Hint: By re-using a previously-defined function, you should be able to write this in a line or two, without any numbers or arithmetic operators.

Exercise 7.7.20 *Develop a function* named `top-half` *that takes in an image and returns the top half of it.*

Hint: See Section 3.5 for functions you'll need.

Exercise 7.7.21 *(Thanks to Leon LaSpina for this problem)*
Develop a function named `splice-pictures` *that takes in two images and combines them by splicing the left half of the first together with the right half of the second.*

Hint: This will work best if you pick pictures of approximately the same height. Try the faces of two famous people ...

Exercise 7.7.22 *Develop a function* named `progress-bar` *that takes in three numbers (*width, height, *and* progress*) and a string (*color*) and produces a horizontal progress bar as in this example, in which the leftmost* progress *pixels are solid and the rest are outlined. You may assume that* width, height, *and* progress *are all positive integers, and that* progress *is no larger than* width.

Exercise 7.7.23 *Develop a function* `bar-graph` *that takes in four numbers and produces a bar-graph with four vertical bars (red, blue, green, and yellow respectively) of those heights.*

Exercise 7.7.24 *Develop a function* `frame-pic` *that takes in an image, a color name, and a positive number, and produces that picture surrounded by a "frame" of the specified color and thickness. For example,*

```
> (frame-pic calendar "blue" 10)
```

Exercise 7.7.25 *My wife wanted to change the background image on her Web page to a repeating image. But she didn't want the image to repeat in a monotonous checkerboard pattern; she wanted each row to be offset from the previous one. Unfortunately, there's no HTML command to do that, so I had to build an image which, when repeated horizontally and vertically, looks like alternating rows offset from one another.*

Develop a function `offset-tile` *which takes in an image and produces an image twice as tall: the top row is the original image, and the bottom row is the image split in half and put back together in reverse order.*

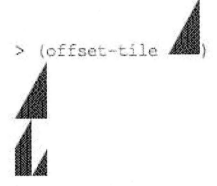

Hint: This is trickier than it seems at first. Be sure to test it on both even-width and odd-width images, and try putting several copies of the result side by side to make sure you haven't created "jaggies".

**This exercise may be easier if you first define two "helper functions" `left-half` and `right-half`. We'll learn more about helper functions in Chapter 11.

7.8   Manipulating colors in images

7.8.1   Images, pixels, and colors

Images on a television or computer screen are actually made up of millions of tiny colored dots, called *pixels* (short for "picture elements"). Look at such a screen up close with a magnifying glass, and you may be able to see them. In many computer systems, including Racket, the color of each dot is represented in *RGB* (or *RGBA*) form: three (or four) numbers representing the amounts of red, green, blue, and perhaps opacity in the dot (the red, green, blue, and alpha *components* of the color). Each of these numbers is conventionally restricted to the integers from 0 to 255. So for example a color with 0 red, 0 green, and 0 blue is black; 255 red, 255 green, and 255 blue is white; 255 red, 0 green, and 0 blue is pure red; the combination of 100 red, 160 green, and 220 blue is a sort of light denim-blue; etc.

7.8.2 Building images pixel by pixel

The `picturing-programs` teachpack includes a function named `build3-image` which builds an image pixel by pixel based on where in the picture you are. Its contract is

```
; build3-image :   number(width) number(height)
;                  function(red-function)
;                  function(green-function)
;                  function(blue-function)
;                  -> image
```

It takes in the width and height of the desired image, and three functions. Each of the three functions takes in the x and y coordinates of a pixel; one computes the red component, one the green component, and one the blue component.

Worked Exercise 7.8.1

Build a rectangle 50 by 50 which shades smoothly from black at the left edge to red (specifically 250 red, 0 green, 0 blue) at the right edge.

Solution: The only way we know to do this is using `build3-image`. Obviously the width and height are both 50, but we'll need three functions to give it. For now, let's name them `red-function`, `green-function`, and `blue-function` (we may come up with better names later).

Each of the three functions *must* have the contract

```
; whatever :   number(x) number(y) -> number
```

Now we need some examples for `red-function`. It doesn't care about the y coordinate given to it, but it should be 0 when the x coordinate is 0, and 250 when the x coordinate is 50. So

```
(check-expect (red-function 0 53) 0)
(check-expect (red-function 50 17) 250)
```

What formula would give us this? Well, there are many ways to do it, but the simplest is $red = 5x$. Let's add another test case in between:

```
(check-expect (red-function 20 40) 100)
```

The skeleton and inventory are straightforward:

```
(define (red-function x y)
  ; x       a number
  ; y       a number
  ...
  )
```

And the formula is easy to translate into Racket:

```
(define (red-function x y)
  ; x        a number
  ; y        a number
  (* 5 x)
  )
```

Test this, and it should work.

Now let's try the green component. We already have the contract. The examples are easy: no matter what x and y coordinates we plug in, the answer should be 0.

```
(check-expect (green-function 7 45) 0)
(check-expect (green-function 118 -3) 0)
```

The skeleton and inventory are exactly the same as for `red-function`, except for renaming the function, and the body is even easier:

```
(define (green-function x y)
  ; x        a number
  ; y        a number
  0
  )
```

Test this, and it should work.

The blue function does *exactly the same thing*; we don't even need to write and test another function for it (although we could if we wished).

We can now build the desired picture as follows:

```
(build3-image 50 50 red-function green-function green-function)
```

Try this and see what comes out.

Note that I've used `green-function` as both the green function and the blue function. This is sorta confusing; it might be better to rename it to say what it *does*, instead of how we intend to *use* it in this problem.

```
(define ( always-zero x y)
  ; x        a number
  ; y        a number
  0
  )
```

```
(build3-image 50 50 red-function always-zero always-zero)
```

For that matter, we could rename `red-function` to better indicate what it does: let's call it **5x**, because it returns 5 times the x coordinate.

```
(define ( 5x x y)
  ; x        a number
  ; y        a number
  (* 5 x)
  )
```

```
(build3-image 50 50 5x always-zero always-zero)
```

∎

Exercise 7.8.2 *Build a rectangle, 50 x 50, which shades smoothly from black at the top-left corner to purple (i.e. red plus blue) in the bottom-right corner. The top-right corner should be blue, and the bottom-left corner red.*

Hint: You can re-use some previously-defined functions, and you'll need to write a new one.

7.8.3 Error-proofing

What happens if you make the image larger than 50 x 50 in the above exercises? 51 is OK, 52 is OK, but 53 produces an error message because one of the color components is outside the range from 0 to 255.

SIDEBAR:

You may be wondering why 52 is OK, since $52 \cdot 5 = 260$. The reason is that the pixel positions are numbered from 0 up to *one less than* the width or height, so the largest number ever actually given to 5x is 51.

One way to solve this problem is to not allow the numbers to get too big, using `min`:

```
; safe-5x :  number(x) number(y) -> number (no more than 255)
(check-expect (safe-5x 0 17) 0)
(check-expect (safe-5x 50 27) 250)
(check-expect (safe-5x 51 7) 255)
(check-expect (safe-5x 89 53) 255)
(define (safe-5x x y)
   ; x      a number
   ; y      a number
   (min 255 (* 5 x)) )
```

This way if $5x \leq 255$, the answer will be $5x$, but if $5x$ is too large, the function will return 255. **Try this** on an image of, say, 100 wide by 75 high. Do you like the result?

Another approach is to multiply by something smaller than 5, *e.g.* if you wanted a 100x75 image that shades *smoothly* from black to red, you might want to multiply by 2.55 instead of 5. This also produces error messages, however, because the components of a color are supposed to be *integers*. Fortunately, there's a function `real->int` that does what it sounds like: it takes in a real number and produces the closest integer to it. For example,

```
; safe-2.55x :  number(x) number(y) -> number
(check-expect (safe-2.55x 0 17) 0)
(check-expect (safe-2.55x 45 27) 115)
(check-expect (safe-2.55x 100 7) 255)
(check-expect (safe-2.55x 189 53) 255)
(define (safe-2.55x x y)
   ; x      a number
   ; y      a number
   (min 255  (real->int (* 2.55 x)) ))
```

Note that this `real->int` trick is only necessary if you're multiplying coordinates by something other than an integer, since an integer times an integer is always an integer.

Exercise 7.8.3 *Is it always clear what "the closest integer" is? Can you think of a kind of number for which there are two different "closest integers"?* **Experiment** *with* `real->int` *to find what it does in this case. Do you have any guesses as to why it works this way?*

Exercise 7.8.4
Build a rectangle, 100 x 100, which shades smoothly from red at the left edge to green

at the right edge. (I'm not giving you a picture of this, since it really doesn't work in a black-and-white printing!)

Exercise 7.8.5

***Build a rectangle**, 100 x 100, which shades smoothly from black at the top-left corner to yellow (i.e. red plus green) at the bottom-right corner. Every point along the diagonal from top-right to bottom-left should be the same color.*

Hint: The formula needs to treat x and y the same, so that increasing *either* of them will increase the amount of color. The red and green functions will be the same.

Exercise 7.8.6

***Build a rectangle**, 100 x 100, which is yellow (i.e. red plus green) in the top-right and bottom-left corners, and black along the diagonal from top-left to bottom-right.*

Hint: Use the `abs` function.

Exercise 7.8.7 ***Experiment** with colors based on*

- *the square of the x or y coordinate,*

- *the square root of the x or y coordinate,*

- *the sine of the x or y coordinate,*

- *the sum, difference, or product of the x and y coordinates*

In all these cases, consider the largest and smallest possible values of the formula, and scale it and convert to integer so the color values are integers between 0 and 255. It may also be easier to see what's happening if you divide the x or y coordinate by something like 10 or 20 before taking the sine of it.

7.8.4 Building images from other images

There's also a built-in function map3-image which is similar to build3-image, but builds a new image *from an existing image*. Its contract is

```
; map3-image :  function(red-function)
;               function(green-function)
;               function(blue-function)
;               image -> image
```

That is, it takes in three functions and an image, and produces a new image. Each of the three functions *must* have the contract

```
; whatever :  number(x) number(y)
;             number(red) number(green) number(blue) -> number
```

The first two parameters are the x and y coordinates, as before. The third, fourth, and fifth are the red, green, and blue components of the pixel at that location in the original picture.

Worked Exercise 7.8.8 *Choose an interesting picture (preferably a photograph) and build a version of it with all the red removed, leaving only the green and blue components.*

Solution: Obviously, we'll need to call map3-image, which means we need three functions to give it. Let's call them red-function, green-function, and blue-function for now. All three have the contract

```
; whatever :  number(x) number(y)
;             number(red) number(green) number(blue) -> number
```

The red function is easy: no matter what x, y, or the old color are, it should return 0:

```
(check-expect (red-function 10 20 30 40 50) 0)
(check-expect (red-function 1000 100 250 125 0) 0)
(define (red-function x y red green blue)
  ; x      a number
  ; y      a number
  ; red    a number
  ; green  a number
  ; blue   a number
  0)
```

The green function simply returns the same amount of green as before:

```
(check-expect (green-function 10 20 30 40 50) 40)
(check-expect (green-function 1000 100 250 125 0) 125)
(define (green-function x y red green blue)
  ; x      a number
  ; y      a number
  ; red    a number
  ; green  a number
  ; blue   a number
  green)
```

and the blue function is similar, but returns the same amount of blue as before (left as an exercise).

Once all three of these are tested, we can simply say

```
(map3-image red-function green-function blue-function my-picture)
```

to get the desired result. ▮

Exercise 7.8.9 *Define a function* `remove-red` *that takes in an image and returns the same image with all the red removed.*

Hint: For this exercise, and most of the exercises in this section, there is no easy way to build "the right answer" other than the function itself. So I suggest describing the right answer in English, rather than using `check-expect`. You still need to write test cases, you just need to check them by eye rather than relying on `check-expect`.

Exercise 7.8.10 *Define a function* `swap-red-blue` *that takes in an image and returns the same image with the red and blue components reversed: wherever there was a lot of red, there should be a lot of blue, and* vice versa.

Exercise 7.8.11 *Define a function* `convert-to-gray` *that takes in an image and returns the same image in* gray-scale. *That is, every pixel should have red, green, and blue components equal to one another. However, the* total *amount of color at each pixel should be roughly the same as the total amount of color at that point in the original picture.*

Exercise 7.8.12 *Define a function* `apply-blue-gradient` *that takes in an image and returns an image with the same red and green components, but with the blue component equal to the y coordinate (so none at the top and the most at the bottom).*

Hint: Test your program with images of a variety of sizes, including some that are more than 255 pixels high.   (It would be nice to have this function always reach full blue just at the bottom of the image, regardless of image height, but that requires some techniques you don't know yet; we'll see how in Chapters 27 and 28.)

Exercise 7.8.13 *Make up some other cool tricks to do with images and their pixels. Go wild.*

7.8.5   A sneak preview

It's sort of inconvenient having to write three separate functions for the red, green, and blue components of the resulting picture (either for `build3-image` or for `map3-image`). There's a function named `build-image`: where `build3-image` takes in three functions that return the red, green, and blue components of a pixel, `build-image` takes in *one* function that returns a whole *color* (with `make-color`).

Exercise 7.8.14 *Re-write some of exercises 7.8.1 through 7.8.7 using* `build-image` *instead of* `build3-image`.

There's also a function `map-image` which takes in only *one* function rather than three. But that function in turn takes in a *color* rather than three numbers, so you can't really use it until you've learned in Chapter 20 how to take colors apart.

7.8.6   A problem with bit-maps

The `build3-image` and `map3-image` functions produce an image in a form called a *bit-map* (or, more precisely, a *pixel-map*). Such images display very nicely "as is", but if you try to enlarge them or rotate them, the results often don't look very good. For example, suppose `my-picture` was a picture you had created in one of these ways. Then `rotate 15 my-picture`, or `scale 5 my-picture`, may well have "jaggies" — visibly jagged, "stairstep" edges that wouldn't happen if you just scaled or rotated a pure geometric shape like a triangle.

Exercise 7.8.15 *Develop a function* `bitmapize` *that takes in a picture and, using* `map3-image`, *returns an image with exactly the same colors.*
Compare the results of

```
(bitmapize (scale 5 (triangle 10 "solid" "blue")))
(scale 5 (bitmapize (triangle 10 "solid" "blue")))
```

Which one looks smoother? Why?

The moral of the story is that if you're going to do bitmap operations (such as `map3-image`), they should be ideally done *after* scaling.

7.9   Randomness

If you were writing a video game, you probably wouldn't want things to always play out the same way; you'd want to give the game a certain amount of *unpredictability*. Likewise, people doing computer simulations of complex systems like traffic patterns, economics, aerodynamics, and drug interactions may want to include some unpredictable events in their simulations.

In Racket, as in most programming languages, this is done with the help of a built-in function called a *random number generator*.[3] There's a Racket function named `random` that takes in a positive integer and returns a "randomly" chosen integer, at least zero and less than the given integer. Here's a sample interaction:

```
> (random 10)
6
> (random 10)
4
> (random 10)
0
> (random 10)
3
> (random 10)
7
> (random 10)
4
> (random 10)
2
```

The answers can be anything from 0, 1, ... 9 (10 choices). In general, the number of possible answers is equal to the argument of `random`. **Try** the `random` function several times each, on several different arguments.

---

[3]Most "random number generators" don't produce *really* random numbers, but rather a predictable sequence of numbers that *look* random unless you know the formula that is used to produce them.

Testing random functions

Since `random` produces an unpredictable result, it's difficult to write test cases for functions that use it. If we write something like

```
(check-expect (random 10) 4)
```

it will fail 90% of the time. For that matter, if we write

```
(check-expect (random 10) (random 10))
```

it will *still* fail 90% of the time. (Why?)

One answer is to use `"should be"` and an English-language description of what's a "reasonable" answer, *e.g.* `"should be an integer from 0 through 9"`. Since random-valued functions may return different answers each time you call them on the same input, make sure to *test them several times interactively*: if you expect different answers each time, but you actually get the *same* answer each time, or if you expect several equally-likely answers but in fact one answer is much more common than another, something may be wrong.

Another way is to use one of `check-expect`'s cousins, `check-member-of` and `check-range`. `check-member-of` takes three or more arguments, and checks whether the first matches *any* of the remaining ones:

```
(check-member-of (random 6) 0 1 2 3 4 5)
```

If you're calling `random` with a large argument, you probably don't want to type in all the possible answers, so `check-range` takes in three numbers and checks that the first is between the second and third (inclusively — that is, it's allowed to be *exactly* the second or the third):

```
(check-range (random 1000) 0 999)
```

The `check-member-of` and `check-range` functions are more convenient to use than "should be", because you don't have to look at the answers yourself. However, they don't help you spot the kind of mistake described above, where a function that's *supposed* to be random actually produces the same answer every time, or produces answers with the wrong probabilities. So even if you decide to use `check-member-of` or `check-range`, you should still have a few "should be"-style tests so you can see whether you're actually getting different answers.

Exercise 7.9.1 *Develop a function named `random-digit` that returns one of the integers 0, 1, ... 9, chosen at random.*

Hint: This function doesn't depend on a parameter, but DrRacket's Beginner Language won't let you write a function without a parameter, so have your function take in something and ignore it.

Exercise 7.9.2 *Develop a function named `roll-die` that returns an integer randomly chosen from 1 to 6 inclusive — no zeroes, no 7's.*

Hint: As before, the function should take a dummy parameter. There are 6 possible answers; how do you make sure that the function never returns 0, but does return 6 some of the time?

Exercise 7.9.3 *Develop a function named `two-dice` that acts like rolling two 6-sided dice and counting the total number of dots.*

Hint: As before, give it a dummy parameter. Note that the possible answers are 2 through 12, but they're not equally likely: 7 should come up much more often than 2 or 12. How can you test this?

Exercise 7.9.4 *Develop a function* named `random-picture` *that takes in a width and a height, and produces a rectangle that size and shape, in which each pixel is a random color (that is, the red, green, and blue components are each chosen randomly).*

7.10   Review of important words and concepts

Racket provides all the usual arithmetic operators: $+$, $-$, $*$, $/$, `sqrt`, *etc.* They obey the same syntax rule as everything else in Racket:

(*function-name argument* ...)

In other words, they are *prefix* operators: we write them *before* whatever they're supposed to work on. This may feel unnatural for people accustomed to the *infix* operators we learned in grade school, but in many ways Racket's syntax is simpler, more consistent, and more flexible; for example, there is no need to memorize precedence rules like PEMDAS, because everything is parenthesized.

Racket distinguishes among different *kinds* of numbers: *integers, fractions, inexact* numbers and *complex* numbers. When testing a function with inexact results, use `check-within` rather than `check-expect`.

Variables and functions can have numeric values, just as they can have image values. The process of defining them is almost exactly as before, except that it's usually easier to construct "right answers" to function examples. There are a few predefined variables in Racket, notably `pi` and `e`, to stand for special numeric values.

Racket, like most programming languages, provides a *random number generator*, which produces (mostly-)unpredictable numbers in a specified range. Since random-valued functions are unpredictable, you can't test them using `check-expect`, but you can specify in English what the allowable values are, or you can use `check-member-of` or `check-range`. Be sure to test such functions several times, both with checking functions and with "should be".

7.11   Reference: Built-in functions on numbers

In this chapter we've introduced a number of functions, many of which you've been using for years:

- $+$, which takes *two or more* parameters

- $-$, which takes *one or more* parameters

- $*$, which takes *two or more* parameters

- $/$

- `add1`

- `sub1`

- `sqrt`

- `min`

- `max`

- `abs`

- `sin`

- `quotient`

- `remainder`

- `random`

- `pi`, which is actually a built-in variable, not a function.

- `check-member-of`

- `check-range`

- `build3-image`

- `build-image`

- `map3-image`

Chapter 8

Animations involving numbers

8.1 Model and view

The examples of Chapter 6 all compute the next picture in the animation from the previous picture. This turns out to be a rather restrictive way to look at things. For example, suppose we wanted an animation of a digital clock. **11:38:49 AM**

How would you go about computing the next picture from the previous one? Well, first you would have to look at the picture and "read" it: from the pattern of dark and light pixels in the picture, recognize each of the digits, interpret the sequence of digits as a number, add 1 to that number, and finally convert the result back into a picture. We're asking the computer to do things that humans do easily, but computers aren't very good at — things that took our eyes millions of years of evolution, and our infant selves years of training.

A more sensible approach would be to store the current time directly as a *number* (which computers are very good at), and add one second to it at every "tick". We'd still need to convert a number to a picture, but this is considerably easier than analyzing a picture and reading a number from it.

In Chapter 6, I said I was simplifying things. The truth is that an event handler doesn't necessarily take in an image; it takes in a "model", which (for now) can be *either an image or a number*. For each animation you write, you'll need to decide which of these to use, and stick to that decision throughout the animation.

You can tell DrRacket what kind of model you're using by adding another event handler to `big-bang`: either `(check-with image?)` or `(check-with number?)` depending on whether you're using images or numbers. This makes no difference if your animation is written perfectly, but if (as will almost certainly happen once or twice) you get confused, and write part of it to work on images and another part to work on numbers, a `check-with` handler allows DrRacket to give you better error messages, so you can figure out more easily what went wrong. We'll explore `check-with` more thoroughly in Chapter 14, but for now suffice it to say that `image?` is a built-in function that checks whether something is an image, and `number?` similarly checks whether something is a number.

The details are in Figure 8.1.

Figure 8.1: Event handlers for animations with image or numeric models

---

The big-bang function has the contract

```
; big-bang :  model (start) handler ... -> model
```

where *model* is either *number* or *image*.

tick handlers must have the contract

```
; function-name :  model (old) -> model (new)
```

They are installed with (on-tick *function-name interval*). The *interval* is the length of time (in seconds) between clock ticks; if you leave it out, the animation will run as fast as it can.

key handlers must have the contract

```
; function-name :  model (old) key -> model (new)
```

The "key" parameter indicates what key was pressed; we'll see how to use it in Chapter 18.

They are installed with (on-key *function-name*).

mouse handlers must have the contract

```
; function-name :  model (old)
;                     number (mouse-x) number (mouse-y) event
;                     -> model (new)
```

The first parameter is the old model; the second represents the *x coordinate*, indicating how many pixels from the left the mouse is; the third number represents the *y coordinate*, indicating how many pixels down from the top the mouse is; and the "event" tells what happened (the mouse was moved, the button was pressed or released, *etc.*); we'll see in Chapter 18 how to use this.

They are installed with (on-mouse *function-name*).

draw handlers must have the contract

```
; function-name :  model (current) -> image
```

and are installed with (on-draw *function-name width height*).

If you leave out the *width* and *height*, the animation window will be the size and shape of the result the first time the draw handler is called.

An especially simple draw handler, show-it, is predefined: it simply returns the same image it was given, and it's useful if you need to specify the width and height of the animation window but don't want to write your own draw handler.

To specify the model type , put in another event handler: either (check-with image?) or (check-with number?), depending on whether your animation uses images or numbers as its model.

8.2 Design recipe for an animation, second version

Now that we know about different types of models, we'll add to the earlier design recipe. The result is in Figure 8.2.

To illustrate it, let's work some examples. Everything in Chapter 6 still works, using images as our models. But we can now do much more. We'll start, as before, with an unmoving "animation".

Worked Exercise 8.2.1 *Develop an animation* *whose "model" is a number, and whose "view" is a blue circle of that radius. For now, it won't change.*

Solution: Since the animation won't actually change, we don't need a tick-handler, a key-handler, or a mouse-handler; we're not sure yet whether we'll need a draw handler.

We've been told to use a number as the model, so that decision is made. Since the model isn't an image, we'll definitely need a draw handler.

The draw handler needs to take in a number and return an image of a blue circle whose radius is that number. Let's name the function `blue-circle-of-size`.

Contract:
```
; blue-circle-of-size :  number(radius) -> image
```

Examples:
```
(check-expect (blue-circle-of-size 2)
              (circle 2 "solid" "blue"))
(check-expect (blue-circle-of-size 37)
              (circle 37 "solid" "blue"))
```

Function skeleton:
```
(define (blue-circle-of-size radius)
  ...)
```

Inventory:
```
(define (blue-circle-of-size radius)
   ; radius        number
   ; "blue"        a string I know I'll need
   ...)
```

Body:
```
(define (blue-circle-of-size radius)
   ; radius        number
   ; "blue"        a string I know I'll need
   (circle radius "solid" "blue")
   )
```

Figure 8.2: Design recipe for an animation, version 2

1. **Identify what handlers you'll need** (check-with, draw, tick, mouse, and/or key).

   - You should always have a `check-with` handler.
   - If your animation needs to change at regular intervals, you'll need a tick handler.
   - If your animation needs to respond to mouse movements and clicks, you'll need a mouse handler.
   - If your animation needs to respond to keyboard typing, you'll need a key handler.
   - You'll always need a draw handler. If your model is exactly the image you want to show in the animation window, you can use `show-it`; if not, you'll need to write your own draw handler.

2. **Decide what type a "model" is** — image or number, for now — and what it "means".

   What kinds of changes do you want to make in response to events? If they're easily described by arithmetic, use a number; if they're image operations (*e.g.* `rotate-cw`), use an image. If neither, see Chapter 10.

   If you decide to use a numeric model, you still need to decide what it *means*: a rectangle's height, a circle's radius, a string's length, something's x coordinate, ...

   If you decide to use an image model, follow the recipe of Chapter 6.

   If you decide to use a number as the model, you'll definitely need to write a draw handler.

3. **Write the contracts** for the handlers, using Figure 8.1. Again, the function names are up to you, but once you've chosen a type for your model, the contracts must be exactly as in Figure 8.1.

4. **Develop each of these functions**, following the usual design recipe for each one. Don't go on to the next one until the previous one passes all of its test cases.

5. **Decide on the initial number** the model should start at.

6. **Decide on the width and height** (if the draw handler doesn't produce something of the right size).

7. **Decide on the time interval between "ticks"** (if you have a tick handler).

8. **Call `big-bang`** with the initial picture and handlers (specified using `check-with`, `on-draw`, `on-tick`, `on-mouse`, and `on-key`). See whether it works.

Test this function to make sure it works correctly by itself.

To run the animation, we need to make some more decisions: what *is* the unchanging radius of the circle? (let's try 7), and what shape and size should the animation window be? I'll pick 100 wide by 50 high, which should be plenty big enough to show a radius-7 circle. The `big-bang` call is now

```
(big-bang 7
          (check-with number?)
          (on-draw blue-circle-of-size 100 50))
```

The result should be an animation window, 100x50, containing a blue circle of radius 7. Notice that when you close the window, it returns the number 7 to the Interactions pane.

∎

Practice Exercise 8.2.2 *Try this* *with different numbers in place of the 100, 50, and 7.*

Try this *with a string like* `"hello"` *instead of a number as the first argument to* `big-bang`. *What error message do you get?*

Take out the `(check-with number?)` *handler, and try that same mistake again. What error message do you get?*

Exercise 8.2.3 *Develop an animation* *of a small picture of your choice on a 200x200 white background. The model should be a number representing the x coordinate of the picture's location; the y coordinate should always be 50.*

Try it with several different numbers as initial models.

The result, like Exercise 8.2.1, won't actually move, but the picture will appear at a distance from the left edge determined by the "initial model" in the `big-bang` call. And, as with Exercise 8.2.1, we'll modify this animation shortly to do more interesting things.

8.3 Animations using `add1`

Recall that for the animation of Exercise 8.2.1, we decided that the model is a number indicating the radius of the circle. How would we *change* the radius? Well, if we wanted the circle to grow over time, we could add 1 to the radius at each clock tick.

A tick handler function, for an animation with a numeric model, must always have a contract of the form

```
function-name :  number -> number
```

Conveniently enough, the `add1` function (introduced in Chapter 7) has exactly this contract, so we can use it as a tick handler without needing to write our own. The result should be a circle that grows larger every tick:

```
(big-bang 7
          (check-with number?)
          (on-draw blue-circle-of-size 100 50)
          (on-tick add1 1/2))
```

(Remember, the 1/2 means the clock should tick every half second.)

Practice Exercise 8.3.1 *Try this.*

Exercise 8.3.2 *Modify* *the display of Exercise 8.3.1 so that the circle appears* centered *and unmoving in a 200x200 white background, so it appears to grow around a fixed center.*

Exercise 8.3.3 *Modify Exercise 8.2.3 so that the picture moves 1 pixel to the right every 1/10 second.*

Hint: This doesn't require writing any new functions at all, only changing the `big-bang` call.

Exercise 8.3.4 *Develop an animation of a square, initially 1x1, which grows by 1 pixel in each dimension at each clock tick, centered in a 200x200 window.*

Note: You may find that the square seems to jiggle slightly from upper-left to lower-right and back. This is because DrRacket uses integers for the positions of images; when the square has an even size, its center is exactly halfway, but when it has an odd size, its "center" for drawing purposes is half a pixel above and to the left of its actual center. Why didn't this problem show up in Exercise 8.3.1?)

Exercise 8.3.5 *Develop an animation of a rectangle, initially 2x1, which grows by 1 pixel in height and 2 in width at each clock tick, centered in a 200x200 window.*

Hint: Have the model represent only the height; put together the right picture from this information.

Exercise 8.3.6 *Develop an animation that displays a small dot or star at a location that varies over time. The x coordinate should be simply t, and the y coordinate $t^2/20$, where t is the number of ticks since the animation started.*

Hint: Write a "helper" function `y-coord` that takes in the current value of t and computes $t^2/20$; use this function in your draw handler.

Exercise 8.3.7 *Modify the animation of Exercise 8.3.6 so that the x coordinate is $100 + 50\cos(t/10)$ and the y coordinate $100 + 30\sin(t/10)$.*

Hint: This will show up better if you use a short tick interval, or leave it out completely so the animation runs as fast as possible.

Exercise 8.3.8 *Add the variable definitions*
```
(define XCENTER 100)
(define YCENTER 100)
(define XSCALE 50)
(define YSCALE 30)
```
to your definitions pane, and replace the formulæ in Exercise 8.3.7 with

$$x = XCENTER + XSCALE * \cos(t/10)$$

and

$$y = YCENTER + YSCALE * \sin(t/10)$$

The animation should still work exactly as before. Check that it does.

Now change the definitions of some of the variables to different numbers and run the animation again. Can you predict what will happen?

There are two other "magic numbers" still in the program: the 1/10's inside the `cos` *and* `sin` *functions. Replace these too with variables; make sure the animation works as before, then try changing these values and predict what will happen. For example, what happens when these two numbers aren't the same: when one is twice the other, or three times the other, or slightly more or less than the other?*

Exercise 8.3.9 *Write an animation that shows a blue progress bar 20 high by 120 wide, initially just an outline but filling in from left to right at 1 pixel per quarter of a second.*

Note: Depending on how you write this, your animation will probably stop changing after 30 seconds, when the progress bar reaches 100% full. In fact, it's still running, but not showing any *visible* change. We'll learn in Chapter 15 how to have it actually stop at a specified point.

8.4 Animations with other numeric functions

Of course, you can do much more interesting things to a numeric model than simply add 1 to it. For example, you can write an add5 function that takes in a number and adds 5 to it, and use this in place of add1 for the examples in Section 8.3, to get a blue circle that grows by 5 pixels at a time, or a digital counter that counts by 5 rather than 1.

Here's another example.

Worked Exercise 8.4.1 *Write an animation of a picture of your choice that moves right 1 pixel whenever the mouse is moved or clicked, and left 4 pixels whenever a key is typed on the keyboard.*

Solution:

What handlers do we need? The animation needs to respond to the mouse and the keyboard, so we'll need a mouse handler and a key handler. If we use a non-image model, we'll also need a draw handler.

Identify the model: The next step in designing an animation is deciding what type the "model" is, and what it "means". The only piece of information that changes in this animation is the x-coordinate of a picture, so let's say our model is a number indicating the x coordinate of the picture.

(You could try to do this animation using an image as the model, moving it to the right with beside and to the left with crop-left. Unfortunately, if it "moved" off the left edge of the screen, the picture would be reduced to nothing, and subsequent attempts to "move it right" wouldn't bring it back. Using a number as the model, we can move it off the left edge, then bring it back onto the screen, as many times as we like.)

Contracts for handlers: Draw handlers always have contract

```
; handle-draw :  model -> image
```

We've decided that for this animation, "model" means "number", so

```
; handle-draw :  number -> image
```

Key handlers always have contract

```
; handle-key :  model key -> model
```

For this animation, that becomes

```
; handle-key :  number key -> number
```

Mouse handlers always have contract

```
; handle-mouse :
  model number(mouse-x) number(mouse-y) event
  -> model
```

In our case, this becomes

```
; handle-mouse :
  number(old) number(mouse-x) number(mouse-y) event
  -> number(new)
```

Write the draw handler: Since our model is a number, we'll need a draw handler to convert it into an image. Let's use our favorite calendar picture, and (since the assignment says it moves only left and right) decide that it'll always be at a y-coordinate of, say, 50. Since it's moving only left and right, a window height of 100 should be plenty, with a window width of (say) 500.

If you did Exercises 8.2.3 and 8.3.3, you've already written a draw handler that will work for this; the only change is the size and shape of the background. Let's suppose you wrote one named `calendar-at-x`.

Write the mouse handler: We need to move right (*i.e.* increase the x coordinate) whenever there's a mouse event, but we don't care about any of the details of the event. So we'll write a function with the **contract**

```
; add1-on-mouse :  number(x)
;                  number(mouse-x) number(mouse-y)
;                  event -> number
```

(Remember, the first parameter to a mouse handler is always the current *model*, which for this animation is a number representing the *x* coordinate of the picture.) We're ignoring `mouse-x`, `mouse-y`, and `event`, so the following examples should be enough:

```
"Examples of add1-on-mouse:"
(check-expect
  (add1-on-mouse 3 29 348 "blarg") 4)
(check-expect
  (add1-on-mouse 15 503 6 "glink") 16)
```

The **skeleton** comes directly from the contract:

```
(define (add1-on-mouse x mouse-x mouse-y event)
  ...)
```

The **inventory** simply adds the four parameters:

```
(define (add1-on-mouse x mouse-x mouse-y event)
  ; x          number
  ; mouse-x    number (ignore)
  ; mouse-y    number (ignore)
  ; event      whatever (ignore)
  ...)
```

In the **body**, we merely need to add 1 to x:

```
(define (add1-on-mouse x mouse-x mouse-y event)
  ; x          number
  ; mouse-x    number (ignore)
  ; mouse-y    number (ignore)
  ; event      whatever (ignore)
  (+ x 1) ; or, if you prefer, (add1 x)
  )
```

Test this, and we can go on to the next handler.

Write the key handler: This is quite similar to the mouse handler. My solution is

```
; sub4-on-key :  number (x) key -> number

(check-expect (sub4-on-key 7 "dummy argument") 3)
(check-expect (sub4-on-key 4 "whatever") 0)

(define (sub4-on-key x key)
  ; x   number
  ; key whatever (ignore)
  (- x 4)
  )
```

Test this, and we can go on to running the animation.

Initial model: Let's start halfway across the window, at an x coordinate of 250.

Call `big-bang`: We've already made all the decisions, so all that's left is

```
(big-bang 250
          (check-with number?)
          (on-draw calendar-at-x)
          (on-mouse add1-on-mouse)
          (on-key sub4-on-key))
```

Exercise 8.4.2 *Write an animation of a picture of your choice that starts at the top of the screen, and moves down by 5 pixels every half second. Use a number, not an image, as your model.*

Exercise 8.4.3 *Write an animation of a dot that doubles in size every 5 seconds, but shrinks by 4 pixels every time a key is typed on the keyboard.*

Exercise 8.4.4 *Write an animation in which a red disk — say,*

```
(circle 15 "solid" "red")
```

— alternates every second between x-coordinate 20 and x-coordinate 60 on a fixed background picture. (Try

```
(beside (circle 20 "solid" "black") (circle 20 "solid" "black"))
```

as the background picture.)

Hint: Use `overlay/xy` or `place-image` to place the dot at a specified x coordinate, which should be the model.

Exercise 8.4.5 *Write an animation of a progress bar (as in Exercise 8.3.9) that starts at 120, and is cut in half every second thereafter: 60, 30, 15, ...*

8.5   Randomness in animations

We can use randomness to make our animations more interesting.

Exercise 8.5.1 *Write an animation of a picture of your choice that appears each second at a different x-coordinate (and the same y-coordinate), chosen from among the five choices 20, 60, 100, 140, 180.*

Hint: There are 5 choices, so you'll need to call (`random 5`) somewhere in the simulation. And your draw handler will have to convert from a 0-4 choice to one of the specified numbers; what algebraic formula would do that? Be sure to *test* your function using `check-member-of`.

Hint: You *can* do this with no model at all, putting all the work in a draw handler that ignores its input. But that goes crazy as soon as the user moves the mouse or types on the keyboard. It's better to put the randomness in the tick handler, not the draw handler.

Exercise 8.5.2 *Write an animation of a picture of your choice that moves either 1 pixel left, 1 pixel right, or not at all, with equal probability, four times a second.*

Hint: How many choices are there? How can you convert them into a modification of the state of the model?

Exercise 8.5.3 *Write an animation that starts with a blank screen, and each half second adds a small dot at a completely random location — both the x coordinate and the y coordinate are chosen at random.*

Hint: Since you need to keep all the previous dots and add one more, your "model" should probably be an image rather than a number. How can you add a dot at a specified location to an existing image?

Hint: It would be especially nice if you could start the animation with *any* image, of any size or shape, and it would sprinkle dots at random all over that background, without rewriting the handlers.

8.6 Review of important words and concepts

Now that we know how to write functions with numeric values, we have a lot more flexibility in creating animations: we can have a number as the "model", change it one way on clock ticks, change it another way on mouse actions, and change it a third way on keyboard actions, as long as we write a suitable draw handler to convert from number to image.

Racket's random number generator can be used to make animations more unpredictable and interesting.

8.7 Reference

There are no new built-in functions or syntax rules in this chapter.

Chapter 9

Working with strings

9.1 Operations

Computer scientists use the term *string*, or *character string*, to mean a sequence of *characters*, which are basically keys on the keyboard. (There are a few exceptions: the arrow keys, function keys, "page up" and "page down" keys, *etc.* don't produce ordinary characters.) You've already learned how to type a literal string: a string starts and ends with double-quote marks, and in between them, you can put numbers, letters, spaces, parentheses, punctuation — anything except other double-quote marks. (In fact, if you *really* need to put a double-quote mark inside a string, you can do it by preceding it with a backslash, *e.g.* `"He said \"Hello,\" and I replied \"Hi there.\""` We won't need to do this very often.) In this section we'll learn to *operate* on strings just as we've already learned to operate on pictures and numbers.

The simplest imaginable string has no characters at all in between the quotation marks:

```
""
```

This is referred to, for obvious reasons, as the "empty string". Whenever you write a function that works on strings, make sure you include the empty string as one of the test cases.

Here are several of the most common operations on strings:

`string-append`
> Contract:

> `; string-append :   string ...-> string`

> It takes in one or more[1] strings, puts them together end to end into a single string, and returns that. For example,

> ```
> (string-append "hello" "there" "friend")
> "hellotherefriend"
> ```

> Note that it does *not* automatically put spaces in between: if you want spaces, you have to put them in:

> ```
> (string-append "hello " "there" " " "friend")
> "hello there friend"
> ```

---

[1]Actually, it even accepts no strings at all; it returns the empty string `""`.

string-length
     Contract:

          ; string-length : string -> integer

     It tells you how many characters (letters, spaces, punctuation marks, *etc.*) are in
     the given string. For example,

          (string-length "hellothere")
          10
          (string-length "Hi there, friend!")
          17

substring
     Contract:

          ; substring : string integer(start) [integer(end)] -> string

     (The "[integer(end)]" notation means that the third parameter is optional; in other
     words, the function takes in a string and one or two integers.) If there is only one
     integer parameter, substring chops off that many characters at the beginning. If
     there are two integer parameters, substring chops off everything *after* the first
     end characters, and then chops off the first start characters. The result will have
     length end-start, unless end is smaller than start, in which case you'll get an error
     message.

number->string
     Contract:

          ; number->string : number -> string

     Converts a number to the sequence of characters used to print it out.

string->number
     Contract:

          ; string->number : string -> number

     If the string can be interpreted as the sequence of characters used to print out a
     number, returns that number. If not, returns the special value false (about which
     we'll learn more in Chapter 13).

Practice Exercise 9.1.1 *Play with these.*

9.2   String variables and functions

You can define variables and functions with string values just as you can define them with
image or numeric values.

Practice Exercise 9.2.1 *Define a variable named me whose value is your full name (first
and last, with a space in between).*
*Write several expressions using this variable and the built-in functions string-append,
string-length, and substring.*

Exercise 9.2.2 *Develop a function named repeat that takes in a string and returns
that string appended to itself (i.e. the resulting string is twice as long).*

Exercise 9.2.3 *Develop a function* `chop-first-char` *that takes in a string and returns all but the first character. (For now, you may assume the string is non-empty; we'll drop this assumption later.)*

Exercise 9.2.4 *Develop a function* `first-char` *that takes in a string and returns a string of length 1, containing just the first character of the given string. (For now, you may assume the string is non-empty; we'll drop this assumption later.)*

Exercise 9.2.5 *Develop a function named* `last-half` *that takes in a string and returns the last half of it.*

Hint: Be sure to test your program on both even-length and odd-length strings. Also try some special cases like the empty string, `""`.

Exercise 9.2.6 *Develop a function named* `first-half` *that takes in a string and returns the first half of it.*

What happens if you concatenate the `first-half` of a string to the `last-half` of the same string? What *should* happen? Again, be sure to test this on both even-length and odd-length strings, and on the empty string.

Exercise 9.2.7 *Develop a function named* `number->image` *that takes in a number and returns an image of that number in (say) 18-point blue font.*

Hint: Combine the built-in functions `text` and `number->string`.

Exercise 9.2.8 *Develop a function named* `digits` *that takes in a positive integer (like 52073; you don't need to deal with fractions or decimals) and tells how many digits long it is, when written in base 10.*

Hint: This doesn't require any arithmetic, only combining functions described in this chapter.

9.3   Review of important words and concepts

Thus far we've seen three important *data types*, or kinds of information: *images*, *strings*, and *numbers* (which can be further broken down into *integers*, *fractions*, *floats*, and *complexes*). Racket provides several built-in functions for working on strings. These functions are used in exactly the same way as functions on images or functions on numbers. Likewise, you can define variables and functions with string values, just as you defined variables and functions with image or number values.

9.4   Reference: Built-in functions on strings

This chapter introduced the following built-in functions:

- `string-append`
- `string-length`
- `substring`
- `number->string`
- `string->number`

Chapter 10

Animations with arbitrary models

10.1   Model and view

In Chapter 8, we saw that an animation involves two pieces of information: a *model* (either an image or a number) and a *view* of that model (always an image). In fact, things are more flexible than that: the *model* can be of *any data type at all*, as long as you're consistent within a given animation. The details are in Figure 10.1.

Note that all the examples of chapters 6 and 8 still work. But now we can also use strings as models, and as we learn more data types in future chapters we'll be able to use those types as models too.

10.2   Design recipe for an animation, version 3

Our design recipe for an animation is now as in Figure 10.2.

Exercise 10.2.1 *Write an animation that initially displays the letter "a" in 18-point green type, and each second adds a "b" onto the end. So after one second it'll say "ab"; after two seconds "abb"; etc.*

Hint: For this animation, your "model" should be a string, and your draw handler will involve the text function.

Exercise 10.2.2 *Add a mouse handler to the previous animation: every time the mouse is moved or clicked, one character will be chopped off the beginning of the string.*

Exercise 10.2.3 *Write an animation that initially displays the word "cat". Each second, it inserts the letters "xyz" in the middle (i.e. between the first half and the second half) of the current word.*

Hint: It may be useful to write a "helper" function insert-in-middle that takes two strings, and inserts one of them into the middle of the other.

Figure 10.1: Event handlers for animations with arbitrary models

The big-bang function has the contract

```
; big-bang :  model(start) handler ... -> number
```

tick handlers must have the contract

```
; function-name :  model (old) -> model (new)
```

They are installed with (on-tick *function-name* *interval*). The *interval* is the length of time (in seconds) between clock ticks; if you leave it out, the animation will run as fast as it can.

key handlers must have the contract

```
; function-name :  model (old) key -> model (new)
```

The "key" parameter indicates what key was pressed; we'll see how to use it in Chapter 18.

They are installed with (on-key *function-name*).

mouse handlers must have the contract

```
; function-name :  model (old)
;                  number (mouse-x) number (mouse-y) event
;                  -> model (new)
```

The first parameter is the old model; the second represents the *x coordinate*, indicating how many pixels from the left the mouse is; the third number represents the *y coordinate*, indicating how many pixels down from the top the mouse is; and the "event" tells what happened (the mouse was moved, the button was pressed or released, *etc.*); we'll see in Chapter 18 how to use this.

They are installed with (on-mouse *function-name*).

draw handlers must have the contract

```
; function-name :  model (current) -> image
```

and are installed with (on-draw *function-name* *width* *height*). (If you leave out the *width* and *height* arguments, the animation window will be the size of the first image.)

An especially simple draw handler, show-it, is predefined: it simply returns the same image it was given, and it's useful if you need to specify the width and height of the animation window but don't want to write your own draw handler.

To specify the model type , use (check-with *type-checker*), where *type-checker* is a function that checks whether something is of a specified type, *e.g.* image?, number?, or string?, depending on what type you've chosen for this animation's model.

Figure 10.2: Design recipe for an animation, version 3

1. **Identify what handlers you'll need** (check-with, draw, tick, mouse, and/or key).

   - You should always have a `check-with` handler.
   - If your animation needs to change at regular intervals, you'll need a tick handler.
   - If your animation needs to respond to mouse movements and clicks, you'll need a mouse handler.
   - If your animation needs to respond to keyboard typing, you'll need a key handler.
   - You always need a draw handler. If your "model" is simply the image you want to show in the animation window, you can use `show-it`; otherwise you'll need to write your own.

2. **Decide what type** a "model" is and what it means.

   The model type should be something that you can easily update in response to events, and also something from which you can figure out what to show on the screen. Choosing an image as the model usually makes the draw handler easy to write, but may make the other handlers more difficult.

   For example, if your response to events is easily described by arithmetic, you probably want a numeric model. If it's easily described by image operations, you probably want an image model. If it's easily described by string operations, you probably want a string model.

   If you decide to use something other than an image as the model, you'll definitely need to write a draw handler.

3. **Write the contracts** for the handlers (using Figure 10.1). Again, the names of the functions are up to you, but once you've chosen a type for your model, the contracts must be exactly as in Figure 10.1.

4. **Develop** each of these functions, following the usual design recipe for each one. Don't go on to the next one until the previous one passes all of its test cases.

5. **Decide** on the initial value of the model.

6. **Decide on the width and height** (if the draw handler doesn't produce something of the right size).

7. **Decide on the time interval between "ticks"** (if you have a tick handler).

8. **Call `big-bang`** with the initial picture and handlers (specified using `check-with`, `on-draw`, `on-tick`, `on-mouse`, and `on-key`). See whether it works.

The following exercise is a step towards the "digital clock" we described earlier:

Exercise 10.2.4 *Develop an animation that displays a digital counter, in 18-point blue numerals. It should start at 0 and increase by 1 each second.*

Hint: Since the change every second is a *numeric* change — adding 1 — you should use a number as the model. But to display it on the screen, you'll need to turn the number into an image. Have you written a function that does this?

Exercise 10.2.5 *Develop an animation that displays a number that starts at 0 and increases by 1 each second, while* simultaneously *moving one pixel to the right each second. So, for example, after 24 seconds you should see the decimal number 24, 24 pixels from the left edge of the window.*

Exercise 10.2.6 *Develop an animation that, at all times, shows the mouse's coordinates as an ordered pair in the animation window. For example, if the mouse were currently 17 pixels from the left and 43 pixels down from the top, the screen would show (17,43)*

10.3   Review of important words and concepts

Interactive programs are generally written following the *model/view framework*: the model changes in response to events, and the view is computed from the model. The model in an animation may be of *any data type you choose*, as long as you pick a type and stick to it consistently for all the relevant handlers.

10.4   Reference

There are no new built-in functions or syntax rules in this chapter, but some previously-defined functions have broader contracts than you knew about before; see Figure 10.1.

Chapter 11

Reduce, re-use, recycle

11.1 Planning for modification and extension

Professional programmers learn very quickly that *program requirements change*. You may be given an assignment, be halfway through writing it, and suddenly be told that the program needs to do something different (usually something additional) from what you were told originally. Even after you've turned in an assignment, or released a piece of software to the public, the requirements can continue to change: either somebody will complain about the way a particular feature works, and ask you to change it, or somebody will think of a neat new feature that they want you to add for the next version. In some of the courses I teach, I warn students in advance "I reserve the right to change the assignment slightly on the day that it's due; you'll have a few hours to accommodate the change."

How can anybody work in such conditions? One thing you can do is, when you first get an assignment, start thinking about likely ways it *might* change. Then you can plan your program in such a way that, if it *does* change in those ways, you can handle the change quickly and easily.

To be more specific, try to design things so that *each likely change affects only one variable or function.* Or, as Parnas writes in "On the Criteria to be Used in Decomposing Systems into Modules" [Par72],

> ... one begins with a list of difficult design decisions or design decisions which are likely to change. Each module is then designed to hide such a decision from the other [modules].

The rest of this chapter will discuss various ways to do this.

11.2 Re-using variables

Worked Exercise 11.2.1 *Design a function named* gas-cost *that estimates how much you'll spend on gasoline for a trip. It should take in the number of miles you're driving, and return how much you expect to spend, in dollars. Your car gets approximately 28 miles per gallon (i.e. this is an inexact number), and gasoline costs $2.459 per gallon. (This example was written in 2006, when that was a reasonable price for gasoline!)*

Solution:
Contract: The function takes in one number and returns another. (The 28 and 2.459 are

important parts of the problem, but they're *fixed* numbers: they'll be the same every time you call the function, so they shouldn't be specified as parameters.) Thus

```
; gas-cost :  number(miles) -> number
```

Examples: As usual, we'll start with easy examples and gradually work up to more complicated ones: 0 miles requires 0 gas, hence costs $0.00. 28 miles requires 1 gallon of gas, so it costs $2.459. And so on.

```
"Examples of gas-cost:"
(check-within (gas-cost 0) 0 .01)
(check-within (gas-cost 28) 2.459 .01) ; i.e.  one gallon
(check-within (gas-cost 56) 4.918 .01) ; i.e.  two gallons
(check-within (gas-cost 77) 6.76 .01) ; 2-3/4 gal; use calculator
(check-within (gas-cost 358) 31.44 .01) ; yecch; use calculator
```

Skeleton:
```
(define (gas-cost miles)
  ...)
```

Inventory:
```
(define (gas-cost miles)
   ; miles        a number
   ; #i28         a fixed number I know I'll need
   ; 2.459        ditto
   ...)
```

Body: If you already see how to write the expression, great. If not, let's try the "inventory with values" trick. Pick a not-too-simple example, *e.g.*

```
(check-within (gas-cost 56) 4.918 .01) ; i.e.  two gallons
```

and fill in values:

```
(define (gas-cost miles)
   ; miles        a number            56
   ; 28           a fixed number      28
   ; 2.459        ditto               2.459
   ; should be    a number            4.918

   ...)
```

The number 4.918 doesn't look much like any of the previous numbers, but the one it resembles most closely is 2.459. In fact, it is exactly twice 2.459. So where did the 2 come from? Well, the number of miles in this example is exactly twice the miles-per-gallon figure, so one might reasonably guess that the formula is

```
(* (/ miles 28) 2.459)
```

Of course, this formula works for *this example*; we still need to **test** it on the remaining examples to be convinced that it works in general. ∎

The arithmetic expression in the body could be simplified somewhat: multiplying by 2.459 and dividing by 28 is equivalent to multiplying by approximately 0.08782142857, so we could have written

```
(define (gas-cost miles)
  ; miles                a number
  ; #i0.08782142857    a fixed number I know I'll need
  (* #i0.08782142857 miles)
  )
```

However, this program is *much harder to understand.* If one of your classmates (or yourself, three months from now) were to look at it, they'd have no idea where the 0.08782142857 came from, whereas in the previous version the algebraic expression "explains itself."

Why is this important? Because *program requirements change.* Imagine that you've worked out this program, and are just about to turn it in, when you learn that the price of gasoline has gone up to $3.899 per gallon. In the original version of the program, you simply replace 2.459 with 3.899 wherever it appears (and change the "right answers" accordingly), and it should work. In the "simplified" version, however, it's not obvious how the number 0.08782142857 needs to be changed, unless you remember that you got it by dividing the gasoline price by the fuel efficiency.

Now suppose you've written not just one but *several* programs that involve the current price of gasoline: say, there's also one that estimates how much money is wasted through spills, and one that estimates how much profit oil companies are making, *etc.* When the price of gasoline rises again, you'll need to change *all* the programs. This is a pain, and it violates the principle that "each change to requirements should affect only one variable or function." So to make our lives easier, let's *define a variable* to represent this number, and rewrite *all* the functions that use the price of gasoline to use the variable name, rather than the number, *e.g.*

```
(define PRICE-PER-GALLON 2.459)

; gas-cost :  number (miles) -> number
(define (gas-cost miles)
  ; miles                a number
  ; #i28                 a fixed number I know I'll need
  ; PRICE-PER-GALLON     ditto
  (* PRICE-PER-GALLON (/ miles #i28))
  )
"Examples of gas-cost:"
(check-within (gas-cost 0) 0 .01)
(check-within (gas-cost 28) 2.459 .01) ; i.e.  one gallon
(check-within (gas-cost 56) 4.918 .01) ; i.e.  two gallons
(check-within (gas-cost 77) 6.76 .01) ; 2-3/4 gal; use calculator
(check-within (gas-cost 358) 31.44 .01) ; yecch; use calculator
```

```
; spillage-cost :  number (gallons spilled) -> number
(define (spillage-cost gallons)
  ; gallons       a number
  (* PRICE-PER-GALLON gallons)
  )
"Examples of spillage-cost:"
(check-within (spillage-cost 0) 0 .01)
(check-within (spillage-cost 1) 2.459 .01)
(check-within (spillage-cost 20000) 49180 1)


; etc.
```

SIDEBAR:

The use of ALL-CAPITALS in the variable name is a convention among Racket programmers (as well as C, C++, and Java programmers) to indicate a variable that represents a "fixed" or "constant" value. Of course, it isn't *really* constant, but it changes much less frequently than the number of miles driven or the number of gallons spilled. In this book, we'll often use ALL-CAPITALS for variables defined in their own right, to distinguish them from function parameters (which are also a kind of variable).

Now, the next time you hear that the price of gasoline has changed, you only need to change the value of PRICE-PER-GALLON in one place, and all the functions should now work with the new price. (You may also need to recalculate the "right answers" to your examples, but if your program worked before, and the only thing that's changed is the price of gasoline, you can be reasonably confident that your program will still work.)

Obviously, there's another "fixed" value in this problem that could change: the 28 miles per gallon.

Exercise 11.2.2 *Replace 28 everywhere it appears in the program with a variable named MILES-PER-GALLON,* **define** *that variable appropriately, and make sure the program still works.*
Change the values *of the variable and the "right answers", and test that the program produces the new correct answers.*

As a general rule, if the same number appears more than once in your program, it deserves a name. Even if it appears only once, it's often a good idea to give it a name; a complex expression with a meaningful name in it is often easier to understand than the same expression with a "magic number" in it.

Of course, by "give it a name" I don't mean something silly like

```
(define TWELVE 12)
```

But if the number 12 appears several times in your program, figure out what each one *means*, and define a variable that makes the *meaning* clear. You may even discover that the same number currently appears in your program for two different reasons: for example, a program dealing with annual orders for a grocery store that sells both eggs and soda pop might include

```
(define MONTHS-PER-YEAR 12)
(define EGGS-PER-CARTON 12)
(define OZ-PER-CAN 12)
```

If the store suddenly started selling eggs in 18-egg cartons, or 16-oz cans of soda pop, you would need to change only one variable definition rather than going through the whole program line by line, looking for twelves and deciding which ones were twelve for which reason.

11.3 Composing functions

Recall Exercise 7.7.17, the `fahrenheit->kelvin` function, which could be written by simply calling one previously-written function (`celsius->kelvin`) on the result of another (`fahrenheit->celsius`). This sort of *re-use* has several benefits:

- `fahrenheit->kelvin` is easy to write, without needing to look up the formulæ or numbers for the other two functions.

- If you make an improvement to the accuracy or efficiency of one of the other functions, `fahrenheit->kelvin` will automatically become more accurate or efficient too. (Remember using `pi` to make `area-of-circle` and `area-of-ring` more accurate?)

- Each of the three functions can be tested and debugged separately (although, since `fahrenheit->kelvin` depends on the other two, there's not much point testing it until you have confidence in the other two).

- If you have confidence in the correctness of the other two functions, but get wrong answers from `fahrenheit->kelvin`, you don't need to look at the other two functions; you can confine your attention to *how they're combined* (*e.g.* perhaps you called them in the wrong order).

- Each of the three functions can be useful in its own right.

- Each of the three functions is shorter, simpler, and easier to understand than if they were all combined into one big function.[1]

Now let's think about `gas-cost` again. Intuitively, it first computes how many gallons of gas we need (from the mileage and the fuel efficiency), and then computes how much money that many gallons of gas cost (from the price of gas). Each of these questions ("how much gas does it take to drive a specified distance?" and "how much does a specified amount of gas cost?") could be useful in its own right. So let's *break the program up* into three separate functions:

---

[1]The human mind seems to have a hard time thinking about more than seven "things" at a time, according to George Miller's famous paper "The Magical Number Seven, Plus or Minus Two" [Mil56]. If your function definition has much more than seven variables and operators in it, it might be a good idea to break it into smaller, simpler pieces so you can hold the whole thing in your mind at once.

```
; gas-needed :  number (miles) -> number
"Examples of gas-needed"
(check-within (gas-needed 0) 0 .01)
(check-within (gas-needed 28) 1 .01)
(check-within (gas-needed 56) 2 .01)
(check-within (gas-needed 77) 2.75 .01)
(check-within (gas-needed 358) 12.8 .01)

; cost-of-gallons :  number (gallons) -> number
"Examples of cost-of-gallons:"
(check-within (cost-of-gallons 0) 0 .01)
(check-within (cost-of-gallons 1) 2.459 .01)
(check-within (cost-of-gallons 2) 4.918 .01)
(check-within (cost-of-gallons 2.75) 6.76225 .01)

; gas-cost :  number (miles) -> number
"Examples of gas-cost:"
(check-within (gas-cost 0) 0 .01)
(check-within (gas-cost 28) 2.459 .01) ; i.e.  one gallon
(check-within (gas-cost 56) 4.918 .01) ; i.e.  two gallons
(check-within (gas-cost 77) 6.76 .01) ; 2-3/4 gal; use calculator
(check-within (gas-cost 358) 31.44 .01) ; yecch; use calculator
```

Each of these functions is easy to write, particularly now that we've given names to the price of gasoline and the fuel efficiency of the car. Note that `gas-cost` shouldn't need to use any numbers *or* those two variables; it should simply use the other two functions.

Exercise 11.3.1 ***Write, test, and debug*** *the* `gas-needed`*,* `cost-of-gallons`*, and (new, improved)* `gas-cost` *functions.*

In general, there are several ways a new function can use an old function:

- rearranging or adding arguments, and passing these to the old function (*e.g.* the `convert-3-reversed` function of Exercise 7.7.19, or the draw handler of Exercise 10.2.1).

- calling one old function on the result of another (such as `fahrenheit->kelvin` and the new `gas-cost`)

- using the same old function several times (*e.g.* the `counterchange` function, which used `beside` twice).

Exercise 11.3.2 ***Develop a function*** `cylinder-volume` *that takes in the radius and height of a cylinder, and computes its volume.*

Hint: Look for a previously-written function you can re-use to do part of the job.

Exercise 11.3.3 ***Develop a function*** `cylinder-area` *that takes in the radius and height of a cylinder, and computes its area.*

Hint: The area includes the vertical sides and both ends.

Exercise 11.3.4 ***Develop a function*** `pipe-area` *that takes in the inner radius of a pipe, the length of the pipe, and the thickness of the walls, and computes its area.*

Hint: The area includes the inner surface, the outer surface, and the narrow top and bottom.

Exercise 11.3.5 *The nation of Progressiva has a simple tax code. The tax you pay is your salary times the tax rate, and the tax rate is 0.5% per thousand dollars of salary. For example, if you make $40,000, your tax rate is 0.5% times 40, which is 20%, so you pay 20% of $40,000, which is $8,000.*

Develop a function to compute the net pay (i.e. pay after taxes) of a person with a given salary.

Hint: You'll probably need two auxiliary functions as well as `net-pay`.

Exercise 11.3.6 *This tax system has the peculiar feature that, beyond a certain income level, if you earn more, you actually get less take-home pay. Use your `net-pay` function to find this income level by experimentation.*

Now imagine the tax rate rises to 0.6% per thousand dollars of salary. What would you need to modify in the program to handle this change? What would be the new income level beyond which you get less take-home pay?

11.4   Designing for re-use

When you're writing a program, sometimes you'll realize that there's an existing program that does most of the work for you. Take advantage of this opportunity (unless your instructor has specifically told you *not* to in a particular case); a good programmer is lazy, and refuses to re-invent the wheel. Recognizing and using such opportunities will save you a lot of time in programming.

But if the previous program was written to solve only one very narrow, specific problem, you may not be able to re-use it for your new problem. So when you're writing a new function, even if you don't immediately see any other application for it, *design it to be easily re-used*; you never know when some future problem will need it. What does this mean?

- Don't make unnecessary assumptions about your parameters.

  Suppose you're writing a function that takes in a string and displays it in an animation window. In the particular animation we're working on, we know that the string in question will always be just a single letter. But unless it's considerably easier or more efficient to write the function for single-letter strings, *don't assume the parameter is a single letter*. In fact, *test* it on different-length strings, even though you'll only need it for single letters in the current project, because a future project might need it for other strings.

  Here's a situation I see often. I've assigned an animation, which will require writing two or three event-handling functions, with (let's say) a number as the model. In the current animation, the model will never be bigger than 100, so one student writes the functions so they only work on numbers less than 100, while another writes them to work for any number. Later in the course, I give another assignment that requires some of the same functions, but no longer guarantees that the model is never bigger than 100. The student who wrote a general, re-usable function in the first place can simply re-use the old function; the one who wrote a "narrower" function has to write a new one from scratch.

- Write each function to do one clear, simple task, not several.

  Suppose the current project requires computing how much I'm going to spend at gasoline stations for a trip, considering that every time I stop for gas I also buy a soda pop. You could write a single function that solves this whole problem, but it would be fairly complicated, and it would "tie up" the solutions to all the sub-problems so you can't solve one without the others. In particular, if a future project needed to compute the amount of gasoline used on a trip or the cost of a specified amount of gasoline, you would have to write those functions (and figure out the right formulæ, and test and debug) then anyway. A better approach is to write several simple functions: how much gas do I need, how much will the gas cost, how much will I spend on soda pop, *etc.* This way I can re-use whichever *parts* of the current project are needed in the future project.

There are whole books written, and whole college courses taught, about "designing programs for re-use", but the above two rules will get you started.

11.5   Designing multi-function programs: a case study

Let's take the gasoline-cost problem a step farther.

Worked Exercise 11.5.1 *Design a function* `road-trip-cost` *which determines the cost of a road trip, given the number of miles you're driving and how many days you'll be away. The car gets roughly 28 miles to the gallon, gasoline costs \$2.459 per gallon, and motels cost \$40 per night. Furthermore, you don't actually* own *a car, so you have to rent one. The car rental agency charges a fixed processing fee of \$10, plus \$29.95 per day, plus \$0.10 per mile . Assume that you're bringing all your own food and drinks, so you don't need to worry about the cost of food on the road. Also assume that the "number of days you'll be away" includes both the day you leave and the day you return.*

Solution: This is a more complicated problem than we've yet seen. If you try to solve the whole thing at once, you'll be overwhelmed. Even if you manage to write a single function that solves the whole problem, it'll be long, complicated, and confusing. We need to take a more careful, methodical approach.

We can write a contract fairly easily:
```
; road-trip-cost :  number (miles) number (days) -> number
```

The examples will be a pain, since they require that *we* solve the whole problem at once, at least in specific cases. So before we jump into that, let's think about how to *break the problem into smaller pieces.*

What are the important values and quantities in the problem?

- the total cost of the road trip

- the number of miles we're driving

- the number of days we'll be away

- the fuel efficiency of the car

- the price of gasoline

- the amount of gasoline we need

- the amount we spend on gasoline

- the cost per night of a motel

- the number of nights we need to stay in a motel

- the amount we spend on motels

- the fixed processing fee for car rental

- the daily charge for car rental

- the per-mile charge for car rental

- the amount we spend on car rental

These quantities fall into several categories: some are *fixed numbers* (for which we probably want to use variables — see Section 11.2) — some are *inputs* (*i.e.* parameters) to the function, some are *output* from the function, and some are *intermediate results* that we need along the way.

Fixed numbers:

- the fuel efficiency of the car

- the price of gasoline

- the cost per night of a motel

- the fixed processing fee for car rental

- the daily charge for car rental

- the per-mile charge for car rental

Inputs to the `road-trip-cost` function:

- the number of miles we're driving

- the number of days we'll be away

Output from the `road-trip-cost` function: the total cost of the road trip
Intermediate results

- the amount of gasoline we need

- the amount we spend on gasoline

- the number of nights we need to stay in a motel

- the amount we spend on motels

- the amount we spend on car rental

The "fixed numbers", at least, should be easy.

```
(define MILES-PER-GALLON #i28)
(define PRICE-PER-GALLON 2.459)
(define MOTEL-PRICE-PER-NIGHT 40)
(define CAR-RENTAL-FIXED-FEE 10)
(define CAR-RENTAL-PER-DAY 29.95)
(define CAR-RENTAL-PER-MILE 0.10)
```

Note that I've given all the variables names that a casual reader could understand. This makes them a bit long, but experience shows that the time saved in figuring out what a variable name means far exceeds the time spent typing long names.

At this point it is useful to figure out *which quantities depend on which others*; see Figure 11.1. Each of these intermediate results is a good candidate for a separate function. Because they aren't the function you originally intended to write, but will help you write it, they're called *auxiliary functions* or *helper functions*. Conveniently enough, we've already written `gas-cost`, `gas-needed`, and `cost-of-gallons`, but if we hadn't, we could write them now in the same way we'll write the rest. [2]

We still have four functions to write: "the total cost of the road trip", "the number of nights we need to stay in a motel", "the amount we spend on motels", and "the amount we spend on car rental". At this point, we know enough about them that we could write contracts and, perhaps, examples for all of them. This is often a good idea, because some of the functions will need to call one another, so it's best to decide *how* they'll be called as early as possible.

We already have a contract for `road-trip-cost`. Next let's try "the amount we spend on motels". Since `road-trip-cost` will depend on this function (among others), let's insert it in the Definitions pane *ahead* of what we've written so far about `road-trip-cost`. Anyway, a good name for this function might be `motel-cost`, and it obviously returns a number in dollars. It depends on the number of nights we stay in motels, and the cost per night of a motel. The latter is a fixed number, and the former is another intermediate value which in turn depends on the number of days of the trip. So

```
; motel-cost :  number (days) -> number
```

Since this depends on another function we haven't dealt with yet, let's postpone its examples until we've handled that other function.

Next: "The number of nights we spend in motels". A good name for the function could be `nights-in-motel`; it returns a integer, like 0, 1, 2, etc. And since `motel-cost` depends on this one, let's insert this one *ahead* of what we've just written about `motel-cost` in the Definitions pane.

This function obviously depends on the number of days of the trip, so

```
; nights-in-motel :  number (days) -> number
```

As usual, we'll pick examples from the easiest to more complicated, and often the easiest number is 0. If the trip involves 0 days, then there *is no* "day that you leave" or "day that you return"; this example doesn't make sense. And a negative number or a fraction certainly wouldn't make sense. We've learned something about the limits of the problem; let's add this as an assumption.

```
; nights-in-motel :  number (days) -> number
; Assumes the number of days is a positive integer.
```

The next simplest integer is 1, which would mean leaving today and coming back today, thus spending *zero* nights in motels. Similarly, if we took a 2-day trip, leaving today and coming back tomorrow, it would mean spending 1 night in a motel. In general, the number of nights is one less than the number of days.

---

[2]For some reason, many of my students seem to think that helper functions don't need contracts or test cases. This is analogous to building a house of cheap, low-quality bricks. If the bricks dissolve in the first rainstorm, the house will fall apart no matter how well designed it is. Similarly, if you're not clear on your helper functions' contracts, or you haven't tested them adequately, your whole program is unlikely to work.

Figure 11.1: Which quantities depend on which

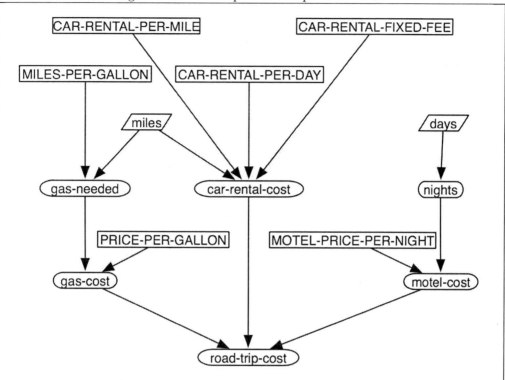

- The fixed numbers don't depend on anything else.

- The inputs (`miles` and `days`) don't depend on anything else.

- "the total cost of the road trip" depends on three other quantities: how much we spend on gas, how much we spend on motels, and how much we spend on car rental.

- "the amount we spend on gasoline" depends on the amount of gasoline and the price of gasoline.

- "the amount of gasoline we need" depends on the number of miles and the fuel efficiency.

- "the number of nights we need to stay in a motel" depends on the number of days (but it's one less: if you leave on Monday and come back Tuesday, you've only stayed over one night).

- "the amount we spend on motels" depends on the number of nights and the cost per night of a motel.

- "the amount we spend on car rental" depends on the fixed fee, the daily charge, the number of days, the per-mile charge, and the number of miles we drive.

```
"Examples of nights-in-motel:"
(check-expect (nights-in-motel 1) 0)
(check-expect (nights-in-motel 2) 1)
(check-expect (nights-in-motel 38) 37)
```

Now we can come back to the examples of `motel-cost`:

```
"Examples of motel-cost:"
(check-expect (motel-cost 1) 0)
(check-expect (motel-cost 2) 40)
(check-expect (motel-cost 38) 1480)
```

(Again, I used a calculator for the last one.)

Next is "the amount we spend on car rental." Let's name it `rental-cost`. It depends on five different quantities, but three of them are fixed numbers, and the other two are the number of miles and the number of days, which we have available as parameters to the main function. So

```
; rental-cost :   number (miles) number (days) -> number
```

The examples will take some arithmetic, but we can pick the numbers to make the arithmetic reasonably easy. Remember that we've already agreed 0 days doesn't make any sense. (One could make a good case that 0 miles doesn't make sense either; however, it's theoretically possible that we might get in the car, turn on the radio, chat for a while, and get out without ever going anywhere.)

As usual, we'll start from the easiest cases:

```
"Examples of rental-cost:"
(check-within (rental-cost 0 1) 39.95 .01)
(check-within (rental-cost 0 2) 69.90 .01)
(check-within (rental-cost 100 1) 49.95 .01)
(check-within (rental-cost 100 2) 79.90 .01)
(check-within (rental-cost 28 1) 42.75 .01)
(check-within (rental-cost 77 2) 77.60 .01)
(check-within (rental-cost 358 3) 135.65 .01)
```

The only function for which we don't have examples yet is `road-trip-cost` itself. So let's write some examples for it, using some of the numbers we've already worked out. The cost of the whole road-trip is found by adding up three other things: the cost of gasoline, the cost of motels, and the cost of car rental.

```
"Examples of road-trip-cost:"
(check-within (road-trip-cost 0 1) 39.95 .01)
; the gas and motels cost 0
(check-within (road-trip-cost 0 2) 109.90 .01)
; gas still 0, motel $40
(check-within (road-trip-cost 28 1) 45.209 .01)
; $42.75 for car, $0 for motel, $2.459 for gas
(check-within (road-trip-cost 77 2) 124.36 .01)
; $77.60 for car, c.  $6.76 for gas, $40 for motel
(check-within (road-trip-cost 358 3) 247.09 .01)
; $135.65 for car, c.  $31.44 for gas, $80 for motel
```

At this point, we've completed the "figure out what you want to do" for all four functions. This will be useful as we go on, because the definitions of some of them will depend on understanding what the others do. The Definitions pane should now look something like Figures 11.2 and 11.3.

Figure 11.2: Constants and old functions

```
 ; Constants for the road-trip-cost problem:
(define MILES-PER-GALLON #i28)
(define PRICE-PER-GALLON 2.459)
(define MOTEL-PRICE-PER-NIGHT 40)
(define CAR-RENTAL-FIXED-FEE 10)
(define CAR-RENTAL-PER-DAY 29.95)
(define CAR-RENTAL-PER-MILE 0.10)


; gas-needed :  number (miles) -> number
(define (gas-needed miles)
  ; miles              a number
  ; MILES-PER-GALLON   a number
  (/ miles MILES-PER-GALLON)
  )
"Examples of gas-needed:"
(check-within (gas-needed 0) 0 .01)
(check-within (gas-needed 28) 1 .01)
(check-within (gas-needed 56) 2 .01)
(check-within (gas-needed 77) 2.75 .01)
(check-within (gas-needed 358) 12.8 .01)


; cost-of-gallons :  number (gallons) -> number
(define (cost-of-gallons gallons)
  ; gallons            number
  ; PRICE-PER-GALLON   number
  (* gallons PRICE-PER-GALLON)
  )
"Examples of cost-of-gallons:"
(check-within (cost-of-gallons 0) 0 .01)
(check-within (cost-of-gallons 1) 2.459 .01)
(check-within (cost-of-gallons 2) 4.918 .01)
(check-within (cost-of-gallons 2.75) 6.76225 .01)


; gas-cost :  number (miles) -> number
(define (gas-cost miles)
  ; miles      number
  (cost-of-gallons (gas-needed miles))
  )
"Examples of gas-cost:"
(check-within (gas-cost 0) 0 .01)
(check-within (gas-cost 28) 2.459 .01) ; i.e.  one gallon
(check-within (gas-cost 56) 4.918 .01) ; i.e.  two gallons
(check-within (gas-cost 77) 6.76 .01) ; 2-3/4 gal; use calculator
(check-within (gas-cost 358) 31.44 .01) ; yecch; use calculator
```

Figure 11.3: Contracts and examples for new functions

```
; nights-in-motel :  number (days) -> number
; Assumes the number of days is a positive integer.
"Examples of nights-in-motel:"
(check-expect (nights-in-motel 1) 0)
(check-expect (nights-in-motel 2) 1)
(check-expect (nights-in-motel 38) 37)


; motel-cost :  number (days) -> number
"Examples of motel-cost:"
(check-expect (motel-cost 1) 0)
(check-expect (motel-cost 2) 40)
(check-expect (motel-cost 38) 1480)


; rental-cost :  number (miles) number (days) -> number
"Examples of rental-cost:"
(check-expect (rental-cost 0 1) 39.95)
(check-expect (rental-cost 0 2) 69.90)
(check-expect (rental-cost 100 1) 49.95)
(check-expect (rental-cost 100 2) 79.90)
(check-expect (rental-cost 28 1) 42.75)
(check-expect (rental-cost 77 2) 77.60)
(check-expect (rental-cost 358 3) 135.65)


; road-trip-cost :  number (miles) number (days) -> number
"Examples of road-trip-cost:"
(check-within (road-trip-cost 0 1) 39.95 .01) ; the gas and motels are 0
(check-within (road-trip-cost 0 2) 109.90 .01) ; gas still 0, motel $40
(check-within (road-trip-cost 28 1) 45.209 .01)
; $42.75 for car, $0 for motel, $2.459 for gas
(check-within (road-trip-cost 77 2) 124.36 .01)
; $77.60 for car, c.  $6.76 for gas, $40 for motel
(check-within (road-trip-cost 358 3) 247.09 .01)
; $135.65 for car, c.  $31.44 for gas, $80 for motel
```

We still have to move each of the four functions through the "skeleton", "inventory", "body", and "testing" stages ... but what to do first?

For the skeletons, inventories, and bodies, it doesn't really matter which function you work on first. Testing and debugging are another story. The `motel-cost` function depends on the `nights-in-motel` function, so we *can't* test the former until we've written the latter, and we certainly can't test the `road-trip-cost` function until everything else works. In other words, we have to build the program from the bottom up, like a brick building: finish the foundation before starting on the walls, and finish the walls before starting on the roof. Don't try to test and debug a function that depends on another function that hasn't been tested and debugged yet.

For clarity, I'll do one function (skeleton, inventory, body, testing) at a time; you could equally well do all the skeletons, then all the inventories, then all the bodies, then test them in order.

We have to start with a function that doesn't rely on any other functions (only fixed numbers and parameters to the main function). According to Figure 11.1, we have two choices: `nights-in-motel`, and `rental-cost`. Let's try `nights-in-motel`.

The skeleton and inventory should be straightforward and routine by now:

```
; nights-in-motel :  number (days) -> number
; Assumes the number of days is a positive integer.
(define (nights-in-motel days)
  ; days      a number
  ...)
```

The formula is obvious:

```
; nights-in-motel :  number (days) -> number
; Assumes the number of days is a positive integer.
(define (nights-in-motel days)
  ; days      a number
  (- days 1)
  )
```

Test this on the already-written examples. (To avoid getting error messages on examples of functions you haven't written yet, use the "Comment Out with Semicolons" menu command to comment out everything not related to `nights-in-motel`.) If it produces correct answers in every case, go on to the next function.

Staying on the same subject, let's do `motel-cost`. Uncomment the lines related to this function, and write the skeleton and inventory:

```
; motel-cost :  number (days) -> number
; Assumes the number of days is a positive integer.
(define (motel-cost days)
  ; days      a number
  ...)
```

In addition, we know from Figure 11.1 that the answer depends on the cost per night, `MOTEL-PRICE-PER-NIGHT`, so let's add that to the inventory. Furthermore, we don't actually care about the number of *days* so much as the number of *nights*, which we can get by calling `nights-in-motel`, so we'll add that to the inventory too:

```
; motel-cost :  number (days) -> number
; Assumes the number of days is a positive integer.
(define (motel-cost days)
   ; days                    a number
   ; MOTEL-PRICE-PER-NIGHT   a number
   ; (nights-in-motel days)  a number
   ...)
```

Now, since `(nights-in-motel days)` represents the number of nights, the formula is straightforward:

```
; motel-cost :  number (days) -> number
; Assumes the number of days is a positive integer.
(define (motel-cost days)
   ; days                    a number
   ; MOTEL-PRICE-PER-NIGHT   a number
   ; (nights-in-motel days)  a number
   (* MOTEL-PRICE-PER-NIGHT (nights-in-motel days))
   )
```

Test this on the already-written examples. If it produces correct answers in every case, go on to the next function. If it doesn't, use the Stepper to decide whether the mistake is in **nights-in-motel** (it shouldn't be, since we've already tested that function) or in this one (much more likely); fix the problem and re-test.

The only function we can do next is **rental-cost**. Uncomment its examples and write a skeleton and (a start on an) inventory:

```
; rental-cost :  number (miles) number (days) -> number
(define (rental-cost miles days)
   ; miles      a number
   ; days       a number
   ...)
```

According to Figure 11.1, it also depends on three fixed numbers: CAR-RENTAL-FIXED-FEE, CAR-RENTAL-PER-DAY, and CAR-RENTAL-PER-MILE, so we'll add these to the inventory:

```
; rental-cost :  number (miles) number (days) -> number
(define (rental-cost miles days)
   ; miles                 a number
   ; days                  a number
   ; CAR-RENTAL-FIXED-FEE  a number
   ; CAR-RENTAL-PER-DAY    a number
   ; CAR-RENTAL-PER-MILE   a number
   ...)
```

The "daily charge" obviously needs to be multiplied by the number of days, and the "per mile charge" obviously needs to be multiplied by the number of miles; add these expressions to the inventory. (If this isn't "obvious", try the "inventory with values" technique.)

```
; rental-cost :  number (miles) number (days) -> number
(define (rental-cost miles days)
  ; miles                        a number
  ; days                         a number
  ; CAR-RENTAL-FIXED-FEE         a number
  ; CAR-RENTAL-PER-DAY           a number
  ; CAR-RENTAL-PER-MILE          a number
  ; (* days CAR-RENTAL-PER-DAY)  >a number
  ; (* miles CAR-RENTAL-PER-MILE) a number
  ...)
```

These last two expressions represent the amount the rental company charges for days, and for miles, respectively. If we add up these two and the fixed fee, we should get the final answer:

```
; rental-cost :  number (miles) number (days) -> number
(define (rental-cost miles days)
  ; miles                         a number
  ; days                          a number
  ; CAR-RENTAL-FIXED-FEE          a number
  ; CAR-RENTAL-PER-DAY            a number
  ; CAR-RENTAL-PER-MILE           a number
  ; (* days CAR-RENTAL-PER-DAY)   a number
  ; (* miles CAR-RENTAL-PER-MILE) a number
  (+  (* days CAR-RENTAL-PER-DAY)
      (* miles CAR-RENTAL-PER-MILE)
      CAR-RENTAL-FIXED-FEE)
)
```

Test this on the already-written examples. If it produces correct answers in every case, go on to the next function. If not, use the Stepper to locate the problem (as before); fix it and re-test.

The only function remaining is `road-trip-cost` itself. We follow the same procedure:

```
; road-trip-cost :  number (miles) number (days) -> number
(define (road-trip-cost miles days)
  ; miles    a number
  ; days     a number
  ...)
```

We know that the answer will involve what we spend on gas, what we spend on motels, and what we spend on car rental. Fortunately, there are functions that compute each of these, and the only inputs those functions require are miles and/or days, both of which we have. So we can add calls to those functions to the inventory:

```
; road-trip-cost :  number (miles) number (days) -> number
(define (road-trip-cost miles days)
  ; miles                    a number
  ; days                     a number
  ; (gas-cost miles)         a number
  ; (motel-cost days)        a number
  ; (rental-cost miles days) a number
  ...)
```

With these expressions in hand, the answer is obvious: add them up.

```
; road-trip-cost :  number (miles) number (days) -> number
(define (road-trip-cost miles days)
   ; miles                     a number
   ; days                      a number
   ; (gas-cost miles)          a number
   ; (motel-cost days)         a number
   ; (rental-cost miles days)  a number
   (+  (gas-cost miles)
       (motel-cost days)
       (rental-cost miles days))

)
```

Test this on the already-written examples. If it produces correct answers in every case, congratulate yourself: we've developed a fairly complex program by breaking it down into small, digestible pieces. ∎

Exercise 11.5.2 *Choose one of the fixed numbers in the above problem: either MILES-PER-GALLON, PRICE-PER-GALLON, etc.* ***Change its numeric value.*** *Before re-running the program,* ***predict*** *which examples are affected, and* ***recalculate*** *(by hand or calculator) their new correct values.* ***Test*** *the program to see if your predictions were right.*

By the way, we *could* in principle have written the whole function at once, without breaking it down into small pieces, and the result might have looked like this:

```
(define (monolithic-rtc miles days)
   (+ (* (/ miles MILES-PER-GALLON) PRICE-PER-GALLON)
      (* MOTEL-PRICE-PER-NIGHT (- days 1))
      (+ (* days CAR-RENTAL-PER-DAY)
         (* miles CAR-RENTAL-PER-MILE)
         CAR-RENTAL-FIXED-FEE)
   ) )
```

If we got everything right on the first try, this would actually be quicker and easier than writing seven separate functions ... but computer programs are almost *never* right on the first try, especially if they're more than two or three lines long. If something were wrong in this definition, it would be quite difficult to track down the mistake(s).

The approach we took, breaking the problem into several small functions, has at least two major advantages: one can test each function individually, and some of the functions may be re-usable from one project to another (*e.g.* the gas-needed, cost-of-gallons, and gas-cost functions which we just copied from a previous problem).

11.6   Practicalities of multi-function programs

As you've seen, a multi-function program is written by applying the design recipe to each of the functions in turn, and testing them "bottom-up" — that is, the functions that don't depend on any others first, then the ones that depend on the first few, and finally the main function that depends on all the others. And you have a certain amount of flexibility how far to go on which function in which order.

However, the final result should look as though you had written one function at a time: the contract, skeleton-turned-body, and examples for one function should appear together with no other function definitions in between. In other words, you may need to do a certain amount of moving forward and backwards to find the right places to type things.

Exercise 11.6.1 *Develop a function* `build-house` *that draws a picture of a house, like*

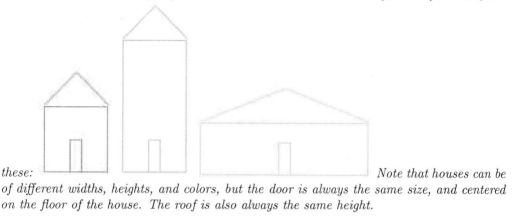

these: _____ *Note that houses can be of different widths, heights, and colors, but the door is always the same size, and centered on the floor of the house. The roof is also always the same height.*

Hint: You may find it helpful to write some auxiliary functions that produce images, and others that produce numbers.

Exercise 11.6.2 *A small commercial airline company wants to figure out how much to charge for its tickets. Specifically, for any given ticket price, they'd like to be able to predict how much profit they'll make. Given that ability, they can try various different ticket prices, see which produces the most profit, and select that as their ticket price.*

Profit, of course, is income minus expenses. There are two major expenses: paying the salaries of the pilot, copilot, and two flight attendants (these four salaries add up to $450 per flight, regardless of how many passengers are on the flight), and jet fuel, at $2.999/gallon. The amount of jet fuel consumed is one gallon per twenty pounds of loaded weight, which is the weight of the airplane itself plus the weight of the people and luggage on it. The airplane itself weighs 50000 pounds. Each passenger and his/her luggage, on average, weighs 250 pounds; same for the four crew members (pilot, copilot, two flight attendants).

The airline is currently charging $200/ticket, and at that price they can typically sell 120 tickets. Raising the price means they make more money on each ticket, but it also causes fewer people to buy tickets; conversely, lowering the price means they take in less money on each ticket, but they can sell more of them. To be precise, they estimate that for each $10 they raise (lower) the ticket price, they'll lose (gain) 4 paying passengers.

Develop a function `airline-profit` *that takes in a proposed ticket price, and returns the estimated profit the airline will make at that price.*

Use your function to determine the profit-maximizing ticket price. Also find the least they could charge and make any profit at all.

Change one or two of the constants (e.g. the price of jet fuel, the number of people who change their minds about buying tickets when the price goes up or down, the size of the crew, the crew salaries, etc.) and repeat the previous paragraph.

Exercise 11.6.3 *Develop a function that takes in the name of a color (e.g.* `"green"`*) and produces that word, followed by a randomly-chosen numeric font size (say, between 10 and 30 points inclusive), in text of that color and font size, surrounded by a box of the same color which is 10 pixels wider and 6 pixels higher than the text. For example,*

```
> (ex963 "blue")
```
```
blue 16
```
```
> (ex963 "purple")
```
```
purple 12
```
```
> (ex963 "purple")
```
```
purple 20
```

11.7   Review of important words and concepts

Program requirements change, so it's in your interest to prepare for such change. One way to do this is to use *symbolic constants*: variables with meaningful names to represent important or likely-to-change values. When these values *do* change, you can just change the variable definition in one place, and all the functions and programs that use this variable will automatically be corrected. Another way is to *design large programs so that each likely change affects only one function.*

To paraphrase John Donne, "no program is an island." Every program you ever write has the potential to be re-used to make subsequent programs easier, and it's in your interest to design the current program to maximize the likelihood that you can re-use it later. In particular, *don't make unnecessary assumptions about your input,* and *design each function to do one clear, simple task.*

A large program is often made up of a "main function" and one or more *auxiliary* or "helper" functions. When faced with a large program to write, *break it down into manageable pieces* Identify the important *quantities* in the problem, and categorize each as an *input,* an *output,* a *fixed value,* or an *intermediate computation.* The inputs will probably become parameters to your main function (and to some of the auxiliary functions); the output will probably be the result of your main function; the fixed values will probably become symbolic constants; and the intermediate computations will probably become auxiliary functions. It's often a good idea to write down contracts (and perhaps examples) for all of these functions at once, so you have a clear idea what they're all supposed to do. Then start writing skeletons, inventories, and bodies, and testing the functions one at a time, starting with the ones that *don't* depend on any other functions.

11.8   Reference

No new functions or syntax rules were introduced in this chapter.

PART II

Definition by Choices

Chapter 12

Defining new types: a bird's-eye view

If you're the sort of person who likes to look at the map before heading out on a trip, this brief chapter should give you an idea of the road we'll be travelling for the next fifteen or twenty chapters. If, on the other hand, you're the sort of person to whom the map doesn't make sense until you've seen some of the road itself, ignore this chapter for now, but come back to it after a few more chapters.

We've learned a bunch of things you can do with images, a bunch of things you can do with numbers, and a bunch of things you can do with strings. These are three important data types that happen to be built into Racket, but for many problems they're not enough and we'll need to *define our own data types*. There are several ways to do this, each with a corresponding new way of writing functions.

First, a new data type can be a *choice* among two or more existing data types, and functions will have to choose among two or more simpler expressions or functions.

Second, a new data type can have *parts* drawn from existing data types, in which case functions will have to dissect data into their parts, and put together parts into new data.

Third, a new data type can (by combining the notions of "definition by choices" and "definition by parts") be defined in terms of itself; functions will likewise be defined in terms of themselves.

Fourth, a new data type can be constructed by "abstraction": observing similarities and intentionally overlooking differences among several existing data types to create a *general* data type that can be specialized to do the job of any of the original types, and more; likewise, from several similar functions one can often construct a single *general* function that does the job of all the original functions and more.

Over 400 years ago, the English philosopher John Locke wrote something eerily close to this, although the match isn't perfect:

> The acts of the mind, wherein it exerts its power over simple ideas, are chiefly these three:
>
> 1. Combining several simple ideas into one compound one, and thus all complex ideas are made.
>
> 2. The second is bringing two ideas, whether simple or complex, together, and setting them by one another so as to take a view of them at once, without uniting them into one, by which it gets all its ideas of relations.

3. The third is separating them from all other ideas that accompany them in their real existence: this is called abstraction, and thus all its general ideas are made.

I might add a fourth, "applying an idea to itself," which has proven to be a powerful — if easily misused — technique in mathematics, computer science, and philosophy.

Chapter 13

Booleans

13.1 A new data type

We've seen several data types so far: images, strings, numbers, and sub-types of number: integers, fractions, inexact numbers, complex numbers. Each data type is suitable for answering a different kind of question:

- images answer the question "what does ... look like?";

- strings answer questions like "what is your name?" or "what is the text of the Gettysburg Address?";

- integers answer questions like "how many ...?";

- fractions and inexact numbers answer questions like "how much ...?"

Now consider "true/false" or "yes/no" questions: "is Joe older than Chris?", "is your name Philip?", and so on. For each of these questions, there are only two possible answers: yes and no. None of the data types above seems quite right for the purpose. So Racket, like most programming languages, has a data type named "boolean", which has exactly two values, written `true` and `false`. You can type either of these into the Interactions pane, hit ENTER, and you'll get back the same value, just as if you had typed a number or a quoted string. Note that `true` is different from `"true"`: the former is a boolean, and the latter is a string.

SIDEBAR:

The word "boolean" is named after the 19th-century mathematician George Boole, who suggested that logical questions of truth and falsity could be addressed by the techniques of algebra, using "numbers" that were restricted to the values 0 and 1 (representing false and true, respectively).

13.2 Comparing strings

Racket has a number of built-in functions that produce Booleans. The first one we'll look at is
```
string=?  :  string string -> boolean
```

For example,
```
(check-expect (string=?  "hello" "goodbye") false)
(check-expect (string=?  "hello" "hello") true)
(check-expect (string=?  "hello" "Hello") false)
(check-expect (string=?  "hello" "hel lo") false)
(check-expect (string=?  "hello" (string-append "hel" "lo")) true)
```
Note that the two strings have to be *exactly* the same, right down to capitalization, spacing, and punctuation. Also note that, by convention, most functions that return Booleans (like string=?) have names ending in a question mark. (Racket doesn't *force* you to do this, but it's a good habit to follow, in order to get along with other Racket programmers.)

So now you know how to tell whether two strings are exactly the same. You can also test how two strings relate in alphabetical order:
```
; string<?  :  string string -> Boolean
; string<=? :  string string -> Boolean
; string>?  :  string string -> Boolean
; string>=? :  string string -> Boolean
```

Practice Exercise 13.2.1 *Make up some examples involving* string<?, string<=?, string>?, *and* string>=?, *and see whether they produce the answer you expect. Try comparing a capitalized word like* "DOG" *with an uncapitalized one like* "cat". *Try comparing either of those with a string made up of punctuation marks, like* "!#., &*", *or a string made up of digits, like* "372.4".

SIDEBAR:

Sometimes it's convenient to treat upper-case, lower-case, and mixed-case words all the same. Racket also provides "case-independent" versions of each of these functions:
```
; string-ci=?  :  string string -> Boolean
; string-ci<?  :  string string -> Boolean
; string-ci<=? :  string string -> Boolean
; string-ci>?  :  string string -> Boolean
; string-ci>=? :  string string -> Boolean
```

To see how these are used in practice, let's write some simple functions.

Worked Exercise 13.2.2 *Develop a function* is-basketball? *that takes in a string representing the name of a game, and returns a Boolean indicating whether the game was* "basketball".

Solution: The **contract** is clearly
```
; is-basketball?  :  string(game) -> boolean
```

For **examples**, we note that there are two possible answers: true and false. To test the program adequately, let's make sure we have an example that produces true, and one that produces false.
```
"Examples of is-basketball?:"
(check-expect (is-basketball?  "basketball") true)
(check-expect (is-basketball?  "cricket") false)
```

Next, we need to write a **skeleton**. The important decisions have already been made in the contract, so
```
(define (is-basketball?  game)
  ...)
```

For the **inventory**, we obviously need the parameter `game`. In addition, since the problem specifically mentions the string `"basketball"`, that string is likely to appear in the function:

```
(define (is-basketball? game)
  ; game              a string
  ; "basketball"      another string
  ...)
```

Now, to fill in the **function body**, we notice that we have two strings (`game` and `"basketball"`) and we want a Boolean; conveniently enough, there's a built-in function `string=?` that takes in two strings and returns a Boolean. So let's use it:

```
(define (is-basketball? game)
  ; game              a string
  ; "basketball"      another string
  (string=? game "basketball")
)
```

Now we can **test** the function on our two examples, and it should work. ∎

Exercise 13.2.3 *Develop a function `is-nintendo?` that takes in a string and tells whether it was `"nintendo"`.*

Exercise 13.2.4 *Develop a function `empty-string?` that takes in a string and tells whether it was `""`.*

Exercise 13.2.5 *Develop a function `in-first-half?` that takes in a (lower-case) string and tells whether it's in the first half of the alphabet (i.e. it comes before `"n"` in alphabetical order)*

Hint: You'll need at least two examples: one in the first half of the alphabet, and one in the second half. It's also a good idea to have an example that's `"n"` itself; this is called a *borderline example*. What do you think is the "right answer" for this example?

13.3 Comparing numbers

Just as `string=?`, `string<?`, *etc.* allow us to compare strings, there are built-in functions that allow us to compare numbers. Here are the most common ones:

```
; = :  number number -> Boolean
; Tells whether the two numbers have the exact same value.

; < :  number number -> Boolean
; Tells whether the first number is less than the second.

; > :  number number -> Boolean
; Tells whether the first number is more than the second.

; <= :  number number -> Boolean
; Tells whether the first number is at most the second.

; >= :  number number -> Boolean
; Tells whether the first number is at least the second.
```

Note that these functions, despite returning Booleans, do *not* have names ending in a question-mark; their traditional mathematical names were so well-established that the designers of Racket decided to keep those names at the expense of the Racket convention.

To get some practice with these functions, let's start by trying some expressions:

```
(check-expect (= 3 4) false)
(check-expect (< 3 4) true)
(check-expect (> 3 4) false)
(check-expect (<= 3 4) true)
(check-expect (>= 3 4) false)
(define age 21)
(check-expect (> age 12) true)
(check-expect (< age 18) false)
(check-expect (= (+ 3 4) 5) false)
(check-expect (= (+ 3 4) 7) true)
```

Feel free to make up and try some more examples of your own.

Now let's try writing some simple functions that use the built-in number comparison operators.

Worked Exercise 13.3.1 *Develop a function* may-drive? *that takes in the age of a person and returns whether that person is old enough to drive a car legally (which in most of the U.S. means "at least 16 years old").*

Solution: For the **contract**, we note that the function "takes in the age of a person", which sounds like it should be a number, "and returns whether ..." The word "whether" in a problem statement almost always means a Boolean. So the contract should be

```
; may-drive?  :  number(age) -> Boolean
```

For the **examples**, we note first that there are two possible answers — true and false — and therefore there must be at least two examples. Furthermore, there's a *borderline* situation between *sub-ranges* of inputs (as there was with in-first-half? above), so we should also test the borderline case.

```
"Examples of may-drive?:"
(check-expect (may-drive?  15) false)
(check-expect (may-drive?  23) true)
(check-expect (may-drive?  16) true) ; borderline case
```

The **skeleton** is straightforward:

```
(define (may-drive? age)
  ...)
```

The **inventory** lists the parameter `age` and the literal 16:

```
(define (may-drive? age)
  ; age        a number
  ; 16         a fixed number we're likely to need
  ...)
```

Now we can fill in the **body**. We have two numbers, and we need a Boolean; conveniently enough, we know of several built-in functions (=, <, >, <=, >=) that take in two numbers and return a Boolean. Let's try >.

```
(define (may-drive? age)
  ; age        a number
  ; 16         a fixed number we're likely to need
  (> age 16)
  )
```

That wasn't too bad. Now we **test** the function ... and we see that it gets one of the answers *wrong*! In particular, it gets the "clear-cut" cases right, but it gets the "borderline" example wrong. This is a common pattern; watch for it! It usually means we've got the direction of the comparison right, but either we should have added an = sign and didn't, or we shouldn't have but did. In this case, it means we should have used >= rather than >.

```
(define (may-drive? age)
  ; age        a number
  ; 16         a fixed number we're likely to need
  ( >= age 16)
  )
```

Now we test this again; it should work correctly for all cases. ∎

Practice Exercise 13.3.2 *Suppose we had mistakenly typed the < operator in the function body instead of > or >=.* **What pattern** *of right and wrong answers would we have gotten?* **Try it** *and see whether your prediction was right.*

Likewise, **what pattern** *of right and wrong answers would we have gotten if we had typed <= instead of >, >=, or <?* **Try it** *and see whether your prediction was right.*

Now, suppose we had chosen the >= operator, but had its arguments in the opposite order: (>= 16 age). **What pattern** *of right and wrong answers would we have gotten?* **Try it** *and see whether your prediction was right.*

Watch for these patterns whenever you're debugging a program that involves sub-ranges of numbers or strings.

Exercise 13.3.3 *Develop a function* `may-drink?` *that takes in a person's age and returns whether the person is old enough to drink alcohol legally. (In most of the U.S., this means "at least 21 years old".)*

Exercise 13.3.4 *Develop a function* `under-a-dollar?` *that takes in the price of an item in dollars (e.g.* `1.49` *or* `.98`*) and tells whether it's less than* `1.00` *.*

Exercise 13.3.5 *Develop a function* `is-17?` *that takes in a number and tells whether it's exactly 17.*

13.4   Designing functions involving booleans

In the above examples, we've used the fact that the function returns a boolean to help us choose test cases: you need at least one test case for which the right answer is `true`, and at least one test case for which the right answer is `false`, or you haven't tested the function adequately. Furthermore, if the input consists of *sub-ranges* with *borderlines* between them, you also need to test right at the borderline. We'll incorporate this idea into the design recipe as follows:

1. Write a contract (and perhaps a purpose statement).

2. *Analyze input and output data types.*

3. Write examples of how to use the function, with correct answers. *If an input or output data type consists of two or more cases, be sure there's at least one example for each case. If an input type involves sub-ranges, be sure there's an example at each borderline.*

4. Write a function skeleton, specifying parameter names.

5. Write an inventory of available expressions, including parameter names and obviously relevant literals, along with their data types (and, if necessary, their values for a specific example).

6. Fill in the function body.

7. Test the function.

We've added one new step: *Analyze input and output data types.* When we were simply writing functions that took in or returned images or numbers, there wasn't much "analysis" to be done. But a function that returns a Boolean can be thought of as distinguishing two sub-categories of input: those inputs for which the right answer is `true`, and those for which it's `false`. And in many cases there are even more sub-categories, as we'll see in Section 13.7. Identifying these sub-categories (and any borderlines between them) early helps you choose good test cases.

Exercise 13.4.1 *Develop a function* `much-older?` *that takes in two people's ages and tells whether the first is "much older" (which we'll define as "at least ten years older") than the second.*

Exercise 13.4.2 *Develop a function* `within-distance?` *that takes in three numbers: x, y, and distance. The function should return whether or not the point* (x, y) *is at most the specified distance from the point* $(0, 0)$*. The formula for the distance of a point to* $(0, 0)$ *is* $\sqrt{x^2 + y^2}$*.*

Hint: You may want to write an auxiliary function to compute the distance.

13.5   Comparing images

Just as we can compare strings or numbers to see whether they're the same, we can also
compare two *images* to see whether they're the same:

```
; image=?  :  image image -> Boolean
```

But images don't have an "order", so there are no image functions analogous to `string<?`,
`string>?`, *etc.*.

Exercise 13.5.1 *Develop a function* `is-green-triangle?` *that takes in an image and
tells whether it is exactly* `(triangle 10 "solid" "green")`.

13.6   Testing types

As we've seen, Racket has several built-in data types: numbers, strings, images, booleans,
etc. It also has built-in functions to *tell whether* something is of a particular type:

```
; number?  :  anything -> boolean
; tells whether its argument is a number.
; image?  :  anything -> boolean
; tells whether its argument is an image.
; string?  :  anything -> boolean
; tells whether its argument is a string.
; boolean?  :  anything -> boolean
; tells whether its argument is a boolean.
; integer?  :  anything -> boolean
; tells whether its argument is an integer.
...
```

You've already seen the `image?`, `number?`, and `string?` functions: we used them in the
`check-with` clause of an animation to specify what type the model is. In fact, `check-with`
can work on *any* function that has contract `anything -> boolean`: if you wanted to write
an animation with a Boolean model, you could say `(check-with boolean?)`. We'll see
more applications of this in Chapter 21.

Practice Exercise 13.6.1 *Try the following expressions in the interactions pane. For
each one,* **predict** *what you think it will return, then see whether you were right. If not,*
experiment *some more until you understand what the function does.* **Make up** *some
similar examples of your own and try them similarly.*

```
(number?  3)
(number?  5/3)
(number?  "3")
(number?  "three")
(number?  true)
(integer?  3)
(integer?  5/3)
(integer?  "3")
(integer?  "three")
(string?  3)
(string?  "3")
(string?  "three")
(image?  3)
(image?  (circle 5 "solid" "green"))
(number?  (+ 3 4))
(number?  (> 3 4))
(boolean?  (> 3 4))
(boolean?  3)
(boolean?  false)
(boolean?  true)
```

SIDEBAR:

Mathematicians use the word *predicate* to mean a function that returns a Boolean, so sometimes you'll hear Racket programmers referring to "type predicates". A type predicate is simply any one of these functions that tell whether something is of a particular type. Another name for *type predicate* is *discriminator*.

Common beginner mistake

Students are often confused by the difference between `string?` and `string=?`, between `image?` and `image=?`, *etc.* All of these functions return Booleans, but they do different things.

The `string=?` function takes *two* arguments (which *must be strings*), and tells whether they're the *same* string. The `string?` function takes *one* argument (which may be of *any type*), and tells whether it is a string at all.

Likewise, `image=?` tells whether two images are the same, while `image?` tells whether something is an image at all.

And `boolean=?` (which you'll almost never need!) tells whether two booleans are the same, while `boolean?` tells whether something is a boolean at all.

Finally, = tells whether two numbers are the same, while `number?` tells whether something is a number at all.

13.7   Boolean operators

Advertisers like to divide the world of consumers into age categories, and one of their favorites is the "18-to-25 demographic": these people are typically living on their own for the first time, spending significant amounts of their own money for the first time, and forming their own spending habits. If an advertiser can get a 19-year-old in the habit of buying a particular brand of shampoo or canned soup, it may pay off in decades of sales.

For this reason, advertisers concentrate their work in places that 18-to-25-year-olds will see it.

Worked Exercise 13.7.1 *Develop a function* that takes in somebody's age, and decides whether the person is in the 18-to-25 demographic.

Solution: The contract is easy:

```
; 18-to-25?  : number (age) -> Boolean
```

Analyzing the data types tells us nothing new about the output type. The input is more interesting: it could be thought of as "18-to-25" and "everything else", but it seems more natural to break it down into *three* categories: under-18, 18-to-25, and over-25.

We'll need at least one example in each of these three categories, plus borderline examples for *both* borderlines — 18 and 25.

```
"Examples of 18-to-25?:"
(check-expect (18-to-25?  15) false)
(check-expect (18-to-25?  18) true)
(check-expect (18-to-25?  20) true)
(check-expect (18-to-25?  25) true)
(check-expect (18-to-25?  27) false)
```

We chose the examples based on the data analysis, and figured out the "right answers" by applying common sense to the problem: if the advertisers want "18-to-25-year-olds", they probably mean to include both 18-year-olds and 25-year-olds (even though somebody may be described as "25 years old" right up to the day before turning 26).

The skeleton is straightforward:

```
(define (18-to-25?  age)
  ...)
```

The inventory throws in a parameter and two literals:

```
(define (18-to-25?  age)
  ; age       a number
  ; 18        a fixed number we'll need
  ; 25        another fixed number we'll need
  ...)
```

In fact, we can predict some things we'll want to do with the numbers: we'll probably want to check whether age is at least 18, and whether age is at most 25:

```
(define (18-to-25?  age)
  ; age          a number
  ; 18           a fixed number we'll need
  ; 25           another fixed number we'll need
  ; (>= age 18)  a Boolean
  ; (<= age 25)  a Boolean
  )
```

But now we face a problem: we have two Booleans, both of which represent *part* of the right answer, but neither of which is the *whole* right answer. We need to *combine* the two, using a *Boolean operator*.

A Boolean operator is a function that takes in one or more Booleans and returns a Boolean. Racket has three common Boolean operators: **and**, **or**, and **not**. The **and** and **or** operators each take in two or more Booleans; the **not** operator takes in exactly one.

Let's try some examples of these in the Interactions pane:

```
(check-expect (or false false) false)
(check-expect (or false true) true)
(check-expect (or true false) true)
(check-expect (or true true) true)
(check-expect (or (= 3 5) (= (+ 3 4) 7)) true)
(check-expect (or (< 3 5) (= (+ 3 4) 5)) true)
(check-expect (or (> 3 5) (= (+ 3 4) 5)) false)
(check-expect (and false false) false)
(check-expect (and false true) false)
(check-expect (and true false) false)
(check-expect (and true true) true)
(check-expect (and (= 3 5) (= (+ 3 4) 7)) false)
(check-expect (and (< 3 5) (= (+ 3 4) 7)) true)
(check-expect (not (= 3 5)) true)
(check-expect (not (< 3 5)) false)
(check-expect (or false true false) true)
(check-expect (or false false false) false)
(check-expect (and false true false) false)
(check-expect (and true true true) true)
```

Now back to our problem. We have two Boolean expressions: one represents whether age is at least 18, and the other represents whether age is at most 25. To find out whether *both* of those things are true simultaneously, we need to combine the expressions using and:

```
(define (18-to-25?  age)
  ; age              a number
  ; 18               a fixed number we'll need
  ; 25               another fixed number we'll need
  ; (>= age 18)      a Boolean
  ; (<= age 25)      a Boolean
  (and  (>= age 18)
        (<= age 25))
)
```

Now we can test the function, and it should work correctly on all five examples. ■

Practice Exercise 13.7.2 *What would have happened if we had used or instead of and in defining the 18-to-25? function?* **Predict** *the pattern of right and wrong answers, then* **change** *the function definition and check whether you were right.*

Exercise 13.7.3 *Develop a function teenage? that takes in a person's age and returns whether the person is at least 13 but younger than 20.*

Exercise 13.7.4 *Develop a function negative-or-over-100? that takes in a number and returns whether it is either negative (i.e. less than zero) or over 100.*

Exercise 13.7.5 *Develop a function may-drive-but-not-drink? that takes in a person's age and tells whether the person is old enough to have a driver's license (in most of the U.S.) but not old enough to drink alcohol (in most of the U.S.).*

Hint: Re-use previously-written functions!

Exercise 13.7.6 *The game of "craps" involves rolling a pair of dice, and (in a simplified version of the game) if the result is 7 or 11, you win.* **Develop a function** *named* `win-craps?` *that takes in a number and tells whether it's either a 7 or an 11.*

Exercise 13.7.7 **Develop a function** *named* `play-craps` *that takes a dummy argument, rolls two dice, adds them up, and returns* `true` *or* `false` *depending on whether you won the roll.*

Hint: Re-use previously defined functions!

SIDEBAR:

How would you test a function like `play-craps`? It ignores its argument, so all you can see directly is that sometimes it returns `true` and sometimes `false`, regardless of the argument. *How much of the time* should it return `true`? *How many runs* would you need to make in order to tell whether it was behaving the way it should?

Exercise 13.7.8 **Develop a function** `not-13?` *that takes a number and tells whether it's not exactly 13.*

Exercise 13.7.9 **Develop a function** `not-single-letter?` *that takes a string and tells whether its length is anything other than 1.*

Exercise 13.7.10 **Develop a function** `over-65-or-teenage?` *that takes in a person's age and tells whether the person is either over 65 or in his/her teens.*

Exercise 13.7.11 **Develop a function** `lose-craps?` *that takes in a number and tells whether it is* not *either 7 or 11. That is, the result should be* `false` *for 7 and 11, and* `true` *for everything else.*

Exercise 13.7.12 **Develop a function** `is-not-red-square?` *that takes in an image and tells whether it is anything other than a solid red square.*

Hint: Use `image-width` to find out how wide the image is.

Exercise 13.7.13 **Develop a function** `any-two-same-pics?` *that takes in three images and tells whether any two (or more) of them are exactly the same.*

Hint: There are at least three different ways the answer could be `true`; test them all, as well as at least one case in which the answer should be `false`.

13.8 Short-circuit evaluation

Technically, `and` and `or` aren't really functions in Racket but rather something called *special forms*; `define` is also a *special form*. The main difference, for now, is that every argument to a function has to have a value, or the function call doesn't make sense. Obviously, `define` can't work that way, because its whole purpose is to define a variable or function that doesn't already have a meaning. The `and` and `or` operators *could* have been regular functions, but the designers of Racket chose to make them special forms in order to get something called *short-circuit evaluation*.

The idea is, if the first argument of an **or** is **true**, you don't really care what the rest of the arguments are; you already know the answer. Suppose you had a variable named x defined, and think about an expression like

```
(or (= x 0) (> (/ 7 x) 2))
```

If **or** were an ordinary function, DrRacket would compute the Boolean values of (= x 0) and (> (/ 7 x) 2), and then apply **or** to the results. If $x = 0$, the sub-expression (/ 7 x) would crash (because you can't divide by zero) before **or** ever got a chance to do its job. Instead, DrRacket computes the Boolean value of (= x 0), and if it's **true**, **or** returns **true** immediately without even looking at its second argument (which doesn't have a value). Only if $x \neq 0$ does DrRacket try to compute (> (/ 7 x) 2), and if $x \neq 0$, this expression is guaranteed to have a value so everything's OK.

Similarly, if the first argument of an **and** is **false**, you already know the answer and don't need to even look at the rest of the arguments. Try typing each of the two expressions

```
(and (> 2 3) y)
(and y (> 2 3))
```

in the Interactions pane of DrRacket. The first should return **false**; the second should complain that it's never heard of the variable y. (If you try these two expressions in the Definitions pane and hit "Step", "Check Syntax", or "Run", *both* will produce error messages, because the Definitions pane checks that all variable names are defined before they are used.)

For most purposes, you can ignore short-circuit evaluation. But on rare occasions, it makes a difference to your programming: you can make a program run faster, or even run without crashing, by putting the arguments of **or** or **and** in a different order.

13.9   Review of important words and concepts

Racket has a *Boolean* data type with two values — **true** and **false** — which is used for yes/no questions. A number of built-in functions allow you to compare strings for equality or order, compare numbers for equality or order, compare images for equality, and combine two or more Booleans into one.

We've added a new step to the design recipe for functions: *analyze the input and output data types*. For now, this means identifying interesting "sub-categories" of input and output. Once you've done this, it helps you in choosing good test cases: make sure to have at least one test case for each sub-category. In addition, if the sub-categories are *ranges* with *borderlines* in between them, make sure to test the function at the borderlines.

If the function doesn't pass all its tests, pay attention to *patterns of right and wrong answers*: was it *always* wrong, or only sometimes? Did it work on the "clear-cut" cases but not the borderlines? The borderlines but not the "clear-cut" cases? These patterns give you valuable clues in figuring out what's wrong with the program.

A *predicate* is any function that returns a Boolean. In Racket, most such functions (by convention) have names ending in a question mark. There are built-in *type predicates* — functions that take in *any type* of argument, and tell whether or not it is, say, a number. They tend to have obvious names: **number?**, **image?**, **string?**, **boolean?**, **integer?**, *etc.*

You can handle much more complicated and sophisticated categories of input by combining Boolean-valued expressions using the Boolean operators **and**, **or**, and **not**.

13.10   Reference: Functions involving Booleans

Here are the new built-in functions (and special forms) we've discussed in this chapter:

- `string=?`
- `string<?`
- `string<=?`
- `string>?`
- `string>=?`
- `string-ci=?`
- `string-ci<?`
- `string-ci<=?`
- `string-ci>?`
- `string-ci>=?`
- `=`
- `<`
- `>`
- `<=`
- `>=`
- `image=?`
- `image?`
- `number?`
- `string?`
- `boolean?`
- `boolean=?`
- `and`
- `or`
- `not`

Chapter 14

Animations with Booleans

The Boolean type allows us to add some new features to our animations. Most obviously, we can use a Boolean as a model, just as we've already learned to use images, numbers, and strings as models. Unfortunately, doing anything interesting with a Boolean model requires *conditionals*, which are introduced in Chapter 15.

However, we can also use Booleans to *stop an animation*. This will give us practice using Booleans before we get to conditionals.

14.1 Stopping animations

Consider the following problem.

Worked Exercise 14.1.1 *Develop an animation that displays the word "antidisestablishmentarianism" in (say) 18-point blue letters. Every half second, the first letter of the word is removed, so the display becomes "ntidisestablishmentarianism", then "tidisestablishmentarianism", etc.*

Solution: Identify the model: Every second we need to chop one letter off the string, which we know how to do using `substring`, and we know how to convert a string to an image with `text`, so let's use a string as our model.

Identify the necessary handlers: Since the model isn't an image, we'll need a draw handler with the contract

```
; show-string :  string -> image
```

And since the model needs to change every half second, we'll need a tick handler with the contract

```
; chop-string :  string -> string
```

Write the handlers: The `show-string` function is straightforward; here's my answer.

```
; show-string :  string -> image
(check-expect (show-string "") (text "" 18 "blue"))
(check-expect (show-string "hello") (text "hello" 18 "blue"))
(define (show-string model)
  ; model      a string
  (text model 18 "blue"))
```

191

Once this works, we can go on to the `chop-string` function. Immediately we face a problem: it's not clear what should happen if its argument is the empty string.

```
; chop-string :  string -> string
(check-expect (chop-string "a") "")
(check-expect (chop-string "hello") "ello")
; (check-expect (chop-string "") what to do here?)
```

So we'll change the contract:

```
; chop-string :  non-empty string -> string
```

Now the problematic example is no longer legal, so we can forget about it — at least for now. The function definition looks like

```
(define (chop-string model)
  ; model      a string
  (substring model 1))
```

We test the function, and it works on all of our test cases.

Size and shape of window: If we don't specify dimensions, the animation window will be the size of the initial picture. Will that work? Well, the initial picture is simply the word "antidisestablishmentarianism" in an 18-point font, and as the word gets shorter, the picture can only get smaller, so it'll still fit in the original animation window; we don't need to specify window size.

Call `big-bang`: The initial model is "antidisestablishmentarianism", so ...

```
(big-bang "antidisestablishmentarianism"
          (check-with string?)
          (on-draw show-string)
          (on-tick chop-string 1/2))
```

This works beautifully until the string is reduced to empty, at which point ... **it crashes!** Remember, `chop-string` doesn't work on an empty string. To avoid this crash, we need a way to *stop the animation* before calling `chop-string` on an empty string.

The `picturing-programs` library provides one more kind of "handler" that we didn't see in Chapter 6: a "stopping condition". You'll write (or use) a function with the contract

```
; function-name :  model -> boolean
```

and install it with

```
(stop-when function-name)
```

The animation will stop as soon as the function returns `true`.

In our case, the model is a string, and we want to stop as soon as the string is empty, so here's my definition:

```
; empty-string? : string -> boolean
(check-expect (empty-string? "") true)
(check-expect (empty-string? "m") false)
(check-expect (empty-string? "n") false)
(check-expect (empty-string? "hello") false)
(define (empty-string? model)
  ; model      a string
  ; ""         a fixed string
  (string=? model ""))
```

Now we can use this to stop the animation as follows:

```
(big-bang "antidisestablishmentarianism"
          (check-with string?)
          (on-draw show-string)
          (on-tick chop-string 1/2)
          (stop-when empty-string?))
```

The animation works exactly as before, except that when the string is reduced to empty, it stops quietly and peacefully instead of showing an ugly error message. ▌

Note that `empty-string?` is called *after* the draw handler and *before* the tick handler. As a result, you'll see the string get gradually shorter, eventually down to nothing, but then the animation will stop before calling `chop-string` on the empty string (which, as we know, would crash).

Exercise 14.1.2 *Recall the animation of Exercise 10.2.1, which initially displayed an "a", then "ab" a second later, then "abb", and so on.* **Modify** *this animation so it stops when the string reaches ten letters long (i.e. "abbbbbbbbb").*

Exercise 14.1.3 **Modify** *the animation of Exercise 14.1.1 so that it stops when the string is reduced to length 3 or less, rather than when it's reduced to the empty string.* **Try** *it with several different initial strings, including some that are already length 3 or less.*

Exercise 14.1.4 **Modify** *the animation of Worked Exercise 6.4.1 so that the animation ends when the image displayed (including white space) is wider than the window.*

Exercise 14.1.5 **Modify** *the animation of Exercise 6.4.3 so that the animation ends when there's nothing left to show in the window.*

Exercise 14.1.6 **Modify** *the animation of Exercise 6.4.4 so that the animation ends when the image (a row of dots) is wider than the window.*

Exercise 14.1.7 **Modify** *the animation of Exercise 6.7.2 or 6.7.3 so that the animation ends when the image (including white space) is wider or taller than the window.*

Exercise 14.1.8 **Modify** *the animation of Exercise 8.3.1 or 8.3.2 so that the animation ends when the circle is wider or taller than the window.*

Hint: Recall that in these animations, the model was a number representing radius; the diameter is twice the radius. Be sure to test the program with a window that's wider than it is tall, or taller than it is wide.

Exercise 14.1.9 *Modify your animation from Exercise 8.4.2 so that the animation ends when the picture reaches the bottom of the window.*

Exercise 14.1.10 *The animation from Exercise 8.4.3 has a problem: it crashes if you type fast enough to reduce the radius of the dot to less than zero.* **Modify** *this animation so it never crashes, but rather stops gracefully when the radius gets too small.*

Exercise 14.1.11 *Your solution to Exercise 8.3.9 probably fills up the progress bar and then just sits there, not making any visible change to the window but not stopping either. (Or, if you did it differently, it may go past filling the progress bar, drawing a bar that's more than 100% full!)*

Modify this animation so it stops gracefully when the progress bar reaches 100%.

Exercise 14.1.12 **Modify** *the animation of Exercise 10.2.4 so that it counts only up to 30, and then stops.*

14.2   Stopping in response to events

A `stop-when` handler works great when the condition for stopping the animation is easily computed from the model. But in some situations, it's more natural to stop the animation in response to a tick, key, or mouse event, using a built-in function named `stop-with`.

```
; stop-with :  model -> stopping-model
; Returns the same thing it was given, but marked so that
; when big-bang sees this result, it stops the animation.
; The draw handler will be called one last time on this value.
```

Worked Exercise 14.2.1 *Modify exercise 10.2.5 so that it stops as soon as the user presses a key on the keyboard. (For now it's "any key"; we'll see in Chapter 18 how to tell if it was, say, the "q" key for "quit".)*

Solution: The model is the same as before: a number that starts at 0 and increases by 1 each second. We still need a tick handler (for the "increases by 1 each second"), and we still need a draw handler (to display the number at the appropriate place), but now we also need a key handler.

The key handler's contract is

```
; key handler stop-on-key :  number key -> number
```

Since we're not worried about *what* key the user pressed, we really only need one test case: if the key handler is called at all, it means the user pressed a key and the animation should end, by calling `stop-with` on some model. Whatever argument we give to `stop-with` will be given to the draw handler "one last time" to decide what picture should stay in the animation window after the animation stops. In many cases, we can just give `stop-with` the current model.

```
(check-expect (stop-on-key 24 "whatever")
              (stop-with 24))

(define (stop-on-key model key)
        ; model number
        ; key   whatever this is (ignore)
        (stop-with model)
        )

(big-bang 0
        (check-with number?)
        (on-tick add1 1)
        (on-draw show-num-at-x 500 100)
        (on-key stop-on-key))
```

▌

Exercise 14.2.2 *Choose a previously-written animation that didn't have a key handler.* **Modify** *it so that it stops as soon as the user types a key.*

Exercise 14.2.3 *Choose a previously-written animation that didn't have a mouse handler.* **Modify** *it so that it stops as soon as the user moves or clicks the mouse.*

Common beginner mistake: stop-with is intended to be called from within a handler; it is *not* a way of installing handlers, like on-tick, on-key, or stop-when. If you call it as one of the arguments to big-bang, as in this example:

```
(big-bang 0
  (check-with number?)
  (on-tick add1)
  (on-draw disk-of-size)
  (stop-with 5)
  )
```

you'll get an error message saying that's not a legal part of a "world description" (remember, big-bang "creates the world").

In order to do more interesting things with stop-with, *e.g.* stop if the user clicks the mouse in a particular part of the screen, or stop if the user types the "q" key, we'll need the techniques of the next few chapters.

14.3 Review of important words and concepts

For situations in which we want an animation to end as soon as the model meets a certain condition, you can provide a stop-when handler — a function from model to Boolean — and as soon as it's true, the animation will end. Note that it is called *after* the draw handler, but *before* the tick, key, and mouse handlers. This means the draw handler has to be written to not crash even if the stopping condition is true, but the tick, key, and mouse handlers may safely assume that the stopping condition is false.

If you want to end the animation in response to a tick, mouse, or key event, it may be more natural to use stop-with from within a tick, mouse, or key handler.

Figure 14.1: Event handlers for animations

The big-bang function has the contract

    ; big-bang : model(start) handler ... -> number

tick handlers must have the contract

    ; *function-name* : model (old) -> model (new)

They are installed with (on-tick *function-name interval*). The *interval* is the length of time (in seconds) between clock ticks; if you leave it out, the animation will run as fast as it can.

key handlers must have the contract

    ; *function-name* : model (old) key -> model (new)

The "key" parameter indicates what key was pressed; we'll see how to use it in Chapter 18.

They are installed with (on-key *function-name*).

mouse handlers must have the contract

    ; *function-name* : model (old)
    ;   number (mouse-x) number (mouse-y) event
    ;   -> model (new)

The first parameter is the old model; the second represents the *x coordinate*, indicating how many pixels from the left the mouse is; the third number represents the *y coordinate*, indicating how many pixels down from the top the mouse is; and the "event" tells what happened (the mouse was moved, the button was pressed or released, *etc.*); we'll see in Chapter 18 how to use this.

They are installed with (on-mouse *function-name*).

draw handlers must have the contract

    ; *function-name* : model (current) -> image

and are installed with (on-draw *function-name width height*). (If you leave out the *width* and *height* arguments, the animation window will be the size of the first image.)

An especially simple draw handler, show-it, is predefined: it simply returns the same image it was given, and it's useful if you need to specify the width and height of the animation window but don't want to write your own draw handler.

stop handlers must have the contract

    ; *function-name* : model (current) -> boolean

and are installed with (stop-when *function-name*).

model type checkers must have the contract

    ; *function-name* : anything -> boolean

and are installed with (check-with *function-name*).

If you're using numbers as your model, use (check-with number?), if you're using strings, use (check-with string?), *etc.*

It's a good idea to include a `check-with` clause in every `big-bang` animation to tell Racket (and future readers of your program) what type you think the model should be. If one of your functions returns the wrong type, you'll get a more informative and useful error message that tells you what went wrong.

14.4 Reference: Built-in functions for making decisions in animations

This chapter has introduced two new bits of syntax:

- `stop-when`

- `stop-with`

(Technically, `stop-with` is a function, while `stop-when` is a special form that works only inside `big-bang`.)

Chapter 15

Conditionals

15.1 Making decisions

We saw in Chapter 13 how to write functions that answer yes/no questions, and we saw in Chapter 14 how to use such a function as the stopping criterion for an animation. But Booleans are used much more generally to *make decisions* about what computation to do.

For example, imagine an e-commerce site that sells games and game equipment of several different kinds: basketballs, baseballs, mitts, bats, Monopoly boards, chess boards and pieces, Nintendo consoles, *etc.*. One part of the site might give a list of the names of different games; a user would select one from the menu, and the site would then display a picture of the selected game.

You know how to display pictures, but this application requires displaying *one of several* pictures, depending on which menu item the user selected. The computer needs to do something like the following:

```
If the user selected "basketball",
  display the picture of a basketball.
If not, see whether the user selected "baseball";
  if so, display the picture of a baseball.
If not, see whether the user selected "Monopoly";
  if so, display the picture of a Monopoly set.
etc.
```

(We'll solve this problem in Exercise 15.3.1.)

This is such a common pattern in programming that Racket (and most other languages) provides a construct to do it, called a *conditional* (or cond for short). A Racket conditional includes a series of "question/answer" pairs: Racket evaluates the first question, and if the result is true, it returns the first answer. If not, it goes on to the second question: if the second question evaluates to true, it returns the second answer; if not, it goes on to the third question, and so on.

Syntax Rule 6 *Anything matching the following pattern is a legal expression:*
```
(cond [question1  answer1]
      [question2  answer2]
      [question3  answer3]
      ...
      [questionn  answern]
      )
```
as long as each of the questions *is an expression of type Boolean, and each* answer *is an expression.*

Note that the questions and answers must come in pairs, surrounded by square brackets. Each question/answer pair is sometimes called a "cond-clause".

SIDEBAR:

In fact, you can use parentheses instead of the square brackets. To avoid confusion, I prefer to use parentheses only for calling functions, as we've been doing so far, and to use square brackets to group together each question/answer pair in a conditional.

Practice Exercise 15.1.1 *Type the following into the Interactions pane:*
```
(cond [(string=?  "hello" "goodbye") "something is wrong!"]
      [(string=?  "snark" "snark") "this looks better"]
      )
```
The result should be the string `"this looks better"`.

Type (or copy-and-paste) the same three lines into the Definitions pane and hit "Run"; you should get the same result.

Then hit "Step" instead of "Run": note that it first evaluates the expression (`string=? "hello" "goodbye"`) *to* `false`, *then throws away the answer* `"something is wrong!"` *and goes on to the second question/answer pair.*

Practice Exercise 15.1.2 *Now try an example in which* none *of the questions comes out* true:
```
(cond [(string=?  "hello" "goodbye") "something is wrong!"]
      [(string<?  "snark" "boojum") "this isn't true either"]
      [(< 5 2) "nor this"]
      )
```
Type this into the Interactions pane; you should get an error message saying cond: all question results were false.

Copy the same four lines into the Definitions pane and hit "Run"; you should get the same error message.

Now try the Stepper; you'll see it evaluate each of the three questions in turn to false, *discard each of the three answers, and then produce the error message.*

Practice Exercise 15.1.3 *Here's an example in which a question other than the last one evaluates to* true:
```
(cond [(= (+ 2 5) (- 10 3))        "yes, this works"]
      [(string=?  "hello" "goodbye") "this shouldn't happen"]
      [(string<?  "goodbye" "hello")
       "this is true but it shouldn't get here"]
      )
```
Note that since the first question evaluates to true, *Racket returns* `"yes, this works"` *and never bothers to even evaluate the other two questions, as you can see by using the*

*Stepper. This demonstrates that cond, like **define**, **and**, and **or**, is a special form rather than a regular function.*

Of course, nobody really uses conditionals directly in Interactions; they're almost always used inside a function. Let's try a more realistic example:

Worked Exercise 15.1.4 *Develop a function reply which recognizes any one of the strings "good morning", "good afternoon", or "good night", and returns either "I need coffee", "I need a nap", or "bedtime!" respectively. If the input isn't any of the three known strings, the function may produce an error message.*

Solution: Contract:
```
; reply :  string -> string
```
If we wished, we could be more specific about what input values are allowed, and what results are possible:
```
; reply:string("good morning","good afternoon",or "good night")->
; string ("I need coffee", "I need a nap", or "bedtime!")
```

Examples: There are exactly three legal inputs, and exactly three legal outputs, so to test the program adequately, we should try all three.
```
"Examples of reply:"
(check-expect (reply "good morning") "I need coffee")
(check-expect (reply "good afternoon") "I need a nap")
(check-expect (reply "good night") "bedtime!")
```

Skeleton: The input represents a greeting, so let's use that name for the parameter:
```
(define (reply greeting)
  ...)
```

Inventory: As usual, we need the parameter `greeting`. Since there are three possible cases, we can be pretty sure the function will need a conditional with three clauses, or question/answer pairs:
```
(define (reply greeting)
  ; greeting       a string
  ...)
```

Skeleton, revisited: Since there are three possible cases, we can be pretty sure the function will need a conditional with three clauses, or question/answer pairs:
```
(define (reply greeting)
  ; greeting      a string
  (cond  [...      ...]
         [...      ...]
         [...      ...]
))
```

To complete the function definition, we need to fill in the "..." gaps. I usually recommend filling in either all the answers, then all the questions, or *vice versa*, depending on which looks easier. In this case, we know exactly what the possible answers are, so let's fill them in first:

```
(define (reply greeting)
  ; greeting        a string
  (cond [...         "I need coffee" ]
        [...         "I need a nap" ]
        [...         "bedtime!" ]
  ))
```

We still need to fill in the questions, each of which should be a Boolean expression, probably involving greeting. Under what circumstances should the answer be "I need coffee"? Obviously, when greeting is "good morning". Filling this in, we get

```
(define (reply greeting)
  ; greeting        a string
  (cond [ (string=? greeting "good morning")   "I need coffee"]
        [...                                    "I need a nap"]
        [...                                    "bedtime!"]
  ))
```

We can do the same thing for the other two cases:

```
(define (reply greeting)
  ; greeting        a string
  (cond [(string=? greeting "good morning")    "I need coffee"]
        [ (string=? greeting "good afternoon") "I need a nap"]
        [ (string=? greeting "good night")     "bedtime!"]
  ))
```

Now **test** the function on the three examples we wrote earlier; it should work. ∎

Incidentally, if you write a function definition with several cond-clauses and you provide test cases for only *some* of them, when you hit "Run" to see the results, the parts of the program you tested will be colored black, and the parts you *didn't* test will be reddish-brown.

Practice Exercise 15.1.5 *Try commenting out one or two of the test cases and hitting "Run" to see this.*

15.2   Else and error-handling

The reply function is unsatisfying in a way: if the input is anything other than one of the three known greetings, the user gets the ugly error message *cond: all question results were false.* It would be friendlier if we could write our program with an "anything else" case, producing a more appropriate message like "I don't understand" or "huh?" if the input isn't something we recognize.

Racket provides a keyword else for just this purpose. If you use else as the *last question* in a cond, it will catch all cases that haven't been caught by any of the earlier questions. For example,

```
(define (reply greeting)
  ; greeting        a string
  (cond [(string=? greeting "good morning")    "I need coffee"]
        [(string=? greeting "good afternoon")  "I need a nap"]
        [(string=? greeting "good night")      "bedtime!"]
        [else                                  "huh?"]
  ))
```

When this function is applied to a string like `"good evening"`, which doesn't match any of the known greetings, Racket will then go on to the last question, which is `else` so Racket returns the corresponding answer `"huh?"` rather than the error message.

SIDEBAR:

Technically, the `else` keyword isn't necessary: if you were to use `true` as the last question, it would (obviously) always evaluate to `true`, so it too would catch all cases that haven't been caught by any earlier question. Try the above function with `true` in place of `else`; it should work exactly as before.

However, `else` is considered easier to read and understand, so most Racket programmers use it in this situation.

By the way, `else` *cannot* appear anywhere in Racket *except* as the last question in a `cond`.

Note that the `else` is *not in parentheses*: it is not a function, and it cannot be applied to arguments. If you *put* it in parentheses, you'll get an error message.

15.3 Design recipe for functions that make decisions

To write functions on data types defined by choices, we'll add a few more details to the design recipe.

1. Write a contract (and perhaps a purpose statement).

2. Analyze input and output data types: *if either or both is made up of several choices, figure out how many and how to describe them.*

3. Write examples of how to use the function, with correct answers. *If an input or output data type is defined by choices, be sure there's at least one example for each choice. If an input type involves sub-ranges, be sure there's an example at the borderline(s).*

4. Write a function skeleton, specifying parameter names.

5. Write an inventory of available expressions, including parameter names and obviously relevant literals, along with their data types (and, if necessary, their values for a chosen example).

6. *Add some details to the skeleton: if an input or output data type is defined by several choices, write a* **cond** *with that many question/answer pairs, with "..." for all the questions and answers.*

7. Fill in the function body. *If the skeleton involves a* **cond***, fill in either all the answers or all the questions, whichever is easier, and then go back to fill in the other column. If one of the choices is "anything else", use* `else` *as the last question in the* **cond***.*

8. Test the function.

To elaborate on step 7,

- if the answers are simple (*e.g.* a fixed set of known values), first fill in all the answers, then go back and figure out what question should lead to each answer; or

- if the questions are simpler than the answers (*e.g.* if the answers are complex expressions, but the questions are simply matching a parameter against a fixed set of known values), first fill in all the questions, then go back and figure out what expression will produce the right answer for each one. In particular, if one of the input choices is "anything else", detect this with `else` as the last question.

Recall that Syntax Rule 6 says the first expression in each `cond`-clause must be an expression of type Boolean, but it doesn't say anything about what type(s) the *second* expressions must be. In most cases, these should all be the same type as the return type of the function you're writing. For example, `reply` is supposed to return a string, so the second expression in each `cond`-clause is a string; in the e-commerce application we discussed earlier, the return type is a picture, so the second expression in each `cond`-clause should be a picture.

Exercise 15.3.1 *Develop a function* `choose-picture` *that takes in a string (either* `"basketball"`, `"baseball"`, `"Monopoly"`, *etc.; you can choose your own names if you wish, but don't choose more than about five) and returns a picture of that object (which you should be able to find on the Web).*

Exercise 15.3.2 *Modify exercise 15.3.1 so that if the input isn't any of the known games, it produces a picture of a question mark (or a person looking puzzled, or something like that).*

Exercise 15.3.3 *Develop a function named* `random-bw-picture` *that takes in a width and a height, and produces a rectangle that size and shape, in which each pixel is randomly either black or white.*

Exercise 15.3.4 *The town of Racketville needs a new computerized voting system. In an early version of the system, we assume there are exactly 4 voters (we'll see later how to handle an arbitrary number of voters).*
Develop a function `count-votes-4` *that takes in five strings. The first is the name of a candidate, and the other four are votes which might or might not be for that candidate. The function should return how many of the votes are for the specified candidate. For example,*
```
(check-expect
  (count-votes-4 "Anne" "Bob" "Charlie" "Bob" "Hortense") 0)
; since there are no votes for Anne
(check-expect
  (count-votes-4 "Anne" "Bob" "Anne" "Phil" "Charlie") 1)
(check-expect
  (count-votes-4 "Anne" "Anne" "Bob" "Anne" "Mary") 2)
(check-expect
  (count-votes-4 "Bob" "Anne" "Bob" "Charlie" "Bob") 2)
```

Hint: Write an auxiliary function that takes in two strings and returns either 1 (if they match) or 0 (if they don't).

Obviously, it's a pain passing around four votes as parameters, and it would be even worse if you had hundreds or thousands of votes. We'll see how to handle larger numbers of data in Chapter 22.

Exercise 15.3.5 *Develop a function* `smallest-of-3` *that takes in three numbers and returns the smallest of them.*

Exercise 15.3.6 *Develop a function* `rough-age` *that takes in a number representing a person's age and returns one of the strings* `"child"`, `"teenager"`, *or* `"adult"` *as appropriate. A "teenager" is at least 13 but less than 20 years old; a "child" is under 13; and an "adult" is at least 20.*

Exercise 15.3.7 *Using* `build3-image`, **build a rectangular image** *150 pixels wide by 100 pixels high which is yellow above the diagonal (from top-left to bottom-right corner) and blue below the diagonal.*

Exercise 15.3.8 *Develop a function* `make-stripes` *that takes in a width and height (in pixels), and produces a rectangle that size and shape in which all the even-numbered rows are red and the odd-numbered rows are blue. The result should be a bunch of narrow stripes.*

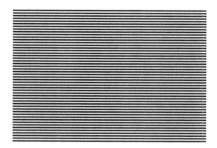

Exercise 15.3.9 *These stripes are really too narrow to see easily.* **Develop a function** `make-wide-stripes` *that does the same thing only with each stripe 5 pixels high: rows 0-4 are red, 5-9 are blue, 10-14 are red, etc.*

Exercise 15.3.10 *Develop a function* `make-diag-stripes` *that takes in a width and height (in pixels), and produces a rectangle that size and shape filled with stripes running from upper-right to lower-left.*

Exercise 15.3.11 *Define a function* `simplify-colors` *that takes in an image and produces an image the same size and shape: for each pixel in the given image, if it has more red than green or blue, make the resulting pixel pure red; if it has more green than red or blue, make it green; and if it has more blue than red or green, make it pure blue. In case of ties, you can decide what to do: pick one of the three colors arbitrarily, or make it white, or something like that.*

Exercise 15.3.12 *Come up with other cool things to do to images using conditionals. Go wild.*

15.4   Case study: bank interest

My bank offers savings accounts with a sliding scale of interest, depending on how much money is in the account: if you have less than $500 in the account, you earn no interest; for $500-$1000, you earn 1% per year interest; for $1000-$4000, you earn 2% per year, and for $4000 and up, you earn 3% per year.

Worked Exercise 15.4.1 *Develop a function* `bank-interest` *that computes the annual interest on a savings account with a specified balance.*

Solution: The function produces the amount of interest earned (a number), based on the balance in the account (a number). And it doesn't make sense, for purposes of this problem, to have a bank balance below 0, so we'll exclude that:

```
; bank-interest :  number(balance) -> number
; assumes balance is at least 0
```

The input and output types are both numbers. The output type doesn't break down in any obvious way into categories, but the input type does: there are four sub-ranges, 0-$500, $500-$1000, $1000-$4000, and $4000-up.

So how many examples will we need? There are four sub-ranges, so we'll need at least four examples; there are also three borderlines, at $500, $1000, and $4000, which need to be tested too. (If we wanted to be especially foolproof, we could test $0 and negative numbers too, but I'll skip that for this example.) So we need at least seven test cases: one inside each sub-range, and one at each borderline.

```
"Examples of bank-interest:"
(check-expect (bank-interest 200) 0)
(check-expect (bank-interest 500)   ? )
(check-expect (bank-interest 800) (* 800 .01)) ; or 8
(check-expect (bank-interest 1000)   ? )
(check-expect (bank-interest 2500) (* 2500 .02)) ; or 50
(check-expect (bank-interest 4000)   ? )
(check-expect (bank-interest 5000) (* 5000 .03)) ; or 150
```

The "right answers" inside each sub-range are obvious: $800 is in the 1% range, so we compute 1% of $800 and get $8, and so on. But the problem statement is rather vague about the borderlines.

For the $500 borderline, the problem actually said "if you have *less than* $500 in the account ...", which suggests that *exactly* $500 should be treated as in the $500-$1000 category. Common sense agrees: if the bank paid no interest on a balance of $500, some customer with a balance of exactly $500 would complain, there'd be a TV news story about it, and the bank would come off looking petty and stingy. The other borderlines are less clear in the problem statement, but for consistency, and for the same public-relations reason as before, let's assume that $1000 is treated as in the $1000-$4000 category, and $4000 is treated as in the $4000-up category. So now we can fill in the rest of the right answers:

```
"Examples of bank-interest:"
(check-expect (bank-interest 200) 0)
(check-expect (bank-interest 500) (* 500 .01)) ; or 5
(check-expect (bank-interest 800) (* 800 .01)) ; or 8
(check-expect (bank-interest 1000) (* 1000 .02)) ; or 20
(check-expect (bank-interest 2500) (* 2500 .02)) ; or 50
(check-expect (bank-interest 4000) (* 4000 .03)) ; or 120
(check-expect (bank-interest 5000) (* 5000 .03)) ; or 150
```

Note that each of these "right answers" is found by multiplying the balance by an appropriate interest rate.

The skeleton is straightforward:

```
(define (bank-interest balance)
  ...)
```

The inventory is easy too:

```
(define (bank-interest balance)
  ; balance        a number, in dollars
  ...)
```

Since the input type is one of four choices, we'll probably need a four-clause cond ... but wait! All the "right answers" match the same "pattern": multiply the balance by the interest rate. So maybe this function should simply apply that formula, and leave the job of choosing the right interest rate to an *auxiliary function*, which might look something like this:

```
; bank-interest-rate :  number -> number
"Examples of bank-interest-rate:"
(check-expect (bank-interest-rate 200) 0)
(check-expect (bank-interest-rate 500) 0.01)
(check-expect (bank-interest-rate 800) 0.01)
(check-expect (bank-interest-rate 1000) 0.02)
(check-expect (bank-interest-rate 2500) 0.02)
(check-expect (bank-interest-rate 4000) 0.03)
(check-expect (bank-interest-rate 5000) 0.03)
```

Let's pretend for a moment that we had this bank-interest-rate function. Then bank-interest would be quite simple: compute the interest rate, and multiply by the balance.

```
(define (bank-interest balance)
  ; balance        a number, in dollars
  (* balance (bank-interest-rate balance))
)
```

We didn't need the four-clause conditional after all.

Of course, we're not done with the problem, since we haven't actually written the bank-interest-rate function. So let's write it. The next step in writing it is a skeleton:

```
(define (bank-interest-rate balance)
  ...)
```

The inventory contains a parameter name:

```
(define (bank-interest-rate balance)
  ; balance           a number, in dollars
  ...)
```

This time there's no obvious "pattern" that all the right answers fit; we actually need the conditional:

```
(define (bank-interest-rate balance)
  ; balance       a number in dollars
  (cond [...        ...]
        [...        ...]
        [...        ...]
        [...        ...]
))
```

Next, we need to fill in the questions and answers. The answers are easy:

```
(define (bank-interest-rate balance)
  ; balance       a number in dollars
  (cond [...        .00 ]
        [...        .01 ]
        [...        .02 ]
        [...        .03 ]
))
```

Next, under what conditions is the right answer 0? When the balance is under $500, *i.e.* (< balance 500). The "$4000-and-up" case is similarly easy: (>= balance 4000):

```
(define (bank-interest-rate balance)
  ; balance       a number in dollars
  (cond [ (< balance 500)       .00]
        [...                    .01]
        [...                    .02]
        [ (>= balance 4000)     .03]
))
```

The other two cases are a little trickier. The $500-$1000 bracket should include all the numbers that are at least 500, but strictly less than 1000, and the $1000-$4000 bracket should include all the numbers that are at least 1000, but strictly less than 4000. This calls for **and**:

```
(define (bank-interest-rate balance)
  ; balance       a number in dollars
  (cond [(< balance 500)            .00]
        [ (and (>= balance 500)
               (< balance 1000))    .01]
        [ (and (>= balance 1000)
               (< balance 4000))    .02]
        [(>= balance 4000)          .03]
))
```

We should now be able to test the `bank-interest-rate` function, and if it works, un-comment and test the `bank-interest` function. ■

15.5 Ordering cases in a conditional

The program could be written somewhat shorter and simpler by taking advantage of the *order* in which DrRacket evaluates the cases of a conditional: it looks at the second question only if the first wasn't true, looks at the third only if the second wasn't true, *etc.* If the first question, (< balance 500), isn't true, then we know that (>= balance 500) *must* be true, so we don't need to ask it. This simplifies the second question to (< balance 1000). Likewise, if this isn't true, then (>= balance 1000) *must* be true, so we can simplify the third question to (< balance 4000). If this in turn isn't true, then the fourth question (>= balance 4000) *must* be true, so we can simplify it to just else. The result is

```
(define (bank-interest-rate balance)
  ; balance       a number in dollars
  (cond [(< balance 500)   .00]
        [ (< balance 1000).01]
        [ (< balance 4000).02]
        [ else            .03]
))
```

This sort of simplification isn't always a good idea. In the original definition, the order of the cases in the cond doesn't matter: we could scramble them up, as in

```
(define (bank-interest-rate balance)
  ; balance       a number in dollars
  (cond [(and (>= balance 500)
              (< balance 1000))    .01]
        [(and (>= balance 1000)
              (< balance 4000))    .02]
        [(>= balance 4000)         .03]
        [(< balance 500)           .00]
))
```

and the function would work just as well, although it might be slightly harder to read. This is because *the cases don't overlap*: there's no possible value of balance for which two different questions would be true, so it doesn't matter in what order we ask the questions. By looking at any one of the cases, you can tell when it will happen.

However, in the "simplified" version above, the second question *includes* the first question, the third includes the second, and the fourth includes everything. As a result, if you scrambled the order of the cases in the "simplified" definition, you would get wrong answers. And to understand when any one of the cases will happen, you need to read not only that case but all the ones before it as well. This is no big deal for this program, which has only four cases, but imagine a program with dozens or hundreds of cases, added by several programmers over the course of weeks or months: to understand under what circumstances the 46th case will happen, you would have to read the first 45 as well!

I generally recommend writing the questions of a conditional so that *no two overlap*, and each one completely describes the situations in which it will happen. I have three exceptions to this rule:

- if one of the cases really is best described as "anything else", then I would use an `else` as the last question;

- if there are only two cases, I would use `else` as the second question rather than repeating the whole first question with a `not` around it (or, better, use another Racket construct named `if` instead of `cond` — look it up!); and

- if I'm extremely concerned about the speed of the program, I'll take full advantage of the order of the questions to simplify the later ones, in order to save a few microseconds.

Different teachers have different opinions on this: if your instructor prefers the version that takes advantage of the order of questions, go ahead and do it that way.

Exercise 15.5.1 *A carpet store needs a function to compute how much to charge its customers. Carpeting costs $5/yard, but if you buy 100 yards or more, there's a 10% discount on the whole order, and if you buy 500 yards or more, the discount becomes 20% on the whole order.*

Develop a function `carpet-price` *that takes in the number of yards of carpeting and returns its total price.*

Exercise 15.5.2 *Develop a function named* `digital-thermometer` *that takes in a temperature (in degrees Fahrenheit) and produces an image of the temperature as a number, colored either green (below 99°), yellow (at least 99° but less than 101°) or red (at least 101°).*

For example,

```
(digital-thermometer 98.3)
98.3
(digital-thermometer 99.5)
99.5
(digital-thermometer 102.7)
102.7
```

(The first one is supposed to be green, the second yellow, and the third red.)

Hint: To convert a number to a string, use `number->string`. However, if you try it on a number like 98.6, you may get a fraction rather than a decimal. If you want it in decimal form, first make it inexact, using `exact->inexact`.

Hint: Use an auxiliary function to choose the color.

Exercise 15.5.3 *Develop a function named* `letter-grade` *that takes in a grade average on a 100-point scale and returns one of the strings* `"A"`, `"B"`, `"C"`, `"D"`, *or* `"F"`, *according to the rule*

- *An average of 90 or better is an A;*

- *An average of at least 80 but less than 90 is a B;*

- *An average of at least 70 but less than 80 is a C;*

- *An average of at least 60 but less than 70 is a D;*

- *An average of less than 60 is an F.*

Exercise 15.5.4 *Three candidates (Anne, Bob, and Charlie) are running for mayor of Racketville, which, by court order, has a new computerized voting system.* **Develop a function** *named who-won that takes in three numbers (the number of votes for Anne, the number of votes for Bob, and the number of votes for Charlie, respectively) and returns a string indicating who won – either "Anne", "Bob", or "Charlie". If two or more candidates tied for first place, the function should return "tie".*

Exercise 15.5.5 **Develop a function** *named 4-votes->winner that takes in four strings representing votes, and returns the name of the winner (or "tie" if there was a tie). You may assume that the only candidates in the race are "Anne", "Bob", and "Charlie" (this makes it much easier!)*

Hint: This should be short and simple if you re-use previously-defined functions.

Exercise 15.5.6 *Some credit card companies give you a refund at the end of the year depending on how much you've used the card. Imagine a company that pays back*

- *0.25% of the first $500 you charge;*

- *0.50% of the next $1000 you charge (i.e. anything you charge between $500 and $1500);*

- *0.75% of the next $1000 you charge (i.e. between $1500 and $2500);*

- *1% of anything you charge over $2500.*

For example, a customer who charged $400 would get back $1.00, which is 0.25% of $400. A customer who charged $1400 would get back 0.25% of the first $500 (making $1.25), plus 0.50% of the next $900 (i.e. $4.50), for a total refund of $5.75.

Develop a function card-refund to determine how much refund will be paid to a customer who has charged a specified amount on the card.

15.6 Unnecessary conditionals

The above recipe may seem to contradict the way we wrote functions in Chapter 13: in most of the problems in that chapter, there were two or more categories of input, and two categories of output (true and false), yet we didn't need any conditionals. For example, recall Worked Exercise 13.3.1, whose definition was

```
(define (may-drive?  age)
  ; age      a number
  ; 16       a fixed number we're likely to need
  (>= age 16)
  )
```

In fact, we could have written this one using a conditional too:

```
(define (may-drive?  age)
  ; age      a number
  ; 16       a fixed number we're likely to need
  (cond   [(>= age 16) true]
          [(< age 16) false]
  ) )
```

and it would work perfectly well, but it's longer and more complicated than the previous version. Indeed, *every* function in Chapter 13 could have been written using a conditional, and would be longer and more complicated that way.

Rule of thumb: Functions that return Boolean can usually be written more simply without a conditional than with one.

Since `string=?`, `=`, and so on return Booleans, their results can be compared using `boolean=?`:

```
(define (reply greeting)
  ; greeting        a string
  (cond [ (boolean=? (string=? greeting "good morning")   true)
          "I need coffee"]
        [ (boolean=? (string=? greeting "good afternoon")   true)
          "I need a nap"]
        [ (boolean=? (string=? greeting "good night")   true)
          "bedtime!"]
  ))
```

This works perfectly well, and passes all its test cases, but it's longer and more complicated than necessary. Likewise

```
(define (not-teenager?  age)
  ; age        a number
  (boolean=? (and (>= age 13) (< age 20))   false)
  )
```

could be more briefly written as

```
(define (not-teenager?  age)
  ; age        a number
  (not (and (>= age 13) (< age 20)))
  )
```

or as

```
(define (not-teenager?  age)
  ; age        a number
  (or ( < age 13) ( >= age 20)))
  )
```

Rule of thumb: If you're using `boolean=?`, you're probably making things longer and more complicated than they need to be.

(The only time I can imagine needing `boolean=?` is when I have two Boolean expressions, and I don't care whether either one is true or false as long as they match. This isn't very common.)

For another example, recall Exercise 13.7.1, which we wrote as follows:

```
(define (18-to-25?  age)
  ; 18                a fixed number we'll need
  ; 25                another fixed number we'll need
  ; (>= age 18)       a Boolean
  ; (<= age 25)       a Boolean
  (and (>= age 18)
       (<= age 25))
  )
```

We *could* have written this using a conditional:

```
(define (18-to-25?  age)
  ; age              a number
  ; 18               a fixed number we'll need
  ; 25               another fixed number we'll need
  ; (>= age 18)      a Boolean
  ; (<= age 25)      a Boolean
  (cond   [(>= age 18) (<= age 25)]
          [(< age 18) false])
)
```

or even (putting one conditional inside another)

```
(define (18-to-25?  age)
  ; age              a number
  ; 18               a fixed number we'll need
  ; 25               another fixed number we'll need
  ; (>= age 18)      a Boolean
  ; (<= age 25)      a Boolean
  (cond   [(>= age 18) (cond   [(<= age 25) true]
                               [(> age 25) false])
          [(< age 18)  false])
)
```

but again, these definitions are longer and more complicated than the one that doesn't use a conditional.

15.7 Nested conditionals

Yes, you can put one conditional inside another. The "answer" part of each cond-clause is allowed to be any expression, and a cond is an expression, so why not? In the example above, it wasn't necessary, and even made the program longer and harder to understand. But there are situations in which nested conditionals are the most natural way to solve a problem.

Worked Exercise 15.7.1 *Imagine that you work for a company that sells clothes over the Internet: a Web page has a menu from which customers can choose which item of clothing, and which color, they're interested in. For simplicity, let's suppose there are only three items of clothing: pants, shirt, and shoes. The pants are available in black or navy; the shirt is available in white or pink; and the shoes are available in pink, burgundy, or navy. Your company photographer has given you pictures of all seven of these items, which you've copied and pasted into DrRacket under the variable names* black-pants, navy-pants, pink-shirt, white-shirt, pink-shoes, burgundy-shoes, *and* navy-shoes.*

   Develop a function show-clothing *that takes in two strings representing the item of clothing and the color, and returns a picture of the item of clothing. If the requested combination of item and color doesn't exist, it should return an appropriate error message.*

Solution: The **contract** is clearly
```
; show-clothing:  string(item) string(color) -> image
```
But wait: sometimes the function is supposed to return an error message instead! There are at least two ways we can handle this: we could either build an image of the error message (using the text function), or we could change the contract to return "image or

string". For now, we'll opt for consistency and always return an image. (In Chapter 19, we'll see another way to handle this.)

There are seven legal **examples**, and to be really confident we should test them all:

```
(check-expect (show-clothing "pants" "black") black-pants)
(check-expect (show-clothing "pants" "navy") navy-pants)
(check-expect (show-clothing "shirt" "white") white-shirt)
(check-expect (show-clothing "shirt" "pink") pink-shirt)
(check-expect (show-clothing "shoes" "pink") pink-shoes)
(check-expect (show-clothing "shoes" "burgundy") burgundy-shoes)
(check-expect (show-clothing "shoes" "navy") navy-shoes)
```

In addition, we should have some illegal examples to test the handling of nonexistent items, unrecognized colors, etc.

```
(check-expect (show-clothing "hat" "black")
  (text "What's a hat?" 12 "red"))
(check-expect (show-clothing "pants" "burgundy")
  (text "We don't have pants in burgundy" 12 "red"))
```

The **skeleton** is easy:

```
(define (show-clothing item color)
  ...)
```

The **inventory** is fairly straightforward too:

```
(define (show-clothing item color)
  ; item          string
  ; color         string
  ; "pants"       string
  ; "shirt"       string
  ; "shoes"       string
  ; "black"       string
  ; "navy"        string
  ; "white"       string
  ; "pink"        string
  ; "burgundy"    string
  ...)
```

(Writing an inventory entry for every one of these literal strings is really boring, and if it's OK with your instructor, feel free to skip this.) We may also need some other expressions in order to build the error messages, but we'll come back to that later.

We know that `item` is supposed to be either `"pants"`, `"shirt"`, or `"shoes"` (or "anything else"), so the body of the function will need a conditional with four cases:

```
(define (show-clothing item color)
  ; item     string
  ; color    string
  (cond [(string=? item "pants")   ...]
        [(string=? item "shirt")   ...]
        [(string=? item "shoes")   ...]
        [else                      ...])
)
```

If the item is in fact "pants", the color can be either "black", "navy", or "anything else", which can be most naturally represented by *another* **cond** *inside the first one*:

```
(define (show-clothing item color)
  ; item     string
  ; color    string
  (cond [ (string=?  item "pants")
          (cond [(string=?  color "black")     ...]
                [(string=?  color "navy")      ...]
                [else  ...])]
        [ (string=?  item "shirt") ...]
        [ (string=?  item "shoes") ...]
        [ else                     ...])
)
```

We can do the same thing for "shirt" and "shoes":

```
(define (show-clothing item color)
  ; item     string
  ; color    string
  (cond [ (string=?  item "pants")
          (cond [(string=?  color "black")     ...]
                [(string=?  color "navy")      ...]
                [else                   ...])]
        [(string=?  item "shirt")
          (cond [(string=?  color "pink")      ...]
                [(string=?  color "white")     ...]
                [else                   ...])]
        [(string=?  item "shoes")
          (cond [(string=?  color "pink")      ...]
                [(string=?  color "burgundy") ...]
                [(string=?  color "navy")      ...]
                [else                   ...])]
        [ else  ...])
)
```

After figuring out all of these conditions, the legal answers are easy:

```
(define (show-clothing item color)
  ; item      string
  ; color     string
  (cond [ (string=?  item "pants")
          (cond [(string=?  color "black")    black-pants ]
                [(string=?  color "navy")     navy-pants ]
                [else                         ...])]
        [(string=?  item "shirt")
          (cond [(string=?  color "pink")     pink-shirt ]
                [(string=?  color "white")    white-shirt ]
                [else                         ...])]
        [(string=?  item "shoes")
          (cond [(string=?  color "pink")     pink-shoes ]
                [(string=?  color "burgundy") burgundy-shoes ]
                [(string=?  color "navy")     navy-shoes ]
                [else                         ...])]
        [ else  ...])
  )
```

All that remains is constructing the error messages, which we can do using text and string-append. But this function definition is getting pretty long already; since building these error messages really is a completely different sort of job from what we've been doing so far, let's have it done by auxiliary functions. Here's one to handle unrecognized items:

```
; bad-item :  string(item) -> image
(define (bad-item item)
  ; item                              string
  ; (string-append "What's a " item "?")    string
  ; 12                                number (font size)
  ; "red"                            string (text color)
  (text (string-append "What's a " item "?") 12 "red")
  )
"Examples of bad-item:"
(check-expect (bad-item "hat") (text) "What's a hat?" 12 "red")
(check-expect (bad-item "belt") (text) "What's a belt?" 12 "red")
```

The analogous function for unrecognized colors is left for you to do; see Exercise 15.7.2 below.

The final definition of show-clothing looks like
```
(define (show-clothing item color)
  ; item      string
  ; color     string
  (cond [ (string=? item "pants")
          (cond [(string=? color "black")    black-pants ]
                [(string=? color "navy")     navy-pants ]
                [else             (bad-color item color) ])]
        [(string=? item "shirt")
          (cond [(string=? color "pink")     pink-shirt ]
                [(string=? color "white")    white-shirt ]
                [else             (bad-color item color) ])]
        [(string=? item "shoes")
          (cond [(string=? color "pink")     pink-shoes ]
                [(string=? color "burgundy") burgundy-shoes ]
                [(string=? color "navy")     navy-shoes ]
                [else             (bad-color item color) ])]
        [ else            (bad-item item) ])
)
```
∎

Exercise 15.7.2 *Write the* bad-color *function needed in the above example.*

Exercise 15.7.3 *Develop a function* make-shape *that takes in three strings: a shape (either* "circle" *or* "triangle"*), a size (either* "small"*,* "medium"*, or* "large"*), and a color (any color that DrRacket recognizes), and produces an appropriate image.*
Note: *Make sure that a "medium circle" and a "medium triangle" are about the same size.*

15.8 Decisions among data types

Most the functions we've written so far have expected one specific type of input, and produced one specific type of output — number, string, image, boolean, *etc.* But sometimes a function needs to be able to handle input of *several different types*. We'll see more useful applications of this ability in the next few chapters, but for now simply imagine a function that takes in a number, which a confused user mistakenly puts in quotation marks. The user would get an unfriendly error message like

+: expects type <number> as 1st argument, given "4"; other arguments were: 3

It would be *really* nice if our program could figure out that by "4" the user probably meant the number 4. Even if we didn't want to go that far, or if there *were* nothing reasonable our program could do with the incorrect input, it would be nice if our program could produce a friendlier message like

This program expects a number, like 3. You typed a quoted string, "4".

To do this, our program would need to recognize that the input was a string rather than a number as expected.

The ability to make decisions based on the types of our inputs (which computer scientists call *polymorphism*) will be useful in a number of ways. In Chapter 19 we'll see how to produce friendly error messages like the above. But first, how do we detect different types?

Recall from Chapter 13 that Racket has built-in *type predicates*, functions that take in *any* type of input (including types you haven't seen yet) and return either `true` or `false` depending on whether the input is of that particular type. For example,

```
; number?  :  anything -> boolean
; image?  :  anything -> boolean
; string?  :  anything -> boolean
; boolean?  :  anything -> boolean
; integer?  :  anything -> boolean
...
```

With these functions in hand, and the decision-making ability provided by `cond`, one can easily write functions that operate differently on different types of inputs.

Worked Exercise 15.8.1 *Develop a function* `classify` *that tells what type its input is, by returning one of the strings* `"image"`, `"string"`, `"number"`, *or* `"other"` *as appropriate.*

(The only "other" type you've seen so far is boolean, *but we'll see more in the next few chapters.)*

Solution: The contract is

```
; classify :  anything -> string
```

In the data analysis step, we observe that not just any string can be produced; the result is always one of four choices, so a more informative contract would be

```
; classify :  anything -> string
; ("image", "string", "number", or "other")
```

(We could write an outventory template for this, but we don't expect to be writing lots of functions that produce this type, so we won't bother.)

For that matter, the input is indeed "anything", but we're interested in which of four categories it falls into (image, string, number, or anything else), so we could even write

```
; classify :  anything (image, string, number, or anything else) ->
; string ("image", "string", "number", or "other")
```

(Again, we could write an inventory template for this, but we don't expect to be writing lots of functions that divide the world up in this particular way, so we won't bother.)

Since the input and output data types each fall into four categories, there should be at least four examples:

```
"Examples of classify:"
(check-expect (classify (circle 5 "solid" "green")) "image")
(check-expect (classify "hello there") "string")
(check-expect (classify 74) "number")
(check-expect (classify true) "other")
```

The skeleton is simple:

```
(define (classify thing)
   ...)
```

For the inventory, we normally start by listing parameters and labeling each one with its type. In this case, we don't *know* what data type `thing` is.

```
(define (classify thing)
  ; thing          anything
  ...)
```

However, we know that there are four categories, both of input and of output, so we can reasonably guess that the body of the function will involve a `cond` with four clauses:

```
(define (classify thing)
  ; thing          anything
  (cond   [...            ...]
          [...            ...]
          [...            ...]
          [...            ...]
        )
)
```

The next step in writing a function involving conditionals is normally to fill in either all the questions or all the answers, whichever is easier. We know that the answers are `"image"`, `"string"`, and so on, so we can fill them in easily:

```
(define (classify thing)
  ; thing          anything
  (cond [...      "image" ]
        [...      "string" ]
        [...      "number" ]
        [...      "other" ]
      )
)
```

We still need to fill in the questions. The only expression we have available to work with is the parameter `thing`, so we must ask questions about it. Under what circumstances is the right answer `"image"`? Obviously, when `thing` is an image. Conveniently, the `image?` function tests this. We can test the other types similarly.

```
(define (classify thing)
  ; thing          anything
  (cond [ (image?  thing)    "image"]
        [ (string? thing)    "string" ]
        [ (number? thing)    "number" ]
        [ else               "other" ]
      )
)
```

Note the `else` in the last clause, which catches any input that hasn't matched any of the previous criteria. ∎

Exercise 15.8.2 *Define a function named size that takes in a number, a string, or an image, and returns "how big it is". For a number, this means the absolute value of the* *number. For a string, it means the length of the string. For an image, it means the number of pixels, i.e. the width times the height.*

Exercise 15.8.3 *Define a function named* `big?` *that takes in either a number or a string, and tells whether the argument is "big". What does "big" mean? For numbers, let's say it means at least 1000, and for strings, let's say it's any string of length 10 or more.*

Hint: The function needs to handle two kinds of input, and for each kind of input there are two possible answers and a "borderline", so you'll need six test cases.

Exercise 15.8.4 *Develop a function named* `same?` *that takes in two arguments, each of which is either a number or a string, and tells whether they're "the same". If one is a number and the other a string, they're obviously* not *"the same"; if both are numbers, you can compare them using =; and if both are strings, you can compare them using* `string=?`*.*

There's actually a built-in function `equal?` that does this and more: it compares *any* two objects, no matter what types, to tell whether they're the same. You may not use it in writing Exercise 15.8.4. You may use it in the rest of the book (except where I specifically tell you not to), but in most cases it's a better idea to use something more specific like =, `string=?`, `key=?`, *etc.* because if you accidentally violate a contract and call one of these on the wrong type of input, you'll get an error message immediately rather than the program going on as if everything were OK. Eventually it would probably produce wrong answers, which are *much harder to track down and fix than error messages.*

Exercise 15.8.5 *Develop a function named* `smart-add` *that takes two parameters and adds them. The trick is that the parameters can be either numbers (like 17) or strings of digits (like "17"); your function has to be able to handle both.*

Hint: There are two parameters, each of which could be either of two types, so you'll need at least four examples.

15.9   Review of important words and concepts

Much of the power of computers comes from their ability to *make decisions* on their own, using *conditionals*. A Racket conditional consists of the word `cond` and a sequence of *question/answer* clauses: it evaluates each *question* in turn is evaluated, and as soon as one comes out `true`, it returns the value of the corresponding *answer*. If none of the *questions* evaluates to `true`, you get an error message. If you want to avoid this error message, you can add another *question/answer* clause at the end, with the *question* being simply the word `else`, which guarantees that if none of the previous *answers* was true, this one will be. This is often used for error-handling.

In order to design functions that make decisions, we add some details to the *skeleton* and *body* steps of the design recipe: we write the skeleton of a `cond`, with the right number of cases, and then fill in the questions and the answers (I recommend either all the questions, then all the answers, or *vice versa*, depending on which is easier).

Functions that return `boolean` can usually be written shorter and simpler *without* a conditional than *with* one. Almost any time you use the `boolean=?` function, you could have accomplished the same thing more simply without it.

If a function has two or more inputs that *each* come in multiple categories, or if a type has sub-categories of a specific category, often the most natural way to write the function is with *nested conditionals*: the *answer* part of a conditional is itself another whole conditional. However, if you find yourself doing this, there may be a shorter and simpler way that *doesn't* require nested conditionals.

People normally write Racket functions to take in particular types of arguments, but you can also design a function to be more flexible, checking for itself what types its arguments were and handling them appropriately. Every built-in Racket type has a *discriminator* function, also known as a *type predicate*, whose name is the name of the type, with a question-mark at the end (*e.g.* `number?`, `string?`, `image?`) which takes in anything and tells whether or not it is of that type. You can use these discriminator functions in a conditional to write *polymorphic functions*, functions that work differently on different types of inputs.

15.10 Reference: Built-in functions for making decisions

In this chapter, we've introduced one new function: `equal?`, which takes in two parameters of *any* types and tells whether they're the same. In general, it's a good idea to use something more specific, like `string=?` or `=`, because you'll catch mistakes faster that way.

This chapter also introduced the Syntax Rule 6, with the *reserved words* `cond` and `else`. (A *reserved word* is a word whose meaning is built into the Racket language and can't be changed, but which isn't called like a function. In particular, the reserved word `else` can *only* appear as the *last question* in a `cond`.)

For the common case of a `cond` with only two cases, the second of which is `else`, there's a shorter form:

```
(if question answer-if-true answer-if-false)
```

Look it up in the Help Desk.

Chapter 16

New types and templates

16.1 Definition by choices

In Exercise 15.1.4, the contract said the input and output types were both *string*. This is a bit over-simplified. In fact, the input is supposed to be one of three possibilities, and the output will also be one of three possibilities.

In a sense, we've invented two new data types *greeting* and *answer*:

```
; A greeting is one of the strings "good morning",
; "good afternoon", or "good night"
; An answer is one of the strings "I need coffee",
; "I need a nap", or "bedtime!"

; reply :  greeting -> answer
; test cases as before
; definition as before
```

This may not seem important yet, but thinking of the input and the output as new data types actually helps us write the program. Since the input and output types are both three-way choices, there must be at least three test cases — one for each possibility — and the body of the method is probably a three-clause conditional. Furthermore, if we ever write *another* function that takes in or returns the *greeting* or *answer* type, it too will need at least three test cases, and its body will probably also involve a three-clause conditional.

The notion of defining a new data type as one of a specified set of choices is called "definition by choices". The predefined Boolean type can also be thought of as defined by choices: it has two choices, `true` and `false`, and as we've already seen, any function that returns a Boolean should have at least two test cases, one returning `true` and one returning `false`.

16.2 Inventories and templates

Suppose we were writing several functions that *each* took in a *greeting*, but all returned different kinds of things. The examples and function definitions would all look pretty similar: there would be three examples, using `"good morning"`, `"good afternoon"`, and `"good night"` respectively, and the function definition would involve a conditional with three clauses, each question comparing the parameter with a different one of these strings.

223

Since so much of the code is identical from one function to another, it might save time to write the identical part once and for all. We'll put it in #| ...|# comments, for reasons that will become clear shortly.

```
#|
(check-expect (function-on-greeting "good morning") ...)
(check-expect (function-on-greeting "good afternoon") ...)
(check-expect (function-on-greeting "good night") ...)

(define (function-on-greeting greeting)
  ; greeting             a greeting, as defined above
  (cond [(string=?  greeting "good morning")    ...]
        [(string=?  greeting "good afternoon") ...]
        [(string=?  greeting "good night")      ...]
))
|#
```

This isn't a "real" function, obviously — the answers to the cond-clauses aren't filled in, and we don't even know what *types* they should be, much less the right answers — but rather a *template* for functions that take in a greeting. The template includes everything we can say about the function and its test cases just by knowing the input data type.

Now, every time you want to write a *real* function that takes in that data type, simply copy-and-paste everything between the #| and |#, change the name of the function, and you're 90% done.

Worked Exercise 16.2.1 *Write a template for functions that operate on bank balances, as defined in Exercise 15.4.1.*

Then use this template to write two functions: bank-interest-rate (as before) and customer-type, which categorizes customers as "rich", "moderate", "poor", or "college student" depending on the size of their bank account, using the same dividing lines.

Solution: We'll start by defining the new data type *bank-balance*:

```
; A bank-balance is a number, in one of the categories
; 0-500 (not including 500); 500-1000 (not including 1000);
; 1000-4000 (not including 4000); and 4000-up.
```

Obviously, there are four choices. The template looks like

```
#|
(check-expect (function-on-bank-balance 200) ...)
(check-expect (function-on-bank-balance 500) ...)
(check-expect (function-on-bank-balance 800) ...)
(check-expect (function-on-bank-balance 1000) ...)
(check-expect (function-on-bank-balance 2000) ...)
(check-expect (function-on-bank-balance 4000) ...)
(check-expect (function-on-bank-balance 7500) ...)

(define (function-on-bank-balance balance)
  ; balance       a bank-balance
  (cond [(< balance 500)           ...]
        [(and (>= balance 500)
              (< balance 1000)     ...]
        [(and (>= balance 1000)
              (< balance 4000)     ...]
        [(>= balance 4000)         ...]
  ))
|#
```

The contract for bank-interest is

```
; bank-interest-rate :  bank-balance ->
                              number (either 0, 0.01, 0.02, or 0.03)
```

Next, copy-and-paste the template and change the name of the function:

```
(check-expect ( bank-interest-rate 200) ...)
(check-expect ( bank-interest-rate 500) ...)
(check-expect ( bank-interest-rate 800) ...)
(check-expect ( bank-interest-rate 1000) ...)
(check-expect ( bank-interest-rate 2000) ...)
(check-expect ( bank-interest-rate 4000) ...)
(check-expect ( bank-interest-rate 7500) ...)

(define ( bank-interest-rate balance)
  ; balance       a bank-balance
  (cond [(< balance 500)           ...]
        [(and (>= balance 500)
              (< balance 1000)     ...]
        [(and (>= balance 1000)
              (< balance 4000)     ...]
        [(>= balance 4000)         ...]
  ))
```

Replace the ... in the examples with the right answers for the problem you're trying to solve:

```
(check-expect (bank-interest-rate 200)    0.00 )
(check-expect (bank-interest-rate 500)    0.01 )
(check-expect (bank-interest-rate 800)    0.01 )
(check-expect (bank-interest-rate 1000)   0.02 )
(check-expect (bank-interest-rate 2000)   0.02 )
(check-expect (bank-interest-rate 4000)   0.03 )
(check-expect (bank-interest-rate 7500)   0.03 )
```

Finally, replace the ... in the cond-clause answers with the right answers for the problem you're trying to solve:

```
(define (bank-interest-rate balance)
  ; balance      a bank-balance
  (cond [(< balance 500)             0.00 ]
        [(and (>= balance 500)
              (< balance 1000)       0.01 ]
        [(and (>= balance 1000)
              (< balance 4000)       0.02 ]
        [(>= balance 4000)           0.03 ]
  ))
```

This should pass all its tests.

Now for customer-type. The contract is

```
; customer-type :  bank-balance -> string
;   ("rich", "moderate", "poor", or "college student")
```

By copying the template and changing the function name, we get

```
(check-expect ( customer-type 200) ...)
(check-expect ( customer-type 500) ...)
(check-expect ( customer-type 800) ...)
(check-expect ( customer-type 1000) ...)
(check-expect ( customer-type 2000) ...)
(check-expect ( customer-type 4000) ...)
(check-expect ( customer-type 7500) ...)

(define ( customer-type balance)
  ; balance      a bank-balance
  (cond [(< balance 500)           ...]
        [(and (>= balance 500)
              (< balance 1000)     ...]
        [(and (>= balance 1000)
              (< balance 4000)     ...]
        [(>= balance 4000)         ...]
  ))
```

We fill in the right answers in the examples:

```
(check-expect (customer-type 200)    "college student" )
(check-expect (customer-type 500)    "poor" )
(check-expect (customer-type 800)    "poor" )
(check-expect (customer-type 1000)   "moderate" )
(check-expect (customer-type 2000)   "moderate" )
(check-expect (customer-type 4000)   "rich" )
(check-expect (customer-type 7500)   "rich" )
```

and then in the body of the function:

```
(define ( customer-type balance)
  ; balance       a bank-balance
  (cond [(< balance 500)               "college student" ]
        [(and (>= balance 500)
              (< balance 1000)         "poor" ]
        [(and (>= balance 1000)
              (< balance 4000)         "moderate" ]
        [(>= balance 4000)             "rich" ]
))
```

This should pass all its test cases. ∎

16.3 Outventories and templates

Likewise, suppose we were writing several functions that each *returned* an *answer*. They would probably all look like

```
#|
(check-expect (function-returning-answer ...)  "I need coffee")
(check-expect (function-returning-answer ...)  "I need a nap")
(check-expect (function-returning-answer ...)  "bedtime!")

(define (function-returning-answer whatever)
  (cond [...    "I need coffee"]
        [...    "I need a nap"]
        [...    "bedtime!"]
))
|#
```

Again, this obviously isn't a "real function", since this time the *questions* aren't filled in; it's only a *template* for functions that return a result of a particular type. It doesn't have an inventory, since we don't even know what type the input is, but it has what we might call an "outventory": the expressions likely to be needed to construct the right kind of answer.

Whereas an "inventory" answers the question "what am I given, and what can I do with it?", an "outventory" answers the question "what do I need to produce, and how can I produce it?". To use the cooking analogy, the "outventory" for a batch of cookies would involve observing that the *last* step of the process is baking, so we'd better find a cookie sheet and preheat the oven. Just as one can write a template based on an inventory, one can also write a template based on an outventory.

When you're writing a real function, you may have to choose between a template based on the input type and one based on the output type. In general, use the *more complicated* one. If the input type is more complicated than the output type, its template will be more detailed so you'll have less work left to do yourself. On the other hand, if the output type is more complicated than the input type (which happens less often), you should use an output-based template because it'll do more of the work for you.

16.4   Else and definition by choices

When we introduced an `else` case into Exercise 15.1.4, we were effectively changing the contract and data analysis: the function no longer took in one of three specific strings, but rather those three *or "any other string"*. In other words, the type definitions became something like

```
; A safe-greeting is one of four possibilities:  "good morning",
; "good afternoon", "good evening", or any other string.
; A safe-answer is one of four possibilities:  "I need coffee",
; "I need a nap", "bedtime!", or "huh?".
```

Technically, we could write the contract as

```
; replay :  string -> safe-answer
```

because the function now accepts *any* string, but it's more useful to think of it as

```
; reply :  safe-greeting -> safe-answer
```

since *safe-greeting*'s four possibilities tell us how to choose test cases: we need a "good morning", a "good afternoon", a "good evening", and some other string. The four possibilities of the input type also tell us how to write the body of the function: a four-way conditional, checking whether the input is "good morning", "good afternoon", "good evening", or any other string (which we can handle naturally using `else`); we need only to fill in the answers.

Alternatively, we could use the four cases of the result type *safe-answer* to tell us that we'll need four test cases — one returning each of the four legal answers. The outventory gives us a conditional with four clauses, with answers "I need coffee", "I need a nap", "bedtime!", and "huh?"; we need only to fill in the questions.

16.5   A bigger, better design recipe

At this point I often find that students get confused between designing a function and designing a data type. Indeed, designing a function often requires that you design one or more data types first. The recipe in Figure 16.5 starts with the difference between function and data type, and then gives a series of steps for each one.

Exercise 16.5.1 *Re-do some of the problems from Chapter 15 in this style.*

16.6   Review of important words and concepts

When we write a function that makes decisions, it often helps to think of the input and/or output type as a *new data type defined by choices*. This helps us choose test cases, and helps again in getting from a function skeleton to a complete function body.

Figure 16.1: Design recipe, with definition by choices

Are you defining a function or a type?	
Functions are analogous to verbs in human languages: they represent *actions* that happen to particular things (the arguments) at a particular time. For example, `+` and `beside` are predefined functions, while `checkerboard2` and `cube` are user-defined functions.	**Data types** are like improper nouns (*e.g.* "computer", "student", "program") in human languages: they represent a *kind of thing*. Racket's built-in data types include "number", "boolean", "string", "image", *etc.* and you can define others like "bank-balance" and "letter-grade". A data type is not "called" at any particular time on any particular arguments, and it doesn't "return" a result; it just *is*.
Write a **contract** (and perhaps a **purpose statement**)	Identify the choices: how many distinct categories or values are there, and how can you detect each one? Are there borderlines to worry about?
Write **examples** of function calls, with correct answers, *e.g.* using `check-expect`. If you have a template for the input or output data type, use it as a starting point for the examples, skeleton and inventory.	Write **examples** of the new data type, one for each category. You don't need "correct answers", since the examples *are* the "correct answers". If your data type consists of sub-ranges, make sure to include examples at the boundaries.
Write a function skeleton and inventory. If you have a template for the input or output data type, use it as a starting point.	If you expect to write more than one function taking in the new type, write an **inventory template**. If you expect to write more than one function returning the new type, write an **outventory template**.
Fill in the function **body**. If it isn't obvious how to put together the pieces to get a right answer, try an **inventory with values** first.	
Proofread for errors that you can spot yourself	
Check Syntax for syntax errors that the computer can spot	
Test the program to make sure it produces correct answers	

If we expect to be writing *several* functions with the same input type or the same output type, it may save us time to write a *function template*: a function skeleton, with an inventory and/or outventory, but no actual code. A template should say as much as you can say about the function by knowing only its input and output types, but not knowing what specific problem it's supposed to solve. Once you've written one, you can copy-and-paste it as a starting point for *every* function you need to write that has that input type or that output type.

16.7   Reference

No new functions or syntax rules were introduced in this chapter.

Chapter 17

Animations that make decisions

17.1 String decisions

Worked Exercise 17.1.1 *Develop an animation* of a simple traffic light. It should initially show a green disk; after 5 seconds, it should change to yellow; after another 5 seconds, to red; after another 5 seconds, back to green, and so on.

Solution: The first step in writing an animation is deciding what handlers we'll need. This problem doesn't mention the mouse or the keyboard, but does mention regularly-scheduled events, so we'll need a tick handler and a draw handler. And as usual, it's a good idea to have a `check-with` clause.

The next step is choosing an appropriate data type for the model. The model represents the current state of the animation, and every 5 seconds we'll need to *make a decision* to choose the *next* state of the model.

There are several different data types we could use for this animation, and we'll compare them in Exercise 17.1.4. For now, let's say our model is a string representing the current color. There are three possible values of the model — "green", "yellow", and "red" — so we could formalize this with the definition by choices

```
; A light-color is any of the strings "green", "yellow", or "red".
```

The next step in designing a new data type is to write down some examples: in our case, they're obviously "green", "yellow", and "red".

We might need to write several functions involving this type, so we'll write an inventory template:

```
#|
(check-expect (function-on-light-color "green") ...)
(check-expect (function-on-light-color "yellow") ...)
(check-expect (function-on-light-color "red") ...)

(define (function-on-light-color c)
  (cond [(string=? c "green")  ...]
        [(string=? c "yellow") ...]
        [(string=? c "red")    ...]
  ))
|#
```

and an "outventory" template:

```
#|
(check-expect (function-returning-light-color ...)  "green")
(check-expect (function-returning-light-color ...)  "yellow")
(check-expect (function-returning-light-color ...)  "red")

(define (function-returning-light-color c)
  (cond [...               "green"]
        [...               "yellow"]
        [...               "red"]
  ))
|#
```

This animation changes every five seconds, so we need a tick handler. Its contract must be *model* → *model*. Since "model" for our purposes means "light-color", our contract will look like

```
; change-light :  light-color -> light-color
```

This function both takes in and returns a "light-color", so we can use both the input-based and output-based templates for "light-color" to help us write the function.

The input and output templates agree that we need at least three examples. The input template says there should be one taking in each of the three colors, and the output template says there should be one returning each of the three colors. Fortunately, we can meet both of these requirements as follows:

```
(check-expect (change-light "green") "yellow")
(check-expect (change-light "yellow") "red")
(check-expect (change-light "red") "green")
```

The inventory template says

```
(define (change-light color)
  ; color                                light-color
  (cond [(string=? color "green")   ...]
        [(string=? color "yellow")  ...]
        [(string=? color "red")     ...]
  ))
```

while the output template says each of the three colors should appear in the *answer* part of a cond-clause. We can satisfy both of them as follows:

```
(define (change-light color)
  ; color                        light-color
  (cond [(string=? color "green")  "yellow" ]
        [(string=? color "yellow") "red" ]
        [(string=? color "red")    "green" ]
        )
  )
```

and the definition is finished (once it passes its tests).

By the way, if we had decided to start with the output-based template rather than the input-based template, we would have gotten

```
(define (change-light color)
  ; color       light-color
  (cond [...    "green" ]
        [...    "yellow" ]
        [...    "red" ]
        ))
```

and then filled in the appropriate questions to get to each answer; the final result would be the same.

We still need a draw handler. Let's name it show-light, since that's what it does. The contract of a draw handler is always *something : model → image*, and we've already decided that "model" for our purposes means "light-color", so our contract will be

```
show-light : light-color -> image
```

Since this function takes in a "light-color" parameter, the input template for "light-color" should help us write it. Filling in the answers for the examples, we get

```
(check-expect (show-light "green") (circle 30 "solid" "green"))
(check-expect (show-light "yellow") (circle 30 "solid" "yellow"))
(check-expect (show-light "red") (circle 30 "solid" "red"))
```

For the skeleton and inventory, the template suggests

```
(define (show-light color)
  ; color                          light-color
  (cond [(string=? color "green")   ...]
        [(string=? color "yellow")  ...]
        [(string=? color "red")     ...]
        ))
```

but a look at the "right answers" in the examples shows that they all match a simple pattern, so there's an easier way:

```
(define (show-light color)
  ; color          light-color
  (circle 30 "solid" color)
  )
```

This is not only shorter and simpler than doing a **cond**, but more flexible: the show-light function will now work equally well on orange, purple, and pink lights, should we ever decide to include those colors in the *light-color* data type.

Hint: Inventory templates and outventory templates give you good advice in writing function definitions, but don't follow them slavishly: sometimes there's an easier way.

We can now test the `show-light` function and, assuming it works, we're done with our draw handler.

The model is a string, so we'll use (check-with string?). (If we wanted to be even safer, we could write a `light-color?` function that checks whether its argument is not only a string, but specifically either "red", "yellow", or "green". See Exercise 17.1.3.) The time interval is obviously 5 seconds. As we The starting model must be either "green", "yellow", or "red"; let's start with "green". We can now run the animation as follows:

```
(big-bang "green"
          (check-with string?)
          (on-draw show-light)
          (on-tick change-light 5)
          )
```

∎

Exercise 17.1.2 *Develop an animation that cycles among several pictures of your choice, changing pictures every two seconds to produce a "slide show" effect.*

Hint: If you use the same pictures as in Exercise 15.3.1, you can re-use a previously-written function to do much of the work for you.

Exercise 17.1.3 *Modify the `change-light` function from Exercise 17.1.1 so that when the input is "red", it returns "purple". (It should now fail one of its test cases.) What happens when you run the animation?*

  Develop a function `light-color?` that takes in anything *and tells whether it is one of the three values "red", "yellow", or "green".*

  Run the animation again with `light-color?` as the `check-with` handler. What happens this time?

Hint: Be sure to test `light-color?` on all three legal light-colors, and on a string that isn't a light-color (*e.g.* "beluga"), and on a non-string (*e.g.* 7). And remember the rule of thumb: functions that return a Boolean can usually be written more simply without a conditional than with one. But you may need to take advantage of short-circuit evaluation (remember section 13.8).

Exercise 17.1.4 *Develop a traffic-light animation like Exercise 17.1.1, but using an image as the model.*

  Develop a traffic-light animation like Exercise 17.1.1, but using a number as the model (say, 1=green, 2=yellow, 3=red).

  Discuss the advantages and disadvantages of each of these three choices.

Exercise 17.1.5 *Develop an animation that cycles among three shapes — a green circle, a yellow triangle, and a blue square — every time the mouse is moved or clicked. Try to make all three shapes approximately the same size.*

Exercise 17.1.6 *Modify the animation of Exercise 17.1.1 so that it more nearly resembles a real traffic light (in most of the U.S, anyway): it'll have three bulbs arranged vertically, of which the top one is either red or black; the middle one is either yellow or black; and the bottom one is either green or black. At every moment, exactly one of the three bulbs is "on", and the other two are black.*

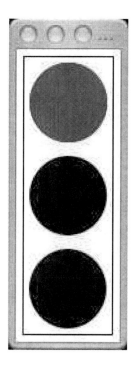

Hint: You may find it helpful to write a helper function which, given a color, finds the *y*-coordinate of the center of that color's light. (They all have the same *x*-coordinate.)

Worked Exercise 17.1.7 *Develop an animation that shows a red triangle for two seconds, then a green triangle for two seconds, then a blue triangle for two seconds, and then stops.*

Solution: The first step in designing an animation is always deciding what handlers you need. In this case, we obviously have to deal with time, so we need a tick handler. We need to stop, so we need either a `stop-when` handler or a `stop-with` inside one of the other handlers; we'll discuss both options. We always need a draw handler, and we should probably have a `check-with` clause.

So what should the model be? We have at least two plausible alternatives: an image (the red, green, or blue triangle) or a string (either `"red"`, `"green"`, or `"blue"`). In either case, we'll have to make a decision based on the current model. We know how to make decisions on images, but comparing strings is usually much more efficient, so we'll choose as our model a string restricted to these three choices.

```
; A shape-color is one of the strings "red", "green", or "blue".
#|
(check-expect (function-on-shape-color "red")   ...)
(check-expect (function-on-shape-color "green") ...)
(check-expect (function-on-shape-color "blue")  ...)

(define (function-on-shape-color c)
  (cond [(string=? c "red")   ...]
        [(string=? c "green") ...]
        [(string=? c "blue")  ...]
  ))

(check-expect (function-returning-shape-color ...)  "red")
(check-expect (function-returning-shape-color ...)  "green")
(check-expect (function-returning-shape-color ...)  "blue")

(define (function-returning-shape-color ...)
  (cond [...              "red"]
        [...              "green"]
        [...              "blue"]
  ))
|#
```

As usual, we'll need a draw handler to convert the model to an image. Assuming we use `stop-when` to decide when to stop, we can now write contracts for all the handlers:

```
; draw handler show-triangle :  shape-color -> image
; tick handler next-color :  shape-color -> shape-color
; stop handler finished?   :  shape-color -> boolean
```

Let's look at the `finished?` function first — the function that decides whether the animation should stop yet. When should the animation stop? Two seconds after the blue triangle appears. Which means the `finished?` function has to recognize whatever the model is at that time.

So what *is* the model at that time? This isn't obvious. It has to be a legal `shape-color`, so it must be either "red", "green", or "blue". And whatever it is, as soon as the model becomes that, the `finished?` function will return `true` and the animation will end. But we don't *want* the animation to end immediately on turning red, or green, or blue; we want it to wait two seconds *after* the triangle turns blue.

So maybe `stop-when` isn't the way to do this, and we should instead eliminate the `finished?` function and call `stop-with` from inside one of the other handlers.

The `show-triangle` function is straightforward, and left as an exercise for the reader.

As for `next-color`, there are three possible examples: "red", "green", and "blue". The next color after red is green, the next color after green is blue ... but what is the next color after blue? Two seconds after the triangle turns blue, the animation should stop, leaving the triangle still blue. So ...

```
(check-expect (next-color "red")   "green")
(check-expect (next-color "green") "blue")
(check-expect (next-color "blue")  (stop-with "blue"))
```

The input template gives us a three-clause conditional with answers to fill in. The answers are straightforward from the above test cases, giving us

```
(define (next-color old-color-name)
  ; old-color-name    shape-color
  (cond [ (string=?  old-color-name "red")   "green" ]
        [ (string=?  old-color-name "green") "blue" ]
        [ (string=?  old-color-name "blue")  (stop-with "blue") ]
))
```

Once this is tested, you can run the animation by calling

```
(big-bang "red"
          (check-with string?)
          (on-draw show-triangle)
          (on-tick next-color 2))
```

(To be even safer, we could write a `shape-color?` function, and use that instead of `string?` in the `check-with` clause. This is left as an exercise for the reader.) ∎

Exercise 17.1.8 *Modify the animation of Exercise 17.1.7 to stop immediately after turning blue.*

Hint: I know of two ways to do this: one is similar to the above but calls `stop-with` in different circumstances, and the other uses a `stop-when` handler instead of the `stop-with` call in `next-color`. Try both.

Exercise 17.1.9 *Modify your animation from exercise 17.1.2 so that each picture is shown only once; after showing the last picture for two seconds, the animation ends.*

17.2 Numeric decisions

Exercise 17.2.1 *Modify your animation from Exercise 10.2.4 so that it only counts up to 59, then starts over at 0.*

Exercise 17.2.2 *Write an animation that places a dot at the mouse location every time the mouse is moved or clicked. The color of this dot should be red if the x coordinate is more than the y coordinate, and green otherwise.*

Hint: You may find that the *answers* in this conditional are two complex expressions, exactly the same except for the color. You can make your function shorter and simpler by moving the conditional *inside* this expression, so the answers in the conditional are just color names.

Exercise 17.2.3 *Write an animation like that of Exercise 8.5.3, but coloring each dot either red, green, or blue, at random.*

Hint: Try writing a helper function that returns one of the three color names at random.

Exercise 17.2.4 *Write an animation a bit like Exercise 8.5.3 and a bit like Exercise 17.2.2: at every time interval, it adds a dot at a random location, but the dot should be red if x > y and green otherwise.*

Hint: Since the coordinates need to be generated randomly once, but used twice (once for choosing color, and once for positioning the dot), write a helper function that takes in the x-coordinate, y-coordinate, and previous image, and adds an appropriately-colored dot at the specified location; call this function on the results of two `random` calls. This function may in turn require another helper function that takes in the x and y coordinates and returns the appropriate color.

Exercise 17.2.5 *Modify the animation of Exercise 17.2.4 so each dot is green if it is within a distance of 50 pixels of the center of the window, and red if it is beyond that distance.*

Exercise 17.2.6 *Modify one of your previous animations by placing a rectangular "Quit" button (a rectangle overlaid with the text "Quit") near the bottom of the window. If the user moves or clicks the mouse inside the button, stop the animation. (We'll see in chapter 18 how to respond* only *to mouse-clicks.)*

Hint: You might want to write a helper function `in-quit-button?` which takes in the x and y coordinates of the mouse and tells whether they represent a point inside the rectangle where you put the "Quit" button.

17.3   Review of important words and concepts

Using conditionals inside the handlers of an animation allows the animations to do much more interesting things. It's not always clear what type to use as the model, as in exercise 17.1.1: each possibility has advantages and disadvantages. That's part of what makes programming interesting.

17.4   Reference: New Functions

No new functions or syntax rules were introduced in this chapter.

Chapter 18

Of Mice and Keys

18.1 Mouse handlers

Recall that the contract for a mouse-handling function must be

```
; model(old) number(x) number(y) event -> model(new)
```

but we didn't explain earlier what an "event" was. Guess what: it's a string. Specifically, it will always be one of the strings in Figure 18.1. And since you already know how to

Figure 18.1: Types of mouse events in DrRacket

`"button-down"`	The user pressed the mouse button.
`"button-up"`	The user released the mouse button.
`"move"`	The user moved the mouse, with the mouse button not pressed.
`"drag"`	The user dragged the mouse while holding the mouse button down.
`"enter"`	The user moved the mouse into the animation window.
`"leave"`	The user moved the mouse out of the animation window.

compare strings, you can write mouse handlers that respond differently to different user actions.

The obvious data analysis for a mouse-handling function would say that the fourth parameter is one of six choices. However, in practice we are usually only interested in one or two of the six, ignoring all the rest; this allows us to considerably simplify our functions. Here's an example:

Worked Exercise 18.1.1 *Write an animation that starts with a blank screen, and adds a small dot at the mouse location every time the mouse button is pressed.*

Solution: Our first question in writing an animation is always what handlers we'll need. There's no mention of time or keyboard, but we'll obviously need a mouse handler, and as usual we'll need a draw handler and a `check-with` handler.

The next question is what type the model should be. We're *adding* dots, and may eventually have dozens or hundreds of them; this problem may remind you of problems 8.5.3 and 17.2.3. As in those problems, the most reasonable model is an *image* showing all the dots added so far. (In Chapter 22, we'll see another way to handle this.)

239

Since the model is an image itself, and that image is all we want to show, we can use
`show-it` as our draw handler rather than writing our own.

The mouse handler has the usual contract:

```
; add-dot-on-mouse-down :
; image(old) number(x) number(y) string(event-type) -> image(new)
```

An event can be any of six possible strings, which would suggest an six-way definition
by choices. However, we're only interested in the "button-down" event, so the fourth
parameter really falls into one of two categories: either "button-down" or "any other
string"; the input template looks like

```
#|
(check-expect (function-on-mouse-press "button-down") ...)
(check-expect (function-on-mouse-press "button-up") ...)

(define (function-on-mouse-press event-type)
  (cond [(string=? event-type "button-down") ...]
        [else                                ...]
  ))
|#
```

We won't bother with an output template because we seldom need to produce a mouse
event.

A simple example starts with an `empty-scene` as the old image. Since there are two
categories for the fourth parameter (and no interesting "categories" for the other three),
we'll need at least two examples:

```
(define WIDTH 300)
(define HEIGHT 200)
(define BACKGROUND (empty-scene WIDTH HEIGHT))
(define DOT (circle 3 "solid" "green"))
(check-expect (add-dot-on-mouse-down BACKGROUND 35 10 "button-down")
              (place-image DOT 35 10 BACKGROUND))
(check-expect (add-dot-on-mouse-down BACKGROUND 35 10 "move")
              BACKGROUND)
```

To make sure the program is actually *adding* a dot to the given image, we should also
try it with a different first argument.
```
(define OTHER-BACKGROUND
  (ellipse 50 30 "solid" "red")
(check-expect (add-dot-on-mouse-down OTHER-BACKGROUND 35 10 "button-down")
              (place-image DOT 35 10 OTHER-BACKGROUND))
(check-expect (add-dot-on-mouse-down OTHER-BACKGROUND 35 10 "button-up")
              OTHER-BACKGROUND)
```

The skeleton and inventory are straightforward, if lengthy:

```
(define (add-dot-on-mouse-down old x y event-type)
   ; old              an image
   ; x                a number (the x coordinate)
   ; y                a number (the y coordinate)
   ; event-type       a string (either "button-down" or not)
   ; DOT              a fixed image we'll need
   ...)
```

Next, the template gives us

```
(define (add-dot-on-mouse-down old x y event-type)
   ; old              an image
   ; x                a number (the x coordinate)
   ; y                a number (the y coordinate)
   ; event-type       a string (either "button-down" or not)
   ; DOT              a fixed image we'll need
   (cond [ (string=?  event-type "button-down")  ...]
         [ else                                   ...]
         )
   )
```

We still need to fill in the answers. The answer in the else case is simple: if the event type is *not* "button-down", we shouldn't do anything, and should simply return the picture we were given. The answer in the "button-down" case is more complicated, but we know the place-image function is useful for adding things to an existing picture. It takes in the image to add (in our case, DOT), two numeric coordinates (obviously x and y), and the picture to add to (in our case, old). The final definition is

```
(define (add-dot-on-mouse-down old x y event-type)
   ; old              an image
   ; x                a number (the x coordinate)
   ; y                a number (the y coordinate)
   ; event-type       a string (either "button-down" or not)
   ; DOT              a fixed image we'll need
   (cond [ (string=?  event-type "button-down")
           (place-image DOT x y old) ]
         [ else   old ]
         )
   )
```

Once this works, we can try it in an animation as follows:

```
(big-bang BACKGROUND
          (check-with image?)
          (on-draw show-it)
          (on-mouse add-dot-on-mouse-down))
```

Does it work the way you expect? Does it work as it should? ∎

Exercise 18.1.2 *Modify this animation so it adds a dot whenever the mouse button is* released, *rather than whenever it is* pressed. *As a user, do you like this version better or worse?*

Exercise 18.1.3 *Modify this animation so it adds a dot whenever the mouse is* dragged *(i.e. moved while holding the mouse button down). The result should be a sort of "sketchpad" program in which you can draw lines and curves with the mouse.*

Exercise 18.1.4 *Modify this animation so it adds a green dot whenever the mouse button is pressed, and a red dot whenever the mouse button is released.*

Hint: You're now interested in *two* of the event types, so there are now *three* interesting categories of input.

Exercise 18.1.5 *Modify the animation of Exercise 17.2.6 so that it stops only if it gets a* `"button-up"` *event inside the button.*

Exercise 18.1.6 *Modify exercise 18.1.1 so that rather than adding a pure-red dot, it adds a drop of red dye at the mouse location. The dye adds a certain amount to the red component of the picture, varying with distance from where it was dropped: for example, if it added 100 to the red component right at the mouse location, it might add 50 to the neighboring pixels, 33 to the pixels 2 units away, 25 to the pixels 3 units away, and so on. The green and blue components of the picture should be unchanged.*

Hint: Use `map3-image`.

18.2   Key handlers

Recall from chapter 6 that the contract for a key-handling function must be

```
; key-handler :  model key-event -> model
```

Chapter 6 was fuzzy on what this "key" parameter is. In fact, it's a string: if a user types "w", your key handler will be called with the string `"w"`, and so on. There are also some special keyboard keys, described in Figure 18.2.   For convenience, DrRacket provides a built-in function named `key=?` which is just like `string=?` except that it works *only* on key-events (this can be useful because if you mistakenly call it on something that isn't a key-event at all, it'll produce an error message immediately rather than letting you go on with a mistake in your program).

Worked Exercise 18.2.1 *Develop an animation of a picture (say, a calendar) that moves left or right by 1 pixel when the user presses the left or right arrow key (respectively). It should ignore all other keys.*

Solution: What handlers do we need? We obviously need to respond to key presses, so we need a key handler. We might or might not need a draw handler, depending on the model type.

So what type should the model be? We've handled similar problems in the past in one of two ways: an image, moving left with `crop-left` and moving right with `beside` and `rectangle`, or a number, moving left with `sub1` and moving right with `add1`. The latter is more efficient, and has the advantage that we can move off the left-hand edge of the screen and come back. So let's use a number to represent the *x*-coordinate of the image.

This tells us that the key handler's contract is

```
; handle-key :  number(x) key-event -> number(new x)
```

Figure 18.2: Special keyboard keys

Key on keyboard	key-event
left arrow	"left"
right arrow	"right"
down arrow	"down"
up arrow	"up"
clear (on number pad)	"clear"
shift	"shift"
control	"control"
caps lock	"capital"
num lock	"num lock"
page up	"prior"
page down	"next"
end	"end"
home	"home"
help	"help"
esc	"escape"
F1, F2, *etc.*	"f1", "f2", *etc.*
+ (on number pad)	"add"
- (on number pad)	"subtract"
* (on number pad)	"multiply"
/ (on number pad)	"divide"
enter (on number pad)	"numpad-enter"

And we'll need a draw handler with contract

```
; calendar-at-x :  number(x) -> image
```

The `calendar-at-x` function is exactly the same as we've used in several previous exercises, so I'll leave it to the reader. Now, about that `handle-key` function...

Data analysis: the first parameter is a number, about which there's not much to say. The second parameter could be a *lot* of different things, but the only categories we're interested in are `"left"`, `"right"`, and anything else (in which case we ignore it). We could write explicit templates for this data type, but we don't expect to be writing lots of functions on it so we'll skip that step.

We'll need at least three examples: one with `"left"`, one with `"right"`, and one key-event that's not either of those: at least three examples in all. Note that if the key isn't `"left"` or `"right"`, we ignore it by returning a new model that's exactly the same as the old one.

```
(check-expect (handle-key 10 "D") 10)
(check-expect (handle-key 10 "left") 9)
(check-expect (handle-key 10 "right") 11)
```

The skeleton and inventory are straightforward:

```
(define (handle-key x key)
  ; x            number
  ; key          key-event (i.e.  string)
  ...)
```

Since there are three main categories (`"left"`, `"right"`, and anything else) of input, we'll need a `cond` with three clauses, with questions to check which one `key` is:

```
(define (handle-key x key)
  ; x            number
  ; key          key-event (i.e.  string)
  (cond  [ (key=? key "right")   ...]
         [ (key=? key "left")    ...]
         [ else                  ...]
         )
  )
```

Now that we've filled in all the questions, we need to fill in the answers. If `key` is anything other than `"left"` or `"right"`, this is easy: return the same x-coordinate we were given, unchanged. In the `"left"` case, we want to subtract 1 from it, and in the `"right"` case, we want to add 1 to it.

```
(define (handle-key x key)
  ; x            number
  ; key          key-event (i.e.  string)
  ; "left"       a fixed string we'll need
  ; "right"      another fixed string we'll need
  (cond [ (key=? key "right")   (+ x 1)  ]
        [ (key=? key "left")    (- x 1)  ]
        [ else                  x ]
        )
  )
```

Once we've tested this and confirmed that the function works on its own, we can run
the animation as follows:
```
(define WIDTH 400)
(define HEIGHT 100)
(define (calendar-at-x x)
   ...
   )
(big-bang (/ WIDTH 2)
          (check-with number?)
          (on-draw calendar-at-x)
          (on-key handle-key))
```

Exercise 18.2.2 *Modify the above animation so it also responds to some ordinary characters: the picture moves 5 pixels to the right in response to the ">" key, and 5 pixels to
the left in response to the "<" key.*

Exercise 18.2.3 *Modify the above animation so it stops when the user types the letter
"q".*

Exercise 18.2.4 *Develop an animation of a disk whose radius increases by 1 when the
user presses the up-arrow key, and decreases by 1 when the user presses the down-arrow
key.*

Exercise 18.2.5 *Develop an animation that allows the user to "type" into the animation window: every time the user types an ordinary character, that character is added to
the right-hand end of the animation window. The program will ignore arrow keys, function
keys, etc.*

Hint: See Exercise 10.2.1 for some ideas, and use `string-length` to check whether the
key is an ordinary character (*i.e.* the *key-event* is a one-character string). Be sure to test
your program with arrow keys as well as ordinary characters.

18.3 Key release

Key handlers are triggered whenever the user presses a key. Sometimes you want something
to happen when the user *releases* a key instead. To handle this situation, you can install
an `on-release` handler, which is just like an `on-key` handler except that it's called when
the key is released rather than when it's pressed. It has contract
```
; handle-release :  model key-event -> model
```
The *key-event* tells you what key was just released.

Exercise 18.3.1 *Modify some of the key-based animations from this chapter so they
trigger on key release rather than on key press.*

Exercise 18.3.2 *Develop an animation which shows the currently-pressed key for just
as long as you hold it down; then it disappears when you release it.*

18.4   Review of important words and concepts

A mouse handler takes in, as its fourth argument, a *mouse-event*, a string which is one of six standard choices, indicating whether the mouse was pressed, released, moved, dragged, *etc.*. A mouse handler, therefore, has as its body a `cond` with up to six cases, handling each different kind of mouse action. More commonly, the handler will only test for one or two kinds of mouse action, then use an `else` clause to handle "all the rest".

A key handler takes in, as its second argument, a *key-event*, a string which is one of several dozen standard choices: single-character strings for ordinary keys, and special strings like `"left"`, `"help"`, *etc.* for special keys. As a convenience for writing key handlers, there's a built-in function `key=?` which works on *only* these strings, and produces an error message on anything else. If your key handler needs to respond only to a short list of specific keys, you can write it using a `cond` with a bunch of `key=?` questions. If you need to handle "all special keys" in one way and "all ordinary keys" in another way, you may need to do something cleverer, like use the fact that all ordinary keys are one-character strings and all the special ones have longer names.

18.5   Reference: Built-in functions for mouse and key handling

One new function was introduced in this chapter: `key=?`

We also introduced `big-bang`'s `on-release` clause, which works just like `on-key` except that it's triggered by releasing a key rather than pressing one.

Chapter 19

Handling errors

19.1 Error messages

Recall Exercise 11.6.1, in which you built pictures of houses. Once `build-house` was working, one could then build a whole village by writing something like
```
(place-image (build-house ...)  30 200
          (place-image (build-house ...)  105 220
                   (place-image (build-house ...)  130 60
                           (empty-scene 300 300))))
```
Now suppose some foolish user provides a width or height that isn't a positive number: you'll get an unfriendly error message like
rectangle: expected <positive number> as second argument, given: -30.
You'd like to make this friendlier by giving the user a more informative message like *House height must be > 0*
instead. One way to do this would be for `build-house` to return that string as its value.

Of course, this violates the contract of `build-house`, which said it returns an image. No problem: now that we know about mixed data types, we can change the contract:
```
; build-house :  number number string -> image-or-string
```

We'll need some extra examples to test that it produces the appropriate string in the appropriate cases; I'll leave that to you. Finally, the body of the function will have an extra conditional somewhere:
```
...
(cond [(> height 0) ...]
      [else "House height must be > 0."])
```
But now when you try to build a village as before, you get the error message
place-image: expected <image> as first argument, given "House height must be > 0"
What happened? The `build-house` function promised, in its original contract, to return an image, and `place-image` only works on images so it relies on this promise. Now we've broken that promise by returning a string instead, so other programs that use `build-house` don't work any more. You could fix this by putting a conditional *everywhere* that `build-house` is used, to check whether it returned an image or a string, but that's a royal pain, and would make your `build-house` function *much* more inconvenient to use.

The problem is that *normally*, the `build-house` function returns an image, which is what `place-image` expects; the only time `build-house` returns a string is when something is very wrong and it doesn't make sense to call `place-image` at all. So the ideal solution would be for `build-house` to produce an error message *and never return to place-image at all.* (In Java, C++, and some other languages, this is referred to as "throwing an exception".) There's a built-in function named `error` that does this. It uses a new data type that we haven't seen before: *symbol*. We'll discuss it more in Chapter 29, but for now, think of it as a function name with an apostrophe in front (but *not* at the end!).

The `error` function has contract

```
; error :  object ...-> nothing
; The first argument is normally a symbol:  the name of the function
; that discovered the error, with an apostrophe in front.
; Any additional arguments go into the error message too.
; The function doesn't return, but stops the program.
```

Worked Exercise 19.1.1 *Modify the* `build-house` *function so that if the width or height is less than 0, it produces an appropriate error message and doesn't return to its caller.*

Solution: We don't need to change the contract, since *if* build-house returns at all, it will still return an image. We need to add some additional test cases:

```
(build-house 0 100 "blue") "should produce an error message:"
"build-house:  House width must be > 0."
(build-house 100 0 "red") "should produce an error message:"
"build-house:  House height must be > 0."
```

The skeleton and inventory don't change, but the body now looks like

```
...
(cond [ (<= width 0)
          (error 'build-house "House width must be > 0.") ]
      [ (<= height 0)
          (error 'build-house "House height must be > 0.") ]
      [ else
          ...])
```

In testing this function, you should get an error message in response to the first "bad" test case. Indeed, you'll never even see the `"should produce an error message:"` because the program stops before getting that far in the definitions pane. Likewise, you'll never get to the second "bad" test case at all, so you don't know whether it works correctly. One way to handle this is to test one "bad" test case, then once it works, comment it out and run again to test the next one. A better way to handle it is described below. ∎

19.2 Testing for errors

You're already familiar with the `check-expect`, `check-within`, `check-member-of`, and `check-range` functions, which compare the actual answer from some expression with what you say it "should be". There's another function, `check-error`, which "expects" the expression to crash with a specific error message, and checks that this actually happens.

```
; check-error :  test-expression string -> nothing
; Checks whether evaluation of the test-expression produces
; the specified string as an error message
```

For example, the above "bad" test cases could be rewritten as

```
(check-error (build-house 0 100 "blue")
             "build-house: House width must be > 0.")
(check-error (build-house 100 0 "red")
             "build-house: House height must be > 0.")
```

and you don't need to comment out either of them, since `check-error` catches the first error, checks that it's correct, and goes on to the next.

Note that `check-error` will complain if the expression produces the wrong error message, or even if it *doesn't* produce an error message: try

```
(check-error (error 'whatever "this error message")
             "that error message")
(check-error (+ 3 4) "something went wrong")
```

19.3 Writing user-proof functions

Exercise 19.3.1 *Modify the solution to Exercise 15.1.4 so that if the input to `reply` isn't any of the known strings, it produces an error message and never returns, rather than returning `"huh?"`.*

Exercise 19.3.2 *Modify the solution to Exercise 9.2.3 so that if the input is an empty string, it produces the error message* chop-first-char: can't chop from an empty string *and never returns.*

Exercise 19.3.3 *Modify the solution to Exercise 9.2.4 so that if the input is an empty string, it produces the error message* first-char: can't get first character of an empty string *and never returns.*

Exercise 19.3.4 *Develop a function `safe-double` that takes in a number, a string, a boolean, or an image. If the input is a number, the function doubles it and returns the result. If the input is anything else, the function produces an appropriate error message, e.g.*

safe-double: This function expects a number, like 3; you gave it a picture.

or (even cooler)

safe-double: This function expects a number, like 3; you gave it the quoted string "five".

Hint: The second example calls for inserting the actual string you were given into your error message. This can be done using `string-append`, or using the `format` function, which I haven't told you about yet. If you wish, look it up and rewrite the function that way.

19.4 Review of important words and concepts

A function contract is a binding promise; if you don't return the type of result you said you would return, other people's programs will crash, and they'll blame you. But sometimes things go wrong, and there *is* no value of the promised return type that would be correct. In this case, often the best answer is to "throw an exception": to bail out of any functions that have called this one, and display an error message in the Interactions pane. The `error` function does this job for you; the `check-error` function in the `testing` teachpack helps you test it.

19.5   Reference: Built-in functions for signaling and testing errors

In this chapter, we introduced two new built-in functions:

- `error`

- `check-error`

(Technically, `check-error` is a special form rather than a function.)

We also mentioned the `format` function, which you are invited to look up for yourself.

PART III

Definition by Parts

Chapter 20

Using Structures

20.1 The posn data type

Recall Exercise 18.2.1, in which a picture moved left or right in response to the left and right arrow keys, respectively. An obvious modification would be to have it move *up or down* in response to *those* arrow keys; this could be easily done by deciding that the model represented the y coordinate rather than the x coordinate. So how would we *combine* these two, allowing the picture to move up, down, left, and right in response to the appropriate arrow keys?

This is harder than it seems at first. For the left/right animation, our model was the x coordinate of the picture; for the up/down animation, it would be the y coordinate. But if the picture is to move in *both* dimensions, the model needs to "remember" *both* the x and y coordinates; it needs to hold *two numbers at once*.

Before explaining how to do this in Racket, let me give an analogy. Last week I went to the grocery store. I like grapefruit, so I picked up a grapefruit in my hand. Then another grapefruit in my other hand. Then another, which I sorta cradled in my elbow... and another, and another, and a quart of milk, and a pound of butter. I made my way to the checkout counter, dumped them all on the conveyor belt, paid for them, picked them up, cradling them one by one between my arms, and carried them precariously out to the car.

What's wrong with this picture? Any sensible person would say "don't carry them all individually; *put them in a bag!*" It's easier to carry one bag (which in turn holds five grapefruit, a quart of milk, and a pound of butter) than to carry all those individual items loose.

The same thing happens in computer programming: it's frequently more convenient to *combine several pieces of information in a package* than to deal with them all individually. In particular, if we want an animation to "remember" both an x and a y coordinate (or, as we'll see in the next chapter, *any* two or more pieces of information), we need to package them up into a single object that can be "the model".

Since (x, y) coordinate pairs are so commonly used in computer programming, DrRacket provides a built-in data type named posn (short for "position") to represent them. A posn can be thought of as a box with two compartments labelled x and y, each of which can hold a number. There are four predefined functions involving posns:

```
; make-posn :  number(x) number(y) -> posn
; posn-x :  posn -> number(x)
; posn-y :  posn -> number(y)
; posn?  :  anything -> boolean
```

253

To create a `posn`, we call the `make-posn` function, telling it what numbers to put in the x compartment and the y compartment: (make-posn 7 12), for example, creates and returns a posn whose x coordinate is 7 and whose y coordinate is 12. For convenience in playing with it, however, we'll store it in a variable. Type the following into the DrRacket Interactions pane:

```
(define where (make-posn 7 12))
where          ; (make-posn 7 12)
```

Now we can use the `posn-x` function to retrieve the x coordinate, and `posn-y` to retrieve the y coordinate:

```
(posn-x where)        ; should be 7
(posn-y where)        ; should be 12
```

This may not look very exciting — after all, we just *put* 7 and 12 into the x and y compartments, so it's not surprising that we can get 7 and 12 out of them. But in a realistic program, the numbers would come from one place (perhaps the user providing arguments to a function, or clicking a mouse) and be used in a completely different place (such as a draw handler).

Practice Exercise 20.1.1 ***Create*** *(in the Interactions pane) several variables containing different posns. Extract their x and y coordinates and make sure they are what you expected.*

*Try the **posn?** function on these variables, and on some expressions that use **make-posn** directly (e.g. (make-posn 13 5)), and on some things that aren't posns.*

Common beginner mistakes
I've seen a lot of students write things like

```
(make-posn here)
(posn-x 7)
(posn-y 12)
(do-something-with here)
```

I know exactly what the student was thinking: "First I create a posn named `here`, then I say that its x coordinate is 7, and its y coordinate is 12, and then I can use it." Unfortunately, this isn't the way the functions actually work: the `make-posn` function does *not* define a new variable, and the `posn-x` and `posn-y` functions *don't change* the x and y coordinates of "the" posn.

To put it another way, the above example doesn't obey the contracts. The `make-posn` function does *not* take in a posn, much less a new variable name; it takes in *two numbers*, and *returns* a posn. The `posn-x` and `posn-y` functions do *not* take in a number; they take in a posn and *return* a number. A correct way to do what this student meant is

```
(define here (make-posn 7 12))
(do-something-with here)
```

or, more simply,

```
(do-something-with (make-posn 7 12))
```

20.2   Definition by parts

In Chapter 16 we learned about "defining a new data type by choices," and in Section 15.8 we saw more examples of definition by choices, of the form "a W is either an X, a Y, or a Z," where X, Y, and Z are previously-defined types.

Another way to define a new data type from previously-defined types is "definition by parts," and `posns` are our first example. A posn has two *parts*, both of which are numbers (a previously-defined type). In Chapter 21, we'll see more examples of definition by parts.

20.3   Design recipe for functions involving posns

Suppose the contract for a function specifies that it takes in a `posn`.

The data analysis (at least for the `posn` parameter) is already done: a `posn` consists of two numbers, x and y. (Although we may have more to say about the numbers themselves, or about other parameters, or about the output type.)

The examples will require creating some `posns` on which to call the function. There are two common ways to do this: either store the `posn` in a variable, as above, and use the variable name as the function argument, or use a call to `make-posn` as the function argument. Both are useful: the former if you're going to use the same `posn` in several different test cases, and the latter if you're just making up one-shot examples.

```
(define where (make-posn 7 12))
(check-expect (function-on-posn where) ...)
(check-expect (function-on-posn (make-posn 19 5)) ...)
```

The skeleton and inventory will look familiar, with the addition of a few expressions you're likely to need in the body:

```
(define (function-on-posn the-posn)
  ; the-posn              a posn
  ; (posn-x the-posn)     a number (the x coordinate)
  ; (posn-y the-posn)     another number (the y coordinate)
  ...)
```

So here's a complete template for functions taking in a posn

```
#|
(define where (make-posn 7 12))
(check-expect (function-on-posn where) ...)
(check-expect (function-on-posn (make-posn 19 5)) ...)

(define (function-on-posn the-posn)
  ; the-posn              a posn
  ; (posn-x the-posn)     a number (the x coordinate)
  ; (posn-y the-posn)     another number (the y coordinate)
  ...)
|#
```

In writing the body, you can now use `the-posn` directly, and (more commonly) you can use the expressions `(posn-x the-posn)` and `(posn-y the-posn)` to refer to its individual coordinates.

20.4   Writing functions on posns

So now let's write some actual functions involving posns.

Worked Exercise 20.4.1 *Develop a function named* `right-of-100?` *that takes in a posn representing a point on the screen, and tells whether it is to the right of the vertical line x = 100. (For example, we might have a 200-pixel-wide window, and want to do one thing for positions in the right half and something else for positions in the left half.)*

(One might reasonably ask "This function only actually uses the x coordinate; why does it take in a posn?" There are at least two answers. First, sometimes the program *has* a posn handy, and doesn't want to take the extra step of extracting the x coordinate from it to pass to `right-of-100?`. Second and more important, what the function actually uses is the function's business, not the business of whoever is calling it. I shouldn't have to think about how to solve a problem myself in order to *call* a function whose job is to solve that problem. I should instead give the function whatever information it *might* need, and it will pick out the parts that it *does* need.)

Solution: The contract is

```
; right-of-100?  :  posn -> boolean
```

Data analysis: there's not much to say about the output type, `boolean`, except that it has two values, so we'll need at least two examples. The input type is `posn`, which consists of two numbers x and y. Of these, we're only interested in the x coordinate for this problem; in particular, we're interested in how the x coordinate compares with 100. It could be smaller, greater, or equal, so we'll actually need *three* examples: one with $x < 100$, one with $x = 100$, and one with $x > 100$. Note that although this function doesn't actually *use* the y coordinate, it still has to be there.

```
(check-expect (right-of-100?  (make-posn 75 123)) false)
(check-expect (right-of-100?  (make-posn 102 123)) true)
(check-expect (right-of-100?  (make-posn 100 123)) false)
; borderline case
```

The template gives us most of the skeleton and inventory. And since it's hard to imagine solving this problem without using the number 100, we'll put that into the inventory too:

```
(define (right-of-100?  the-posn)
  ; the-posn            a posn
  ; (posn-x the-posn)   a number (the x coordinate)
  ; (posn-y the-posn)   another number (the y coordinate)
  ; 100                 a fixed number we'll need
  ...)
```

Body: We don't actually need `(posn-y where)` in this problem, so we can drop it from the inventory. Of the remaining available expressions, there's a posn and two numbers. The obvious question to ask is whether one of those numbers (the x coordinate) is larger than the other (100):

```
(> (posn-x where) 100)
```

This expression returns a Boolean, so we could use it in a `cond` to make a decision... but this function is supposed to return a Boolean, so a `cond` is probably overkill. In fact, if this expression is true, the function right answer true, and if this expression is false, it right answer false, so we can just use this expression itself as the body:

```
(define (right-of-100?  the-posn)
  ; the-posn           a posn
  ; (posn-x the-posn) a number(x)
  ;-(posn-y-the-posn)-a-number(y)
  ; 100                 a fixed number we know we'll need
  (> (posn-x the-posn) 100)
  )
```

When we test this function on the three examples we wrote earlier, it works.   ∎

Common beginner mistakes

Many students think of a **posn** as the same thing as two numbers, so if I had written the **right-of-100?** function above, they would call it in either of the following ways:

```
(right-of-100?  (make-posn 75 112))
(right-of-100?  75 112)
```

In fact, only the first of these passes a syntax check in Racket. The **right-of-100?** function defined above expects one parameter of type **posn**, *not* two parameters of type **number**. Try each of the function calls above, and see what happens.

Exercises: writing functions on posns

Exercise 20.4.2 *Develop a function named* **above-diagonal?** *that takes in a posn representing a point on the screen, and tells whether it's above the diagonal line* $x = y$.

Hint: Remember that in computer graphics, positive y-values are usually *down*, so this diagonal line is from the top-left to bottom-right of the window. Pick some specific positions, described in (x, y) coordinates, and decide whether they're above the diagonal or not; then generalize this to a test that tells whether *any* **posn** is above the diagonal (by looking at its x and y coordinates).

Worked Exercise 20.4.3 *Write a function named* **distance-to-top-left** *that takes in a posn representing a point on the screen, and computes the straight-line distance from this point to the top-left corner (i.e. coordinates* $(0, 0)$*) of the screen, in pixels.*

Hint: The formula for the distance is $\sqrt{x^2 + y^2}$.

Solution: Contract:

```
; distance-to-top-left:  posn -> number
```

Data analysis: we already know what **posn** and **number** mean, and there are no sub-categories of either one to worry about, only arithmetic.

For the examples, we'll start with really easy ones we can do in our heads, then work up to gradually more complicated ones that require a calculator. Note that since there are square roots involved, the answers may be inexact, so we use **check-within** rather than **check-expect**.

```
(check-within (distance-to-top-left (make-posn 0 0)) 0 .1)
(check-within (distance-to-top-left (make-posn 6 0)) 6 .1)
(check-within (distance-to-top-left (make-posn 0 4.3)) 4.3 .1)
(check-within (distance-to-top-left (make-posn 3 4)) 5 .1)
```
; $3^2 + 4^2 = 9 + 16 = 25 = 5^2$
```
(check-within (distance-to-top-left (make-posn 4 7)) 8.1 .1)
```
; $4^2 + 7^2 = 16 + 49 = 65 > 8^2$

Skeleton and inventory (from the template):

```
(define (distance-to-top-left the-point)
  ; the-point              a posn
  ; (posn-x the-point)     a number (x)
  ; (posn-y the-point)     a number (y)
  ...)
```

Body: We   have   two   numeric   expressions,   (posn-x the-point)   and
(posn-y the-point), which represent the x and y coordinates respectively. We need
to square each of them:

```
(define (distance-to-top-left the-point)
  ; the-point              a posn
  ; (posn-x the-point)     a number (x)
  ; (posn-y the-point)     a number (y)
  ; (* (posn-x the-point) (posn-x the-point))     a number (x²)
  ; (* (posn-y the-point) (posn-y the-point))     a number (y²)
  ...)
```

Note that there's getting to be a fuzzy line between inventory and body: we've added
these expressions in comments, because they're not the final body but we know they're a
step along the way.

Then we need to add those two squares:

```
(define (distance-to-top-left the-point)
  ; the-point              a posn
  ; (posn-x the-point)     a number (x)
  ; (posn-y the-point)     a number (y)
  ; (* (posn-x the-point) (posn-x the-point))     a number (x²)
  ; (* (posn-y the-point) (posn-y the-point))     a number (y²)
  ; (+ (* (posn-x the-point) (posn-x the-point))
  ;    (* (posn-y the-point) (posn-y the-point)))  a number (x² + y²)
  ...)
```

and finally square-root that, using sqrt:

```
(define (distance-to-top-left the-point)
  ; the-point              a posn
  ; (posn-x the-point)     a number (x)
  ; (posn-y the-point)     a number (y)
  ; (* (posn-x the-point) (posn-x the-point))      a number (x²)
  ; (* (posn-y the-point) (posn-y the-point))      a number (y²)
  ; (+ (* (posn-x the-point) (posn-x the-point))
  ;    (* (posn-y the-point) (posn-y the-point)))  a number (x² + y²)
  (sqrt (+ (* (posn-x the-point) (posn-x the-point))
           (* (posn-y the-point) (posn-y the-point))))
)
```

We can now test this on the examples we wrote earlier, and it should work.

Of course, as you get more comfortable with writing functions on posns, you won't need to write down all these intermediate steps, and can simply write

```
(define (distance-to-top-left the-point)
  (sqrt (+ (* (posn-x the-point) (posn-x the-point))
           (* (posn-y the-point) (posn-y the-point))))
)
```

instead. But for now, I'd like you to use the inventory; discuss with your instructor when you can get away with skipping it. ∎

Exercise 20.4.4 *Develop a function* named `coordinate-difference` *which takes in a **posn** and gives back the* difference *between the coordinates (which tells you, in a sense, how far the point is from the diagonal line $x = y$).*

Hint: The answer should never be negative, so use the built-in `abs` (absolute-value) function to ensure this.

Exercise 20.4.5 *Develop a function* named `distance` *that takes in* two *posns (call them* **here** *and* **there**), *and computes the straight-line distance between them. The formula is*

$$\sqrt{(x_{here} - x_{there})^2 + (y_{here} - y_{there})^2)}$$

Hint: Since your function will have two parameters **here** and **there**, both of which are posns, the skeleton will include

```
; here                  a posn
; there                 a posn
; (posn-x here)         a number(x coordinate of here)
; (posn-y here)         a number(y coordinate of here)
; (posn-x there)        a number(x coordinate of there)
; (posn-y there)        a number(y coordinate of there)
```

Exercise 20.4.6 *Develop a function* named `posn=?` *that takes in two *posns* and tells whether they're the same (i.e. they have the same x coordinate and the same y coordinate).*

Hint: Be sure your examples include two posns that are the same, two that differ only in x, two that differ only in y, and two that differ in both x and y coordinates.

You may *not* use the built-in `equal?` function to solve this problem.

Exercise 20.4.7 *Develop a function* named `distance-to-origin` *that takes in* either *a number or a posn and tells how far it is from the appropriate "origin". For numbers, that's 0; for posns, that's (make-posn 0 0).*

20.5   Functions that return posns

Since `posn` is a data type, like `number`, `image`, *etc.*, you can write functions that *return* a posn too. Such functions will almost always use `make-posn` somewhere in the body. In other words, the output template for `posn` looks like this:

```
#|
(check-expect (function-returning-posn ...)  (make-posn 3 8))
...

(define (function-returning-posn ...)
  (make-posn ...    ...)
  )
|#
```

Worked Exercise 20.5.1 *Develop a function* named `diagonal-point` *that takes in a number and returns a posn whose x and y coordinate are both that number.*

Solution: Contract:

```
; diagonal-point :  number -> posn
```

Data analysis: the input is a number, about which there's not much to say. The output is a posn, which has two numeric parts x and y.

Examples:

```
(check-expect (diagonal-point 0) (make-posn 0 0))
(check-expect (diagonal-point 3.7) (make-posn 3.7 3.7))
```

Skeleton/inventory (from the output template for `posn`):

```
(define (diagonal-point coord)
  ; coord    a number
  (make-posn ...    ...)
  )
```

At this point we'll apply the "inventory with values" technique.

```
(define (diagonal-point coord)
  ; coord           a number       3.7
  ; right answer    a posn         (make-posn 3.7 3.7)
  (make-posn ...    ...)
  )
```

Body: The "inventory with values" makes this really easy: the only reasonable way we can get `(make-posn 3.7 3.7)` from a parameter `coord` with the value 3.7 is `(make-posn coord coord)`, so that becomes the body:

```
(define (diagonal-point coord)
  ; coord          a number     3.7
  ; right answer   a posn       (make-posn 3.7 3.7)
  (make-posn coord coord)
  )
```

We run the test cases on this definition, and it works. ▮

The "inventory with values" technique tends to be more useful the more complicated the function's *result type* is. It doesn't really help when the result type is Boolean, it helps a little when the result type is a number, even more when the result type is a string or an image, and it's *extremely* helpful for functions that return a posn or the other complex data types we'll see in the next few chapters.

Exercise 20.5.2 *Develop a function* named swap-x-y *that takes in a posn and returns a new posn with the coordinates swapped: the x coordinate of the output should be the y coordinate of the input, and vice versa.*

Hint: This function both takes in and returns a posn, but they're not the same posn, so you'll need to use both the input and output templates for posn.

Exercise 20.5.3 *Develop a function* named scale-posn *that takes in a number and a posn, and returns a posn formed by multiplying the number by each of the coordinates of the input posn.*
 For example,

```
(check-expect (scale-posn 3 (make-posn 2 5)) (make-posn 6 15))
```

Exercise 20.5.4 *Develop a function* named add-posns *that takes in two posns and returns a new posn whose x coordinate is the sum of the x coordinates of the two inputs, and whose y coordinate is the sum of the y coordinates of the two inputs.*

Exercise 20.5.5 *Develop a function* named sub-posns *that takes in two posns and returns a new posn whose x coordinate is the difference of the x coordinates of the two inputs, and whose y coordinate is the difference of the y coordinates of the two inputs.*

Exercise 20.5.6 *Redefine* the distance *function from Exercise 20.4.5 to be much shorter and simpler, by re-using functions you've already seen or written in this chapter.*

Hint: You should be able to do this in two fairly short lines of Racket code.

Exercise 20.5.7 *Develop a function* named choose-posn *that takes in a string and two posns. The string should be either* "first" *or* "second". *The* choose-posn *function right answer either the first or the second of its two posns, as directed by the string.*

Hint: Although this function returns a posn, it can be written *without* using make-posn (except for the examples); indeed, it's much shorter, simpler, and easier without using make-posn. This situation doesn't happen often, but it does happen, so don't use make-posn blindly.

20.6   Writing animations involving posns

Now we can finally solve the problem that started this chapter.

Worked Exercise 20.6.1 *Write an animation of a picture that moves up, down, left, and right in response to the "up", "down", "left", and "right" arrow keys. It should ignore all other keys.*

Solution: The model has to represent *both* the x and y coordinates of the object, so we'll use a posn. Since the model is a posn, we'll need a draw handler with contract

```
; show-picture :  posn -> image
```

and a key handler with contract

```
; handle-key :  posn key -> posn
```

Draw handler

Let's do the `show-picture` function first. We have its contract already, and there's not much to say about the data types.

```
(define WIDTH 300)
(define HEIGHT 300)
(define BACKGROUND (empty-scene WIDTH HEIGHT))
(define DOT (circle 3 "solid" "blue"))
...
(check-expect (show-picture (make-posn 15 12))
  (place-image DOT 15 12 BACKGROUND))
(check-expect (show-picture (make-posn 27 149))
  (place-image DOT 27 149 BACKGROUND))
```

The skeleton and inventory are similar to those we've seen before involving posns:

```
(define (show-picture where)
  ; where              a posn
  ; (posn-x where)     a number(x)
  ; (posn-y where)     a number(y)
  ; DOT                a fixed image (to be placed)
  ; BACKGROUND         a fixed image (to use as background)
  ...)
```

Now let's try the "inventory with values" technique, using the "moderately complicated" example of (make-posn 27 149).

```
(define (show-picture where)
  ; where              a posn           (make-posn 27 149)
  ; (posn-x where)     a number(x)      27
  ; (posn-y where)     a number(y)      149
  ; DOT                a fixed image    (to be placed)
  ; BACKGROUND         a fixed image    (to use as background)
  ; right answer       an image         (place-image DOT 27 149 BACKGROUND)
  ...)
```

This makes the body pretty easy:

```
(define (show-picture where)
  ; where           a posn        (make-posn 27 149)
  ; (posn-x where)  a number(x)   27
  ; (posn-y where)  a number(y)   149
  ; DOT             a fixed image (to be placed)
  ; BACKGROUND      a fixed image (to use as background)
  ; right answer    an image      (place-image DOT 27 149 BACKGROUND)
  (place-image DOT
               (posn-x where) (posn-y where)
               BACKGROUND)
)
```

We can test this on the known examples, and it works.

Key handler

Now for the key handler. Recall that the contract is

```
; handle-key :  posn key -> posn
```

where "key" is really a string, but limited to certain specific strings. In this problem we're interested in four specific keys — "left", "right", "up", and "down" — plus "any other key," which we'll ignore.

```
(check-expect (handle-key (make-posn 12 19) "e") (make-posn 12 19))
; ignore "e" by returning the same model we were given
(check-expect (handle-key (make-posn 12 19) "left") (make-posn 11 19))
; move left by decreasing the x coordinate
(check-expect (handle-key (make-posn 12 19) "right") (make-posn 13 19))
(check-expect (handle-key (make-posn 12 19) "up") (make-posn 12 18))
; remember that positive y-values are down
(check-expect (handle-key (make-posn 12 19) "down") (make-posn 12 20))
```

The skeleton is easy. The inventory will show the expressions we have available (based on the data type posn):

```
(define (handle-key where key)
  ; where           a posn
  ; key             a string
  ; (posn-x where)  a number(x)
  ; (posn-y where)  a number(y)
  ...)
```

We could also add the "outventory" line

```
; (make-posn some-number-x some-number-y)
```

because we know that `handle-key` is supposed to return a posn.

There are four specific values of `key` that we care about: "up", "down", "left", and "right". So we'll need a conditional with five cases: one for each of these, and one for "anything else".

```
(define (handle-key where key)
  ; where            a posn
  ; key              a key
  ; (posn-x where)   a number(x)
  ; (posn-y where)   a number(y)
  (cond [(key=? key "up")      ...]
        [(key=? key "down")    ...]
        [(key=? key "left")    ...]
        [(key=? key "right")   ...]
        [else                  ...]
        )
  ...)
```

We still need to fill in the answers. In the "ignore" case, we can simply return where unchanged:

```
(define (handle-key where key)
  ; where            a posn
  ; key              a key
  ; (posn-x where)   a number(x)
  ; (posn-y where)   a number(y)
  (cond [(key=? key "up")      ...]
        [(key=? key "down")    ...]
        [(key=? key "left")    ...]
        [(key=? key "right") ...]
        [else               where ]
  ))
```

The other four cases all require producing a posn that's similar to where, but moved slightly in either the x or the y dimension. The formulæ for these may be obvious to you, but in case they're not, let's try an "inventory with values" for each case.

```
(define (handle-key where key)
  ; where            a posn         (make-posn 12 19)
  ; key              string
  ; (posn-x where)   a number(x)     12
  ; (posn-y where)   a number(y)     19
  (cond [ (key=? key "up")     ; right answer (make-posn 12 18)
         ]
        [ (key=? key "down")   ; right answer (make-posn 12 20)
         ]
        [ (key=? key "left")   ; right answer (make-posn 11 19)
         ]
        [ (key=? key "right")  ; right answer (make-posn 13 19)
         ]
        [ else             where ]
  ))
```

From these "right answers", it's pretty easy to write the formulæ using make-posn:

```
(cond [ (key=? key "up")     ; right answer (make-posn 12 18)
        (make-posn (posn-x where) (- (posn-y where) 1)) ]
      [ (key=? key "down")   ; right answer (make-posn 12 20)
        (make-posn (posn-x where) (+ (posn-y where) 1)) ]
      [ (key=? key "left")   ; right answer (make-posn 11 19)
        (make-posn (- (posn-x where) 1) (posn-y where)) ]
      [ (key=? key "right")  ; right answer (make-posn 13 19)
        (make-posn (+ (posn-x where) 1) (posn-y where)) ]
      [ else                 where ]
      ))
```

Alternatively, we could realize that moving up, moving down, moving left, and moving right can *all* be thought of as the same problem: *adding* something to *both* dimensions of the posn, and we've already written a function to do that, in Exercise 20.5.4. So assuming you've done that exercise, we can solve the problem as follows:

```
(cond [ (key=? key "up")     ; right answer (make-posn 12 18)
        (add-posns where (make-posn 0 -1)) ]
      [ (key=? key "down")   ; right answer (make-posn 12 20)
        (add-posns where (make-posn 0 1)) ]
      [ (key=? key "left")   ; right answer (make-posn 11 19)
        (add-posns where (make-posn -1 0)) ]
      [ (key=? key "right")  ; right answer (make-posn 13 19)
        (add-posns where (make-posn 1 0)) ]
      [ else                 where ]
      ))
```

which is shorter and clearer.

In either case, after testing this, we can put together the animation:

```
(big-bang (make-posn (/ WIDTH 2) (/ HEIGHT 2))
          (check-with posn?)
          (on-draw show-picture)
          (on-key handle-key))
```

∎

Exercise 20.6.2 *You may notice that four of the five cases in the final version of the definition share the pattern*

```
(add-posns where some-posn)
```

Even the remaining example could be fit into this pattern by adding (make-posn 0 0). *This common pattern suggests that the function definition could be simplified by "factoring out" the* **add-posns**, *moving it outside the* **cond** *so the* **cond** *decides only what to use as the second argument to* **add-posns**. *Try this. Compare the length of the resulting function with the length of the function definition in Exercise 20.6.1 above.*

Exercise 20.6.3 **Develop an animation** *of a dot that jumps randomly around the window: every half second, it disappears from where it was and appears at a completely random location with $0 \le x \le WIDTH$ and $0 \le y \le HEIGHT$.*

Hint: This is easier than Exercise 20.6.1, since you don't need to worry about what key was pressed.

Use a `posn` as the model. You *can* get this to work with an image as the model, but Exercise 20.6.4 builds on this one, and it's *much* easier if you use a `posn` as the model.

Exercise 20.6.4 *Modify Exercise 20.6.3 so that if the user clicks the mouse on the dot (i.e. within a distance of 3 from its current center), the animation ends with the message "Congratulations!" This forms a sort of video-game, which will get harder if you shorten the time between ticks.*

The following five exercises list several fun features to add to these animations. They're independent of one another; you can do any or all of them, in whatever order you wish.

Exercise 20.6.5 *Modify Exercise 20.6.1 or 20.6.3 so that if the user types the letter "q", the animation ends.*

Exercise 20.6.6 *Modify Exercise 20.6.1 or 20.6.3 so that whenever the user clicks the mouse, the dot jumps immediately to the mouse location .*

Exercise 20.6.7 *Modify Exercise 20.6.1 or 20.6.3 so that the display is a green dot if it's within 50 pixels from the center of the window (i.e. (make-posn (/ WIDTH 2) (/ HEIGHT 2)), and a red dot if it's farther away.*

Hint: Re-use a function we've seen earlier in this chapter.

Exercise 20.6.8 *Modify Exercise 20.6.1 so that in addition to responding to arrow keys, the dot moves slowly and randomly around the screen every half second: with equal probability, it moves up one pixel, down one pixel, left one pixel, or right one pixel.*

Hint: You'll obviously need to use `random`. Since all four random choices result in adding something to the current posn, you could write a helper function `choose-offset` that takes in a number (either 0, 1, 2, or 3) and returns the appropriate posn to add. Alternatively, you could write a function `random-offset` that takes in a dummy parameter, ignores it, picks a random number (either 0, 1, 2, or 3), and returns the appropriate posn to add. The latter approach is easier to use, but harder to test.

Exercise 20.6.9 *Modify Exercise 20.6.1 so that if the dot reaches an edge of the window, it "wraps around". That is, if it's at x coordinate 0, and tries to move left, its x coordinate becomes WIDTH; if it's at x coordinate WIDTH and tries to move right, its x coordinate becomes 0. Likewise, if the y coordinate is 0 and it tries to move up, the y coordinate becomes HEIGHT, while if the y coordinate is HEIGHT and the dot tries to move down, it jumps to y coordinate 0.*

Hint: It may be easiest to just move the posn, without worrying about whether it's outside the window, and then call a helper function that takes in the "attempted" position of the dot and returns a "corrected" position with $0 \leq x \leq$ WIDTH and $0 \leq y \leq$ HEIGHT.

20.7 Colors

20.7.1 The `color` data type

The `posn` type is just one example of a *structure*, about which we'll learn more in Chapter 21. The `posn` type wraps up two numbers that need to travel together and must be kept in the right order (the position $(3, 5)$ is very different from $(5, 3)$).

Recall from Section 7.8 that the color of each pixel in an image is represented by three numbers: the red, green, and blue components. This is another classic situation that calls for a structure: three pieces of information that always travel together and need to be kept in the correct order. And in fact, DrRacket has a predefined structure named `color`, for which the following functions are predefined:

```
; make-color :  number(r) number(g) number(b) [number(alpha)] -> color
; color-red :   color -> number
; color-green :  color -> number
; color-blue :  color -> number
; color-alpha :  color -> number
; color?  :  anything -> boolean
```

You've been using `make-color` since Chapter 3 to *put together* colors, but now you can also use `color-red`, `color-green`, `color-blue`, and `color-alpha` to *take them apart*.

As before, each of the color components should be an integer from 0 through 255, and (as you know), the alpha component defaults to 255 if you leave it out. For example, `(make-color 0 0 0)` is black, `(make-color 255 255 255)` is white, `(make-color 0 200 250)` is a light greenish blue, *etc.*

Most of the functions in Chapter 3 that accept a color name also accept a `color`, so for example one could write

```
(overlay (text "hello" 20 (make-color 200 200 50))
         (ellipse 100 60 "solid" (make-color 50 50 200)))
```

Practice Exercise 20.7.1 *Play with this.*

Exercise 20.7.2 *Write an animation* *that displays a large disk whose color changes with the clock and the mouse position: the x coordinate of the mouse should control the amount of red, the y coordinate should control the amount of blue, and the clock should control the amount of green.*

Hint: As in Section 7.8.3, use `min` to make sure you never pass numbers larger than 255 to `make-color`.

There's a built-in function `color?` which tells whether something is a color.

Exercise 20.7.3 *Develop a function* `color=?` *that takes in two colors and tells whether they're the same.*

Exercise 20.7.4 *Extend* *the function* `color=?` *so that each argument can be either a color or a string (color name). You'll need at least eight test cases: the first argument can be a string or a* `color`, *the second argument can be a string or a* `color`, *and the right answer can be* **true** *or* **false***. Your function should also not crash if it's given a string that isn't a recognized color name:*

```
(check-expect (color=?  "forest green" (make-color 34 139 34))
              true)
(check-expect (color=?  (make-color 58 72 14) (make-color 58 72 14))
              true)
(check-expect (color=?  "plaid" "orange")
              false)
```

20.7.2   Building images pixel by pixel

Recall the `build3-image` function of Section 7.8. There's a simpler version, `build-image`, which takes in *one* function rather than three:

```
; build-image :  number(width) number(height) function -> image
; The function argument to build-image must have the contract
; whatever :  number(x) number(y) -> color
```

For example, Exercise 7.8.1 can be re-done using `build-image` as follows:

```
; red-gradient-pixel :  number(x) number(y) -> color
(check-expect (red-gradient-pixel 0 53) (make-color 0 0 0))
(check-expect (red-gradient-pixel 7 45) (make-color 35 0 0))
(check-expect (red-gradient-pixel 50 17) (make-color 250 0 0))

(define (red-gradient-pixel x y)
  ; x      a number
  ; y      a number
  (make-color (* 5 x) 0 0))

(build-image 50 50 red-gradient-pixel)
```

Exercise 20.7.5 *Re-do some of the exercises from Section 7.8 using `build-image` instead of `build3-image`.*

20.7.3   Building images pixel by pixel from other images

Similarly, there's a `map-image` function that's like `map3-image`, but takes in only *one* function:

```
; map-image :  function image -> image
; The function argument must have contract
; whatever :  number(x) number(y) color -> color
```

Exercise 20.7.6 *Re-do some of the exercises from Section 7.8 using `map-image` instead of `map3-image`.*

Exercise 20.7.7 *Develop a function `replace-green-white` which replaces every pure-green pixel in an image with a pure-white pixel.*

Hint: This will be easier than it would be with `map3-image` because you can use `color=?`.

```
                              SIDEBAR:
```
It would be nice to generalize some of these functions, *e.g.* generalize `replace-green-white` to `replace-colors`, which takes in two colors and an image and replaces every pixel of the first color with the second. Unfortunately, that would mean the helper function depends on the parameters of `replace-color`, and we don't know how to do that yet. We'll see how in Chapters 27 and 28.

The `get-pixel-color` function allows you to get the color of *any* pixel in a given image, rather than only the one at the same location as the pixel you're currently computing.

Practice Exercise 20.7.8 *Look it up in the Help Desk. Play with it. Go wild.*

20.8 Review of important words and concepts

Sometimes an animation (or other kind of program) needs to store *several* pieces of data together in a "package"; we call this *definition by parts*. DrRacket has a predefined data type `posn` to represent (x,y) coordinate pairs, perhaps the most common example of this situation. There are several predefined functions — `make-posn`, `posn-x`, `posn-y`, `posn?` — that work with `posn`s. When writing a function that takes in a `posn`, the inventory should list not only the parameter itself but the *x* and *y parts* of the parameter.

The "inventory with values" technique is especially helpful for functions with a complicated return type like `posn`, the other structures in the next chapter, lists, *etc.*)

One can also write functions that *return* a `posn`, typically (though not always) using `make-posn` inside the body of the function.

An animation can use a `posn` as its model; this gives you a great deal more power to write fun animations that move around the screen.

Another built-in structure type is `color`. If you think of a `posn` as a box with two compartments labelled *x* and *y*, then a `color` is a box with three compartments labelled `red`, `green`, and `blue`. The `map-image`, `build-image`, *etc.* functions allow you to operate on the colors of an image.

20.9 Reference: Built-in functions on posns and colors

In this chapter we've introduced or mentioned the following built-in functions:

- `make-posn`
- `posn-x`
- `posn-y`
- `posn?`
- `make-color`
- `color-red`
- `color-green`
- `color-blue`
- `color?`

- color=?

- map-image

- build-image

- get-pixel-color

Chapter 21

Inventing new structures

21.1 Why and how

Chapter 20 showed how to store two numbers — an x coordinate and a y coordinate —
in a single object of type `posn`. This enabled us to write animations that "remember" a
two-dimensional position, and can change either or both of the coordinates.

Likewise, we saw how to store three numbers — the red, green, and blue components
of a color — in an object of type `color`.

But what if you have *more* than three pieces of information to remember? Or what if
one of them isn't a number? The `posn` and `color` data types won't help you much in those
situations.

Let's review what a `posn` is, then see how to generalize the idea.

- A posn is a package containing two "parts" (also known as *fields* or *instance variables*)
  named x and y, each of which is a number.

- posn itself is a data type (like `number` or `image`), but there may be many *instances*
  of this data type. For example, 2/3, 5, and -72541 are all instances of `number`, while
  (make-posn 3 4) and (make-posn 92 -3/4) are both instances of `posn`.

- There's a built-in function named `make-posn` that takes in two numbers and puts
  them together into a `posn` package. (Computer scientists call this a *constructor*.)

- There are two built-in functions named `posn-x` and `posn-y` that pull out the individual numbers from such a package. (Computer scientists call these *getters* or
  selectors.)

- There's a built-in function named `posn?` that takes in *any* Racket object and tells
  whether or not it is a posn. (Computer scientists call this a *discriminator*.)

Exercise 21.1.1 *What are the parts, fields, constructor, selectors, and discriminator of
the* `color` *data type?*

If we were trying to represent something other than a two-dimensional coordinate pair
or an RGB color, we might need more fields, and they might have different names and
types. We would still need a "constructor" function that takes in the values of the parts
and puts them together into a package. We would still need several "getter" functions (one
for each "part") that retrieve the individual parts from a package. And we would still need

a "discriminator" function which tells us whether a given object is this kind of package at all.

Racket provides a way to define other data types analogous to posn, with fields, constructor, getters, and discriminator. Here's the syntax rule:

Syntax Rule 7 *Anything matching the pattern*

```
(define-struct struct-name (field-name-1 ... field-name-n))
```

is a legal expression, as long as struct-name *is a previously undefined name. (The field-names may or may not already be defined elsewhere; it doesn't matter.)*

The expression has no value, but the side effect of defining a new data type struct-name *and several functions with contracts*

```
; make-struct-name :   n objects -> struct-name
; struct-name-field-name-1 :  struct-name -> object
; ...
; struct-name-field-name-n :  struct-name -> object
; struct-name? :  object -> boolean
```

There's a lot going on in there, so let's see how it applies to the two structs we've already seen — posn and color. The posn type happens to be predefined in the HtDP languages of DrRacket, but if it weren't, we could define it ourselves as follows:

```
(define-struct posn (x y))
```

The *struct-name* is posn. There are two fields, named x and y. So we've defined a new data type named posn, as well as the following functions:

```
; make-posn :  object(x) object(y) -> posn
; posn-x :  posn -> object
; posn-y :  posn -> object
; posn? :  object -> boolean
```

which (mostly) agrees with what we learned in the previous chapter.

Exercise 21.1.2 *How would you define the* color *type if it weren't predefined?*

There's one difference between these contracts and those you learned in Chapter 20: the "parts" of a posn here are just "objects", rather than specifically numbers. In fact, you *can* build a posn whose "*x* coordinate" is a string and whose "*y* coordinate" is an image, and you won't get any error messages — but as soon as you try to *use* that posn in a function that expects the coordinates to be numbers, it'll crash. To avoid this, we agree to follow the *convention* that the coordinates in a posn are always numbers, so in practice the contracts really are

```
; make-posn :  number(x) number(y) -> posn
; posn-x :  posn -> number
; posn-y :  posn -> number
; posn? :  object -> boolean
```

exactly as we learned in the previous chapter.

Worked Exercise 21.1.3 *Define a structure to represent a person, with first and last names and age.*

Solution: The structure has three parts, which can naturally be called *first*, *last*, and *age*. We'll agree to the convention that *first* and *last* are both strings, while *age* is a number. So the struct definition looks like

```
(define-struct person (first last age))
```

This has the effect of defining a new data type `person`, along with the functions

```
; make-person :  string(first) string(last) number(age) -> person
; person-first :  person -> string
; person-last :  person -> string
; person-age :  person -> number
; person?  :  object -> boolean
```

To see that this definition actually works, we put the `define-struct` line (and, ideally, the comments about function contracts) in the definitions pane, hit "Run", and we can now use the `person` type as follows:

```
> (make-person "Joe" "Schmoe" 19)
(make-person "Joe" "Schmoe" 19)
> (define author (make-person "Stephen" "Bloch" 46))
> (define lambda-guy (make-person "Alonzo" "Church" 107))
> (person-first author)
"Stephen"
> (person-last author)
"Bloch"
> (person-last lambda-guy)
"Church"
> (person-first lambda-guy)
"Alonzo"
> (person-first (make-person "Joe" "Schmoe" 19))
"Joe"
> (person-age lambda-guy)
107
> (person?  author)
true
> (person?  "Bloch")
false
> (person?  (make-person "Joe" "Schmoe" 19))
true
```

SIDEBAR:

Alonzo Church (1903-1995) invented a model of computation called the "lambda calculus" (no relation to the "calculus" that's about derivatives and integrals) which later became the inspiration for the Lisp, Scheme, and Racket languages. This is why there's a Greek letter lambda (λ) in the DrRacket logo; we'll learn more about lambda in Chapter 28. He was also my advisor's advisor's advisor; so there.

Note that you don't need to *define* the `make-person`, `person-first`, `person-last`, `person-age`, or `person?` functions; they "come for free" with `define-struct`. We wrote down their contracts only so we would know how to *use* them. ∎

21.2 A Recipe for Defining a Struct

Back in Chapter 5, we learned a step-by-step recipe for defining a function, and in Chapter 10 we learned a step-by-step recipe for writing an animation. A step-by-step recipe for defining a struct is in Figure 21.1.

Figure 21.1: Design recipe for defining a struct

1. **Identify the parts** of the desired data types: how many parts should it have, and what are their names and their types?

2. **Write a** `define-struct` according to Syntax Rule 7.

3. Write down (in comments) the **contracts** for the functions that "come for free":

   - a constructor, whose name is `make-` followed by the name of the struct;
   - several *getters* or *selectors* (one for each field) whose names are the name of the struct, a hyphen, and the name of one of the fields;
   - a discriminator whose name is the name of the struct, followed by a question mark.

4. Write some **examples** of objects of the new data type.

5. Write input and output templates for functions that work on the new type.

Worked Exercise 21.2.1 *Define a data type to represent an employee of a business, including the employee's name (we won't bother with first and last names), ID number, and salary.*

Solution:

Identify the parts

```
; An employee has three parts:  name, id, and salary.
; The name is a string, while id and salary are numbers.
```

Write a `define-struct`

```
(define-struct employee (name id salary))
```

Write contracts for the functions that "come for free"

```
; make-employee:
    string(name) number(id) number(salary) -> employee
; employee-name:  employee -> string
; employee-id:  employee -> number
; employee-salary:  employee -> number
; employee?:  object -> boolean
```

Write examples of the new data type

```
(make-employee "Joe" 348 42995)
(make-employee "Mary" 214 49500)
(define emp1 (make-employee "Bob" 470 36000))
(define emp2 (make-employee "Chris" 471 41000))
(check-expect (employee-name emp1) "Bob")
(check-expect (employee-id emp2) 471)
(check-expect (employee-salary emp2) 41000)
(check-expect (employee-salary (make-employee "Mary" 214 49500))
              49500)
(check-expect (employee? emp1) true)
(check-expect (employee? "Mary") false)
```

Write templates

The input template is

```
#|
(check-expect (function-on-employee emp1) ...)
(check-expect (function-on-employee
                  (make-employee "Joe" 348 42995))
              ...)

(define (function-on-employee emp)
  ; emp                  an employee
  ; (employee-name emp)  a string
  ; (employee-id emp)    a number
  ; (employee-salary emp) a number
  ...)
|#
```

and the output template

```
#|
(check-expect (function-returning-employee ...) emp1)
(check-expect (function-returning-employee ...)
              (make-employee "Joe" 348 42995))

(define (function-returning-employee ...)
  (make-employee ... ... ...)  ; name, id, salary
  )
|#
```

Common beginner mistakes

Students often get confused between `define-struct` and `make-person` (and other constructors like `make-employee`).

By way of analogy, imagine an inventor who has invented a new kind of cell phone. The inventor probably doesn't actually build cell phones herself; instead, she produces *blueprints, diagrams, etc.* for how the new kind of cell phone is supposed to go together.

Based on these blueprints and diagrams, somebody builds a *factory* which then builds millions of individual cell phones.

In our setting, `define-struct` is like the inventor. The `make-person`, `make-employee`, *etc.* functions are like factories: they don't even exist until the inventor has done her work, but then they can be used to build as many instances of `person` or `employee` respectively as you wish.

I often see students write things like

```
(define-struct employee (name id salary))
(define emp1 (make-employee "Bob" 470 36000))
(check-expect emp1-salary 36000)
(check-expect (emp1-salary employee) 36000)
```

There is no variable or function named `emp1-salary`, nor is there a variable named `employee`, so the last two lines both produce error messages. But there *is* a function named `employee-salary`, which *takes in* an `employee` object; the student probably meant

```
(check-expect (employee-salary emp1) 36000)
```

Another pitfall: the same student writes

```
(check-expect (employee-salary "Bob") 36000)
```

What's wrong with this? Well, there *is* a function named `employee-salary`, but its contract specifies that it takes in an `employee`, not a string. What this student is trying to do is *look up* a previously-defined employee by one of its field values; we'll learn how to do this in Section 22.6.

21.3   Exercises on Defining Structs

Exercise 21.3.1 *Define a structure named my-posn to represent an (x, y) coordinate pair. The result should behave just like the built-in posn, except for its name.*

Exercise 21.3.2 *Define a data type to represent a CD in your audio library, including such information as the title, performer, what year it was recorded, and how many tracks it has.*

Exercise 21.3.3 *Define a data type to represent a candidate in an election. There should be two fields: the candidate's name and how many votes (s)he got.*

Exercise 21.3.4 *Define a data type to represent a course at your school, including the name of the course, the name of the instructor, what room it meets in, and what time it meets. (For now, assume all courses start on the hour, so you only need to know what hour the course starts.)*

Hint: You'll need to decide whether a "room" is best represented as a number or a string.

Exercise 21.3.5 *Define a data type to represent a basketball player, including the player's name, what team (s)he plays for, and his/her jersey number.*

Exercise 21.3.6 *Define a data type to represent a dog (or a cat if you prefer), with a name, age, weight, and color.*

Exercise 21.3.7 *Define a data type to represent a mathematical rectangle, whose properties are length and width.*

Hint: There's already a function named `rectangle`, so if you try to write

```
(define-struct rectangle ...)
```

you'll probably get an error message. Name your struct `rect` instead.

Hint: This data type has *nothing to do with images*. A `rect` has no color, it is not outlined or solid, it has no position, *etc.*; it has *only* a length and a width.

Exercise 21.3.8 *Define a data type to represent a time of day, in hours, minutes, and seconds. (Assume a 24-hour clock, so 3:52:14 PM would have hours=15, minutes=52, seconds=14.)*

21.4 Writing functions on user-defined structs

Writing functions using a struct you've defined yourself is no more difficult than writing functions using `posns`.

Worked Exercise 21.4.1 *Define a function that takes in an **employee** (from Exercise 21.2.1) and tells whether or not the employee earns over $100,000 per year.*

Solution: Before you type any of this stuff, make sure you've got the definition of the `employee` data type, and perhaps its examples, in the definitions pane. The following stuff should all appear *after* that definition.

Contract:

```
; earns-over-100k?  :  employee -> boolean
```

Examples:

```
(check-expect
  (earns-over-100k?  (make-employee "Phil" 27 119999)) true)
(check-expect
  (earns-over-100k?  (make-employee "Anne" 51 100000))
  false ; (borderline case)
(check-expect (earns-over-100k?  emp1) false)
  ; assuming the definition of emp1 from before
```

Skeleton and inventory:

```
(define (earns-over-100k? emp)
  ; emp                      employee
  ; (employee-name emp)      string
  ; (employee-id emp)        number
  ; (employee-salary emp)    number
  ; 100000                   fixed number
  ...)
```

Body:

We don't actually need the employee name or id, only the salary.

```
(define (earns-over-100k? emp)
  ; emp                      employee
  ; (employee-name emp)      string
  ; (employee-id emp)        number
  ; (employee-salary emp)    number
  ; 100000                   fixed number
  (> (employee-salary emp) 100000)
)
```

Testing:

Hit "Run" and see whether the actual answers match what you said they "should be". ∎

Exercise 21.4.2 *Choose a function you've already written that operates on* posn, *and* **rewrite** *it to operate on a* my-posn *instead.*

Exercise 21.4.3 *Develop a function* rec-before-1980? *that takes in a CD and returns* true *or* false *depending on whether it was recorded before 1980.*

Exercise 21.4.4 *Develop a function* older? *that takes in two* person *structs and tells whether the first is older than the second.*

Exercise 21.4.5 *Develop a function* person=? *that takes in two* person *structs and tells whether they have the exact same name and age. You may* not *use the built-in* equal? *function to solve this problem.*

Exercise 21.4.6 *Develop a function* same-team? *that takes in two basketball-player structs and tells whether they play for the same team.*

Exercise 21.4.7 *Develop a function* full-name *that takes in a* person *struct and returns a single string containing the person's first and last names, separated by a space.*

Exercise 21.4.8 *Develop a function* rect-area *that takes in a* rect *struct and returns the area of the rectangle (i.e. length times width).*

Exercise 21.4.9 *Develop a function* `larger-rect?` *that takes in two* `rect` *structs and tells whether the first has a larger area than the second.*

Hint: Copying the input template for the `rect` structure will take care of *one* of the two parameters; for the other, you'll need to copy the inventory again and change the parameter name.

Exercise 21.4.10 *Develop a function* `seconds-since-midnight` *that takes in a time-of-day struct and returns how many seconds it has been since midnight.*

Exercise 21.4.11 *Develop a function* `seconds-between` *that takes in two time-of-day structs and returns the difference between them, in seconds.*

Hint: For example, the time 11:01:14 is 124 seconds after the time 10:59:10.

Exercise 21.4.12 *Develop a function named* `who-won` *that takes in three candidate structures (from Exercise 21.3.3) and returns the name of the one with the most votes, or the word "tie" if two or more of them tied for first place.*

Hint: Obviously, this resembles Exercise 15.5.4, but it doesn't assume that the candidates' names are always "Anne", "Bob", and "Charlie"; it'll work with *any* names.

21.5   Functions returning user-defined structs

Just as you can write a function to return a `posn` or a `color`, you can also write a function that returns a `name`, `cd`, `employee`, or any other type you've defined. As in Section 20.5, you'll usually (but not always!) need a `make`-whatever in the body of your function. Use the output template.

Worked Exercise 21.5.1 *Define a function* `change-salary` *that takes in an employee (from Exercise 21.2.1) and a number, and produces a new employee just like the old one but with the salary changed to the specified number.*

Solution:

Contract:

```
; change-salary :  employee number -> employee
```

Examples:

```
(check-expect
  (change-salary (make-employee "Joe" 352 65000) 66000)
  (make-employee "Joe" 352 66000))
(check-expect
  (change-salary (make-employee "Croesus" 2 197000) 1.49)
  (make-employee "Croesus" 2 1.49))
```

Skeleton and Inventory

Since this function both takes in *and* returns an `employee`, we can use both the input and output templates to help us write it.

```
(define (change-salary emp new-salary)
  ; emp                        employee
  ; (employee-name emp)        string
  ; (employee-id emp)          number
  ; (employee-salary emp)      number
  ; new-salary                 number
  (make-employee ... ... ...))
```

Since this function returns something of a complex data type, we'll use an **inventory with values**:

```
(define (change-salary emp new-salary)
  ; emp                    employee  (make-employee "Joe" 352 65000)
  ; (employee-name emp)    string    "Joe"
  ; (employee-id emp)      number    352
  ; (employee-salary emp)  number    65000
  ; new-salary             number    66000
  ; right answer                employee (make-employee "Joe" 352 66000)
  (make-employee ... ... ...))
```

This makes the **Body** fairly obvious:

```
(define (change-salary emp new-salary)
  ; emp                    employee (make-employee "Joe" 352 65000)
  ; (employee-name emp)    string   "Joe"
  ; (employee-id emp)      number   352
  ; (employee-salary emp)  number   65000
  ; new-salary             number   66000
  ; right answer           employee (make-employee "Joe" 352 66000)
  (make-employee (employee-name emp)
                 (employee-id emp)
                 new-salary )
)
```

Now test the function and see whether it works correctly on both examples.   ∎

Exercise 21.5.2 *Develop a function* `change-jersey` *that takes in a basketball player struct and a number and produces a basketball player with the same name and team as before, but the specified jersey number.*

Exercise 21.5.3 *Develop a function* `birthday` *that takes in a person struct and returns a person with the same first and last name, but one year older.*

Exercise 21.5.4 *Develop a function* `change-name-to-match` *that takes in two person structs and returns a person just like the first one, but with the last name changed to match the second one.*

Exercise 21.5.5 *Develop a function* `raise-salary-percent` *that takes in an employee structure and a number, and produces a copy of the employee with the specified percentage increase in salary.*

Exercise 21.5.6 *Develop a function* `add-a-vote` *that takes in a candidate structure and adds one to his/her vote count.*

Exercise 21.5.7 *Develop a function* `swap-length-width` *that takes in a* `rect` *structure and produces a new* `rect` *whose length is the width of the given* `rect`, *and vice versa.*

21.6 Animations using user-defined structs

Worked Exercise 21.6.1 *Write an animation of a picture that moves steadily to the right or left, say 3 pixels per second; if the user presses the right-arrow key, the picture starts moving to the right, and if the user presses the left-arrow key, the picture starts moving to the left.*

Solution:

Handlers
Since the picture needs to "move steadily" at a fixed rate per second, we'll need a tick handler. Since it needs to respond to key presses, we'll need a key handler. And as usual, we'll need a check-with handler and a draw handler.

Model
Since the picture only needs to move left and right, we need only the x coordinate of its location (we'll probably want to define a named constant for its y coordinate). However, we also need to keep track of which *direction* it's moving — left or right — so that a tick handler can move it in the appropriate direction every second. One way to do that is with a string which will always be either `"left"` or `"right"`. So our model needs to have two fields, which we can call `x` (a number) and `dir` (a string). We'll name such a data structure a `moving-x`.

Combining this English-language description with a `define-struct`, we get

```
; A moving-x consists of x (a number) and
;   dir (a string, either "left" or "right")
```

```
(define-struct moving-x (x dir))
```

which gives us the following functions "for free":

```
; make-moving-x :  number string -> moving-x
; moving-x-x :  moving-x -> number
; moving-x-dir :  moving-x -> string
; moving-x?  :  object -> boolean
```

Some examples of the new data type:

```
(define state1 (make-moving-x 10 "right"))
(define state2 (make-moving-x 29 "left"))
(check-expect (moving-x-x state1) 10)
(check-expect (moving-x-dir state2) "left")
```

An input template:

```
#|
(define (function-on-moving-x current)
  ; current                 moving-x
  ; (moving-x-x current)    number
  ; (moving-x-dir current) string
  ...)
|#
```

And an output template:

```
#|
(define (function-returning-moving-x whatever)
  (make-moving-x ... ...))
|#
```

Contracts for handlers
We'll need a draw handler, a tick handler, and a key handler, with contracts

```
; handle-draw :  moving-x -> image
; handle-tick :  moving-x -> moving-x
; handle-key :  moving-x key -> moving-x
```

Writing the draw handler
We already have a contract. To make the examples easy, we can revive the `calendar-at-x` function from Chapter 8 and say

```
(check-expect (handle-draw state1) (calendar-at-x 10))
(check-expect (handle-draw state2) (calendar-at-x 29))
```

The skeleton and inventory are easy from the input template:

```
(define ( handle-draw current)
  ; current                 moving-x
  ; (moving-x-x current)    number
  ; (moving-x-dir current)  string
  ...)
```

If you already see what to do, great. If not, we'll add an "inventory with values":

```
(define (handle-draw current)
  ; current                 moving-x  (make-moving-x 10 "right")
  ; (moving-x-x current)    number    10
  ; (moving-x-dir current) string    "right"
  ; right answer            image     (calendar-at-x 10)
  ...)
```

This makes the body easy:

```
(define (handle-draw current)
  ; current              moving-x (make-moving-x 10 "right")
  ; (moving-x-x current) number   10
  ; (moving-x-dir current) string "right"
  ; right answer         image    (calendar-at-x 10)
  (calendar-at-x (moving-x-x current))
)
```

Test this function on the above test cases before going on. Once it works, and if it's OK with your instructor, you *might* want to take out the "scratch work", leaving only the real code, which is quite short:

```
(define (handle-draw current)
  (calendar-at-x (moving-x-x current))
)
```

Writing the tick handler

We already have a contract. Since the speed of motion is a fixed number, let's define a constant for it:

```
(define SPEED 3)
```

And since part of the input data type has two cases ("left" and "right"), we'll need at least two examples, one for each. To be really bulletproof, we should also have a case that handles illegal moving-x objects:

```
(check-expect (handle-tick (make-moving-x 10 "right"))
              (make-moving-x (+ 10 SPEED) "right"))
(check-expect (handle-tick (make-moving-x 29 "left"))
              (make-moving-x (- 29 SPEED) "left"))
(check-error (handle-tick (make-moving-x 53 "fnord"))
             "handle-tick:  Direction is neither left nor right!")
```

For the skeleton and inventory, we copy the template, change the name, and add some special values:

```
(define ( handle-tick current)
  ; current              moving-x
  ; (moving-x-x current) number
  ; (moving-x-dir current) string
  ; SPEED                fixed number
  ; "left", "right"      fixed strings
  ...)
```

Clearly, we'll need to do something different depending on whether the current direction is "left" or "right", so we'll need a conditional with those two cases (plus an error-handling case). To figure out what to do in each case, let's copy the relevant parts of the inventory into each case and do an "inventory with values" for each:

```
(define (handle-tick current)
  ; ...
  (cond  [  (string=?  (moving-x-dir current) "left")
            ; (moving-x-x current)        number    29
            ; (moving-x-dir current)      string    "left"
            ; right answer                moving-x
            ;       (make-moving-x (- 29 SPEED) "left")
            ...
            ]
         [ (string=?  (moving-x-dir current) "right")
            ; (moving-x-x current)        number    10
            ; (moving-x-dir current)      string    "right"
            ; right answer                moving-x
            ;       (make-moving-x (+ 10 SPEED) "right")
            ...
            ]
         [ else (error 'handle-tick
                       "Direction is neither left nor right!")]
         )
  )
```

Which makes the "answer" part of each cond-clause pretty easy:

```
(define (handle-tick current)
  ; ...
  (cond [(string=?  (moving-x-dir current) "left")
         ; (moving-x-x current)        number    29
         ; (moving-x-dir current)      string    "left"
         ; right answer                moving-x
         ;    (make-moving-x (- 29 SPEED) "left")
         (make-moving-x (- (moving-x-x current) SPEED) "left")
         ]
        [ (string=?  (moving-x-dir current) "right")
         ; (moving-x-x current)        number    10
         ; (moving-x-dir current)      string    "right"
         ; right answer                moving-x
         ;    (make-moving-x (+ 10 SPEED) "right")
         (make-moving-x (+ (moving-x-x current) SPEED) "right")
         ]
        [else (error 'handle-tick
                     "Direction is neither left nor right!")]
        )
  )
```

Test this function on the above test cases before going on.

Again, if you delete the scratch work, the function definition is fairly short:

```
(define (handle-tick current)
  (cond [(string=?  (moving-x-dir current) "left")
         (make-moving-x (- (moving-x-x current) SPEED) "left")
         ]
        [ (string=?  (moving-x-dir current) "right")
         (make-moving-x (+ (moving-x-x current) SPEED) "right")
         ]
        [else (error 'handle-tick
                     "Direction is neither left nor right!")]
        )
  )
```

Writing the key handler

We already have a contract. One of the inputs is a *key*, which for our purposes can be broken down into `"left"`, `"right"`, and anything else.

```
(check-expect (handle-key state1 "up") state1)
(check-expect (handle-key state1 "right") state1)
  ; since state1 is already going right
(check-expect (handle-key state1 "left")
  (make-moving-x 10 "left"))
(check-expect (handle-key state2 "right")
  (make-moving-x 29 "right"))
```

For the skeleton and inventory, we have a choice: since the function takes in *both* a moving-x and a *key*, we could use the template for either one. In fact, we'll probably need elements of both:

```
(define (handle-key current key)
  ; current                 moving-x
  ; (moving-x-x current)     number
  ; (moving-x-dir current)   string
  ; key                     string
  ; "left", "right"          fixed strings
  (cond [ (key=?  key "left")  ...]
        [ (key=?  key "right") ...]
        [ else                 ...]
        )
  )
```

The "else" case is easy: return **current** without modification. For the other two, we can use an "inventory with values":

```
(cond [(key=?  key "left")
       ; (moving-x-x current)    number   10
       ; (moving-x-dir current)  string   "right"
       ; right answer            moving-x (make-moving-x 10 "left")
       ...]
      [ (key=?  key "right")
       ; (moving-x-x current)    number   10
       ; (moving-x-dir current)  string   "right"
       ; right answer            moving-x (make-moving-x 10 "right")
       ...]
      [ else                     current ]
      )
)
```

To fill in the first of the "…" gaps, we clearly need (make-moving-x (moving-x-x current) key). For the second, there are two places we could get a "right" from: (moving-x-dir current) and key. Which one should we use? One way to decide would be to do another "inventory with values", using an example that was traveling to the left … but since we've already said (make-moving-x (moving-x-x current) key) in the "left" case, it seems plausible to do the same thing in the "right" case:

```
(cond [(key=?  key "left")
       ; (moving-x-x current)    number   10
       ; (moving-x-dir current)  string   "right"
       ; right answer            moving-x (make-moving-x 10 "left")
       (make-moving-x (moving-x-x current) key) ]
      [ (key=?  key "right")
       ; (moving-x-x current)    number   10
       ; (moving-x-dir current)  string   "right"
       ; right answer            moving-x (make-moving-x 10 "right")
       (make-moving-x (moving-x-x current) key) ]
      [ else                     current ]
      )
)
```

Notice that we're returning the exact same expression in the "left" and "right" cases. Recognizing this, we can simplify the program by combining them into one:

```
(define (handle-key current key)
  ; ...
  (cond [ (or (key=?  key "left") (key=?  key "right"))
          (make-moving-x (moving-x-x current) key) ]
        [ else                     current ]
        )
  )
```

Test this before going on.

Running the animation
Now that we know each of the handlers works by itself, we can put them together:

```
(big-bang
  (make-moving-x (/ WIDTH 2) "right") ; start at middle, moving right
  (check-with moving-x?)
  (on-draw handle-draw)
  (on-tick handle-tick 1)
  (on-key handle-key)
  )
```

which, when I test it, works as it's supposed to. ∎

Exercise 21.6.2 *Modify the animation of Exercise 21.6.1 so that if the x coordinate becomes less than 0, the direction switches to "right", and if the x coordinate becomes more than WIDTH, the direction switches to "left" — in other words, the picture "bounces" off the walls.*

Exercise 21.6.3 *Modify the animation of Exercise 20.6.4 so that it keeps track of how many clicks you've done before successfully clicking on a dot. Once you do, it should replace the contents of the animation window with something like "Congratulations! It took you 13 clicks to hit a dot."*

Hint: Your model needs to "remember" the current x and y coordinates of the dot, as well as how many clicks there have been so far (initially zero). The tick handler will generate a new set of random coordinates but keep the click count unchanged. The mouse handler will add one to the click count, but leave the coordinates unchanged (unless the click was close enough, in which case it builds an appropriate stop-with message using `number->string` and `string-append`).

Hint: This is easier to do using `stop-with` than `stop-when`.

21.7 Structs containing other structs

In Exercise 21.6.3, you probably defined a struct with three fields: x, y, and `clicks`. Two of the three happen to be the exact same fields as in a `posn`, so an alternative way to define this struct would be as *two* fields, one of which is a posn. (Fields of a struct can be *any* type, even another struct.) This has some advantages: any function you've previously written to work on posns can be re-used without change. It also has some disadvantages: building an example is more tedious, *e.g.* `(make-click-posn (make-posn 3 4) 5)` rather than `(make-click-posn 3 4 5)`.

Exercise 21.7.1 *Modify the animation of Exercise 21.6.3 to use this sort of a model. It should behave exactly as before. Is the code shorter or longer? Easier or harder to understand?*

(If you did Exercise 21.6.3 using a nested struct, try it with three fields instead. Is the code shorter or longer? Easier or harder to understand?)

Exercise 21.7.2 *Define a data type `placed-circ` to represent a mathematical circle with its two-dimensional location. It should have a posn for its center, and a number for its radius.*

Exercise 21.7.3 *Define a data type* `placed-rect` *to represent a mathematical rectangle with its two-dimensional location. It should have a* `posn` *for the "top-left corner" (a common way of representing rectangles in computer graphics), and two numbers for the width and height.*

Exercise 21.7.4 *Define a function* `circs-overlap?` *that takes in two* `placed-circ` *structures and tells whether they overlap.*

Hint: Use the distance between their centers, together with their radii.

Exercise 21.7.5

Write an animation in which a particular (small) picture moves with the mouse over a (large) background picture, and every time the user clicks and releases the mouse button, the small picture is added to the background picture at that location. For example, if the small picture were a smiley-face, you could place a bunch of smiley-faces in various places around the background picture, with a smiley-face always moving with the mouse so you can see what it'll look like in advance.

Exercise 21.7.6 *Write an animation of a dot that moves around the screen at a constant speed until it hits the top, left, right, or bottom edge of the window, at which time it "bounces off".*

Hint: You'll need a `posn` to represent the current location, plus two numbers (or a `posn`, if you prefer) to represent the current *velocity* — how fast is it moving to the right, and how fast is it moving down? When you hit a wall, one component of the velocity should be reversed, and the other should stay as it was. You may find it easier to break your tick handler into *three* functions: one to move the dot, one to decide whether it should bounce in the x dimension, and one to decide whether it should bounce in the y dimension.

Exercise 21.7.7 *Modify the animation of Exercise 21.7.6 so that if you press any of the arrow keys, it accelerates the dot in that direction (that is, it changes the velocity, not the location). You now have a rocket-ship simulation.*

Exercise 21.7.8 *Modify the animation of Exercise 21.7.6 so that every second, the dot slows down a little bit (call it friction) — say, 5% per second. You now have a billiards simulation.*

Exercise 21.7.9 *Modify Exercise 18.2.5 (typing into the animation window) so there's a vertical-bar cursor showing where you're currently typing. The right-arrow key should move the cursor one character to the right (unless it's already at the end of the text), left-arrow one character to the left (unless it's already at the beginning), any ordinary character you type should be inserted into the text where the cursor is (and the cursor should move to the right), and the key "backspace" should delete the character just before the cursor.*

Hint: You'll need to define a structure to represent both the string that appears in the window and the location of the cursor. One good way to do this is to store two strings: the text before the cursor and the text after the cursor.

Exercise 21.7.10

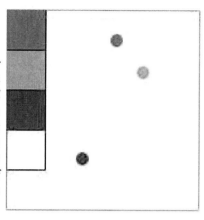

Write an animation with a "palette" containing four colored panels (say, red, green, blue, and white) down the left-hand side, and a "picture region", initially all white, filling the rest of the animation window. When you click on any of the colored panels, a dot of that color starts moving with your mouse, and when you click the mouse anywhere in the picture region, the dot is left there; then you can go on and add more dots of that color, or pick up a different color and add some different-colored dots.

21.8 Decisions on types, revisited

In section 15.8, we learned to define a new data type "by choices", *e.g.* "an X is either a Y or a Z". But in that chapter, Y and Z were always predefined types like string, number, image, *etc.*. The technique of "definition by choices" becomes more useful when Y and Z are themselves defined "by parts", *i.e.* structs.

Recall that to write a function on a type defined by choices, we needed *discriminator functions* (*e.g.* `number?`, `string?`, `image?`) to tell which type something was. Conveniently enough, `define-struct` gives you a discriminator function for the newly-defined type, with the obvious name (`posn?`, `person?`, `employee?`, `candidate?`, ...).

Worked Exercise 21.8.1 *Define a data type* named placed-shape *which is either a* placed-circ *(from Exercise 21.7.2) or a* placed-rect *(from Exercise 21.7.3).*

Develop a function `perimeter` *which works on a* placed-shape *and returns the length of the boundary of the shape.*

Develop a function `move-shape` *that takes in a* placed-shape *and two numbers dx and dy, and returns another* placed-shape *just like the given one but moved by dx in the x dimension and dy in the y dimension.*

Solution: The data definition is simply "A placed-shape is either a placed-circ or a placed-rect." However, for this definition to be useful, we need some examples of the data type, and we need templates. Examples are easy: any `placed-circ` or any `placed-rect` will do (and to test a function on *placed-shape*, we should have at least one of each). Depending on exactly how you did Exercises 21.7.2 and 21.7.3, this could look like

```
(define shape-1 (make-placed-circ (make-posn 3 8) 5))
(define shape-2 (make-placed-rect (make-posn 15 21) 12 8))
```

The input template looks like

```
#|
(define (function-on-placed-shape s)
  (cond [(placed-circ?  s) (function-on-placed-circ s)]
        [(placed-rect?  s) (function-on-placed-rect s)]
  ))
|#
```

where `function-on-placed-circ` and `function-on-placed-rect` indicate functions written based on the input templates for those data types. If these functions are fairly short and simple, it may be more practical to combine all three into one, following a combined template like

```
#|
(define (function-on-placed-shape s)
  (cond [(placed-circ?  s)
          ; s                         placed-circ
          ; (placed-circ-center s)    posn
          ; (placed-circ-radius s)    number
          ...]
        [(placed-rect?  s)
          ; (placed-rect-top-left s)  posn
          ; (placed-rect-width s)     number
          ; (placed-rect-height s)    number
          ...]
  ))
|#
```

Again, some of the details may vary depending on how you did Exercises 21.7.2 and 21.7.3.

We can also write an output template:

```
#|
(define (function-returning-placed-shape ...)
  (cond [... (function-returning-placed-circ ...)]
        [... (function-returning-placed-rect ...)]
  ))
|#
```

As with the input template, if the relevant functions returning a *placed-circ* and a *placed-rect* are short and simple, it makes more sense to combine them all into one template:

```
#|
(define (function-returning-placed-shape ...)
  (cond [... (make-placed-circ ... ...)]
        [... (make-placed-rect ... ... ...)]
  ))
|#
```

To define the `perimeter` function, we have a choice: either we write three separate functions `circ-perimeter`, `rect-perimeter`, and `perimeter`, each of which is fairly short, or we combine them into one larger function. We'll do both here, so you can see the advantages and disadvantages of each approach.

```
; circ-perimeter :  placed-circ -> number
(define empty-circ (make-placed-circ (make-posn 0 0) 0))
(define circ-1 (make-placed-circ (make-posn 10 4) 1))
(check-within (circ-perimeter empty-circ) 0 .01)
(check-within (circ-perimeter circ-1) 6.28 .01)
(check-within (circ-perimeter shape-1) 31.4 .1)
(define (circ-perimeter c)
  ; c                     placed-circ
  ; (placed-circ-center c) posn
  ; (placed-circ-radius c) number
  (* pi 2 (placed-circ-radius c)))
```

Note that since the formula for the perimeter of a circle involves π, which can be represented only approximately in a computer, the answer is approximate so we use `check-within` rather than `check-expect`.

```
; rect-perimeter :  placed-rect -> number
(define empty-rect (make-placed-rect (make-posn 0 0) 0 0))
(define horiz-line (make-placed-rect (make-posn -1 0) 2 0))
(define square-2
  (make-placed-rect (make-posn 1 1) (sqrt 2) (sqrt 2)))
(check-expect (rect-perimeter empty-rect) 0)
(check-expect (rect-perimeter horiz-line) 4)
(check-within (rect-perimeter square-2) 5.66 .01)
(check-expect (rect-perimeter shape-2) 40)
(define (rect-perimeter r)
  ; r                     placed-rect
  ; (placed-rect-top-left r)posn
  ; (placed-rect-width r)   number
  ; (placed-rect-height r) number
  (* 2 (+ (placed-rect-width r) (placed-rect-height r))))
```

The function on *placed-shapes* is now fairly simple:

```
; perimeter :  placed-shape -> number
(check-within (perimeter empty-circ) 0 .01)
(check-within (perimeter empty-rect) 0 .01)
(check-within (perimeter circ-1) 6.28 .01)
(check-within (perimeter square-2) 5.66 .01)
(check-within (perimeter shape-1) 31.4 .1)
(check-within (perimeter shape-2) 40 .1)
(define (perimeter s)
  (cond [(placed-circ? s) (circ-perimeter s)]
        [(placed-rect? s) (rect-perimeter s)]
  ))
```

If we wanted to write the whole thing as one big function, it would look more like this (the contract and examples are unchanged):

```
(define (perimeter s)
  (cond [(placed-circ?  s)
         ; s                          placed-circ
         ; (placed-circ-center s) posn
         ; (placed-circ-radius s) number
         (* pi 2 (placed-circ-radius s))]
        [(placed-rect?  s)
         ; s                          placed-rect
         ; (placed-rect-top-left s)posn
         ; (placed-rect-width s)  number
         ; (placed-rect-height s) number
         (* 2 (+ (placed-rect-width s) (placed-rect-height r)))]
  ))
```

If you were sure you would only need the `perimeter` function, not the more specific versions of it for the placed-circ and placed-rect types, and if you were confident of your programming skills, the single-function solution would probably be quicker and easier to write. On the other hand, three little functions are generally easier to test and debug (one at a time!) than one big function, and they can be individually re-used. For example, if in some future problem you wanted the perimeter of something you *knew* was a placed-circ, not a placed-rect, you could use `circ-perimeter` rather than the more general, but slightly less efficient, `perimeter`. In the long run, you should know both approaches.

For the `move-shape` function, we need at least two examples — a rectangle and a circle:

```
(check-expect
  (move-shape (make-placed-circ (make-posn 5 12) 4) 6 -3)
  (make-placed-circ (make-posn 11 9) 4))
(check-expect
  (move-shape (make-placed-rect (make-posn 19 10) 8 13) -5 6)
  (make-placed-rect (make-posn 14 16) 8 13))
```

The `move-shape` function both *takes in* and *returns* a placed-shape, so we'll use both input and output templates.

```
(define (move-shape it dx dy)
  ; it      placed-shape
  ; dx      number
  ; dy      number
  (cond [(placed-circ?  it) (function-returning-placed-circ ...)]
        [(placed-rect?  it) (function-returning-placed-rect ...)]
  ))
```

We could write two other functions `move-placed-circ` and `move-placed-rect`, but this time let's try a single-function solution. The templates give us the following:

```
(define (move-shape it dx dy)
  ; it        placed-shape
  ; dx        number
  ; dy        number
  (cond [(placed-circ?  it)
         ; (placed-circ-center it) posn
         ; (placed-circ-radius it) number
         (make-placed-circ ......)  ]
        [(placed-rect?  it)
         ; (placed-rect-top-left it) posn
         ; (placed-rect-width it)    number
         ; (placed-rect-height it)   number
         (make-placed-rect ........)  ]
  ))
```

The width and height of the rectangle shouldn't change, and the radius of the circle shouldn't change, but we need a new top-left corner for the rectangle, and a new center for the circle. The obvious way to get these is with add-posns (Exercise 20.5.4):

```
(define (move-shape it dx dy)
  ; it                         placed-shape
  ; dx                         number
  ; dy                         number
  (cond [(placed-circ?  it)
         ; (placed-circ-center it) posn
         ; (placed-circ-radius it) number
         (make-placed-circ (add-posns (placed-circ-center it)
                                      (make-posn dx dy))
                           (placed-circ-radius it)) ]
        [(placed-rect?  it)
         ; (placed-rect-top-left it) posn
         ; (placed-rect-width it)    number
         ; (placed-rect-height it)   number
         (make-placed-rect (add-posns (placed-rect-top-left it)
                                      (make-posn dx dy))
                           (placed-rect-width it)
                           (placed-rect-height it)) ]
  ))
```

∎

Exercise 21.8.2 *Develop a function* area *which works on a* placed-shape *and returns the area of the shape.*

Exercise 21.8.3 *Develop a function* contains? *that takes in a* placed-shape *and a* posn *and tells whether the* posn *is inside the shape. Consider the shape to include its border, so a point exactly on the border is "contained" in the shape.*

Exercise 21.8.4 *Develop a function* shapes-overlap? *that takes in two* placed-shapes *and tells whether they overlap.*

Hint: This problem is a little harder. Since *each* of the two parameters can be either a circle or a rectangle, you have four cases to consider. The "both circles" case is handled by

Exercise 21.7.4; the "both rectangles" case can be handled by using a previously-defined function on *placed-shapes*; and the "circle and rectangle" cases will require some geometrical thinking.

Exercise 21.8.5 *Develop an animation* like Exercise 20.6.4 or 21.6.3, but with each shape being either a circle (with random location and radius) or a rectangle (with random location, width, and height), with a 50% probability of each shape. I recommend testing this with a slow clock tick, e.g. 5 seconds, so you have time to try clicking in several places just outside various sides of the shape to make sure they don't count as hits.

Exercise 21.8.6 *Define a data type* zoo-animal *which is either a monkey, a lion, a sloth, or a dolphin. All four kinds have a name and a weight. Lions have a numeric property indicating how much meat they need per day (in kilograms). Monkeys have a string property indicating their favorite food (e.g. "ants", "bananas", or "caviar"). Sloths have a Boolean property indicating whether they're awake.*

Exercise 21.8.7 *Develop a function* underweight? *that takes in a* zoo-animal *and returns whether the animal in question is underweight. For this particular kind of monkey, that means under 10 kg; for lions, 150 kg; for sloths, it's 30 kg; for dolphins, 50 kg.*

Exercise 21.8.8 *Develop a function* can-put-in-cage? *that takes in a* zoo-animal *and a number (the weight capacity of the cage) and tells whether the animal in question can be put into that cage. Obviously, if the weight of the animal is greater than the weight capacity of the cage, the answer is* false. *But sloths cannot be moved when they're asleep, and dolphins can't be put in a cage at all.*

Exercise 21.8.9 *Define a data type* vehicle *which is either a car, a bicycle, or a train. All three types of vehicle have a weight and a top speed; a bicycle has a number of gears; a train has a length; and a car has a horsepower (e.g. 300) and a fuel-economy rating (e.g. 28 miles/gallon).*

Exercise 21.8.10 *Develop a function* range? *on vehicles. It should take in the number of hours you're willing to travel, and will return how far you can go in that much time on this vehicle.*

21.9   Review of important words and concepts

A *struct* is a data type made up of several "parts", also called *fields* or *instance variables*. An *instance* of a data type is an individual object of that type — for example, 2/3, 5, and -72541 are all instances of the type number, while (make-posn 3 4) is an instance of the type posn. The built-in function define-struct allows you to define a new struct type, and also provides several functions to allow you to manipulate the new type: a *constructor* which builds individual instances of the new data type; several *getters* or *selectors* (one for each field) which retrieve the value of that field from an instance of the new type; and a *discriminator* which tells whether something is of the new type at all.

There's a step-by-step recipe for defining a struct, just as for defining a function or writing an animation:

1. Identify the parts, their names and types

2. Write a define-struct

3. Write the contracts for the constructor, getters, and discriminator

4. Write some examples

5. If you expect to write several functions involving the data type, write input and output templates.

A function can not only take in but *return* instances of user-defined struct types, as with posn. If you need to write such a function, the "inventory with values" technique will be very useful.

Many animations need more than just two numbers in their models, so you often need to define a struct type for the purpose.

The fields of a struct can be of *any* type, even another struct. This sometimes allows you to better re-use previously-written functions (especially for posns).

Definition by choices becomes much more interesting when the choices can themselves be user-defined types. Functions written to operate on such types may be written in one of two ways: either one function per type, with a short "main" function that simply decides which choice the input is and calls an appropriate helper function, or as one big function with the helper functions "collapsed" into the main function. The single-function approach may be more convenient if the helper functions are all very short and simple, and if they are unlikely to be needed on their own; otherwise, it's usually safer and more flexible to write one function per type.

21.10 Reference: Built-in functions for defining structures

The only new syntax introduced in this chapter is define-struct.

PART IV

Definition by Self-reference

Chapter 22

Lists and functions on them

22.1 Limitations of structs

When we define a struct, among the first questions we ask is "how many parts does the struct have?" This question assumes that the struct *has* a fixed number of parts: a posn has two numbers, a color has three numbers, a person has two strings and a number, a moving-x has a number and a string, ... In general, a struct is a way to collect a fixed number of related pieces of information into one "package" that we can pass around as a single object, and store in a single variable.

But what if we wanted to collect an *unknown number* of related pieces of information into one "package", pass it around as a single object, and store it in a single variable? For example, consider the collection of students registered for a particular course: if a student adds (or drops) the course, does that require redefining the struct with one more (or fewer) field, then rewriting and retesting every function that operated on the struct, since there are now one more (or one fewer) getter functions, and every constructor call must now have one more (or one fewer) argument than before? That seems ridiculous: one should be able to write software once and for all to work on a collection of students, allowing the number of students to change while the program is running.

There are many other ways to collect related pieces of information into a package, of which the simplest is a "list".

22.2 What is a list?

You're all familiar with lists in daily life: lists of friends, lists of schools or jobs to apply to, lists of groceries to buy, lists of things to pack before going on a trip. In each case, a list is not changed in any fundamental way by changing the number of items in it. A list can be reduced to 1 or 0 items, and then have more items added to it later; reducing it to 1 or even 0 items didn't make it stop being a list.

This fact — that a list can have as few as 0 elements — underlies the way we'll define lists in Racket. Here are three apparently-obvious facts about lists:

1. **A list is either empty or non-empty.**

   Not terribly exciting, although it suggests that we'll do some kind of definition by choices with two cases: empty and non-empty.

2. **An empty list has no parts.**

   Again, not terribly exciting. The next one is a little more interesting:

3. **A non-empty list has a first element. It also has "the rest" of the list,** *i.e.* **everything after the first element.**

   This looks like a definition by parts: there are two parts, the "first" element and the "rest". What types are these parts? If we were defining a list of numbers, obviously, the "first" element would be a number; in a list of strings, the "first" element would be a string. But what about the "rest"? If the list consists of only one element, the "rest" should be empty; if the list consists of two elements, the "rest" contains one element; and so on. In other words, the "rest" of a non-empty list is a list (either empty or non-empty).

When we introduced "definition by choices" and "definition by parts", we said they were ways to define a new data type *from previously-defined data types*. We've loosened that requirement a bit now: the *list* data type is defined by choices from the *non-empty-list* data type, which is defined by parts from (among other things) the *list* data type. Neither data type can be "previous" to the other, because each depends on the other. However, if we're willing to define both at once, we can get a tremendous amount of programming power.

The following diagram shows the relationships among types in a list of numbers: a "list" is defined by choices as either "empty list" or "non-empty list", while "non-empty list" is defined by parts as a number and a "list".

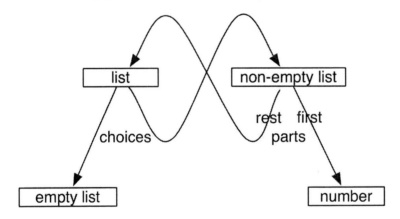

22.3   Defining lists in Racket

In this section we'll develop a definition of lists, and learn to write functions on them, using only what you already know about definition by parts and by choices. The resulting definition is a little awkward to work with, so in section 22.4 we'll discuss the more practical version of lists that's built into Racket. If you prefer to "cut to the chase," you can skip this section.

For concreteness, we'll define a list of strings; you can also define a list of numbers, or booleans, or even lists similarly. We'll use "los" as shorthand for "list of strings".

22.3.1 Data definitions

Recall our first fact about lists: "a list [of strings] is either empty or non-empty." This is a definition by choices with two choices. It tells us that for any function that takes in a list of strings, we'll need an empty test case and at least one non-empty test case. (In fact, we'll usually want at least three test cases: an empty example, an example of length 1, and at least one longer list.) It also tells us that the body of a function on lists of strings will probably involve a two-way `cond`, deciding between the empty and non-empty cases:

```
#|
(define (function-on-los L)
  ; L                     a list of strings
  (cond [...    ...]
        [...    ...]
  ))
|#
```

The second fact about lists, "An empty list has no parts," can be represented in Racket by defining a struct with no parts:

```
; An empty list has no parts.
(define-struct empty-list ())
; make-empty-list :  nothing -> empty-list
; empty-list?  :  anything -> boolean
#|
(define (function-on-empty-list L)
  ; L     an empty-list
  ...)
|#
```

This looks a little weird, admittedly: we've never before defined a struct with no parts, but there's no rule against it. Since there are no parts, there are no getters; there's only a constructor (which takes no parameters) and a discriminator. In other words, we can create an empty list, and recognize it when we see it.

Note that I haven't specified that an empty-list is an empty-list *of strings*: since it doesn't contain anything anyway, an empty-list of strings can be exactly the same as an empty-list of numbers or anything else.

In practice, there's seldom much point in writing a function whose only input is an empty list. All empty lists contain exactly the same information, so such a function would have to return the same answer in all cases, so why bother writing a function? So we'll skip the *function-on-empty-list* template from now on.

Now for the third fact about lists: "A non-empty list has two parts: the first element and the rest." More specifically: "A non-empty list of strings has two parts: the first element (a string) and the rest (a list of strings)." This seems to call for definition by parts. I'll use "nelos" as shorthand for "non-empty list of strings".

```
; A nelos has two parts:  first (a string) and rest (a los)
(define-struct nelos (first rest))
; make-nelos :  string los -> nelos
; nelos-first :  nelos -> string
; nelos-rest :  nelos -> los
; nelos?  :  anything -> boolean
#|
(define (function-on-nelos L)
  ; L                                 a nelos
  ; (nelos-first L)                   a string
  ; (nelos-rest L)                    a los
  ; (function-on-los (nelos-rest L)) whatever this returns
  ...)
|#
```

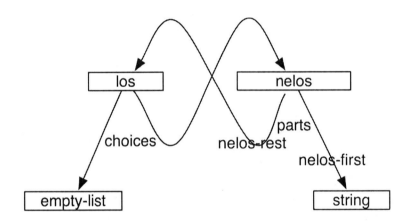

Since (nelos-rest L) is a list of strings, the obvious thing to do to it is call some function that works on a list of strings, like function-on-los. It's quite useful to include this in the inventory, as we'll see shortly.

With this information, we can write the complete data definition, with input templates for both *los* and *nelos*, fairly concisely:

```
; A los is either (make-empty-list) or a nelos
#|
(define (function-on-los L)
  ; L   a list of strings
  (cond [ (empty-list? L)  ...]
        [ (nelos? L)       (function-on-nelos L) ]
  ))
|#
```

```
; A nelos looks like
; (make-nelos string los)

#|
(define (function-on-nelos L)
  ; L                                a cons
  ; (nelos-first L)                  a string
  ; (nelos-rest L)                   a los
  ; (function-on-los (nelos-rest L)) whatever this returns
  ...)
|#
```

(We'll come back to the output template in Chapter 23.)

Note that once a *los* has been determined to be non-empty, the obvious thing to do to it is call some function that works on non-empty lists, like `function-on-nelos`.

Note also that because the *los* and *nelos* data types each refer to one another, the `function-on-los` and `function-on-nelos` templates refer to one another in a corresponding way.

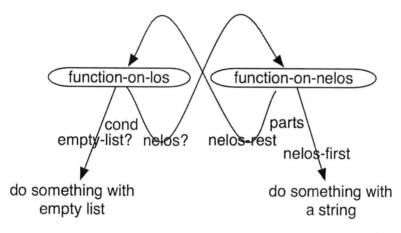

22.3.2   Examples of the los data type

As with any new data type, we should make up some examples to make things feel more real and concrete. We'll need at least one empty example, which we can build with `make-empty-list`:

```
(define nothing (make-empty-list))
```

and at least one non-empty example, which we can build with `make-nelos`. The `make-nelos` function expects two arguments: a string and a *los*. The only *los* we already have is `nothing`, so

```
(define english (make-nelos "hello" nothing))
```

This represents a list of strings whose first element is `"hello"` and whose rest is an empty list, so there is no second element.

Suppose we wanted a list with `"bonjour"` as its first element and `"hello"` as the second and last. This is easy by calling `make-nelos`:

```
(define fr-eng (make-nelos "bonjour" english))
```

We can go on to build even longer lists, as shown in Figure 22.1.

Figure 22.1: Defining and using list-of-strings

```
; An empty list has no parts.
(define-struct empty-list ())
; make-empty-list :  nothing -> empty-list
; empty-list?  :  anything -> boolean

; A nelos has two parts:  first (a string) and rest (a los).
(define-struct nelos (first rest))
; make-nelos :  string los -> nelos
; nelos-first :  nelos -> string
; nelos-rest :  nelos -> los
; nelos?  :  anything -> boolean
#|
(define (function-on-nelos L)
   ; L                             a nelos
   ; (nelos-first L)               a string
   ; (nelos-rest L)                a los
   ; (function-on-los (nelos-rest L)) whatever this returns
   ...)
|#

; A los is either an empty-list or a nelos.
#|
(define (function-on-los L)
   ; L                             a los
   (cond [(empty-list? L) ...]
         [(nelos? L)      (function-on-nelos L)]
   ))
|#
(define nothing (make-empty-list))
(define english (make-nelos "hello" nothing))
(define fr-eng (make-nelos "bonjour" english))
(define heb-fr-eng (make-nelos "shalom" fr-eng))
(define shfe (make-nelos "buenos dias" heb-fr-eng))
(define ashfe (make-nelos "salaam" shfe))
(define dwarfs (make-nelos "sleepy" (make-nelos "sneezy"
  (make-nelos "dopey" (make-nelos "doc" (make-nelos "happy"
  (make-nelos "bashful" (make-nelos "grumpy" nothing)))))))))
```

Practice Exercise 22.3.1 *Copy Figure 22.1 into your Definitions pane (it should be available as a download from the textbook Web site), and try the following expressions. For each one,* predict *what it will return before hitting ENTER, and see whether you were* *right. If not, figure out why it came out as it did.*

```
(empty-list? nothing)
(nelos? nothing)
(nelos-first nothing)
(nelos-rest nothing)
(empty-list? english)
(nelos? english)
(nelos-first english)
(nelos-rest english)
(empty-list? (nelos-rest english))
(nelos? fr-eng)
(nelos-first fr-eng)
(nelos-rest fr-eng)
(nelos? (nelos-rest fr-eng))
(nelos-first (nelos-rest fr-eng))
(nelos-rest (nelos-rest fr-eng))
(nelos? ashfe)
(nelos-first ashfe)
(nelos-rest ashfe)
(nelos-first (nelos-rest (nelos-rest ashfe))))
(nelos-first (nelos-rest (nelos-rest (nelos-rest dwarfs))))
```

22.3.3 Writing a function on los

How would we write a function on the *los* data type? In a way, this is the wrong question: our templates above show *two* functions, *function-on-los* and *function-on-nelos*, which depend on one another, so when we write a specific function, it too will probably consist of two functions that depend on one another.

Worked Exercise 22.3.2 *Define a function* `count-strings` *that takes in a* los *and returns how many strings are in it: 0 for an empty list, 1 for a list of one element, and so on.*

Solution: We'll write two functions: one that works on a *los* and one that works on a *nelos*.

Contracts:

```
; count-strings : los -> number
; count-strings-on-nelos : nelos -> number
```

The data analysis is already done.

Test cases:

```
(check-expect (count-strings nothing) 0)
(check-expect (count-strings english) 1)
(check-expect (count-strings fr-eng) 2)
(check-expect (count-strings ashfe) 5)
(check-expect (count-strings dwarfs) 7)
```

```
; can't call (count-strings-on-nelos nothing)
; because nothing isn't a nelos
(check-expect (count-strings-on-nelos english) 1)
(check-expect (count-strings-on-nelos fr-eng) 2)
(check-expect (count-strings-on-nelos ashfe) 5)
(check-expect (count-strings-on-nelos dwarfs) 7)
```

Skeletons and Inventories:

Conveniently, we already have templates that do most of the work for us:

```
(define ( count-strings L)
  ; L    a los
  (cond [(empty-list?  L) ...]
        [(nelos?  L)      ( count-strings-on-nelos  L)]
))

(define ( count-strings-on-nelos  L)
  ; L                              a nelos
  ; (nelos-first L)                a string
  ; (nelos-rest L)                 a los
  ; ( count-strings (nelos-rest L) a number
  ...)
```

Note that count-strings and count-strings-on-nelos refer to one another in the same way function-on-los and function-on-nelos refer to one another, which in turn corresponds to the way *los* and *nelos* refer to one another.

Now we just need to fill in everywhere that there's a "...". The first one, the answer in the (empty-list? L) case, is easy: an empty list has a length of 0. (We *could* write a count-strings-on-empty-list function to do this, but that seems like too much work just to get the answer 0.)

```
(define (count-strings L)
  ; L    a los
  (cond [(empty-list?  L) 0 ]
        [(nelos?  L)      (count-strings-on-nelos L)]
))
```

The other "..." is the body of count-strings-on-nelos. From the inventory, we have an expression for the number of strings in the rest of the list. So how many strings are there in the *whole* list? If you see immediately how to do this, great; if not, let's try an **inventory with values**. We'll pick a moderately complicated example:

```
(define (count-strings-on-nelos L
  ; L                      a nelos  (cons "a" (cons "b" (cons "c" empty)))
  ; (nelos-first L)        a string "a"
  ; (nelos-rest L)         a los    (cons "b" (cons "c" empty))
  ; (count-strings (nelos-rest L))  a number  2
  ; right answer                    a number  3
```

How could you get the right answer, 3, from the things above it? The one that most closely resembles 3 is 2; you can get 3 from 2 by adding 1. This suggests the body

```
(define (count-strings-on-nelos L)
  ; L                     a nelos  (cons "a" (cons "b" (cons "c" empty)))
  ; (nelos-first L)       a string "a"
  ; (nelos-rest L)        a los    (cons "b" (cons "c" empty))
  ; (count-strings (nelos-rest L))   a number 2
  ; right answer                     a number 3
  (+ 1 (count-strings (nelos-rest L)))  )
```

Does this make sense? It says the number of strings in the whole list is one more than the number of strings in the rest of the list, which is certainly true.

Run the test cases, and they should all work. Use the Stepper to watch the computation for some non-trivial examples, like (count-strings shfe). ∎

22.3.4   Collapsing two functions into one

We've written functions before that depended on auxiliary functions; the only new thing here is that the auxiliary function depends on the original function in turn. And it's perfectly natural that when we're working with two different data types, we have to write two different functions. However, the only place count-strings-on-nelos is used is inside count-strings, so if we prefer, we can replace the call to count-strings-on-nelos with its body:

```
(define (count-strings L)
  ; L   a los
  (cond [(empty-list?  L)                    0]
        [(nelos?  L)
         ; L                                  a nelos
         ; (nelos-first L)                    a string
         ; (nelos-rest L)                     a los
         ; (count-strings (nelos-rest L))     a number
         (+ 1 (count-strings (nelos-rest L))) ]
        ))
```

Note that now the count-strings function *calls itself*. Some of you may have written functions in the past that called themselves, and the most likely result was something called an "infinite loop": the function called itself to answer the same question, then called itself to answer the same question, then called itself to answer the same question, and never accomplished anything. What we've done here is different: rather than calling the function to answer the *same* question, we're calling it to answer a *smaller* question, then using the result to figure out the answer to the original question.

The single-function solution is usually shorter and simpler, but later on we'll encounter situations in which we *have* to use the two-function solution, so you should know both approaches.

In order to write functions on lists as a single function rather than two, we must likewise collapse the two templates into one:

```
 #|
(define (function-on-los L)
   ; L    a los
   (cond [(empty-list?  L)                      ...]
         [(nelos?  L)
          ; L                                   a nelos
          ; (nelos-first L)                     a string
          ; (nelos-rest L)                      a los
          ; (function-on-los (nelos-rest L))    whatever this returns
          ...]))
 |#
```

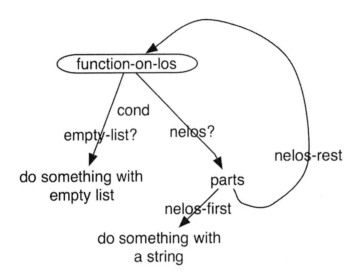

22.4 The way we really do lists

The approach taken in Section 22.3 works, but it's rather awkward to work with. Lists
are so common and useful that they're built into Racket (and some other languages). In
reality, most Racket programmers use the built-in list functions rather than defining a list
data type themselves.

As in section 22.3, we'll define a list of strings for concreteness. You can also define a
list of numbers, or booleans, or even lists similarly. We'll use "los" as shorthand for "list
of strings".

22.4.1 Data definitions

Recall our first fact about lists: "a list [of strings] is either empty or non-empty." This is
a definition by choices, with two choices. It tells us that for any function that takes in a
list of strings, we'll need an empty test case and at least one non-empty test case. (In fact,
we'll usually want at least three test cases: an empty example, an example of length 1, and
at least one longer list.) It also tells us that the body of a function on lists of strings will
probably involve a two-way cond, deciding between the empty and non-empty cases:

```
#|
(define (function-on-los L)
  ; L                      a list of strings
  (cond [...      ...]
        [...      ...]
  ))
|#
```

The second fact about lists is "An empty list has no parts." Racket provides a built-in constant `empty` and a built-in function `empty?` to represent and recognize empty lists, respectively.

```
; empty :  a constant that stands for an empty list
; empty?  :  anything -> boolean
```

Now for the third fact about lists: "A non-empty list has two parts: the first element and the rest." Let's make it more specific: "A non-empty list of strings has two parts: the first element (a string) and the rest (a list of strings)." This seems to call for definition by parts. For convenience, Racket has a built-in data type to represent a non-empty list. Since putting one non-empty list inside another is the usual way to "construct" a large list, we use the word `cons` (short for "construct"). Racket provides the following built-in functions:

```
; A non-empty list, or cons, has two parts:
;   first (whatever type the elements are) and
;   rest (a list)
; cons :  element list -> non-empty-list
; first :  non-empty-list -> element
; rest :  non-empty-list -> list
; cons?  :  anything -> boolean
```

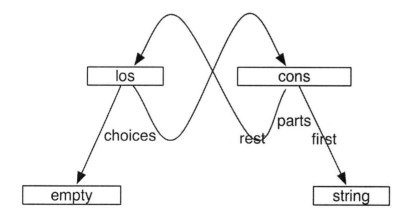

With this information, we can write the complete data definition, with input templates for both *los* and *nelos*, fairly concisely:

```
; A los is either empty or a nelos
#|
(define (function-on-los L)
  ; L   a list of strings
  (cond [(empty?  L)        ...]
        [(cons?  L)         (function-on-nelos L)]
  ))
|#

; A nelos looks like
; (cons string los)

#|
(define (function-on-nelos L)
  ; L                             a cons
  ; (first L)                     a string
  ; (rest L)                      a los
  ; (function-on-los (rest L))    whatever this returns
  ...)
|#
```

(We'll come back to the output template in Chapter 23.)

Note that because the *los* and *nelos* types refer to one another, the function-on-los and function-on-nelos templates refer to one another in a corresponding way.

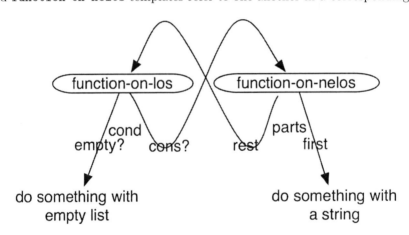

22.4.2   Examples of the los data type

As with any new data type, we should make up some examples to make things feel more real and concrete. We have empty to provide an empty example. We'll need to build non-empty examples using cons, which (in our list-of-strings example) expects a string and a list of strings. The only list of strings we already have is empty, so we'll use that:

```
(define english (cons "hello" empty))
```

This represents a list of strings whose first element is "hello" and whose rest is an empty list, so there is no second element.

Suppose we wanted a list with "bonjour" as its first element and "hello" as the second and last. This is easy by calling cons:

```
(define fr-eng (cons "bonjour" english))
```

We can go on to build even longer lists, as shown in Figure 22.2.

Figure 22.2: Lists of strings, using built-in Racket features

```
; An empty list has no parts.
; empty :  a constant
; empty?  :  anything -> boolean

; A cons has two parts:  first (a string) and rest (a los).
; cons :  string los -> nelos
; first :  nelos -> string
; rest :  nelos -> los
; cons?  :  anything -> boolean
#|
(define (function-on-nelos L)
  ; L                               a nelos
  ; (first L)                       a string
  ; (rest L)                        a los
  ; (function-on-los (rest L))      whatever this returns
  ...)
|#

; A los is either an empty-list or a nelos.
#|
(define (function-on-los L)
  ; L                               a los
  (cond [(empty-list? L)    ...]
        [(nelos? L)         (function-on-nelos L)]
  ))
|#
(define english (cons "hello" empty))
(define fr-eng (cons "bonjour" english))
(define heb-fr-eng (cons "shalom" fr-eng))
(define shfe (cons "buenos dias" heb-fr-eng))
(define ashfe (cons "salaam" shfe))
(define dwarfs (cons "sleepy" (cons "sneezy" (cons "dopey" (cons "doc"
  (cons "happy" (cons "bashful" (cons "grumpy" empty)))))))))
```

Practice Exercise 22.4.1 *Copy Figure 22.2 into your Definitions pane (it should be available as a download from the textbook Web site), and try the following expressions. For each one,* predict *what it will return before hitting ENTER, and see whether you were right. If not, figure out why it came out as it did.*

```
(empty? empty)
(cons? empty)
(first empty)
(rest empty)
(empty? english)
(cons? english)
(first english)
(rest english)
(empty? (rest english))
(cons? fr-eng)
(first fr-eng)
(rest fr-eng)
(cons? (rest fr-eng))
(first (rest fr-eng))
(rest (rest fr-eng))
(cons? ashfe)
(first ashfe)
(rest ashfe)
(first (rest (rest ashfe))))
(first (rest (rest (rest dwarfs)))))
```

22.4.3   Writing a function on los

How would we write a function on the *los* data type? In a way, this is the wrong question: our templates above show *two* functions, *function-on-los* and *function-on-nelos*, which depend on one another, so when we write a specific function, it too will probably consist of two functions that depend on one another.

Worked Exercise 22.4.2 *Define a function* `count-strings` *that takes in a los and returns how many strings are in it: 0 for an empty list, 1 for a list of one element, and so on.*

Solution: We'll write two functions: one that works on a *los*, and one that works on a *nelos*.

Contracts:

```
; count-strings : los -> number
; count-strings-on-nelos : nelos -> number
```

The data analysis is already done.

Test cases:

```
(check-expect (count-strings empty) 0)
(check-expect (count-strings english) 1)
(check-expect (count-strings fr-eng) 2)
(check-expect (count-strings ashfe) 5)
(check-expect (count-strings dwarfs) 7)


; can't call (count-strings-on-nelos empty)
; because empty isn't a nelos
(check-expect (count-strings-on-nelos english) 1)
(check-expect (count-strings-on-nelos fr-eng) 2)
(check-expect (count-strings-on-nelos ashfe) 5)
(check-expect (count-strings-on-nelos dwarfs) 7)
```

Skeletons and Inventories:
Conveniently, we already have templates that do most of the work for us:

```
(define ( count-strings L)
  ; L   a los
  (cond [(empty? L)    ...]
        [(cons? L)     ( count-strings-on-nelos L)]
))

(define ( count-strings-on-nelos L)
  ; L                            a nelos
  ; (first L)                    a string
  ; (rest L)                     a los
  ; ( count-strings (rest L))    a number
  ...)
```

Note that count-strings and count-strings-on-nelos refer to one another in the same way function-on-los and function-on-nelos refer to one another, which in turn corresponds to the way *los* and *nelos* refer to one another. The "main" function, the one we're really interested in, is count-strings, but we need a helper function count-strings-on-nelos.

Now we just need to fill in everywhere that there's a "...". The first one, the answer in the (empty? L) case, is easy: an empty list has a length of 0. (We *could* write a count-strings-on-empty-list function to do this, but that seems like too much work just to get the answer 0.)

```
(define (count-strings L)
  ; L   a los
  (cond [(empty? L)    0 ]
        [(cons? L)     (count-strings-on-nelos L)]
))
```

The other "..." is the body of count-strings-on-nelos. From the inventory, we have an expression for the number of strings in the *rest* of the list. So how many strings are there in the *whole* list? If you see immediately how to do this, great; if not, let's try an **inventory with values**. We'll pick a moderately complicated example:

```
(define (count-strings-on-nelos L)
   ; L               a nelos  (cons "a" (cons "b" (cons "c" empty)))
   ; (first L)       a string "a"
   ; (rest L)        a los    (cons "b" (cons "c" empty))
   ; (count-strings (rest L))   a number  2
   ; right answer               a number 3
```

How could you get the right answer, 3, from the things above it? The one that most closely resembles 3 is 2; you can get 3 from 2 by adding 1. This suggests the body

```
(define (count-strings-on-nelos L)
   ; L               a nelos  (cons "a" (cons "b" (cons "c" empty)))
   ; (first L)       a string "a"
   ; (rest L)        a los    (cons "b" (cons "c" empty))
   ; (count-strings (rest L))   a number 2
   ; right answer               a number 3
   (+ 1 (count-strings (rest L)))  )
```

Does this make sense? It says the number of strings in the whole list is one more than the number of strings in the rest of the list, which is certainly true.

Run the test cases, and they should all work. Use the Stepper to watch the computation for some non-trivial examples, like (count-strings shfe). ■

22.4.4   Collapsing two functions into one

We've written functions before that depended on auxiliary functions; the only new thing here is that the auxiliary function depends on the original function in turn. And it's perfectly natural that when we're working with two different data types, we have to write two different functions. However, the only place count-strings-on-nelos is used is inside count-strings, so if we prefer, we can replace the call to count-strings-on-nelos with its body:

```
(define (count-strings L)
   ; L   a los
   (cond [(empty?  L)                          0]
         [(cons?  L)
          ; L                                a nelos
          ; (first L)                        a string
          ; (rest L)                         a los
          ; (count-strings (rest L))         a number
          (+ 1 (count-strings (rest L)))  ]
   ))
```

Note that now the count-strings function *calls itself.* Some of you may have written functions in the past that called themselves, and the most likely result was something called an "infinite loop": the function called itself to answer the same question, then called itself to answer the same question, then called itself to answer the same question, and never accomplished anything. What we've done here is different: rather than calling the function to answer the *same* question, we're calling it to answer a *smaller* question, then using the result to figure out the answer to the original question.

SIDEBAR:

Computer scientists use the word "recursion" for the notion that a function can call itself, or two or more functions can call one another. Such functions are described as "recursive". Generations of computer science students have been mystified by recursion, often because they try to think through the entire computation at once. It seems to work better to think about only one level at a time. Concentrate on making sure that

- the answer to the empty case is right, and

- if you have a correct answer for the rest of the list, you can construct a correct answer for the whole list.

If this bothers you, here's a way to justify it. Suppose we wrote a function this way and it *didn't* work correctly, *i.e.* there were some legal inputs on which it produced a wrong answer; call these "bad" inputs. In particular, there must be a *shortest* bad input. We know the function works correctly on the empty list, so the shortest bad input must be non-empty, and thus have a "first" and a "rest". The "rest" of this list is shorter than the shortest bad input, so it's not bad, *i.e.* the function works correctly on it. We know the function produces a correct answer for the whole list from a correct answer for the rest of the list. Since the answer on the rest of the list *is* correct, that means the answer to the shortest bad input is correct too, which means this isn't a "bad" input after all. So the shortest "bad" input can't be empty, and it can't be one item longer than a "good" input, so it can't exist at all, *i.e.* the function is always correct.

In order to write functions on lists as a single function rather than two, we must likewise collapse the two templates into one:

```
#|
(define (function-on-los L)
  ; L    a los
  (cond [(empty? L)              ...]
        [(cons? L)
         ; L                     a nelos
         ; (first L)             a string
         ; (rest L)              a los
         ; (function-on-los (rest L))   whatever this returns
         ...]))
|#
```

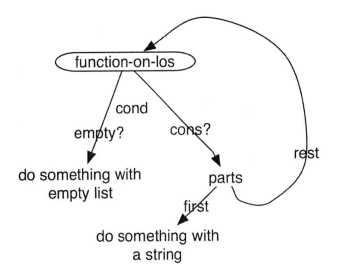

Again, it's a matter of personal preference whether you solve a problem like this with two functions that call one another, or one that calls itself; do whichever makes more sense to you. They both work.

Whether you use two functions that call one another or one function that calls itself, there will be somewhere that checks whether the list is empty, and returns an answer *without* calling itself. This is called the *base case* of the recursion.

22.5   Lots of functions to write on lists

So far we've seen how to solve only one problem on lists, *i.e.* counting how many strings are in a list of strings. We've seen slightly different definitions depending on whether we define our own structs or use Racket's built-in list features, and on whether we write it as two functions that call one another or one function that calls itself, but it's still only one problem. To really get the hang of writing functions on lists, you'll need to practice on a number of examples.

I've described these examples using Racket's built-in list features; they could of course be written to use the `empty-list` and `nelos` structures defined in section 22.3, but the definitions would be longer and harder to understand.

Worked Exercise 22.5.1 *Define a data type* list-of-numbers *(or* lon *for short), including a template for functions operating on lists of numbers.* ***Develop*** *a function* `count-numbers` *that takes in a list of numbers and returns a number.*

Solution: The data definition is similar to that for *list-of-strings*:

```
; A list-of-numbers is either
;    empty or
;    a nelon (non-empty list of numbers).
#|
(define (function-on-lon L)
  ; L    a list of numbers
  (cond [ (empty? L)      ...]
        [ (cons?  L)      (function-on-nelon L) ]
  ))
|#

; A nelon looks like
; (cons number lon)

#|
(define (function-on-nelon L)
  ; L                            a cons
  ; (first L)                    a number
  ; (rest L)                     a lon
  ; (function-on-lon (rest L))   whatever this returns
  ...)
|#
```

And not surprisingly, the function definition is quite similar to that of count-strings:

```
; count-numbers :  lon -> number
(check-expect (count-numbers empty) 0)
(check-expect (count-numbers (cons -4 empty)) 1)
(check-expect
  (count-numbers (cons 5 (cons 2 (cons 8 (cons 6 empty)))))
  4)
(check-expect (count-numbers-on-nelon (cons -4 empty)) 1)
(check-expect
  (count-numbers-on-nelon (cons 5 (cons 2 (cons 8 (cons 6 empty)))))
  4)

(define (count-numbers L)
  ; L    a lon
  (cond [(empty? L)     0]
        [(cons?  L)      (count-numbers-on-nelon L)]
  ))

(define (count-numbers-on-nelon L)
  ; L                          a nelon
  ; (first L)                  a string
  ; (rest L)                   a lon
  ; (count-numbers (rest L))   a number
  (+ 1 (count-numbers (rest L))) )
```

or, writing it more simply as a single function,

```
(define (count-numbers L)
  ; L                                    a lon
  (cond    [(empty?  L)                  0]
           [(cons?  L)
            ; L                          a nelon
            ; (first L)                  a number
            ; (rest L)                   a lon
            ; (count-numbers (rest L))   a number
            (+ 1 (count-numbers (rest L)))]
  ))
```

In fact, aside from its name, this function is *identical* to `count-strings`: neither one actually makes any use of the type of the elements, so either one would work on a list of any type. There's a built-in Racket function `length` that does the same job, and now that you've seen how you could have written it yourself, you should feel free to use the built-in `length` function. ∎

The next example is more interesting, and depends on the type of the elements.

Worked Exercise 22.5.2 *Develop a function* `add-up` *that takes in a list of numbers and returns the result of adding them all together. For example,*

```
(check-expect (add-up (cons 4 (cons 8 (cons -3 empty)))) 9)
```

Solution: We already have the data definition for *list-of-numbers*, so we'll go on to the function. The contract, examples, skeleton, and inventory are easy:

```
; add-up :  list-of-numbers -> number
(check-expect (add-up empty) 0)
(check-expect (add-up (cons 14 empty)) 14)
(check-expect (add-up (cons 3 (cons 4 empty))) 7)
(check-expect (add-up (cons 4 (cons 8 (cons -3 empty)))) 9)
```

```
(define (add-up L)
  ; L                         a lon
  (cond [(empty?  L)          ...]
        [(cons?  L)           (add-up-nelon L)]
  ))
```

```
(define (add-up-nelon L)
  ; L                    a nelon
  ; (first L)            a number
  ; (rest L)             a lon
  ; (add-up (rest L))    a number
  ... )
```

We need to fill in the two "..." gaps. The answer to the empty case is obviously 0. For the other "...", let's try an inventory with values:

```
(define (add-up-nelon L)
  ; L                   nelon    (cons 4 (cons 8 (cons -3 empty)))
  ; (first L)           number   4
  ; (rest L)            lon       (cons 8 (cons -3 empty))
  ; (add-up (rest L))   number   5
  ; right answer        number   9
  ... )
```

So how can you get the right answer, 9, from the things above it? The two lists don't look promising, but the numbers 4 and 5 do: we can get 9 by adding the 4 (*i.e.* (first L)) and the 5 (*i.e.* (add-up (rest L))). This suggests the definition

```
(define (add-up-nelon L)
  ; L                   nelon    (cons 4 (cons 8 (cons -3 empty)))
  ; (first L)           number   4
  ; (rest L)            lon      (cons 8 (cons -3 empty))
  ; (add-up (rest L))   number   5
  ; right answer        number   9
  (+ (first L) (add-up (rest L))) )
```

Does this make sense? Should the sum of a list of numbers be the same as the first number plus the sum of the rest of the numbers? Of course. Test the function, and it should work on all legal inputs.

Here's a shorter single-function version, developed the same way.

```
(define (add-up L)
  ; L                               lon
  (cond [(empty?  L)                0]
        [(cons?  L)
          ; L                       nelon
          ; (first L)               number
          ; (rest L)                lon
          ; (add-up (rest L))       number
          (+ (first L) (add-up (rest L)))
        ]
  ))
```

∎

Exercise 22.5.3 *Suppose you work for a toy company that maintains its inventory as a list of strings, and somebody has come into the store looking for a doll. You want to know whether there are any in stock.* **Develop** *a function* contains-doll? *that takes in a list of strings and tells whether any of the strings in the list is* "doll".

Exercise 22.5.4 **Develop** *a function* any-matches? *that takes in a string and a list of strings and tells whether any of the strings in the list is the same as the given string. For example,*

```
(check-expect
  (any-matches?  "fnord" (cons "snark" (cons "boojum" empty)))
  false)
(check-expect
  (any-matches?  "fnord" (cons "snark" (cons "fnord" empty)))
  true)
```

Hint: The templates for operating on lists use a conditional to decide whether you've got an empty or a non-empty list. This function needs to make another decision: does the current string match the target or not? You can do this with another conditional, or (since this function returns a boolean), you can do it more simply without the extra conditional.

Exercise 22.5.5 *Develop a function* `count-matches` *that takes in an object and a list of objects and tells* how many *(possibly zero) of the objects in the list are the same as the given object. For example,*
```
(check-expect
  (count-matches "cat" (cons "dog" (cons "cat" (cons "fish"
    (cons "cat" (cons "cat" (cons "wombat" empty)))))))
  3)
(check-expect
  (count-matches 1 (cons 3 (cons 1 (cons 4
                        (cons 1 (cons 5 (cons 9 empty)))))))
  2)
```

Hint: For this one, you probably *will* need a nested conditional.

There's an additional difference: this function is supposed to work on *any kind of object,* not just strings. So instead of `string=?`, you'll need to use the built-in function `equal?`.

Exercise 22.5.6 *Develop a function* `count-votes-for-name` *that takes in a string (the name of a candidate) and a list of strings (the votes cast by a bunch of voters) and tells how many of the voters voted for this particular candidate.*

Hint: This is really easy if you re-use previously-written functions.

Exercise 22.5.7 *Develop a function* `count-over` *that takes in a number and a list of numbers, and tells how many of the numbers in the list are larger than the specified number.*

Exercise 22.5.8 *Develop a function* `average` *that takes in a list of numbers and returns their average, i.e. their sum divided by how many there are. For this problem, you may assume there is at least one number in the list.*

Hint: Not *every* function on lists can best be written by following the templates . . .

Exercise 22.5.9 *Develop a function* `safe-average` *that takes in a list of numbers and returns their average; if the list is empty, it should signal an error with an appropriate and user-friendly message.*

Exercise 22.5.10 *Develop a function* `convert-reversed` *that takes in a list of numbers. You may* assume *that all the numbers are integers in the range 0-9, i.e. decimal digits. The function should interpret them as digits in a decimal number, ones place first (trust me, this actually makes the problem easier!), and returns the number they represent. For example,*
```
(check-expect
  (convert-reversed (cons 3 (cons 0 (cons 2 (cons 5 empty)))))
  5203)
```
Do **not** *use the built-in* `string->number` *function for this exercise.*

Exercise 22.5.11 *Develop a function* `multiply-all` *that takes in a list of numbers and returns the result of multiplying them all together. For example,*
`(check-expect (multiply-all (cons 3 (cons 5 (cons 4 empty)))) 60)`

Hint: What is the "right answer" for the empty list? It may not be what you think at first!

Exercise 22.5.12 *A "dollar store" used to mean a store where everything cost less than a dollar. Develop a function* `dollar-store?` *that takes in a list of numbers (the prices of various items), and tells whether the store qualifies as a "dollar store".*

Exercise 22.5.13 *Develop a function* `all-match?` *that takes in a string and a list of strings, and tells whether all the strings in the list match the given string. For example,*
```
(check-expect
  (all-match? "cat" (cons "cat" (cons "dog" (cons "cat" empty))))
  false)
(check-expect
  (all-match? "cat" (cons "cat" (cons "cat" empty)))
  true)
```

Exercise 22.5.14 *Develop a function* `general-bullseye` *that takes in a list of numbers and produces a white image with black concentric rings at those radii.*

Hint: I recommend using an empty image like (`circle 0 "solid" "white"`) as the answer for the empty case.

Exercise 22.5.15 *Develop an animation that displays a bull's-eye pattern of black rings on a white background. Each second, an additional ring will be added, three pixels outside the previous outer ring.*

Hint: Use a list of numbers as the model. For your tick handler, write a function that takes in a list of numbers and sticks one more number onto the front of the list, equal to three times the length of the existing list.

Exercise 22.5.16 *Develop an animation that displays a bull's-eye pattern, as in Exercise 22.5.15, but each second, an additional ring will be added at a* random *radius.*

In section 22.4.4, why did we move the body of `function-on-nelos` inside the body of `function-on-los`, rather than the other way around? Because in most cases, we want the resulting function to work on *all* lists, including empty. But sometimes it works better to move `function-on-los` inside `function-on-nelos` instead.

Exercise 22.5.17 *Develop a function* `largest` *that takes in a list of numbers and returns the largest one.*

Hint: This function doesn't really make sense on an empty list, so the input data type is really "non-empty list of numbers," and the simplest test case should be a one-element list. Since `largest` doesn't make sense on an empty list, you should be careful never to call it on an empty list.

If you use the two-function approach, the "main" function here is the one for non-empty lists; the one for possibly-empty lists is the helper function. And if you use a one-function approach, you'll need to move the function for possibly-empty lists inside the function for non-empty lists, *e.g.*

```
(define (function-on-nelos L)
  ; (first L) a string
  ; (rest L)  a list
  (cond [(empty?  (rest L)) ...]
        [(cons?  (rest L))
         ; (function-on-nelos (rest L))    whatever this returns
         ...]))
```

Exercise 22.5.18 *Develop a function* `count-blocks` *that takes in a list of numbers, which may contain some repetitions, and tells how many* blocks *of repeated numbers there are. A* block *is one or more copies of the same number appearing in the list, with no other numbers in between. For example,*

```
(check-expect (count-blocks
  (cons 3 (cons 3 (cons 2 (cons 7 (cons 7 (cons 7
    (cons 2 (cons 2 empty))))))))
  4)
```

because this list has a block of 3's, then a block of 2's, then a block of 7's, then another block of 2's: four blocks in all.

Hint: I know of at least two ways to solve this problem. Both involve useful techniques that you should know; try both.

First, try writing a version of this function that only works on non-empty lists; as in Exercise 22.5.17, the base case becomes "is the list one element long?". For one-element lists, the answer is easy; for longer lists, you know that the list has both a first and a second element, and can reasonably ask whether they're the same. Once this works on all non-empty lists, add an "empty" case.

The other approach is to write a helper function that takes in not only a list of numbers but also the number we're "already looking at:" if the list is non-empty, you can reasonably check whether its first number is the same as the one you're already looking at.

Exercise 22.5.19 *Develop a function* `count-even-odd-blocks` *that takes in a list of integers and tells how many blocks of consecutive even or consecutive odd numbers there are. For example,*

```
(check-expect (count-even-odd-blocks
  (cons 3 (cons 9 (cons 2 (cons 7 (cons 1 (cons 1
    (cons 2 (cons 4 empty))))))))
  4)
```

because the numbers 3 and 9 form a block of odd numbers; 2 is a block of even numbers; 7, 1, and 1 form a block of odd numbers; and 2 and 4 are a block of even numbers, for four blocks in all.

Hint: Obviously, this is similar to Exercise 22.5.18, but if you use the "helper function" approach, it doesn't need to take in a specific "already seen" number, but only whether the previous number was even or odd. Instead of passing in the previous number, therefore, try writing two separate (but similar) helper functions `even-helper` and `odd-helper`. This approach is a little longer, but it's a powerful technique that you can use for many problems in the future. Try it.

```
                          SIDEBAR:
There are many problems that call for scanning through a list from left to right,
looking for particular patterns. The above approach is one that computer scientists
call a finite-state machine or finite-state automaton.
```

Exercise 22.5.20 *Develop a function* `random-element` *that takes in a non-empty list and returns a randomly chosen element of it. Ideally, each element should be equally likely to be chosen.*

Hint: You'll probably need the built-in `list-ref` function, which takes in a non-empty list and a number, and returns the element that far away from the beginning of the list. For example,

```
(check-expect
  (list-ref (cons "a" (cons "b" (cons "c" empty))) 0)
  "a")
(check-expect
  (list-ref (cons "a" (cons "b" (cons "c" empty))) 1)
  "b")
(check-expect
  (list-ref (cons "a" (cons "b" (cons "c" empty))) 2)
  "c")
```

`list-ref` produces an error message if you give it too large a number, so make sure you don't do that.

Since `random-element` is unpredictable, you won't be able to test it with `check-expect`, but you can call it a bunch of times with the same list and see whether each element is chosen roughly the same number of times.

Warning: The `list-ref` function is useful when you need to get the element of a list at an *arbitrary numeric position.* That's actually not a common thing to need; 95% of the time, you'll be better off using `first` and `rest`.

Exercise 22.5.21 *Write a data definition, including templates, for a* list of lists of strings. *Write several examples of this data type.*

Develop a function `total-length` *that takes in a list of lists of strings and returns the total number of strings appearing in all the lists put together.*

Develop a function `longest` *that takes in a non-empty list of lists of strings and returns the longest of the lists. If there are two or more of the same maximum length, it may return either one at your choice.*

22.6 Lists of structs

As we've seen, writing a function to work on a list of numbers is almost exactly like writing a function to work on a list of strings. Not surprisingly, writing a function to work on a list of posns, or employees, or other types like that isn't much harder.

Worked Exercise 22.6.1 *Develop a function* `any-on-diag?` *that takes in a list of* `posn` *structures and tells whether any of them are "on the diagonal," i.e. have x and y coordinates equal to one another.*

Solution: The data definition is straightforward:

```
; A list-of-posns is either
;   empty or
;;  a nelop (non-empty list of posns).
#|
(define (function-on-lop L)
  ; L    a list of posns
  (cond [ (empty? L)       ...]
        [ (cons? L)        (function-on-nelop L) ]
  ))
|#

; A nelop looks like
; (cons posn lop)

#|
(define (function-on-nelop L)
  ; L                               a cons
  ; (first L)                       a posn
  ; (posn-x (first L))              a number
  ; (posn-y (first L))              a number
  ; (rest L)                        a lop
  ; (function-on-lop (rest L))      whatever this returns
  ...)
|#
```

For test cases, we need an empty list and at least two or three non-empty lists: at least one with right answer `true` and at least one with right answer `false`.

```
(check-expect (any-on-diag?  empty) false)
(check-expect (any-on-diag?  (cons (make-posn 5 6) empty)) false)
(check-expect (any-on-diag?  (cons (make-posn 5 5) empty)) true)
(check-expect (any-on-diag?  (cons (make-posn 5 6)
                             (cons (make-posn 19 3) empty)))
              false)
(check-expect (any-on-diag?  (cons (make-posn 5 6)
                             (cons (make-posn 19 19) empty)))
              true)
(check-expect (any-on-diag?  (cons (make-posn 5 5)
                             (cons (make-posn 19 3) empty)))
              true)
```

The function templates give us a good start on writing the `any-on-diag?` function:

```
(define (  any-on-diag?  L)
  ; L    a list of posns
  (cond [  (empty?  L)        ...]
        [  (cons?  L)         (any-on-diag-nelop?  L) ]
  ))

(define (  any-on-diag-nelop?  L)
  ; L                               a cons
  ; (first L)                       a posn
  ; (posn-x (first L))              a number
  ; (posn-y (first L))              a number
  ; (rest L)                        a lop
  ; (  any-on-diag?  (rest L))      a boolean
  ...)
```

The right answer for the empty list is **false** (that was one of our test cases), so we can fill that in immediately. And the obvious question to ask about the posn is "are the x and y coordinates equal?", *i.e.* (= (posn-x (first L)) (posn-y (first L))), so we'll add that to the template too:

```
(define (any-on-diag?  L)
  ; L    a list of posns
  (cond [(empty?  L)        false ]
        [(cons?  L)         (any-on-diag-nelop?  L)]
  ))
(define (any-on-diag-nelop?  L)
  ; L                                              a cons
  ; (first L)                                      a posn
  ; (posn-x (first L))                             a number
  ; (posn-y (first L))                             a number
  ; (= (posn-x (first L)) (posn-y (first L)))      a boolean
  ; (rest L)                                       a lop
  ; (any-on-diag?  (rest L))                       a boolean
  ...)
```

Now let's try an inventory with values. In fact, since the function has to return a boolean, we'll do *two* inventories-with-values, one returning **true** and one returning **false**:

```
(define (any-on-diag-nelop?  L)
  ; L   a cons    (cons (make-posn 5 6) (cons (make-posn 19 3) empty))
  ; (first L)              a posn    (make-posn 5 6)
  ; (posn-x (first L))     a number  5
  ; (posn-y (first L))     a number  6
  ; (= (posn-x (first L)) (posn-y (first L)))  a boolean    false
  ; (rest L)               a lop     (cons (make-posn 19 3) empty)
  ; (any-on-diag?  (rest L)) a boolean false
    ; right answer          a boolean false
  ...)
```

```
(define (any-on-diag-nelop?  L)
  ; L   a cons    (cons (make-posn 5 5) (cons (make-posn 19 3) empty))
  ; (first L)              a posn    (make-posn 5 5)
  ; (posn-x (first L))     a number  5
  ; (posn-y (first L))     a number  5
  ; (= (posn-x (first L)) (posn-y (first L)))  a boolean    true
  ; (rest L)               a lop     (cons (make-posn 19 3) empty)
  ; (any-on-diag?  (rest L)) a boolean false
    ; right answer          a boolean true
  ...)
```

What expression could we fill in for the "..." that would produce the right answer in both cases? Well, the right answer is a boolean, and there are two booleans above it in the inventory. The most common ways to combine booleans to get another boolean are **and** and **or**. In this case **or** gives the right answer:

```
(define (any-on-diag-nelop?  L)
  ; L                                            cons
  ; (first L)                                    posn
  ; (posn-x (first L))                           number
  ; (posn-y (first L))                           number
  ; (= (posn-x (first L)) (posn-y (first L)))    boolean
  ; (rest L)                                     lop
  ; (any-on-diag?  (rest L))                     boolean
  (or  (= (posn-x (first L)) (posn-y (first L)))
       (any-on-diag?  (rest L))))
```

Test the function(s), and you should get correct answers.

If you prefer to solve this as a single function, the process is similar, but the end result is

```
(define (any-on-diag? L)
  ; L                                                    list of posns
  (cond[(empty? L)         false]
       [(cons? L)
        ; L                                              a cons
        ; (first L)                                      posn
        ; (posn-x (first L))                             number
        ; (posn-y (first L))                             number
        ; (= (posn-x (first L)) (posn-y (first L)))      boolean
        ; (rest L)                                       lop
        ; (any-on-diag? (rest L))                        boolean
        (or (= (posn-x (first L)) (posn-y (first L)))
            (any-on-diag? (rest L)))
       ]))
```

Exercise 22.6.2 *Develop a function* `any-over-100K?` *that takes in a list of* `employee` *structures (from Exercise 21.2.1) and tells whether any of them earn over $100,000 per year.*

Exercise 22.6.3 *Develop a function* `lookup-by-name` *that takes in a string and a list of* `employee` *structures (from Exercise 21.2.1) and returns the first one whose name matches the string. If there is none, it should return* `false`.

Exercise 22.6.4 *Develop a function* `total-votes` *that takes in a list of* `candidate` *structures (from Exercise 21.3.3) and returns the total number of votes cast in the election.*

Exercise 22.6.5 *Develop a function* `avg-votes` *that takes in a list of* `candidate` *structures and returns the* average *number of votes for each candidate.*

Hint: This doesn't have a reasonable answer if there are no candidates. How do you want to handle this case?

Exercise 22.6.6 *Develop a function* `winner` *that takes in a list of* `candidate` *structures and returns the one with the most votes. If there are two or more tied for first place, you can return whichever one you wish.*

Hint: This doesn't have a reasonable answer if there are no candidates. How do you want to handle this case?

Exercise 22.6.7 *Develop an animation similar to Exercise 20.6.4, but every few seconds a dot is added to the screen (in addition to whatever dots are already there), and if you click inside any of the existing dots, the game ends. (The game will be easy to win, since pretty soon the screen fills with dots so it's hard not to hit one.)*

Hint: Use a list of posns as the model.

22.7   Strings as lists

Worked Exercise 22.7.1 *Develop a function* `count-e` *that takes in a string and returns the number of times the letter "e" appears in it. You may assume there are no capital letters (i.e. you don't need to count "E").*

Solution: The contract and examples are fairly straightforward:

```
; count-e :  string -> number
(check-expect (count-e "") 0)
(check-expect (count-e "a") 0)
(check-expect (count-e "e") 1)
(check-expect (count-e "ab") 0)
(check-expect (count-e "ae") 1)
(check-expect (count-e "ea") 1)
(check-expect (count-e "ee") 2)
(check-expect
  (count-e "Tweedledum and Tweedledee were going to a fair")
  10)
```

But how do we write the function?

In a way, this looks similar to the `count-matches` function. Intuitively, a string is a sequence of characters, which "feels" sort of like a list. But we don't have a template for writing functions on a string, looking at each letter one at a time.

There are two ways to handle this. One is to develop such a template so we can write functions that operate directly on strings. The other is to convert a string into a list and then use functions on lists to handle it. Both approaches are useful to know, so let's try both.

A template for strings

To develop a template for operating on strings, we'll proceed by analogy with lists. A string is either empty or non-empty; if it's non-empty, it has a first character and "the rest".

If only we had built-in functions analogous to `empty?`, `cons?`, `first`, and `rest`... Wait: Exercise 13.2.4 defines a function that tells whether a string is empty. We could easily write a `non-empty-string?` function from it using `not` (or we could just use `else`, and not define `non-empty-string?` at all). Exercise 19.3.3 defines a `first-char` function analogous to `first`, while exercises 9.2.3 and 19.3.2 define a `chop-first-char` function analogous to `rest`. So with these, the template is easy:

```
#|
(define (function-on-string str)
  ; str a string
  (cond [(empty-string?  str)      ...]
        [(non-empty-string?  str)  (function-on-nes str)]
  ))
|#
```

```
#|
(define (function-on-nes str)
  ; str                                    non-empty string
  ; (first-char str)                       length-1 string
  ; (chop-first-char str)                  string
  ; (function-on-string (chop-first-char str)) whatever
  ...)
|#
```

or, collapsing the two functions into one,

```
#|
(define (function-on-string str)
  (cond [(empty-string? str)              ...]
        [(non-empty-string? str)
         ; str                                    non-empty string
         ; (first-char str)                       length-1 string
         ; (chop-first-char str)                  string
         ; (function-on-string (chop-first-char str)) whatever
         ...]))
|#
```

With this template, the solution is pretty easy:

```
(define (count-e str)
  (cond [(empty-string? str)              0 ]
        [(non-empty-string? str)
         ; str                                    non-empty string
         ; (first-char str)                       length-1 string
         ; (chop-first-char str)                  string
         ; (count-e (chop-first-char str))
         (cond [(string=? (first-char str) "e")
                (+ 1 (count-e (chop-first-char str)))]
               [else (count-e (chop-first-char str))])]))
```

The char data type

Before we can discuss the other approach, we need to learn about another data type: *char*. Strings in Racket and most other languages are built from *characters*, which are actually another data type you can work with directly. There are built-in functions char=?, which compares two characters to see if they're the same, and char?, which checks whether something is a character at all.

Recall that to type in a string, regardless of length, you surround it in double-quotes. To type in a character, you put #\ in front of it. For example, the first (and only) character in the string "e" is #\e; the third character in the string "5347" is #\4; and the third character in the string "Hi there" is #\ , which can also be written more readably as #\space.)

Converting strings to lists

There's a built-in function string->list which converts a string into a list of chars. So using this approach, we could define count-e very simply as follows:

```
(define (count-e str)
  (count-matches #\e (string->list str)))
```

Note that `count-matches` works on a list of *any* type of object, including `char`. ▮

I recommend trying some of the following problems using the template, and some using conversion to a list, so you're comfortable using both techniques.

Exercise 22.7.2 *Develop a function* `count-vowels` *that takes in a string and returns how many vowels (any of the letters "a", "e", "i", "o", or "u") it contains. You may assume there are no capital letters.*

Exercise 22.7.3 *Develop a function* `has-spaces?` *that takes in a string and tells whether it contains any blanks.*

Exercise 22.7.4 *Develop a function* `count-words` *that takes in a string and tells how many words are in it. A "word" is a sequence of letters; whether it's one letter or ten, it counts as a single word. Note also that there might be punctuation marks, spaces, multiple spaces, numbers, etc. in between words.*

Hint: This problem is similar to Exercise 22.5.19. In addition, you'll probably want the built-in function `char-alphabetic?`. Look it up in the Help Desk.

22.8 Arbitrarily nested lists

In Exercise 22.5.21 we saw that the elements of a list can themselves be lists (of strings, numbers, *etc.*). There is also no rule that all the elements of a list are the same type: one can have a list of which *some* elements are strings, others are lists of strings, and others even lists of lists of strings. For example, suppose we were working with English sentences, and had decided to represent a sentence as a list of words, *e.g.* the sentence "Bob likes Mary" could be stored in the computer as (cons "Bob" (cons "likes" (cons "Mary" empty))). But how should we represent a sentence like "Jeff said "Bob likes Mary" yesterday"? The thing that Jeff said is in itself a whole sentence, so it would be nice to represent it the same way we represent sentences ... but it fits into the grammar of the whole sentence in exactly the same way as if he had said only one word.

```
(cons "Jeff" (cons "said" (cons
    (cons "Bob" (cons "likes" (cons "Mary" empty)))
  (cons "yesterday" empty)))))
```

Exercise 22.8.1 *Write a data definition, including templates, for a nested string list, in which each element may be either a string or another nested string list.*

Exercise 22.8.2 *Translate the following English sentences into nested string lists, using a list to represent each quotation.*

- *"We watched "Rudolph the Red-Nosed Reindeer" and "Frosty the Snowman" on Christmas Eve."*

- *" "This is silly," said Mary."*

- *"Grandpa said "I'll read you a book called "The Princess Bride", one of my favorites. "Once upon a time, there was a beautiful princess named Buttercup. The stable-boy, Wesley, was in love with her, but never said anything but "As you wish." " " The boy was already asleep."*

Exercise 22.8.3 *Ingredient lists on food packaging sometimes get deeply nested. I found a package of ice cream with the following ingredients list (I am not making this up!) :*

> *Milk, skim milk, cream, hazelnut swirl (praline paste (hazelnuts, sugar, milk chocolate (sugar, cocoa butter, milk, chocolate, natural flavor, soy lecithin), bittersweet chocolate (sugar, chocolate, cocoa butter, butter oil, natural flavor, soy lecithin)), corn oil, powdered sugar (sugar, corn starch), dark chocolate (sugar, chocolate, cocoa butter, butter oil, natural flavor, soy lecithin), corn starch, cocoa processed with alkali, coconut oil, mono- and di-glycerides, salt, soy lecithin), sugar, chocolate truffle cake (semi-sweet chocolate (sugar, chocolate, cocoa butter, soy lecithin), cream, chocolate cookie crumbs (enriched flour (flour, niacin, reduced iron, thiamine mononitrate, riboflavin, folic acid), sugar, partially hydrogenated soybena, cottonseed, and canola oil, cocoa processed with alkali, high fructose corn syrup, yellow corn flour, chocolate, salt, dextrose, baking soda, soy lecithin), corn syrup, butter, chocolate, sugar, natural flavor), bittersweet chocolate (sugar, chocolate, cocoa butter, butter oil, natural flavor, soy lecithin), cocoa processed with alkali, egg yolks, natural flavor, guar gum, carob bean gum, carrageenan, dextrose*

We could represent this in Racket as follows:

```
(define milk-chocolate (cons "sugar" (cons "cocoa-butter"
  (cons "milk" (cons "chocolate" (cons "natural flavor"
  (cons "soy lecithin" empty)))))))
(define bittersweet-chocolate (cons "sugar" (cons "chocolate"
  (cons "cocoa butter" (cons "butter oil" (cons
  "natural flavor" (cons "soy lecithin" empty)))))))
(define praline-paste (cons "hazelnuts" (cons "sugar"
  (cons milk-chocolate (cons bittersweet-chocolate empty)))))
  ...
```

Note how I've defined Racket variables for the ingredients that have ingredient lists of their own.

    Finish *translating this ingredient list to Racket.*

Exercise 22.8.4 *Develop a function* `count-strings-nested` *that takes in a nested string list and returns the total number of simple strings in it, no matter how many levels of nested lists they're inside.*

Exercise 22.8.5 *Develop a function* `max-nesting-depth` *that takes in a nested string list and returns its maximum nesting depth:* `empty` *has a nesting depth of 0, a list of strings has a nesting depth of 1, a list that contains some lists of strings has a nesting depth of 2, etc.*

It can be difficult to read and write such nested lists and the test cases for Exercises 22.5.21, 22.8.1, 22.8.3, 22.8.4, and 22.8.5. In Section 23.3 we'll learn a more compact notation for lists that makes this easier.

22.9   Review of important words and concepts

Whereas a structure collects a *fixed* number of related pieces of information into one object, a list allows you to collect a *variable* number of related pieces of information into one object. The *list* data type is defined by combining techniques we've already seen: definition by choices (is it empty or not?) and definition by parts (if it's non-empty, it has a first and a rest, which is itself a list).

We already know how to write functions on data types defined by choices, and defined by parts; the new feature is that since a list really involves two interdependent data types, a function on lists is often written as two interdependent functions. However, since one of these is generally only used in one place in the other, we can often make the program shorter and simpler by combining the two functions into one that calls itself on the rest of the list.

A list can contain *any* kind of data: numbers, strings, structs, or even other lists. The template for functions that work on lists is almost the same for all of these; the only difference is what you can do with (`first the-list`). In particular, if the first element of a list is itself a list, you may need to call the same function on it.

Operating on strings is much like operating on lists. A function that takes in a string can test whether it's the empty string or not, extract its first character and the remaining characters, and so on ... or it can use the built-in function `string->list` to convert the whole string into a list of characters, and then use the usual list template to work with this list of characters.

22.10   Reference: Built-in functions on lists

This chapter introduced the following built-in constants and functions:

- `empty`
- `empty?`
- `cons`
- `first`
- `rest`
- `cons?`
- `string->list`
- `char=?`
- `char?`
- `char-alphabetic?`
- `list-ref`

Chapter 23

Functions that return lists

If you did exercises 22.5.15 or 22.5.16, you've already written some functions that return lists, but only in a very simple way: adding one new element to the front of an existing list. In this chapter we'll discuss functions that construct an entire list as their results.

23.1 Doing something to each element

Worked Exercise 23.1.1 *Develop a function add1-each that takes in a list of numbers and returns a list of numbers of the same length, with each element of the answer equal to 1 more than the corresponding element of the input. For example,*

```
(check-expect (add1-each (cons 3 (cons -12 (cons 7 empty))))
              (cons 4 (cons -11 (cons 8 empty))))
```

Solution: For brevity, I'll write this as a single function; the two-function version is quite similar. The contract, test cases, skeleton, and inventory are straightforward:

```
; add1-each : list-of-numbers -> list-of-numbers
(check-expect (add1-each empty) empty)
(check-expect (add1-each (cons 3 empty)) (cons 4 empty))
(check-expect (add1-each (cons 3 (cons -12 (cons 7 empty))))
              (cons 4 (cons -11 (cons 8 empty))))

(define (add1-each nums)
  ; nums                       lon
  (cond [(empty? nums)      ...]
        [(cons? nums)
         ; nums                       nelon
         ; (first nums)               number
         ; (rest nums)                lon
         ; (add1-each (rest nums)) lon
         ...]
))
```

The answer to the empty case is obviously `empty` (since the result has to be the same length as the input). To fill in the non-empty case, let's do an inventory with values:

333

```
  [(cons?  nums)
   ; nums                    (cons 3 (cons -12 (cons 7 empty)))
   ; (first nums)            3
   ; (rest nums)             (cons -12 (cons 7 empty))
   ; (add1-each (rest nums)) (cons -11 (cons 8 empty))
   ; right answer            (cons 4 (cons -11 (cons 8 empty)))
   ...]
  ))
```

Notice that the recursive call (add1-each (rest nums)) gives you most of the right answer, but it's missing a 4 at the front. Where could the 4 come from? Since (first nums) in this example is 3, an obvious choice is (+ 1 (first nums)).

```
  [(cons?  nums)
   ; nums                    (cons 3 (cons -12 (cons 7 empty)))
   ; (first nums)            3
   ; (rest nums)             (cons -12 (cons 7 empty))
   ; (add1-each (rest nums)) (cons -11 (cons 8 empty))
   ; right answer            (cons 4 (cons -11 (cons 8 empty)))
   (cons  (+ 1 (first nums))
          (add1-each (rest nums))) ]
  ))
```

Test this, and it should work on all legal inputs. ▮

Exercise 23.1.2 *Develop a function* square-each *that takes in a list of numbers and returns a list of their squares, in the same order.*

Exercise 23.1.3 *Develop a function* string-lengths *that takes in a list of strings and returns a list of their (numeric) lengths, in the same order.*

Exercise 23.1.4 *Develop a function* salaries *that takes in a list of* employee *structures (from Exercise 21.2.1) and returns a list containing only their salaries, in the same order.*

Exercise 23.1.5 *Develop a function* give-10%-raises *that takes in a list of* employee *structures and returns a list of the same* employees, *but each earning* 10% *more than before.*

Exercise 23.1.6 *Develop a function* stutter *that takes in a list of anything (it doesn't matter whether they're strings, numbers, or something else) and returns a list twice as long, with each element repeated twice in a row. For example,*
(check-expect (stutter (cons 5 (cons 2 (cons 9 empty))))
  (cons 5 (cons 5 (cons 2 (cons 2 (cons 9 (cons 9 empty)))))))

Exercise 23.1.7 *Develop a function* list-each *that takes in a list (of numbers, strings, it doesn't matter) and returns a* list of one-element lists, *each containing a different one of the elements in the original list. For example,*
(check-expect (list-each (cons "a" (cons "b" empty)))
  (cons (cons "a" empty) (cons (cons "b" empty) empty)))

Exercise 23.1.8 *Develop a function* suffixes *that takes in a list (of numbers, strings, it doesn't matter) and returns a* list *of lists comprising all the* suffixes *of the list (that is, "the last 3 elements," "the last 17 elements,", "the last 0 elements," etc. of the given list). For example,*

```
(check-expect (suffixes (cons "a" (cons "b" (cons "c" empty))))
  (cons (cons "a" (cons "b" (cons "c" empty)))
        (cons (cons "b" (cons "c" empty))
              (cons (cons "c" empty)
                    (cons empty
                          empty))))))
```

Exercise 23.1.9 *Recall the built-in* string-append *function, which takes in two strings and produces a single string by combining them end to end.* *Develop a function* list-append *that takes in two* lists *(of numbers, strings, it doesn't matter) and combines them end-to-end into one list. For example,*

```
(check-expect
  (list-append (cons "a" (cons "b" (cons "c" empty)))
               (cons "d" (cons "e" empty)))
  (cons "a" (cons "b" (cons "c" (cons "d" (cons "e" empty)))))))
```

Hint: This function takes in *two* lists, so one might wonder what template to use. We'll discuss this more fully in Chapter 25, but for now, use the template on the first of the two lists, treating the second as just a simple variable.

There's a built-in function append that does this, but you are *not* allowed to use append in writing your function; the point is that if append weren't built in, you could have written it yourself. After you've finished this exercise, feel free to use append in the rest of the book.

Exercise 23.1.10 *Define a function* backwards *that takes in a list (of anything) and returns a list of the same objects in the opposite order.*

There's a built-in function named reverse which does this, but I want you to define it yourself without using reverse. After you've finished this exercise, feel free to use reverse in the rest of the book.

23.2 Making decisions on each element

In some problems, you need to make a decision about each element of a list, using a conditional. As with Exercises 22.5.5, 22.5.7, *etc.*, this conditional is usually nested inside the one that decides whether the list is empty or not.

Exercise 23.2.1 *Develop a function* substitute *that takes in two strings and a list of strings, and returns a list the same length as the given list, but with all occurrences of the first string replaced by the second. For example,*

```
(check-expect
  (substitute "old" "new" (cons "this" (cons "that" (cons "old"
    (cons "new" (cons "borrowed" (cons "old" (cons "blue"
    empty)))))))
  (cons "this (cons "that" (cons "new" (cons "new"
    (cons "borrowed" (cons "new" (cons "blue" empty))))))))
```

Exercise 23.2.2 *Develop a function* `remove-all` *that takes in a string and a list of strings, and returns the same list but with all occurrences (if there are any) of the given string removed. For example,*
```
(check-expect
  (remove-all "old" (cons "this" (cons "that" (cons "old"
    (cons "new" (cons "borrowed" (cons "old"
    (cons "blue" empty))))))))
  (cons "this" (cons "that" (cons "new" (cons "borrowed"
    (cons "blue" empty))))))
```

Exercise 23.2.3 *Develop a function* `remove-first` *that takes in a string and a list of strings, and returns the same list but with the first occurrence (if any) of the given string removed. For example,*
```
(check-expect
  (remove-first "old" (cons "this" (cons "that" (cons "old"
    (cons "new" (cons "borrowed" (cons "old"
    (cons "blue" empty))))))))
  (cons "this" (cons "that" (cons "new" (cons "borrowed"
    (cons "old" (cons "blue" empty)))))))
```

Exercise 23.2.4 *Develop a function* `unique` *that takes in a list of objects and returns a list of the same objects, but each appearing only once each.*

Hint: There are several ways to do this. Probably the easiest way, given what you've seen so far, produces a result in the order in which each string *last* appeared in the input; for example,
```
(check-expect (unique (cons "a" (cons "b" (cons "a" empty))))
  (cons "b" (cons "a" empty)))
; not (cons "a" (cons "b" empty)))
(check-expect
  (unique (cons 3 (cons 8 (cons 5 (cons 5 (cons 8 empty))))))
  (cons 3 (cons 5 (cons 8 empty))))
; not (cons 3 (cons 8 (cons 5 empty)))
```
We'll discuss other approaches in later chapters.

Since you don't know what kind of objects you're dealing with, you'll need to use `equal?` to compare them.

Exercise 23.2.5 *Develop a function* `fire-over-100K` *that takes in a list of* `employee` *structures and returns a list of those who earn at most $100,000/year, leaving out the ones who earn more. The remaining employees should be in the same order they were in before.*

Exercise 23.2.6 *Develop a function* `add-vote-for` *that takes in a string (representing a candidate's name) and a list of* `candidate` *structures, and returns a list of* `candidate` *structures in which that candidate has one more vote (and all the others are unchanged). You may assume that no name appears more than once in the list.*

Hint: What should you do if the name doesn't appear in the list at all?

Exercise 23.2.7 *Develop a function* `tally-votes` *that takes in a list of strings (Voter 1's favorite candidate, Voter 2's favorite candidate, etc.) and produces a list of* `candidate` *structures in which each candidate's name appears once, with how many votes were cast for that candidate.*

23.3 A shorter notation for lists

23.3.1 The list function

Writing (cons "a" (cons "b" (cons "c" empty))) for a three-element list is technically correct, but it's tedious. Fortunately, Racket provides a shorter way to accomplish the same thing. There's a built-in function named list that takes zero or more parameters and constructs a list from them. For example,

```
> (list "a" "b" "c")
(cons "a" (cons "b" (cons "c" empty)))
```

Note that list is *just a shorthand*: it produces the exact same list as the cons form, and any function that works on one of them will still work on the other.

Common beginner mistake

I've frequently seen students simply replace every cons in their code with list, getting results like

```
(list "a" (list "b" (list "c" empty)))
```

Think of cons as *adding one element to the front* of a list, whereas list builds a list from scratch. If you call cons on two arguments, the result will be a list one element longer than the second argument was; if you call list on two arguments, the result will be a list of exactly two elements. For example,

```
> (define my-list (list "x" "y" "z"))
> (cons "w" my-list)
(cons "w" (cons "x" (cons "y" (cons "z" empty))))
> (list "w" my-list)
(cons "w" (cons (cons "x" (cons "y" (cons "z") empty) empty))
```

Practice Exercise 23.3.1 *Translate* each of the following lists from *list* notation into *nested-cons* notation. **Check** that your answers are correct by typing each expression into DrRacket (Beginning Student language) and comparing the result with your answer.

```
(list)
(list "a")
(list "a" "b")
(list (list "Mary" "Joe") (list "Chris" "Phil"))
(list empty "a" empty)
```

23.3.2 List abbreviations for display

The list function makes it easier and more convenient to *type in* lists (especially lists of structs, lists of lists, *etc.*), but it's still a pain to *read* them. If you want lists to *print out* in list notation rather than nested-cons notation, simply go to the "Language" menu in DrRacket, select "Choose Language", and then (under the *How to Design Programs* heading) select "Beginning Student with List Abbreviations".

```
> (list "a" "b" "c")
(list "a" "b" "c")
> (cons "a" (cons "b" (cons "c" empty)))
(list "a" "b" "c")
> (define my-list (list "x" "y" "z"))
> (cons "w" my-list)
(list "w" "x" "y" "z")
> (list "w" my-list)
(list "w" (list "x" "y" "z"))
```

Again, note that this is only a change in output convention: both `cons` and `list` still work, and any correct function on lists will still work no matter which way you type in the examples, and no matter which language you're in.

Practice Exercise 23.3.2 *Translate each of the following lists from nested-`cons` notation into `list` notation.* **Check** *that your answers are correct by typing each expression into DrRacket (Beginning Student with List Abbreviations language) and comparing the result with your answer.*

```
(cons "a" empty)
empty
(cons 3 (cons 4 (cons -2 empty)))
(cons (cons 3 empty) empty)
```

There's an even shorter form called "quasiquote notation", using the apostrophe:

```
> '(1 2 (3 4) 5)
(list 1 2 (list 3 4) 5)
> '("abc" "de" ("f" "g") "h")
(list "abc" "de" (list "f" "g") "h")
> '()
empty
```

Quasiquote notation is *not* available in Beginning Student language.

SIDEBAR:

If you want to see your *output* in this even-shorter notation, "Choose Language", choose "Beginning Student with List Abbreviations", click "Show Details" at the bottom of the window, find the "Output Style" section on the right, choose "Quasiquote", then click "OK" and then "Run" (which you have to do whenever you change languages).

   You'll notice that the output has not an ordinary apostrophe but rather a "backquote". For now, you can treat these two characters as the same. Backquote allows you to do some other neat things, but we won't use it in this textbook; if you're really curious, look it up in the Help Desk.

Practice Exercise 23.3.3 *For each exercise from Chapters 22 and 23 that you've already done, rewrite the test cases using `list` or `quasiquote` notation, and try the function again. The results should be especially nice for functions that take in or return lists of lists or lists of structs, like Exercises 22.8.5 and 23.1.8.*

23.4 Animations with lists

Exercise 23.4.1 *Write an animation of a bunch of balls, each moving around the screen with constant velocity and bouncing off walls. Pressing the + key should create one more ball, with random initial location (inside the animation window) and random velocity (say, from -10 to +10 in each dimension). Pressing the − key should remove the most recently-added ball, unless there are no balls, in which case it should do nothing. Clicking with the mouse inside a ball should remove the ball you clicked on, leaving the rest of the balls unchanged.*

Hint: You'll need each ball to have a location and a velocity, as in exercise 21.7.6, and use a list of structs as your model, as in exercise 22.6.7.

Hint: What should happen if you click with the mouse in a place where two or more balls overlap? The assignment doesn't say exactly; you should decide in advance what you *want* to happen in this case, and make it work.

23.5 Strings as lists

In Section 22.7, we showed two different ways to write functions on strings: using an input template for them analogous to the input template for lists, and using the built-in function `string->list`, which converts a string to a list of characters.

One can do the exact same thing for functions that *return* a string: either use an output template analogous to that for returning a list, or use the built-in function `list->string`, which converts a list of characters to a string. (If any of the things in the list is *not* a character, it produces an error message.) I recommend trying some of the following problems each way.

Exercise 23.5.1 *Develop a function `string-reverse` that takes in a string and returns a string of the same characters in reverse order.*

Exercise 23.5.2 *Develop a function `string-suffixes` that takes in a string and returns a list of all its suffixes. For example,*

```
(check-expect (string-suffixes "abc")
   (list "abc" "bc" "c" ""))
```

Exercise 23.5.3 *Develop a function `replace-char` that takes in a character and two strings (*replacement *and* target*). It returns a string formed by replacing each occurrence of the character in* target *with the entire string* replacement*. For example,*

```
(check-expect (replace-char #\r "fnord" "reference librarian")
   "fnordefefnordence libfnordafnordian")
```

Exercise 23.5.4 *Develop a function named `ubby-dubby` which translates a given string into "ubby-dubby talk". This is defined as follows: insert the letters "ubb" in front of each vowel in the original string. For example,*

```
(check-expect (ubby-dubby "hello there")
              "hubbellubbo thubberubbe")
```

You may assume *for simplicity that all the letters are lower-case. You may find it useful to write a* vowel? *helper function.*

Exercise 23.5.5 *Modify your solution to exercise 23.5.4 so it inserts the letters "ubb" only once in front of each* group of consecutive *vowels. For example,*

```
(check-expect (ubby-dubby "hello friends out there")
  "hubbellubbo frubbiends ubbout thubberubbe")
```

Hint: See Exercise 22.7.4.

Exercise 23.5.6 *Develop a function* words *that takes in a string and returns a* list *of strings, one for each word in the input string, leaving out any spaces, punctuation, numbers, etc. A "word" is defined as in Exercise 22.7.4: a sequence of one or more letters. For example,*

```
(check-expect (words "This is chapter 26, or is it 25?")
              (list "This" "is" "chapter" "or" "is" "it"))
```

Exercise 23.5.7 *Develop a function* pig-latin *that takes in a string and converts it to "Pig Latin": for each word, if it starts with a vowel, add "way" at the end of the word, and if it starts with a consonant, move that consonant to the end of the word and add "ay". You may* assume *that the input string has no upper-case letters, numbers, or punctuation. For example,*

```
(check-expect (pig-latin "hi boys and girls")
              "ihay oysbay andway irlsgay")
```

Exercise 23.5.8 *Modify your solution to exercise 23.5.7 so that if a word starts with more than one* consonant, *the function moves* all *of them to the end, followed by "ay". For example,*

```
(check-expect (pig-latin "this is a strange function")
              "isthay isway away angestray unctionfay")
```

Exercise 23.5.9 *Modify your solution to exercise 23.5.7 or 23.5.8 to handle capital letters correctly: any word that started with a capital letter before should still start with a capital letter after converting it to Pig Latin, and capital letters moved from the start to the end of a word should no longer be capitalized. For example, if you made both this modification and the one in exercise 23.5.8,*

```
(check-expect (pig-latin "My name is Stephen Bloch")
  "Ymay amenay isway Ephenstay Ochblay")
```

Hint: To do this, you may need some of the built-in functions char-upper-case?, char-lower-case?, char-upcase, and char-downcase. Look them up in the Help Desk.

Exercise 23.5.10 *Design a function* basic-mad-lib *that takes in a string (the template and a non-empty list of strings), and returns a string. The template may contain ordinary words and punctuation, as well as the hyphen character (-). The output of the function should be based on the template, but it should replace each - with a randomly-chosen word from the list of words. For example,*

```
(basic-mad-lib "The - bit the - and took a - home."
  (list "dog" "cat" "senator" "taxi" "train" "chair"))
; could be "The chair bit the dog and took a senator home."
```

Exercise 23.5.11 *Design a function* mad-lib *similar to the above, but it takes a string (the* template*) and* three *non-empty lists (which we'll call* nouns, verbs, *and* adjectives*). The template may contain the "special" words* -noun-, -verb-, *and* -adjective-; *each* -noun- *should be replaced by a randomly chosen element of* nouns, *and so on. For example,*

```
(mad-lib
  "The -noun- -verb- the -adjective- -noun- and -verb- quickly."
  (list "dog" "cat" "senator" "taxi" "train" "chair")
  (list "tall" "green" "expensive" "chocolate" "overrated")
  (list "ate" "drank" "slept" "wrote"))
; could be
"The senator slept the overrated cat and drank quickly."
```

23.6 More complex functions involving lists

Lists and recursion allow us to solve much more interesting and complicated problems than we could solve before. Sometimes such problems require "helper" or "auxiliary" functions. For each of the following problems, you'll need *at least* one helper function. To figure out what helper functions you need, just start writing the main function, following the design recipe. When you reach the "inventory with values" point, you'll probably find that there is no built-in function to produce the right answer from the available expressions. So decide what such a function would need to do. Then write it, following the design recipe. This function in turn may need yet another helper function, and so on.

Exercise 23.6.1 *Develop a function* sort *that takes in a list of numbers and returns a list of the same numbers in increasing order.*

Hint: There are several possible ways to do this. If you use an input template, you'll probably need a helper function that inserts a number in order into an already-sorted list. If you use an output template, you'll probably need two helper functions: one to find the smallest element in an unsorted list, and one to remove a specified element from an unsorted list. In either case, I recommend treating list-of-numbers and sorted-list-of-numbers as two separate types: when a function produces a sorted list, or assumes that it is given a sorted list, say so in the contract and inventory, and make sure your test cases satisfy the assumption.

Exercise 23.6.2 *Develop a function named* sort-candidates *that takes in a list of* candidate *structures and returns a list of the same* candidate *structures in decreasing order by number of votes, so the winner is first in the list, the second-place winner is second, etc.. In case of ties, either order is acceptable.*

Exercise 23.6.3 *Develop a function* subsets *that takes in a list (of numbers, strings, it doesn't matter) and returns a list of lists representing* all possible subsets *of the elements in the original list, once each. For example,* (subsets (list "a" "b" "c")) *should produce something like*

```
(list (list)
      (list "a")
      (list "b")
      (list "a" "b")
      (list "c")
      (list "a" "c")
      (list "b" "c")
      (list "a" "b" "c"))
```

You may assume *that all the things in the input list are different.*

Exercise 23.6.4 *Develop a function* scramble *that takes in a list (of numbers, strings, it doesn't matter) and returns a list of lists representing* all possible orderings *of the elements in the original list, once each. For example, (*scramble *(list "a" "b" "c"))* should produce something like

```
(list (list "a" "b" "c")
      (list "b" "a" "c")
      (list "a" "c" "b")
      (list "c" "a" "b")
      (list "b" "c" "a")
      (list "c" "b" "a"))
```

Again, you may assume *that all the things in the input list are different. Even better, decide* what the function should do if there are duplicate elements in the input list, and make sure it does the right thing.

Hint: This will probably require *more than one* helper function. Take it one step at a time: try to write the main function, figure out what you need to do to the recursive result, invent a function to do that, and repeat until what you need to do is built-in.

Exercise 23.6.5 *Develop a function* scramble-word *that takes in a string and returns a list of strings representing* all possible orderings *of the characters in the string.*

*For a basic version of this function, you may include the same string more than once: for example, (*scramble-word *"foo") might produce (list "foo" "ofo" "oof" "foo" "ofo" "oof") Once you have this working, try rewriting it so it doesn't produce any duplicates: (*scramble-word *"foo") might produce (list "foo" "ofo" "oof") instead.*

Hint: Re-use functions you've already written!

Exercise 23.6.6 *Modify the* scramble-word *function so that, even if there are repeated characters in the string, the result won't contain the same word twice: (*scramble-word *"foo") might produce (list "foo" "ofo" "oof").*

23.7   Review of important words and concepts

Many of the most interesting things one can do with a list involve producing another list. Sometimes we do the same thing to every element of a list, producing a list of the results. Sometimes we select some of the elements of a list, producing a shorter list. And sometimes we do more complicated things like scramble or subsets.

Recall from Chapter 20 that the inventory-with-values technique tends to be more useful the more complicated the output type is. Lists, and especially lists of lists or lists of structs, are the most complicated types we've seen yet, and the inventory-with-values technique is extremely helpful in writing these functions.

23.8 Reference: built-in functions that return lists

We've seen several new built-in functions in this chapter:

- append
- `char-upper-case?`
- `char-lower-case?`
- `char-upcase`
- `char-downcase`
- `append`
- `reverse`
- `list->string`

Chapter 24

Whole numbers.

24.1 What is a whole number?

A *whole number*[1] is a non-negative integer: any of the numbers $0, 1, 2, 3, \ldots$.

What does the "..." in the above definition mean? It basically means "and so on," or "you know the rest." But what if you were talking to somebody who *really didn't* "know the rest"? Perhaps an alien from another planet, whose mathematical background was so different from yours that he/she/it couldn't fill in the "and so on". How would you define whole numbers to someone who didn't already know what whole numbers were?

In the 1880's, two mathematicians named Richard Dedekind and Giuseppe Peano addressed this problem more or less as follows:

- 0 is a whole number

- If α is a whole number, then so is $S(\alpha)$

The S was intended to stand for "successor" — for example, 1 is the successor of 0, and 2 is the successor of 1. However, the above definition doesn't require that you already know what 0, or 1, or 2, or "successor", or "plus" mean.

24.1.1 Defining wholes from structs

Imagine that Racket didn't already know about whole numbers. We could *define* them as follows:

```
; A built-whole is either 0 or (S built-whole).
(define-struct successor [previous])
(define (S x) ; shorter name for convenience
  (make-successor x))
(define (P x) ; shorter name for convenience
  (successor-previous x))
```

(I use the name *built-whole* to distinguish it from "ordinary wholes", which we'll use in the next section.)

We would then start constructing examples of the data type:

---

[1] Actually, I was brought up to call these "natural numbers", and Racket includes a `natural?` function to tell whether something is one of them. But some books define "natural numbers" to start at 1 rather than 0. By contrast, everybody seems to agree that the "whole numbers" start at 0, so that's the term I'll use in this book.

- 0

- (S 0), which "means" 1

- (S (S 0)), which "means" 2

- (P (S (S 0))), another way to represent 1

- (S (S (S (S (S 0))))), which "means" 5

and so on.

The above definition should remind you of the definition of a list in Chapter 22: a list is either empty or (cons *object list*). We defined lists by choices; one of the choices had two parts (which we could get by using first and rest), one of which was itself a list.

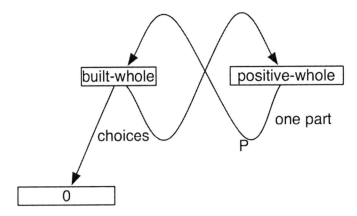

This combination of definition by choices and by parts led us to a standard way to write functions on lists.

Following that analogy, how would one write functions on this *built-whole* data type? The data type is defined by two choices, one of which has one part, which is another built-whole. So the template (collapsed into a single function) looks like

```
(define (function-on-built-whole n)
  (cond [(equal? n 0) ...]
        [(successor? n)
          ; n                              successor
          ; (P n)                          built-whole
          ; (function-on-built-whole (P n)) whatever this returns
        ]))
```

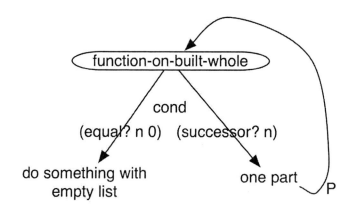

Worked Exercise 24.1.1 *Develop a function* spams *that takes in a* built-whole *and returns a list with that many copies of the string* "spam".

Solution: The contract is clearly

```
; spams :  built-whole -> list-of-string
```

Since the data type has two choices, we need to make sure we've got an example of each, and a more complex example

```
(check-expect (spams 0) empty)
(check-expect (spams (S 0)) (list "spam"))
(check-expect (spams (S (S (S 0)))) (list "spam" "spam" "spam"))
```

For the function skeleton, we'll start by copying the single-function template from above, changing the function name:

```
(define ( spams n)
  (cond [(equal?  n 0) ...]
        [(successor?  n)
         ; n                 successor
         ; (P n)             built-whole
         ; ( spams  (P n)) list of strings
        ]))
```

The answer in the 0 case is obviously empty. For the non-zero case, let's try an inventory with values:

```
(define (spams n)
  (cond [(equal?  n 0)   empty ]
        [(successor?  n)
         ; n                 successor      3
         ; (P n)             built-whole    2
         ; (spams (P n)) list of strings (list "spam" "spam")
         ; right answer  list of strings
                            ; (list "spam" "spam" "spam")
        ]))
```

The obvious way to get from (list "spam" "spam") to (list "spam" "spam" "spam")
is by cons-ing on another "spam", so ...

```
(define (spams n)
  (cond [(equal? n 0)      empty]
        [(successor? n)
         ; n               successor      3
         ; (P n)           built-whole    2
         ; (spams (P n))   list of strings (list "spam" "spam")
         ; right answer    list of strings
                           ; (list "spam" "spam" "spam")
         (cons "spam" (spams (P n)))
        ]))
```

Test this on the examples, and it should work. Make up some examples of your own;
does it do what you expect? ▮

SIDEBAR:

The word "spam" today means "commercial junk e-mail". Have you ever wondered
how it got that meaning?

"Spam" was originally a brand name for a "Spiced Ham" product sold by the Hormel
meat company. In 1970, the British TV show "Monty Python's Flying Circus" aired
a comedy sketch about a restaurant that was peculiar in two ways: first, every item
on its menu included Spam, and second, one table of the restaurant was occupied by
Vikings who, on several occasions during the sketch, started singing "Spam, spam,
spam, spam ..."

In 1970, there was no such thing as e-mail. By 1980, e-mail was a well-known
phenomenon, although not many people had it, and comics could start joking "If we
have electronic mail, pretty soon we'll have electronic junk mail." By 1990, it was
no longer a joke but a nuisance. Legend has it that somebody (I don't know who or
when — probably in the 1980's) was going through his/her inbox deleting junk mail
and muttering "junk ...junk ...junk ..." when the Monty Python sketch popped
into his/her head and (s)he replaced the word "junk" with the word "spam". And the
rest is history.

Exercise 24.1.2 *Develop a function* copies *that takes in a string and a* built-whole,
and produces a list of that many copies of the string.

Exercise 24.1.3 *Develop a function* whole-value *that takes in a* built-whole *and returns the ordinary number that it "means". For example,*

```
(check-expect (whole-value 0) 0)
(check-expect (whole-value (S 0)) 1)
(check-expect (whole-value (P (S (S (S (S (S 0)))))) 4)
```

24.1.2   Wholes, the way we really do it

One can do a lot with this definition of wholes, but writing (S (S (S (S (S 0))))) for
5 is a royal pain. In fact, Racket already knows about numbers, including whole numbers,
so we can use Racket's predefined arithmetic operations.

A *whole* is either 0 or (add1 *whole*).

We can replace

(equal? n 0) with the predefined (zero? n) or (= n 0);

(S n) with the predefined (add1 n) or (+ n 1);

(P n) with the predefined (sub1 n) or (- n 1); and

(successor? n) with the predefined (positive? n) or > n 0).

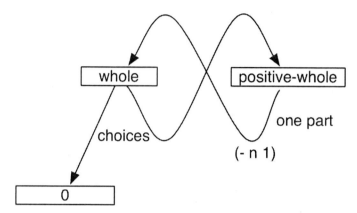

The resulting template looks like

```
(define (function-on-whole n)
  (cond [(= n 0) ...]
        [(> n 0)
         ; n                              positive whole
         ; (- n 1)                        whole
         ; (function-on-whole (- n 1))    whatever this returns
        ]))
```

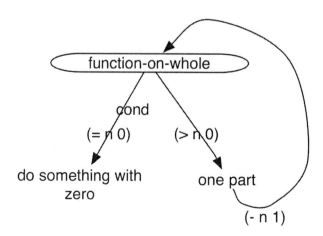

Worked Exercise 24.1.4 *Re-write the spams function of Exercise 24.1.1 to work on ordinary, built-in whole numbers.*

Solution: The contract changes to take in an ordinary whole number:

```
; spams :  whole-number -> list-of-strings
```

The examples change to use ordinary number notation:

```
(check-expect (spams 0) empty)
(check-expect (spams 1) (list "spam"))
(check-expect (spams 3) (list "spam" "spam" "spam"))
```

The function definition is exactly the same as before, but replacing the *built-whole* functions with standard Racket arithmetic functions:

```
(define (spams n)
  (cond [ (= n 0)        empty]
        [ (> n 0)
          ; n                    positive whole 3
          ;   (- n 1)            whole          2
          ; (spams  (- n 1) ) list of strings(list "spam" "spam")
          ; right answer         list of strings
                                 ; (list "spam" "spam" "spam")
          (cons "spam" (spams (- n 1)))
        ]))
```

Try this and make sure it still works. ∎

Exercise 24.1.5 *Re-write the* `copies` *function of Exercise 24.1.2 to take in a string and an (ordinary) whole number.*

Exercise 24.1.6 *Develop a function* `count-down` *that takes in an (ordinary) whole number and produces a list of the whole numbers from it down to 0. For example,*

```
(check-expect (count-down 4) (list 4 3 2 1 0))
```

Exercise 24.1.7 *Develop a function* `add-up-to` *that takes in a whole number and returns the sum of all the whole numbers up to and including it.*

Hint: The formula $n(n+1)/2$ solves the same problem, so you can use it to check your answers. But you should write your function by actually adding up all the numbers, not by using this formula.

Exercise 24.1.8 *Develop a function* `factorial` *that takes in a whole number and returns the product of all the whole numbers from 1 up to and including it.*

Hint: What is the "right answer" for 0? There are at least two possible ways to answer this: you could decide that the function *has* no answer at 0 (so the base case is at 1, not 0), or you could pick an answer for 0 so that the other answers all come out right. Mathematicians generally choose the latter.

Exercise 24.1.9 *Develop a function* `fibonacci` *that takes in a whole number n and produces the n-th Fibonacci number. The Fibonacci numbers are defined as follows: the 0-th Fibonacci number is 0, the 1st Fibonacci number is 1, and each subsequent Fibonacci number is the sum of the previous two Fibonacci numbers. For example,*

```
(check-expect (fibonacci 0) 0)
(check-expect (fibonacci 1) 1)
(check-expect (fibonacci 2) 1)
(check-expect (fibonacci 3) 2)
(check-expect (fibonacci 4) 3)
(check-expect (fibonacci 5) 5)
(check-expect (fibonacci 6) 8)
(check-expect (fibonacci 7) 13)
```

Hint: The usual template involves calling `(fibonacci (- n 1))` inside the body of `fibonacci`. In this case, you'll probably want to call `(fibonacci (- n 2))` as well. However, that doesn't make sense unless you know that `(- n 2)` *is* a whole number, so your base case needs to handle both 0 and 1.

Note: The definition of `fibonacci` that you get by following the template for whole numbers is correct, but extremely slow. On my computer, `(fibonacci 30)` takes about a second; `(fibonacci 35)` takes about ten seconds; and `(fibonacci 37)` takes almost thirty seconds. Try watching it in the Stepper, and you'll see that it asks the same question over and over. See if you can find a way to solve the same problem much more efficiently, using a helper function with some extra parameters. We'll see another way to fix this problem in Section 30.3.

SIDEBAR:

"Fibonacci" is the modern name for Leonardo filius Bonacci ("son of Bonaccio"), a mathematician who lived in Pisa, Italy in the 12th and 13th centuries. He is best known today for this sequence of numbers, which has surprising applications in biology, number theory, architecture, *etc.* But his most significant impact on the world was probably persuading European scholars to switch from Roman numerals by showing how much easier it is to do arithmetic using Arabic numerals.

Exercise 24.1.10 *Develop a function named* `dot-grid` *(remember this from Chapter 5?) that takes two whole numbers* `width` *and* `height` *and produces a rectangular grid of circles with* `width` *columns and* `height` *rows.*

> `(dot-grid 5 3)`

Exercise 24.1.11 *Develop a function named* `randoms` *that takes in two whole numbers* `how-many` *and* `limit` *and produces a list of* `how-many` *numbers, each chosen randomly from 0 up to* `limit`.

Hint: Use the template on `how-many`, not on `limit`.

Exercise 24.1.12 *Develop a function named* `random-posns` *that takes in three whole numbers* `how-many`, `max-x`, *and* `max-y` *and produces a list of* `how-many` *posns, each with x chosen randomly between 0 and* `max-x`, *and y chosen randomly between 0 and* `max-y`.

Exercise 24.1.13 *Develop a function* named `table-of-squares` *that takes in a whole number and returns a list of* **posns** *representing a table of numbers and their squares from the given number down to 0. For example,*

```
(check-expect (table-of-squares 4)
  (list (make-posn 4 16)
        (make-posn 3 9)
        (make-posn 2 4)
        (make-posn 1 1)
        (make-posn 0 0)))
```

Note: I've put these in descending order because it's easier to write the function that way. It would be nice to produce the table in increasing order instead. We'll see how to do that in the next section.

24.2   Different base cases, different directions

Recall Exercise 24.1.7, a function that adds up the positive integers from a specified number down to 0. What if we wanted to add up the positive numbers from a specified number down to, say, 10 instead?

Worked Exercise 24.2.1 *Develop a function* `add-up-from-10` *that takes in a whole number* $n \geq 10$ *and returns the sum* $10 + 11 + \ldots + n$.

Generalize this to a function `add-up-between` *that takes in two whole numbers* m *and* n *and returns the sum* $m + (m + 1) + \ldots + n$.

Solution: The function takes in a "whole number ≥ 10", which is a new data type. Here's its data definition:

```
; A whole-num>=10 is either 10, or (add1 whole-num>=10)
```

The contract and examples are easy:

```
; add-up-from-10 :  whole-number>=10 -> number
(check-expect (add-up-from-10 10) 10)
(check-expect (add-up-from-10 11) 21)
(check-expect (add-up-from-10 15) 65)
```

Since we've changed the data type, we'll need a new template:

```
(define (function-on-nn>=10 n)
  (cond [(= n 10) ...]
        [(> n 10)
         ; n                              whole number > 10
         ; (- n 1)                        whole number >= 10
         ; (function-on-nn>=10 (- n 1))   whatever this returns
        ]))
```

With this, the definition is easy:

```
(define (add-up-from-10 n)
  (cond [(= n 10) 10]
        [(> n 10)
         ; n                          whole number > 10
         ; (- n 1)                    whole number >= 10
         ; (add-up-from-10 (- n 1)) number
         (+ n (add-up-from-10 (- n 1)))
        ]))
```

It feels a bit inelegant to have $n \geq 10$ be part of the contract; could we reasonably make the function work correctly on *all* whole numbers? We would have to choose a "right answer" for numbers less than 10. In that case, there are no numbers to add up, so the answer should be 0.

```
; add-up-from-10 :  whole-number -> number
(check-expect (add-up-from-10 8) 0)
(check-expect (add-up-from-10 10) 10)
(check-expect (add-up-from-10 11) 21)
(check-expect (add-up-from-10 15) 65)
(define (add-up-from-10 n)
  (cond [ (< n 10) 0]
        [(= n 10) 10]
        [(> n 10)
         ; n                          whole number > 10
         ; (- n 1)                    whole number >= 10
         ; (add-up-from-10 (- n 1)) number
         (+ n (add-up-from-10 (- n 1)))
        ]))
```

This passes all its tests, but on further consideration, we realize that the right answer to the (= n 10) case is the same as 10 plus the right answer to the (< n 10) case; we could leave out the (= n 10) case, replacing (> n 10) with (>= n 10), and it would *still* pass all its tests. **Try this** for yourself.

The more general add-up-between function differs from add-up-from-10 only by replacing the 10 with the extra parameter m:

```
;  add-up-between :  whole-number(m)  whole-number(n) -> number
(check-expect (add-up-between 8 6) 0)
(check-expect (add-up-between 8 8) 8)
(check-expect (add-up-between 7 9) 24)
(define (add-up-between  m n)
  (cond [(< n  m ) 0]
        [(> n  m )
         ; n                          whole number >  m
         ; (- n 1)                    whole number >= m
         ; (add-up-between  m (- n 1))number
         (+ n (add-up-between  m (- n 1)))
        ]))
```

Exercise 24.2.2 *Develop a function count-down-to that takes in two whole numbers* low *and* high *and produces a list of the numbers* high, high-1, ... low *in that order. If* low > high, *it should return an empty list.*

What if we wanted the list in *increasing* order? Rather than treating high as a "whole number $\geq$ low", and calling the function recursively on (sub1 high), we instead treat low as a "whole number $\leq$ high", and calling the function recursively on (add1 low).

Exercise 24.2.3 *Develop a function count-up-to that takes in two whole numbers* low *and* high *and produces a list of the numbers* low, low+1, ... high. *If* low > high, *it should return an empty list.*

Exercise 24.2.4 *Develop a function* increasing-table-of-squares *which takes in a whole number n and returns a list of posns representing a table of numbers and their squares from 0 up to the given number.*

24.3   Peano arithmetic

Imagine that for some reason the + function wasn't working correctly on your computer (although add1 and sub1 still worked). Could we make do without +?

It would be pretty easy to write a function to add 2:

```
; add2 :  number -> number
(check-expect (add2 0) 2)
(check-expect (add2 1) 3)
(check-expect (add2 27) 29)
(define (add2 x)
  (add1 (add1 x)))
```

But can we write a function that takes in *two* whole numbers as parameters and adds them?

Worked Exercise 24.3.1 *Develop a function* wn-add *to add two whole numbers, without using any built-in arithmetic operators except* add1, sub1, zero?, *and* positive?.

Solution: The contract and examples are straightforward:

```
; wn-add :  whole-num (m) whole-num (n) -> whole-num
(check-expect (wn-add 0 0) 0)
(check-expect (wn-add 0 1) 1)
(check-expect (wn-add 0 3) 3)
(check-expect (wn-add 1 0) 1)
(check-expect (wn-add 3 0) 3)
(check-expect (wn-add 3 8) 11)
```

We have *two* whole-number parameters. In Chapter 25, we'll discuss how to handle this sort of situation in general, but for now let's just follow the template on one of them, pretending the other one is simple:

```
(define (wn-add m n)
  (cond [(zero?  n) ...]
        [(positive?  n)
         ; m                        whole
         ; n                        positive whole
         ; (sub1 n)                 whole
         ; (wn-add m (sub1 n))      whole
         ...
        ]))
```

Now we need to fill in the ... parts. The "zero" case is easy: if $n = 0$, then $m + n = m + 0 = m$. For the nonzero case, we'll do an inventory with values:

```
(define (wn-add m n)
  (cond [(zero?  n)    m ]
        [(positive?  n)
         ; m                        whole         3
         ; n                        positive whole 8
         ; (sub1 n)                 whole         7
         ; (wn-add m (sub1 n))      whole         10
         ; right answer             whole         11
         ...
        ]))
```

Remember that we can only use add1 and sub1, not + or -. So the obvious way to get 11 from 10 is add1:

```
(define (wn-add m n)
  (cond [(zero?  n) m]
        [(positive?  n)
         ; m                        whole 3
         ; n                        positive whole
         ; (sub1 n)                 whole 7
         ; (wn-add m (sub1 n))      whole 10
         ; right answer             whole 11
         (add1 (wn-add m (sub1 n)))
        ]))
```

Does this make sense? Is it always true that $m + n = 1 + (m + (n - 1))$? Of course; that's simple algebra. ∎

Exercise 24.3.2 *Develop a function wn-mult which multiplies two whole numbers together without using any built-in arithmetic operators except add1, sub1, zero?, and positive?. You are allowed to use wn-add, because it's not built-in; we just defined it from these operators.*

All the remaining exercises in this section are subject to the same restriction: "without using any built-in arithmetic operators except add1, sub1, zero?, and positive?." You may, of course, re-use the functions you've already written in this section.

Exercise 24.3.3 *Develop a function wn-raise which, given two whole numbers m and n, computes m^n.*

Exercise 24.3.4 *Develop a function* nn<= *which, given two whole numbers m and n, tells whether* $m \leq n$.

Exercise 24.3.5 *Develop a function* nn= *which, given two whole numbers m and n, tells whether they're equal or not.*

Exercise 24.3.6 *Develop a function* wn-sub *which, given two whole numbers m and n, computes* $m - n$.

Hint: In this chapter, we've defined whole numbers, but not negative numbers, and we haven't promised that sub1 works on anything other than a positive whole number. There are two ways you can write this function:

- The "purist" way uses sub1 only on positive whole numbers, and produces an error message if you try to subtract a larger number from a smaller (this was actually a common mathematical practice in the 18th century)

- The "pragmatist" way relies on the fact that Racket *really does* know about negative numbers, and sub1 *really does* work on any number, not only positive wholes. This way you can write wn-sub to work on *any* two whole numbers. The problem is that the result may not be a whole number, so code like (wn-sub x (wn-sub y z)) may not work.

Exercise 24.3.7 *Develop two functions* wn-quotient *and* wn-remainder *which, given two whole numbers m and n, compute the quotient and remainder of dividing m by n. Both should produce an error message if* $n = 0$.

Exercise 24.3.8 *Develop a function* wn-prime? *which tells whether a given whole number is prime.*

Hint: There are several ways to do this. One way is to define a helper function not-divisible-up-to? which, given two whole numbers m and n, tells whether m is "not divisible by anything up to n" (except of course 1).

Racket also knows about *fractions*, but if it didn't, we could define them ourselves, just as we've defined wholes, addition, multiplication, and so on.

Exercise 24.3.9 *Define a struct* frac *that represents a fraction in terms of whole numbers (as we've defined them).*

Exercise 24.3.10 *Develop a function* frac= *that takes in two* frac *objects and tells whether they're equal. (**Careful!** What does it mean for two fractions to be equal?)*

Exercise 24.3.11 *Develop a function* reduce-frac *that takes in a* frac *and returns an equivalent* frac *in lowest terms, i.e. with no common factors between numerator and denominator.*

Exercise 24.3.12 *Develop a function* frac-mult *that takes in two* fracs *and returns their product, as a* frac.

Exercise 24.3.13 *Develop a function* frac-add *that takes in two* fracs *and returns their sum, as a* frac.

24.4 The wholes in binary

Dedekind and Peano's definition of the wholes isn't the only way to define them. Here's another approach.

Almost every computer built since about 1950 has used *binary* or *base-two* notation to represent numbers: for example, the number 19 is written 10011, indicating $1 \cdot 2^4 + 0 \cdot 2^3 + 0 \cdot 2^2 + 1 \cdot 2^1 + 1 \cdot 2^0$. In decimal notation, it's really easy to multiply by 10 (just write a 0 at the end of the number). Similarly, in base two, it's really easy to multiply by 2 (just write a 0 at the end of the number). This inspires the following data definition:

A binary-whole-number is either

- 0, or

- $S_0(whole)$, or

- $S_1(whole)$

where $S_0(x)$ is intended to correspond to writing a 0 at the end of the number x, and $S_1(x)$ to writing a 1 at the end of x.

24.4.1 Defining binary wholes from structs

Let's try this in Racket.

```
A built-binary-whole is either
0,
(S0 built-binary-whole), or
(S1 built-binary-whole).

(define-struct s0 (half))
(define-struct s1 (half))
(define (S0 x) (make-s0 x)) ; for short
(define (S1 x) (make-s1 x)) ; for short
```

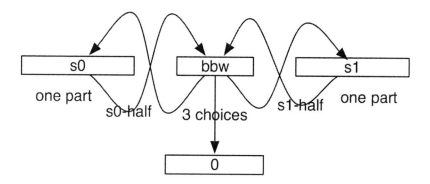

Some examples of this data type are

- 0

- (S1 0), which "means" 1

- (S0 (S1 0)), which "means" 2

- (S1 (S1 0)), which "means" 3

- (S1 (S1 (S0 (S0 (S1 0))))), which "means" 19

Obviously, it's a lot easier to write 19 as
(S1 (S1 (S0 (S0 (S1 0)))))
than as
(S(S(S(S(S(S(S(S(S(S(S(S(S(S(S(S(S(S(S 0))))))))))))))))))),
the way we would have written 19 in section 24.1.1.

A template based on this data definition has three cases: is it zero, is it an s0 structure, or is it an s1 structure? I'll use *bbw* as shorthand for *built-binary-whole*.

```
(define (function-on-bbw n)
  (cond [(equal?  n 0) ...]
        [(s0?  n)
         ; (s0-half n)                    bbw
         ; (function-on-bbw (s0-half n))  whatever
         ...]
        [(s1?  n)
         ; (s1-half n)                    bbw
         ; (function-on-bbw (s1-half n))  whatever
         ...]
        ))
```

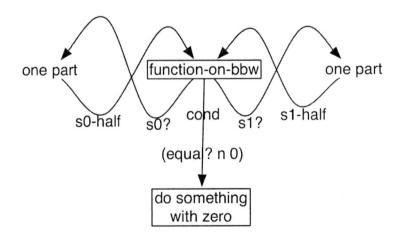

Worked Exercise 24.4.1 *Re-write the* `spams` *function to take in a* built-binary-whole.

Solution: The contract and examples are straightforward:

```
; spams :  built-binary-whole -> string-list
(check-expect (spams 0) empty)
(check-expect (spams (S1 0)) (list "spam"))
(check-expect (spams (S0 (S1 0))) (list "spam" "spam"))
(check-expect (spams (S0 (S1 (S1 0)))))
  (list "spam" "spam" "spam" "spam" "spam" "spam"))
(check-expect (spams (S1 (S1 (S1 0)))))
  (list "spam" "spam" "spam" "spam" "spam" "spam" "spam"))
```

The template gives us

```
(define ( spams  n)
  (cond [(equal?  n 0) ...]
        [(s0?  n)
         ; (s0-half n)          whole
         ; ( spams  (s0-half n)) string-list
         ...]
        [(s1?  n)
         ; (s1-half n)          whole
         ; ( spams  (s1-half n)) string-list
         ...]
        ))
```

Obviously, the right answer to the zero case is `empty`. For the other cases, we'll use an inventory with values.

```
(define (spams n)
  (cond [(equal?  n 0)   empty ]
        [(s0?  n)
         ; n              whole    (S0 (S1 (S1 0))), i.e. 6
         ; (s0-half n)    whole    (S1 (S1 0)), i.e. 3
         ; (spams (s0-half n))
         ;               string-list (list "spam" "spam "spam")
         ; right answer string-list
         ; (list "spam" "spam" "spam" "spam" "spam" "spam")
         ...]
        [(s1?  n)
         ; n              whole    (S1 (S1 (S1 0))), i.e. 7
         ; (s1-half n)    whole    (S1 (S1 0)), i.e. 3
         ; (spams (s1-half n))
         ;               string-list (list "spam" "spam" "spam")
         ; right answer string-list
         ; (list "spam" "spam" "spam" "spam" "spam" "spam "spam")
         ...]
        ))
```

Now, how can you get a list of 6 spams from a list of 3 spams? There are a number of ways, but the most obvious one is to append two copies of it together. Which seems appropriate, since the recursive call is supposed to return "half as many" spams.

How to get a list of 7 spams from a list of 3 spams? Since the recursive call is on "half" of an odd number, it's really $(n-1)/2$. So to get n from $(n-1)/2$, you make two copies and add one more. The function definition becomes

```
(define (spams n)
  (cond [(equal? n 0) empty]
        [(s0? n)
         ; n              whole      (S0 (S1 (S1 0))), i.e. 6
         ; (s0-half n)  whole      (S1 (S1 0)), i.e. 3
         ; (spams (s0-half n))
         ;              string-list (list "spam" "spam" "spam")
         ; right answer string-list
         ; (list "spam" "spam" "spam" "spam" "spam" "spam")
         (append  (spams (s0-half n))
                  (spams (s0-half n))) ]
        [(s1? n)
         ; n       whole      (S1 (S1 (S1 0))), i.e. 7
         ; (s1-halfhn)whole      (S1 (S1 0)), i.e. 3
         ; (spams (s1-half n))
         ;       string-list (list "spam" "spam" "spam")
         ; right answering-list
         ; (list "spam" "spam" "spam" "spam" "spam" "spam" "spam")
         (cons "spam" (append  (spams (s1-half n))
                               (spams (s1-half n)))) ]
        ))
```

Exercise 24.4.2 *Rewrite the `copies` function to take in a* built-binary-whole.

Exercise 24.4.3 *Develop a function `binary-add1` that takes in a* built-binary-whole *and returns the next larger* built-binary-whole. *For example, the next larger whole after 5 is 6, so*

```
(check-expect (binary-add1 (S1 (S0 (S1 0)))) (S0 (S1 (S1 0))))
```

Exercise 24.4.4 *Develop a function `bbw-value` that takes in a* built-binary-whole *and returns the (ordinary) whole number that it represents. For example,*

```
(check-expect (binary-whole-value 0) 0)
(check-expect (binary-whole-value (S1 0)) 1)
(check-expect (binary-whole-value (S0 (S1 (S1 (S0 (S1 0)))))) 22)
```

24.4.2   Binary whole numbers, the way we really do it

Again, Racket already knows about numbers and arithmetic, so instead of the structures s0 and s1, we might use

```
(define (S0 x) (* x 2))
(define (S1 x) (+ 1 (* x 2)))
(define (half x) (quotient x 2))
```

plus the built-in functions zero?, even?, and odd?.

The template becomes (using *rbw* as shorthand for "real binary whole")

```
#|
(define (function-on-rbw n)
  (cond [(zero?  n) ...]
        [(even?  n)
         ; (half n)                          rbw
         ; (function-on-rbw (half n))        whatever
         ...]
        [(odd?  n)
         ; (half n)                          rbw
         ; (function-on-rbw (half n))        whatever
         ...]
        ))
|#
```

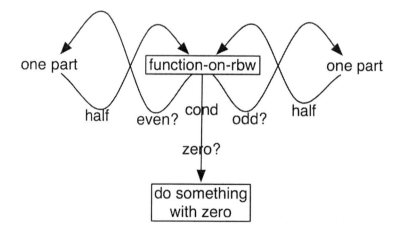

Worked Exercise 24.4.5 *Re-write the* spams *function to take in an ordinary whole number, using the binary template.*

Solution: The contract and examples are the same as in Exercise 24.1.4. The definition becomes

```
(define (binary-spams n)
  (cond [( zero? n) empty]
        [( even? n)
         ; n               whole      6
         ; ( half n)       whole      3
         ; (binary-spams ( half n))
         ;                 string-list (list "spam" "spam "spam")
         ; right answer   string-list
         ; (list "spam" "spam" "spam" "spam" "spam" "spam")
         (append (binary-spams ( half n))
                 (binary-spams ( half n))) ]
        [( odd? n)
         ; n               whole      7
         ; ( half n)       whole      3
         ; (binary-spams ( half n))
         ;                 string-list (list "spam" "spam" "spam")
         ; right answer   string-list
         ; (list "spam" "spam" "spam" "spam" "spam" "spam" "spam")
         (cons "spam" (append (binary-spams ( half n))
                              (binary-spams ( half n)))) ]
        ))
```

∎

Exercise 24.4.6 *Re-write the* copies *function of Exercise 24.4.2 so that it takes in an ordinary whole number, but is still written using the binary template.*

Exercise 24.4.7 *Re-write the* binary-add1 *function of Exercise 24.4.3 so that it takes in an ordinary whole number, but is still written using the binary template rather than calling the built-in* add1 *or* +. *For example,*

```
(check-expect (binary-add1 5) 6)
```

Exercise 24.4.8 *Re-write the* dot-grid *function of Exercise 24.1.10 by using the binary template.*

Exercise 24.4.9 *Re-write the* randoms *function of Exercise 24.1.11 by using the binary template.*

Exercise 24.4.10 *Re-write the `random-posns` function of Exercise 24.1.12 by using the binary template.*

Exercise 24.4.11 *Essay question: Notice that I've picked some of the functions from Section 24.1 to re-do using the binary template. Why did I pick these and not the others? What kind of function lends itself to solving with the binary template, and what kind doesn't?*

24.5 Review of important words and concepts

Programmers often want a computer to do something a specified number of times. If the "number of times" is driven by a list of data, we can use the techniques of Chapters 22 and 23, but if it really is just a number, as in `copies` or `dot-grid`, we can use the analogous technique of *whole-number recursion*.

Racket, like most other programming languages, has built-in support for arithmetic on whole numbers and other kinds of numbers. (Most languages don't handle fractions, or very large whole numbers, as well as Racket does, but that's a separate issue.) However, in this chapter we've shown how to *define* arithmetic, whole numbers, and fractions. Along the way, we've learned a useful technique for writing functions that do things a specified number of times, like `copies` or `dot-grid`.

The whole numbers can be defined either using "successor", as Dedekind and Peano did, or using binary notation, as most modern computers do.

24.6 Reference: Built-in functions on whole numbers

In this chapter, we've introduced the built-in functions

- `zero?`

- `positive?`

- `sub1`

Chapter 25

Multiple recursive data

The inventories and template functions we've been using so far are generally based on the data type of an input (or, in a few cases, on the data type of the result). If an input is a list, we can use the input template of Chapter 22; if the output is a list, we can use the output template of Chapter 23; if the input is a natural number, we can use the input template of Chapter 24; *etc.*

But what template should we use when we have *two or more* inputs of complex types?

If your function takes two parameters x and y of complex types, there are four possibilities:

		y	
		simple	complex
x	simple	1	2
	complex	3	4

1. x and y are both simple;

2. x is simple but y is complex;

3. x is complex but y is simple;

4. x and y are both complex.

25.1   Separable parameters

In exercise 23.1.9, we wrote a `list-append` function that took in two list parameters. We used the usual list template for the first and pretended the second was of a simple type. In other words, we lumped cases 1 and 2 together, and cases 3 and 4 together.

		list2	
		simple	complex
list1	simple	1	2
	complex	3	4

Likewise, in exercise 24.3.1, we wrote an `wn-add` function that took in two natural number parameters. In that case, we used the usual natural-number template for one of them and pretended the other one was of a simple type. The rest of the exercises in section 24.3 can also be done in this way: a function that does different things depending on whether x is simple or complex, perhaps calling a helper function that does different things depending on whether y is simple or complex.

I call this situation "separable parameters", because we can separate the question of whether x is simple or complex from the question of whether y is simple or complex.

25.2 Synchronized parameters

That approach works frequently, but not all the time. For example,

Worked Exercise 25.2.1 *Develop a function* `pay-list` *that takes in two lists: one specifies the number of hours worked by each of a bunch of employees, and the other specifies the corresponding hourly wage for each of those employees. It should produce a list of the amounts each employee should be paid, in the same order.*

Solution: The contract is straightforward:

```
; pay-list :  list-of-numbers(hours)
              list-of-numbers(hourly-wages)
              -> list-of-numbers
```

For test cases, as usual, we'll start with the simplest cases and then build up:

```
(check-expect (pay-list empty empty) empty)
(check-expect (pay-list (list 3) empty)  ???)
```

The two lists we were given are of different sizes, and it's not clear from the problem assignment what should happen in this case. In fact, the problem doesn't even make sense if the lengths of the two lists are different. So let's revise the contract:

```
; pay-list :  list-of-numbers(hours)
              list-of-numbers(hourly-wages)
              -> list-of-numbers
; Assumes the two input lists are the same length.
; Result will be the same length.
```

Now that we've excluded inputs that make no sense, we can get back to the test cases:

```
(check-expect (pay-list empty empty) empty)
(check-expect (pay-list (list 30) (list 8)) (list 240))
(check-expect (pay-list (list 30 20 45) (list 8 10 10))
              (list 240 200 450))
```

The skeleton is easy. For the inventory, we'll try the usual list template on `hours`, and treat `hourly-wages` as simple.

```
(define (pay-list hours hourly-wages)
  ; hours                list of numbers (list 30 20 45)
  ; hourly-wages         list of numbers (list 8 10 10)
  (cond [(empty? hours) ...]
        [(cons? hours)
         ; (first hours) number           30
         ; (rest hours)  list of numbers (list 20 45)
         ; (pay-list (rest hours) hourly-wages)
         ;              list of numbers ???
         ; right answer list of numbers (list 240 200 450)
         ]))
```

What is the "right answer" to the recursive call? It doesn't *have* a right answer, because it's being called on two lists of different lengths!

We'll have to try something different. It doesn't make sense to call (pay-list (rest hours) hourly-wages), or for that matter (pay-list hours (rest hourly-wages)), because both of those calls break the contract by passing in lists of different lengths. But (pay-list (rest hours) (rest hourly-wages)) *would* make sense, if we knew that both of those things existed — that is, if *both* hours and hourly-wages were non-empty lists. Similarly, if *both* of them were empty lists, the answer would be empty. So here's a revised inventory:

```
(define (pay-list hours hourly-wages)
   ; hours                      list of numbers (list 30 20 45)
   ; hourly-wages               list of numbers (list 8 10 10)
   (cond [ (and (empty? hours) (empty? hourly-wages)) ...]
         [ (and (cons? hours) (cons? hourly-wages))
           ; (first hours)             number          30
           ; (first hourly-wages) number              8
           ; (rest hours)            list of numbers (list 20 45)
           ; (rest hourly-wages)  list of numbers (list 10 10)
           ; (pay-list (rest hours)  (rest hourly-wages))
           ;                          list of numbers (list 200 450)
           ; right answer           list of numbers (list 240 200 450)
         ]))
```

Now it's easy:

```
(define (pay-list hours hourly-wages)
   ; hours                      list of numbers (list 30 20 45)
   ; hourly-wages               list of numbers (list 8 10 10)
   (cond [(and (empty? hours) (empty? hourly-wages))   empty ]
         [(and (cons? hours) (cons? hourly-wages))
           ; (first hours)             number          30
           ; (first hourly-wages) number              8
           ; (rest hours)            list of numbers (list 20 45)
           ; (rest hourly-wages)  list of numbers (list 10 10)
           ; (pay-list (rest hours) (rest hourly-wages))
           ;                          list of numbers (list 200 450)
           ; right answer           list of numbers (list 240 200 450)
           (cons  (* (first hours) (first hourly-wages))
                  (pay-list (rest hours) (rest hourly-wages)))
         ]))
```

One thing might bother you about this definition. (At least it bothers *me*!) We're checking whether *both* parameters are empty (case 1), and whether *both* parameters are non-empty (case 4), but what if one is empty and the other isn't (cases 2 and 3)? That would of course be an illegal input, but if some user tried it, (s)he would get an unfriendly error message like *cond: all question results were false*, and the user might conclude that *our program* was wrong, when in fact it's the user's fault. Instead, let's handle this case specifically with a more-informative error message:

```
(define (pay-list hours hourly-wages)
  (cond [(and (empty? hours) (empty? hourly-wages)) ...]
        [(and (cons? hours) (cons? hourly-wages))
         (cons (* (first hours) (first hourly-wages))
               (pay-list (rest hours) (rest hourly-wages)))
         ]
        [else
          (error  'pay-list
                  "Number of hours and hourly wages must match.")
         ]))
```

```
(check-error (pay-list (list 3) empty)
      "pay-list:  Number of hours and hourly wages must match.")
(check-error (pay-list (list 3) (list 8 7.50))
      "pay-list:  Number of hours and hourly wages must match.")
```

In this example, it wasn't enough to treat one of the two list inputs as if it were simple: we had to go through the two lists *in lock-step*, looking at the **first** of both at the same time, and the **rest** of both at the same time. It's usually easy to spot such situations, because they *don't make sense unless the inputs are the same size*. When you see such a problem, not only can you use an inventory like the above, but you can also include an error-check that produces an informative error message if the inputs *aren't* the same size.

For this sort of problem, cases 2 and 3 (in which one of x and y is simple and the other complex) are lumped together — they're both illegal — and we only really need to worry about cases 1 and 4.

		hourly-wages	
		simple	complex
hours	simple	1	2
	complex	3	4

25.3   Interacting parameters

There are problems that don't seem to fit either of the preceding patterns: it's reasonable for either of the parameters to be simple and the other complex, and whatever one of them is, it makes a difference what the other one is. The parameters *interact* with one another.

Worked Exercise 25.3.1 *Suppose the* `list-ref` *function weren't built into DrRacket; how would we write it? Since* `list-ref` *is built in, we'll name ours* `pick-element` *instead.*

Develop a function `pick-element` *that takes in a natural number and a non-empty list, and returns one of the elements of the list. If the number is 0, it returns the first element of the list; if 1, it returns the second element; etc. If there is no such element, it should produce an appropriate error message.*

Solution: The contract is

```
; pick-element :  natural non-empty-list -> object
```

A *non-empty list* is defined to be either (cons `object` empty) or (cons `object` `non-empty list`); the template for it looks like

```
#|
(check-expect (function-on-nel (list "a")) ...)
(check-expect (function-on-nel (list "a" "b")) ...)
(check-expect (function-on-nel (list 3 1 4 1 5)) ...)

(define (function-on-nel L)
  (cond [(empty?  (rest L)) ...]
        [(cons?  (rest L))
         ; L                           non-empty list
         ; (first L)                   object
         ; (rest L)                    non-empty list
         ; (function-on-nel (rest L))  whatever
         ...
        ]))
|#
```

For our problem, the test cases clearly need to include long-enough and not-long-enough lists.

```
(check-expect (pick-element 0 (list "a")) "a")
(check-expect (pick-element 0 (list 5 -2 17)) 5)
(check-error (pick-element 1 (list "a"))
             "pick-element:  no such element")
(check-expect (pick-element 1 (list 5 17)) 17)
(check-expect (pick-element 1 (list 5 -2 17)) -2)
(check-error (pick-element 4 (list "a"))
             "pick-element:  no such element")
(check-expect
   (pick-element 4 (list "a" "b" "c" "d" "e"))
   "e")
(check-expect
   (pick-element 4 (list "a" "b" "c" "d" "e" "f" "g"))
   "e")
```

As a first attempt, let's try the separable-parameters approach, treating n as complex and the list as simple.

```
(define (pick-element n things)
  ; n                                  natural
  ; things                             non-empty list
  (cond [(zero?  n) ...]
        [(positive?  n)
         ; (sub1 n)                     natural
         ; (pick-element (sub1 n) things) object
         ...
        ]))
```

In the base case ($n = 1$), the right answer is either (`first things`) or an error message, depending on whether `things` is empty. We can do that if necessary, using a nested cond.

The recursive case is a problem: knowing the answer to (pick-element (sub1 n) things) tells you *nothing* about the right answer to (pick-element n things). This won't work.

Maybe if, instead of treating *n* as complex and the list as simple, we treat the list as complex and *n* as simple?

```
(define (pick-element n things)
  ; n                                  natural
  ; things                             non-empty list
  (cond [(empty? (rest things)) ...]
        [(cons? (rest things))
         ; things                      non-empty list
         ; (rest things)               list
         ; (pick-element n (rest things)) object
         ...
         ])))
```

The base case, again, will need a nested conditional to check whether *n* is 1 or larger. The recursive case still has a problem: knowing the answer to (pick-element n (rest things)) tells you nothing about the right answer to (pick-element n things).

There seems to be a sort of synchronization going on here: the list length doesn't have to be *exactly the same* as the number, but it does have to be *at least as much*. So let's try the synchronized approach. I'll also throw in an "inventory with values" while we're at it.

```
(define (pick-element n things)
  ; n                     natural        1
  ; things                non-empty list (list "a" "b" "c")
  (cond [(and (zero? n) (empty? (rest things)))
         (first things)]
        [(and (positive? n) (cons? (rest things)))
         ; (sub1 n)        natural        0
         ; (rest things) non-empty list (list "b" "c")
         ; (pick-element (sub1 n) (rest things))
         ;                 object         "b"
         ; right answer   object         "b"
         ...]
        [else (error 'pick-element "no such element")]))
```

This looks a little more promising: the result of the recursive call is the same as the right answer to the problem at hand. So let's make that the answer in the second **cond** clause:

```
(define (pick-element n things)
  ; n                    natural         1
  ; things               non-empty list (list "a" "b" "c")
  (cond [(and (zero? n) (empty? (rest things)))
         (first things)]
        [(and (positive? n) (cons? (rest things)))
         ; (sub1 n)         natural         0
         ; (rest things) non-empty list (list "b" "c")
         ; (pick-element (sub1 n) (rest things))
         ;                 object          "b"
         ; right answer  object          "b"
         (pick-element (sub1 n) (rest things)) ]
        [else (error 'pick-element "no such element")]))
```

This passes several of its tests, but not all: in particular, it fails tests in which the element to be picked *isn't the last*. By following the "synchronized" approach, we've effectively forced the length of the list to be *exactly one more* than the number. To get this function to work right, it must be more permissive: if the number is down to 0 and the list isn't only one element, that's fine.

```
(define (pick-element n things)
  ; n                    natural         1
  ; things               non-empty list (list "a" "b" "c")
  (cond [(and (zero? n) (empty? (rest things)))
         (first things)]
        [(and (positive? n) (cons? (rest things)))
         (first things)]
        [(and (positive? n) (cons? (rest things)))
         ; (sub1 n)         positive-natural0
         ; (rest things) non-empty list (list "b" "c")
         ; (pick-element (sub1 n) (rest things))
         ;                 object          "b"
         ; right answer  object          "b"
         (pick-element (sub1 n) (rest things)) ]
        [else (error 'pick-element "no such element")]))
```

The conditional now explicitly identifies and deals with *all four* cases:

		simple	complex
		simple	complex
things	simple	1	2
	complex	3	4

For this particular problem, two of the cases produce the same answer, so we can combine them. Removing the inventory comments, we're left with

```
(define (pick-element n things)
  (cond [ (zero? n)     (first things)]
        [(and (positive? n) (cons? (rest things)))
         (pick-element (sub1 n) (rest things)) ]
        [else (error 'pick-element "no such element")]))
```

which does in fact pass all its tests.

In this case, we've actually combined cases 1 and 3:

		n	
		simple	complex
things	simple	1	2
	complex	3	4

But in other situations, we might actually need all four cases to do four different things. See the Exercises below.

The above function definition isn't foolproof, in that if someone violates the contract by passing in the number 0, or a negative number, or an empty list, it'll produce an ugly error message. We could remedy this by re-formulating the problem as accepting *any* number and *any* list; the result would be

```
(define (pick-element n things)
  (cond [(< n 0)
         (error 'pick-element "illegal element number")]
        [(empty? things)
         (error 'pick-element "no such element")]
        [(zero? n)                        (first things)]
        [(and (positive? n) (cons? things))
         (pick-element (sub1 n) (rest things))]))
```

■

25.4   Exercises

Some of these exercises involve separable parameters; some involve synchronized parameters; some involve interacting parameters, and may require treating all four possible combinations of simple and complex separately.

Exercise 25.4.1 *Develop a function* cart-prod *(short for "Cartesian product") that takes in two lists and returns a list of two-element lists, each with an element from the first input list and an element from the second in that order. The result should include* all possible *pairs of elements. You may assume that there are no duplicate elements in the first list, and no duplicate elements in the second list (although there might be things that are in both input lists.)*

Hint: You'll need a helper function.

Exercise 25.4.2 *Develop a function* make-posns *that takes in two lists of numbers, the same length, and produces a list of* posns *with x coordinates taken from the first list, in order, and y coordinates from the corresponding elements of the second list.*

Exercise 25.4.3 *Develop a function* `label-names` *that takes in a list of strings and a natural number, which should be how many strings there are. It produces a list of two-element lists, each comprising a different natural number and one of the strings from the list. The numbers should be in decreasing order, starting with the given number and ending with 1, and the strings should be in the order they were given. For example,*
```
(check-expect (label-names (list "anne" "bob" "charlie") 3)
  (list (list 3 "anne") (list 2 "bob") (list 1 "charlie")))
```

If the above exercise feels sorta strange and artificial, here's a more natural (but slightly harder) version, which will probably require a helper function:

Exercise 25.4.4 *Develop a function* `label-names-2` *that takes in a list of strings, and produces a list of two-element lists, each comprising a different natural number and one of the strings from the list. The numbers should be in increasing order, starting with 1 and ending with the number of strings in the list, and the strings should be in the order they were given. For example,*
```
(check-expect (label-names-2 (list "anne" "bob" "charlie"))
  (list (list 1 "anne") (list 2 "bob") (list 3 "charlie")))
```

Exercise 25.4.5 *Develop a function* `intersection` *that takes in two lists of strings and returns a list of the strings that appear in* both *of them, leaving out any string that appears in only one or the other. The strings in the result should be in the same order that they appeared in the first list. You may assume that no string appears more than once in either list.*

Exercise 25.4.6 *Develop a function* `union` *that takes in two lists of strings and returns a list of the strings that appear in* either *list, but only once each. You may assume that no string appears more than once in either list.*

Exercise 25.4.7 *Develop a function* `set-diff` *that takes in two lists of strings and returns a list of the strings that appear in* the first but not the second. *You may assume that no string appears more than once in either list.*

Exercise 25.4.8 *Re-do exercises 25.4.5, 25.4.6, and 25.4.7 without the assumption that there are no duplicates in the inputs.*

Exercise 25.4.9 *Develop a function* `binary-add` *that takes in two natural numbers and returns their sum, using the binary template (and not using the built-in + function).*

Note: Somebody had to do this, not in Racket but in wires and transistors, in order for your computer to be able to add.

Exercise 25.4.10 *Develop a function* `binary-mult` *that takes in two natural numbers and returns their product, using the binary template (and not using the built-in + or * functions).*

Note: Somebody had to do this, not in Racket but in wires and transistors, in order for your computer to be able to multiply.

Exercise 25.4.11 *Develop a function* `binary-raise` *that takes in two natural numbers m and n and returns m^n, using the binary template (and not using the built-in +, *, or* `expt` *functions).*

Exercise 25.4.12 *Develop a function* `substring?` *that takes in two strings and tells whether the first one appears in the second as a substring. For example,*
```
(check-expect (substring? "bob" "") false)
(check-expect (substring? "" "bob") true)
(check-expect (substring? "b" "bob") true)
(check-expect (substring? "c" "bob") false)
(check-expect (substring? "bob" "bob") true)
(check-expect (substring? "bob" "bobs") true)
(check-expect (substring? "bob" "brats and snobs") false)
(check-expect (substring? "no rat" "brats and snobs") false)
(check-expect (substring? "bob" "thingbobs") true)
(check-expect (substring? "bob" "I botched it but bob fixed it")
   true)
(check-expect (substring? "bob" "I botched it but amy fixed it")
   false)
```

(There is a function in some dialects of Racket that does this job, but I want you to do it using only `char=?`, *comparing one character at a time.)*

Exercise 25.4.13 *Develop a function* `subsequence?` *that takes in two strings and tells whether the characters of the first appear in the same order in the second (but possibly with some other characters in between). For example,*
```
(check-expect (subsequence? "bob" "") false)
(check-expect (subsequence? "" "bob") true)
(check-expect (subsequence? "b" "bob") true)
(check-expect (subsequence? "c" "bob") false)
(check-expect (subsequence? "bob" "bob") true)
(check-expect (subsequence? "bob" "bobs") true)
(check-expect (subsequence? "bob" "brats and snobs") true)
(check-expect (subsequence? "no rat" "brats and snobs") false)
(check-expect (subsequence? "bob" "thingbobs") true)
(check-expect (subsequence? "bob" "I botched it but bob fixed it")
true)
(check-expect (subsequence? "bob" "I botched it but amy fixed it")
   true)
```
I don't think there's a built-in Racket function that will help much with this, but in any case, I want you to do this using only `char=?`, *comparing one character at a time.*

Hint: Perhaps surprisingly, this problem is *easier* than `substring?`.

Exercise 25.4.14 *Develop a function* `lcsubstring` *("longest common substring") that takes in two strings and returns the longest string which is a substring of both of them. For example,*
```
(check-expect (lcsubstring "mickey mouse" "minnie mouser") "mouse")
```

The answer may not be unique: for example,
```
(lcsubstring "mickey mouse" "minnie moose")
```
could legitimately be either `"mi"`, `" m"`, *or* `"se"`.

Hint: Different approaches to this can differ radically in efficiency. My first attempt took several *minutes* to solve the (`lcsubstring "mickey mouse" "minnie moose"`) problem. A different approach, using only things that you've seen already, solved the same problem in 0.01 seconds; the difference is even more dramatic for longer strings.

Exercise 25.4.15 *Develop a function* `lcsubsequence` *("longest common subsequence") that takes in two strings and returns the longest string which is a subsequence of both of them. For example,*

```
(check-expect (lcsubsequence "mickey mouse" "minnie moose")
  "mie mose")
```

The answer may not be unique: for example, (`lcsubsequence "abc" "cba"`) *could legitimately be any of the strings* `"a"`, `"b"`, *or* `"c"`.

Hint: As in exercise 25.4.14, your program may be slow. My first attempt took about 2.5 seconds to solve (`lcsubsequence "mickey mouse" "minnie moose"`), and I don't know of a more efficient way to do it using what you've already seen. A technique called *dynamic programming* or *memoization*, which we'll discuss in Chapter 30, enabled me to do it in about 0.01 seconds. Again, the difference is more dramatic for longer strings.

Exercise 25.4.16 *A common task in computer science is* pattern-matching: *given a pattern, ask whether a particular string matches it. In our pattern language, a* `"?"` *stands for "any single character," while* `"*"` *stands for "any zero or more characters." For example, the pattern* `"c?t"` *would match "cat" and "cut" but not "colt", "cats", or "dog". Similarly, the pattern* `"cat*"` *would match the strings "cat", "cats", "catastrophe", etc. but not "caltrop" or "dog". The pattern* `"a??a*r"` *would match "abbatoir", "akbar", and "araaar", etc. but not "almoner", "alakazam", or "fnord". The pattern* `"*.docx"` *would match the name of any Word 2007 file (and thus could be used to decide which filenames to show in a file dialog).*

Define a function `pattern-match?` *that takes in two strings: the* pattern *and the* target, *and tells whether the target matches the pattern.*

Note that the special characters `"?"` *and* `"*"` *are special only when they appear in the* pattern; *if they appear in the* target, *they should be treated as ordinary characters.*

SIDEBAR:

Exercises 25.4.12 through 25.4.16 resemble problems that come up in biology: the "strings" in that case are sequences of DNA bases in a gene, or sequences of amino acids in a protein. The efficiency of such programs determines how quickly a genome can be sequenced, a drug interaction predicted, a virus identified, *etc.*

25.5　Review of important words and concepts

When you have to write a function that takes in two or more complex parameters (lists, strings, natural numbers, *etc.*), you can take several different approaches.

- If the problem "doesn't make sense" unless the parameters are "the same size" (or have some particular relationship to one another), then you can generally take the "synchronized parameters" approach: your function will check whether both are simple (the base case) and whether both are complex (the recursive case). If one is simple but the other complex, it produces an error message.

		p2	
		simple	complex
p1	simple	1	2
	complex	3	4

```
(define (function-on-synch-params p1 p2)
  (cond [(and (simple? p1) (simple? p2)) ...]
        [(and (complex? p1) (complex? p2))
         ; (function-on-synch-params (simplify p1)
                                     (simplify p2))
         ...]
        [else (error ...)]))
```

(The functions *simple?*, *complex?*, and *simplify* in the above aren't real functions; they stand for however you identify simple and complex elements of the data type in question, and how you simplify it. For example, if you were dealing with lists, *simple?* would stand for `empty?`; *complex?* for `cons?`; and *simplify* for `rest`.)

- If the expression necessary to produce the right answer is the same for both simple and complex second parameters, we call the parameters "separable", and you can just use a template on the first parameter, treating the second parameter as a simple type.

		p2	
		simple	complex
p1	simple	1	2
	complex	3	4

```
(define (function-on-separable-params p1 p2)
  (cond [(simple? p1) ...]
        [(complex? p1)
         ; (function-on-separable-params (simplify p1) p2)
         ...]))
```

Likewise, if the expression is the same for simple and complex *first* parameters, you can use a template on the second parameter, treating the first as a simple type.

- If neither of the previous situations applies, you'll probably need to identify all four possible combinations of simple and complex parameters and treat them individually. Furthermore, in the case that both are complex, there are several different reasonable recursive calls you could make.

		p2	
		simple	complex
p1	simple	1	2
	complex	3	4

```
(define (function-on-interacting-params p1 p2)
  (cond [(and (simple? p1) (simple? p2)) ...]
        [(and (simple? p1) (complex? p2))
         ; (function-on-interacting-params p1 (simplify p2))
         ...]
        [(and (complex? p1) (simple? p2))
         ; (function-on-interacting-params (simplify p1) p2)
         ...]
        [(and (complex? p1) (complex? p2))
         ; (function-on-interacting-params p1 (simplify p2))
         ; (function-on-interacting-params (simplify p1) p2)
         ; (function-on-interacting-params
                ; (simplify p1) (simplify p2))
         ...]))
```

Some functions that you can write using these techniques are correct, but surprisingly slow and inefficient; a technique called *dynamic programming* or *memoization*, which we can't discuss until chapter 30, can improve the efficiency enormously.

25.6   Reference

No new functions or syntax rules were introduced in this chapter.

PART V

Miscellaneous topics

Chapter 26

Efficiency of programs

For this chapter, switch languages in DrRacket to "Intermediate Student Language".

26.1 Timing function calls

Computer programs, of course, *must* produce correct answers. But that's not enough: the main reason computers were invented was to produce correct answers *quickly*. If a program doesn't run fast enough, you can buy a more expensive, faster computer. But perhaps surprisingly, you can often get much more dramatic improvements by changing the *program*.

In Intermediate Student Language, there's a built-in function named `time` that allows you to measure how long something takes. For example, type (`time (* 3 4)`) in the Interactions pane of DrRacket. You should see something like

```
cpu time:  0 real time:  0 gc time:  0
12
```

The 12, of course, is the result of (`* 3 4`); the previous line shows how much time the computation took, by three different measures. "CPU time" is how much time (in milliseconds) the computer's processor spent actually solving the problem (as opposed to managing the operating system, managing memory, managing DrRacket itself, *etc.*). "Real time" is the total time (in milliseconds) from when you hit ENTER to when the answer came out. "GC time" is how much time (in milliseconds) DrRacket spent "garbage-collecting", *i.e.* releasing things from memory that are no longer needed.

In the case of (`* 3 4`), all three are well under a millisecond, so the answers are all 0. To see nonzero times, you need to use some of the functions defined in Chapters 22, 23, 24, and 25.

Recall the `add-up-to` function of Exercise 24.1.7, and type the following lines into the Definitions pane (after the definition of `add-up-to`):

```
(time (add-up-to 10))
(time (add-up-to 100))
(time (add-up-to 1000))
(time (add-up-to 10000))
(time (add-up-to 100000))
(time (add-up-to 1000000))
```

Hit "Run" and see what happens. Each of the examples shows a line of timing figures. Not surprisingly, it takes longer to solve a larger problem than a smaller one.

Try running `(time (add-up-to 100000))` several times, writing down the CPU time, real time, and GC time each time. How much do they vary from one trial to the next? How well can you predict them? Can you predict how long it'll take to compute `(add-up-to 200000)`?

Exercise 26.1.1 *Choose some functions defined in Chapters 22, 23, 24, and 25, and try timing them on various sizes of arguments. How much does the time vary from one trial to the next? From timing a few arguments, can you predict how long it'll take on a new argument?*

Hint: *You can use `randoms`, from Exercise 24.1.11, to generate large lists of numbers. Make sure you don't count the time to generate the numbers in the time to run the function. One way to do this is to define a variable to hold a list of, say, 10000 random numbers, and then call `(time (the-function-I'm-testing lotsa-numbers))`.*

Some good ones to try are
`convert-reversed`, *exercise 22.5.10*
`all-match?`, *exercise 22.5.13*
`largest`, *exercise 22.5.17*
`count-blocks`, *exercise 22.5.18*
`stutter`, *exercise 23.1.6*
`backwards`, *exercise 23.1.10*
`unique`, *exercise 23.2.4*
`tally-votes`, *exercise 23.2.7*
`sort`, *exercise 23.6.1*
`subsets`, *exercise 23.6.3*
`scramble`, *exercise 23.6.4*
`factorial`, *exercise 24.1.8*
`fibonacci`, *exercise 24.1.9*
`wn-add`, *exercise 24.3.1*
`wn-mult`, *exercise 24.3.2*
`wn-raise`, *exercise 24.3.3*
`wn-prime?`, *exercise 24.3.8*
`binary-add`, *exercise 25.4.9*
`binary-mult`, *exercise 25.4.10*
`binary-raise`, *exercise 25.4.11*
`substring?`, *exercise 25.4.12*
`subsequence?`, *exercise 25.4.13*
`lcsubstring`, *exercise 25.4.14*
`lcsubsequence`, *exercise 25.4.15*

26.2   Review of important words and concepts

A computer is generally doing a lot of things at once, only some of which are running the program you just wrote. Some of a computer's time goes into managing the operating system (Windows, MacOS, *etc.*), some goes into managing DrRacket, some goes into reclaiming memory that is no longer needed ("garbage collection"), and some goes into solving your problem.

A computer typically takes longer to evaluate a function on a large or complicated argument than on a small or simple one. *How much* longer is an important area of research in computer science: for some problems, doubling the size of the argument roughly doubles the time it takes (as you might expect), but other problems behave differently. Furthermore, different programs to solve the same problem can have dramatically different efficiencies.

26.3 Reference: New syntax for timing

This chapter introduced one new function (technically a "special form"), `time`, which evaluates an expression, prints out how long it took, and then returns the result.

Chapter 27

Local definitions

For this chapter, switch languages in DrRacket to "Intermediate Student Language" or higher.

27.1 Using locals for efficiency

Suppose we wanted to write a function `smallest` to find the smallest of a list of numbers. A straightforward solution, based on what you've already seen, would be

```
; smallest: non-empty-list-of-numbers -> number
(check-expect (smallest (list 4)) 4)
(check-expect (smallest (list 4 7)) 4)
(check-expect (smallest (list 7 4)) 4)
(check-expect (smallest (list 6 9 4 7 8 3 6 10 7)) 3)
(define (smallest nums)
  (cond [(empty? (rest nums))     (first nums)]
        [(cons? (rest nums))
         ; (first nums)               number
         ; (rest nums)                non-empty list of numbers
         ; (smallest (rest nums))  number
         (cond [(<= (first nums) (smallest (rest nums)))
                (first nums)]
               [else (smallest (rest nums))])])))
```

This definition works, and produces right answers, but consider the following two examples:

```
(check-expect
  (smallest (list 1 2 3 4 5 6 7 8 9 10 11 12 13 14 15 16 17 18))
  1)
(check-expect
  (smallest (list 18 17 16 15 14 13 12 11 10 9 8 7 6 5 4 3 2 1))
  1)
```

On my computer (as of 2009), the former takes about 3 milliseconds; the latter takes almost 9 seconds — 3000 times longer, even though both examples find the smallest of the same set of numbers! What's going on?

To figure this out, let's pick some simpler examples:

```
(check-expect (smallest (list 1 2 3 4)) 1)
(check-expect (smallest (list 4 3 2 1)) 1)
```

and use the Stepper to see what's happening. The former example calls

```
(smallest (list 1 2 3 4))
  (smallest (list 2 3 4))
    (smallest (list 3 4))
      (smallest (list 4))
        return 4
      return 3
    return 2
  return 1
```

The latter example behaves differently:

```
(smallest (list 4 3 2 1))
  (smallest (list 3 2 1))
    (smallest (list 2 1))
      (smallest (list 1))
        return 1
      (smallest (list 1)) again!
        return 1
    (smallest (list 2 1)) again!
      (smallest (list 1)) a third time!
        return 1
      (smallest (list 1)) a fourth time!
        return 1
      return 1
  (smallest (list 3 2 1)) again!
    (smallest (list 2 1)) a third time!
      (smallest (list 1)) a fifth time!
        return 1
      (smallest (list 1)) a sixth time!
        return 1
    (smallest (list 2 1)) a fourth time!
      (smallest (list 1)) a seventh time!
        return 1
      (smallest (list 1)) an eighth time!
        return 1
      return 1
    return 1
  return 1
return 1
```

In other words, the function is calling itself on the exact same question over and over, wasting a lot of time. Any time that (first nums) is larger than (smallest (rest nums)), it calls (smallest (rest nums)) all over again.

How can we avoid this waste of time? One reasonable approach is to compute (smallest (rest nums)), *save* the result in a variable, then use that result twice without re-computing it. Unfortunately, the syntax rules we've seen so far don't allow us to define a variable inside a function definition.

There is a way to do it, however.

Syntax Rule 8

```
(local [definition definition ...]
  expression)
```

is an expression. Each definition *can be a variable definition (rule 4), a function definition (rule 5), or a struct definition (rule 7).*

The effect is to apply all the definitions *temporarily*, evaluate the inner expression, and then *forget* all the new definitions; the result is the value of the inner expression.

Here's a simple, unrealistic example:

```
(local [(define y 5)]
  (* y y)) ; returns 25
y ; produces an error message, because y is undefined
```

In fact, a "local" definition can *temporarily hide* a definition that's already in effect:

```
(define y 17)
y ; returns 17
(local [(define y 5)] (* y y)) ; returns 25
y ; returns 17 again
```

More realistically, the main reason people use `local` is to define a variable inside a function definition:

```
; smallest: non-empty-list-of-numbers -> number
(check-expect (smallest (list 4)) 4)
(check-expect (smallest (list 4 7)) 4)
(check-expect (smallest (list 7 4)) 4)
(check-expect (smallest (list 6 9 4 7 8 3 6 10 7)) 3)
(define (smallest nums)
  (cond [(empty? (rest nums))          (first nums)]
        [(cons? (rest nums))
         ; (first nums)                number
         ; (rest nums)                 non-empty list of numbers
         ; (smallest (rest nums))      number
         (local [(define winner (smallest (rest nums)))]
           (cond [(<= (first nums) winner) (first nums)]
                 [else winner]))]))
```

Now *both* of the examples

```
(check-expect
  (smallest (list 1 2 3 4 5 6 7 8 9 10 11 12 13 14 15 16 17 18))
  1)
(check-expect
  (smallest (list 18 17 16 15 14 13 12 11 10 9 8 7 6 5 4 3 2 1))
  1)
```

run in about 3 milliseconds on my computer; we've sped up the latter by a factor of 3000.

Exercise 27.1.1 *Re-write the spams function from Exercise 24.4.5 using* `local` *to call itself only once. Does it work correctly? Is it significantly faster?*

Exercise 27.1.2 *Re-write the* copies *function from Exercise 24.4.2 or 24.4.6 by using* local *to call itself only once. Does it work properly? Is it significantly faster?*

Exercise 27.1.3 *Re-write the* dot-grid *function from Exercise 24.4.8 using* local *to call itself only once. Does it work properly? Is it significantly faster?*

Exercise 27.1.4 *Re-write the* randoms *function from Exercise 24.4.9 using* local *to call itself only once. Does it work correctly? Is it significantly faster?*

Exercise 27.1.5 *Consider the functions* binary-add1 *from Exercise 24.4.3,* binary-add *from Exercise 25.4.9,* binary-mult *from Exercise 25.4.10, and* binary-raise *from Exercise 25.4.11. Which of these (if any) would benefit from this treatment? Why?*

27.2   Using locals for clarity

Consider a distance function that takes in two posns and computes the distance between them:

```
; distance :  posn posn -> number
(check-expect (distance (make-posn 3 5) (make-posn 3 5)) 0)
(check-expect (distance (make-posn 3 5) (make-posn 6 5)) 3)
(check-expect (distance (make-posn 3 5) (make-posn 3 -10)) 15)
(check-expect (distance (make-posn 3 5) (make-posn 6 9)) 5)
(check-within (distance (make-posn 3 5) (make-posn 4 4)) 1.41 .1)
(define (distance here there)
   (sqrt (+ (* (- (posn-x here) (posn-x there))
               (- (posn-x here) (posn-x there)))
            (* (- (posn-y here) (posn-y there))
               (- (posn-y here) (posn-y there)))))))
```

This passes all its tests, and it's reasonably efficient, but the definition is long, complicated, and hard to read. The formula computes the difference of x coordinates, squares that, computes the difference of y coordinates, squares that, adds the squares, and square-roots the result.

It would arguably be easier to read if we had *names* for "the difference of x coordinates" and "the difference of y coordinates". We can do that with local:

```
(define (distance here there)
   (local [(define xdiff (- (posn-x here) (posn-x there)))
           (define ydiff (- (posn-y here) (posn-y there)))]
      (sqrt (+ (*  xdiff xdiff ) (*  ydiff ydiff )))))
```

The expression on the last line is much shorter and clearer: one can easily see that it's the square root of the sum of two squares. (It may also be slightly more efficient, but not the dramatic improvement we saw for `smallest` above.)

Exercise 27.2.1 *Develop a function* `rotate-colors` *that takes in an image and (using* `map-image`*) creates a new image whose red component is the old green component, whose green component is the old blue component, and whose blue component is the old red component. Use* `local` *to give names to the old red, green, and blue components.*

Exercise 27.2.2 *What other functions have you written that would benefit from this technique? Try rewriting them and see whether they're shorter and clearer.*

27.3 Using locals for information-hiding

Another approach to making `smallest` more efficient would have been to write a helper function `smaller`:

```
; smaller :  number number -> number
; returns the smaller of two numbers
(check-expect (smaller 3 8) 3)
(check-expect (smaller 9 7) 7)
(check-expect (smaller 2 2) 2)

(define (smaller a b)
  (cond   [(<= a b) a]
          [else b]))

(define (smallest nums)
  (cond [(empty?  (rest nums)) (first nums)]
        [(cons?  (rest nums))
          (  smaller (first nums) (smallest (rest nums)))]))
```

This definition, too, calls itself recursively only once, so it doesn't have the efficiency problems of the first version above. But it requires a helper function, which may be of no use in the rest of the program.

As mentioned above, you can also define a *function*, or even a *struct*, locally. So if we wanted, we could *hide* the definition of `smaller` inside that of `smallest`:

```
(define (smallest nums)
  (local [(define (smaller a b) (cond [(<= a b) a] [else b]))]
    (cond [(empty?  (rest nums)) (first nums)]
          [(cons?  (rest nums))
            (smaller (first nums) (smallest (rest nums)))])))
```

I recommend moving `smaller` into a local definition only *after* you've tested and debugged it as usual.

Suppose you were hired to write a `sort` function like that of Exercise 23.6.1. It needed a helper function `insert` which inserts a number in order into an already-sorted list of numbers. But "insert" is a fairly common word, and your customer might want to write a function by the same name herself, which would be a problem because DrRacket won't allow you to define two functions with the same name. So again, one could hide the `insert` function inside the definition of `sort`:

```
(define (sort nums)
   (local [(define (insert num nums) ...)]
      (cond [(empty? nums) empty]
            [(cons? nums)
             (insert (first nums) (sort (rest nums)))])))
```

For another example, the `wn-prime?` function of Exercise 24.3.8 needed a helper function `not-divisible-up-to?`, which nobody would ever want to use unless they were writing a prime-testing function. So after you've tested and debugged both functions, you can *move* the definition of `not-divisible-up-to?` function inside the definition of `wn-prime?`:

```
(define (wn-prime? num)
   (local [(define (not-divisible-up-to? m n) ...)]
      (not-divisible-up-to? num (- num 1))))
```

For one more example, recall exercise 11.5.1, a `road-trip-cost` function which depended on six other functions: `gas-cost`, `cost-of-gallons`, `gas-needed`, `motel-cost`, `nights-in-motel`, and `rental-cost`. Any of those other functions could conceivably be useful in its own right, but suppose we knew that they *wouldn't* be used on their own. It would still be useful to write and test the functions individually, but once they all work, they (and the constants) could be *hidden* inside the definition of `road-trip-cost`:

```
(define (road-trip-cost miles days)
  (local [ (define MPG 28)
           (define PRICE-PER-GALLON 2.459)
           (define MOTEL-PRICE-PER-NIGHT 40)
           (define CAR-RENTAL-FIXED-FEE 10)
           (define CAR-RENTAL-PER-DAY 29.95)
           (define CAR-RENTAL-PER-MILE 0.10)
           (define (gas-needed miles)
                   (/ miles MPG))
           (define (cost-of-gallons gallons)
                   (* PRICE-PER-GALLON gallons))
           (define (gas-cost miles)
                   (cost-of-gallons (gas-needed miles)))
           (define (nights-in-motel days)
                   (- days 1))
           (define (motel-cost days)
                   (* MOTEL-PRICE-PER-NIGHT (nights-in-motel days)))
           (define (rental-cost miles days)
                   (+ CAR-RENTAL-FIXED-FEE
                      (* days CAR-RENTAL-PER-DAY)
                      (* miles CAR-RENTAL-PER-MILE))) ]
     (+ (gas-cost miles)
        (motel-cost days)
        (rental-cost miles days))))
```

Of course, since each of the helper functions is called only once, there's not much point in defining them as functions at all. For this problem, it would be simpler and more realistic to define them as *variables* instead:

```
(define (road-trip-cost miles days)
  (local [(define MPG 28)
          (define PRICE-PER-GALLON 2.459)
          (define MOTEL-PRICE-PER-NIGHT 40)
          (define CAR-RENTAL-FIXED-FEE 10)
          (define CAR-RENTAL-PER-DAY 29.95)
          (define CAR-RENTAL-PER-MILE 0.10)
          (define  gas-needed  (/ miles MPG))
          (define  gas-cost  (* PRICE-PER-GALLON gas-needed))
          (define  motel-cost  (* MOTEL-PRICE-PER-NIGHT (- days 1)))
          (define  rental-cost
             (+ CAR-RENTAL-FIXED-FEE
                (* days CAR-RENTAL-PER-DAY)
                (* miles CAR-RENTAL-PER-MILE)))]
     (+  gas-cost motel-cost rental-cost )))
```

We're now using local partly for information-hiding (it's a convenient place to put the constants PRICE-PER-GALLON, MPG, *etc.* without the rest of the program seeing those names) and partly for clarity (gas-needed, gas-cost, *etc.* are just intermediate steps in calculating the answer).

27.4   Using locals to insert parameters into functions

In all of the above examples, we've written helper functions as usual, tested and debugged them, then moved them into local definitions inside the main function. In this section, we'll see problems for which the helper function *must* be defined locally inside another function — it doesn't work by itself.

Worked Exercise 27.4.1 *Modify the solution to Exercise 7.8.12 so the amount of blue increases smoothly from top to bottom, regardless of the height of the image.*

Solution: The `apply-blue-gradient` function will use the `map-image` function, which requires a function with the contract

```
; new-pixel :  number(x) number(y) color -> color
```

Let's write some examples of this function. We'll want one at the top of the image, one at the bottom, and one in between. The one at the top is easy:

```
(check-expect (new-pixel 40 0 (make-color 30 60 90))
              (make-color 30 60 0))
```

But how can we write an example at the bottom or in between when we don't know how tall the given image is?

Let's pretend for a moment the image was 100 pixels tall. Then we would choose examples

```
(check-expect (new-pixel 36 100 (make-color 30 60 90))
              (make-color 30 60 255))
(check-expect (new-pixel 58 40 (make-color 30 60 90))
              (make-color 30 60 102))
```

because 40 is 40% of the way from top to bottom, and 102 is 40% of the way from 0 to 255. The function would then look like

```
(define (new-pixel x y old-color)
  ; x          a number
  ; y          a number
  ; old-color a color
  (make-color (color-red old-color)
              (color-green old-color)
              (real->int (* 255 (/ y 100)))))

(define (apply-blue-gradient pic)
  ; pic        an image
  (map-image new-pixel pic))
```

This works beautifully for images that happen to be 100 pixels high. To make it work in general, we'd like to replace the 100 in the definition of `new-pixel` with `(image-height pic)`, but this doesn't work because `new-pixel` has never heard of `pic`: `pic` won't even be defined until somebody calls `apply-blue-gradient`. As a step along the way, let's define a variable `pic` directly in the Definitions pane:

```
(define pic (ellipse 78 100 "solid" "green"))
(check-expect (new-pixel ...)  ...)
(define (new-pixel x y old-color)
  (make-color (color-red old-color)
              (color-green old-color)
              (real->int (* 255 (/ y  (image-height pic) )))))

(map-image new-pixel pic)
```

Now we can run the check-expect test cases for new-pixel, and also look at the result of the map-image to see whether it looks the way it should. But it still doesn't work in general.

So we'll get rid of the pic variable, comment out the check-expect test cases, and *move the definition* of new-pixel *inside* the apply-blue-gradient function:

```
(define (apply-blue-gradient pic)
  ; pic      an image
  (local [(define (new-pixel x y old-color)
            (make-color (color-red old-color)
                        (color-green old-color)
                        (real->int (* 255 (/ y (image-height pic))))))]
    (map-image new-pixel pic)))
```

Note that when the variable name pic appears in new-pixel, it refers to the parameter of apply-blue-gradient.

Try this definition of apply-blue-gradient on a variety of pictures of various sizes.

■

A disadvantage of writing a function inside another function is that you can't test an inner function directly, so I recommend the process above: define global variable(s) for the information from the outer function that the inner function needs, test the inner function in the presence of these variables, and once it passes all the tests, move the inner function inside a function with parameters with the same names as those variables (and now you can get rid of the global variables).

Exercise 27.4.2 *Develop a function* add-red *that takes in a number and an image, and adds that number to the red component of every pixel in the image. (Remember to keep the red component below 256.)*

Exercise 27.4.3 *Develop a function* substitute-color *that takes in two colors and an image, and replaces every pixel which is the first color with the second color.*

Exercise 27.4.4 *Develop a function* horiz-stripes *that takes in a width, a height, a stripe width, and two colors, and produces a rectangular image of the specified width and height with horizontal stripes of the specified width and colors.*

Exercise 27.4.5 *Develop a function* smooth-image *that takes in an image and replaces each color component of each pixel with the* average *value of that color component in the pixel and its four neighbors (up, down, left, and right).*

Hint: Use the get-pixel-color function to get the values of the neighboring pixels. Use another local to give names (*e.g.* up, down, left, and right) to these values, for clarity.

You'll need to decide what to do at the borders. The easiest answer is to just call `get-pixel-color` even though the position may be outside the borders; it will return black in that case, so the resulting picture will have darkened edges. A more proper, and more difficult, solution is to average together only the neighboring pixels that actually exist. This will probably require two or three helper functions and a *list* of neighboring colors. These helper functions will also help you with Exercise 27.4.8.

A "higher-order function" is a function that takes in functions as parameters, and/or returns a function as its value. (We'll learn how to write such functions in Chapter 28.) Some examples are `map3-image`, `build3-image`, `map-image`, and `build-image`. We've seen how to write a function that (locally) defines another function from its parameters, then passes that new function as an argument to a higher-order function.

What other higher-order functions have we seen? How about `on-tick`, `on-draw`, `on-key`, `on-mouse`, *etc.*? The same technique now allows us to write a function that uses its parameters to construct event handlers and run an animation on them.

Exercise 27.4.6 *Recall Exercise 6.5.2, which placed a stick-figure at a fixed location on a background scene and had the stick figure turn upside-down every second or so.*

Develop a function `flipping-figure` *that takes in a background scene and the x and y coordinates where you want the figure to be, and runs an animation with the figure flipping upside-down every second or so at that location on that background.*

Exercise 27.4.7 *Develop a function* `add-dots-with-mouse` *that takes in a color and a number, and runs an animation that starts with a white screen, and every time the mouse is clicked, adds a circular dot of the specified color and radius at the mouse location.*

Exercise 27.4.8 *Look up John Conway's "Game of Life" on the Web (e.g. Wikipedia).*

Develop a function `life-gen` *that takes in an image representing a grid of cells (think of the color white as "dead" and any other color as "alive"), and produces the grid of cells one generation later. If a pixel has fewer than two or more than three "live" neighbors (from among its eight neighbors — above, below, left, right, and the four diagonals), it dies. If it has exactly two, it stays the same as it was (alive or dead). If it has exactly three, it becomes alive (or stays alive, if it already was). You may want to use another* `local` *to give names to the eight neighboring pixels, or to a list of their colors, or something.*

Define an animation with `life-gen` *as its tick handler.*

Start it with a random image (see Exercise 15.3.3) as the initial model.

If you want more control over the animation, recall that `big-bang` *returns its final model. Try starting this "life" animation with the result of* `add-dots-with-mouse` *(see Exercise 27.4.7).*

SIDEBAR:

Most programming languages allow you to define local variables. Some (like Java and Pascal) allow you to define local structs and functions. Some of these allow you to write a function whose parameters are then inserted into locally-defined functions, although they require more complicated syntax and put extra restrictions on what you can do with these parameters. Racket makes this stuff easier than any other language I know of.

27.5 Review of important words and concepts

Racket (like most programming languages) allows you to define variables *locally*: you introduce a new variable, work with it for a little while, and then *forget* it. This is used for four common reasons:

- for efficiency: suppose a function calls itself more than once on the same argument(s). We call it only once, store the result in a local variable, and use the variable more than once.

- for clarity: suppose a particular long expression, an intermediate step in computing a function, appears several times in the function definition. Define a local variable to hold the result of that expression, and the resulting definition may be significantly shorter and easier to understand.

- for information-hiding: suppose a constant, struct, or function is only needed within a particular function, especially if it has a common name that somebody might want to use somewhere else in a large program. Define it locally, use it in this function as many times as you want, and be confident it won't conflict with or be confused with things by the same name defined elsewhere.

- for defining functions that can be passed to a higher-order function like `build-image`, `map-image`, `on-draw`, *etc.* In particular, the ability to define a function inside another function, using the parameters of the outer one, enables you to do image manipulations and animations that you couldn't do before. We'll see another way to do this in Section 28.6.

27.6 Reference: New syntax for local definitions

This chapter introduced one new syntax rule, Rule 8 introducing **local** definitions of variables, functions, and even structs.

Chapter 28

Functions as objects

For this chapter, switch languages in DrRacket to "Intermediate Student Language with Lambda" or higher. (We'll discuss `lambda` in Section 28.6.)

28.1 Adding parameters

The original reason for defining functions was to avoid writing almost the same expression over and over. Recall the rule from Chapter 4, *if you write almost the exact same thing over and over, you're doing something wrong.* So we *parameterized* the expression: made it a function definition with one or more *parameters*. The part of those expressions that was *always the same* became the *body* of the function definition, and the part that was *different* became a *parameter* to the function.

Recall Exercise 22.5.3, a function `contains-doll?` which checked whether the string `"doll"` occurs in a given list. Now imagine `contains-baseball?`, which checks whether the string `"baseball"` occurs in a given list. The definitions of these two functions would be almost identical, except that the word `"doll"` in one is replaced with `"baseball"` in the other.

We respond, again, by *parameterizing* — in this case, *adding a parameter* to a function that already has one. In Exercise 22.5.4, we wrote a function `any-matches?` that took in an extra parameter and searches for *that object* in a given list. Once we've written, tested, and debugged that more *general* function, `contains-doll?` and `contains-baseball?` and anything else like them is trivial.

Now suppose we had written a function `any-over-10?` that took a list of numbers and tells whether any of the numbers are larger than 10. (This should be an easy exercise by now.) An obvious variant on this would be `any-over-5?`, whose definition would be exactly the same, only with the number 5 replacing the number 10. To avoid having to write each of these nearly-identical functions, we again *add a parameter*:

```
; any-over?  :   number  list-of-numbers -> boolean
(check-expect (any-over? 5 empty) false)
(check-expect (any-over? 5 (list 3)) false)
(check-expect (any-over? 5 (list 5)) true)
(check-expect (any-over? 5 (list 6)) true)
(check-expect (any-over? 5 (list 7 2 4)) true)
(check-expect (any-over? 5 (list 3 2 4)) false)
(check-expect (any-over? 5 (list 3 2 5)) true)
```

```
(define (any-over?   threshold numbers)
  (cond [(empty? numbers) false]
        [(cons? numbers)
         (or (> (first numbers)  threshold )
             (any-over?   threshold (rest numbers)))]))
```

28.2 Functions as parameters

What if we wanted to find whether any of the elements of a list were *greater than or equal to* a particular threshold? Or if any of the elements of a list were *smaller* than a particular threshold? any-over? won't do it; the obvious analogues would be any-at-least? and any-under?, which would be just like any-over? but with a $>=$ or $<$ in place of the $>$ in the above definition.

Again, we're writing *almost exactly the same code over and over*, which probably means we're *doing something wrong*. And as before, the answer is to add a parameter. But this time the "part that's different" is a *function* rather than a number or a string. Which means that our general function will have to *take a function as a parameter*.

You've already seen some functions — on-tick, on-draw, check-with, map-image, build-image, *etc.* — that take in a function as an argument. But you haven't been allowed to *write* such functions yourself. This is because, for absolute beginning programmers, confusing a function with a variable is a very common mistake. But now that you're past those beginning mistakes, **switch languages** to DrRacket's "Intermediate Student Language with lambda".

In Racket, *function* is a data type, just like *number* or *string* or *list*. If you can pass a number or a list as an argument, there's no reason not to pass a function as an argument. Functions that operate on other functions are called *higher-order functions*.

The following exercise generalizes any-over? to allow for any-under?, any-at-least?, any-equal?, *etc.*

Worked Exercise 28.2.1 *Develop a function* any-compares? *that takes in a function, a number, and a list of numbers, and tells whether any of the numbers in the list has the specified relationship to the fixed number.*

Solution: The contract and examples look like

```
; any-compares? :   function number list-of-numbers -> boolean
(check-expect (any-compares?  >= 5 (list 2 5 1)) true)
(check-expect (any-compares?  > 5 (list 2 5 1)) false)
(check-expect (any-compares?  = 5 (list 2 5 1)) true)
(check-expect (any-compares?  = 5 (list 2 6 1)) false)
(check-expect (any-compares?  < 5 (list 2 6 1)) true)
(check-expect (any-compares?  < 5 (list 7 6 8)) false)
```

Before we go on with developing the function, let's look again at the contract. The first argument to any-compares? is supposed to be a function, so let's try some other functions.

What would (any-compares? + 5 (list 7 6 8)) do? Well, it compares each number in the list with 5, using the + operator, and if any of these questions returns true ... but wait! The + operator doesn't return a boolean at all! Calling any-compares? doesn't make sense unless the function you give it returns a boolean.

What would (any-compares? positive? 5 (list 7 6 8)) do? It should compare each number in the list with 5, using positive? ... but wait! The positive? function only takes one parameter, so how can it possibly "compare" two numbers? In fact, calling any-compares? doesn't make sense unless the function you give it takes exactly two parameters.

To rule out such nonsensical uses of any-compares?, let's make the contract more precise: instead of just saying "function", we'll write down (in parentheses) the *contract* that the function must satisfy:

```
; any-compares?  :   (number number -> boolean)
                     number
                     list-of-numbers
                     -> boolean
```

The skeleton looks like

```
(define (any-compares?    compare? num nums)
  ; compare?             number number -> boolean
  ; num                  number
  ; nums                 list of numbers
  (cond [(empty? nums) ...]
        [(cons? nums)
         ; (first nums) number
         ; (rest nums)  list of numbers
         ; (any-compares?   compare? num (rest nums))   boolean
         ...]))
```

So what can we do with compare?? It's a function on two numbers, returning a boolean, so the obvious thing to do with it is to call it on two numbers. Conveniently, we have two numbers in the inventory: num and (first nums). There are two ways we could call the function:

```
; (compare?  (first nums) num) boolean
; (compare?  num (first nums)) boolean
```

To see which one (or both) will actually help us, let's use an inventory with values. We'll pick the example (any-compares? < 5 (list 2 6 7)) in which the first comparison should be true, and the others false.

```
(define (any-compares? compare? num nums)
  ; compare?          number number -> boolean        <
  ; num                             number             5
  ; nums                            list of numbers  (list 2 6 7)
  (cond [(empty? nums) ...]
        [(cons? nums)
         ; (first nums)             number             2
         ; (rest nums)              list of numbers  (list 6 7)
         ; (compare? (first nums) num) boolean         true
         ; (compare? num (first nums)) boolean         false
         ; (any-compares? compare? num (rest nums))
                                     boolean            false
         ; right answer             boolean            true
         ...]))
```

So of the two, we seem to need (compare? (first nums) num). The final definition (with the scratch work removed) is

```
(define (any-compares? compare? num nums)
  (cond [(empty? nums) false ]
        [(cons? nums)
         (or (compare? (first nums) num)
             (any-compares? compare? num (rest nums)))]))
```

∎

Now that we've written any-compares?, if we *want* any-over?, any-greater?, any-less?, any-over-5?, *etc.*, we can write them easily:

```
(define (any-over? num nums)
  (any-compares? > num nums))
(define (any-at-least? num nums)
  (any-compares? >= num nums))
(define (any-less? num nums)
  (any-compares? < num nums))
(define (any-over-5? nums)
  (any-compares? > 5 nums))
```

With the aid of a helper function, we can go even farther:

```
(define (divisible-by? x y)
  (zero? (remainder x y)))
(define (any-even? nums)
  (any-compares? divisible-by? 2 nums))
```

Or, if divisible-by? isn't likely to be used anywhere else, we could wrap it up in a local:

```
(define (any-even? nums)
  (local [(define (divisible-by? x y)
            (zero? (remainder x y))) ]
    (any-compares? divisible-by? 2 nums)))
```

What if we had defined `prime?`, as in Exercise 24.3.8, and wanted to know whether any of the numbers in the list are prime? There's no obvious way to use `any-compares?` to solve this problem, because `any-compares?` insists on comparing each element of the list with a particular fixed value. In fact, a more natural function than `any-compares?` would be

```
; any-satisfies? (number -> boolean) list-of-numbers -> boolean
(check-expect (any-satisfies? even? (list 3 5 9)) false)
(check-expect (any-satisfies? even? (list 3 5 8)) true)
(define (over-5? x) (> x 5))
(check-expect (any-satisfies? over-5? (list 2 3 4)) false)
(check-expect (any-satisfies? over-5? (list 2 6 4)) true)
(check-expect (any-satisfies? prime? (list 2 6 4)) true)
(check-expect (any-satisfies? prime? (list 8 6 4)) false)
```

The definition (after taking out the scratch work) is

```
(define (any-satisfies? test? nums)
  (cond [(empty? nums) false]
        [(cons? nums)
         (or (test? (first nums))
             (any-satisfies? test? (rest nums)))]))
```


Worked Exercise 28.2.2 *Suppose we had written* `any-satisfies?` *first.* **Define the** *function* `any-compares?`, *taking advantage of having already written the more general function.*

Solution: Since `any-satisfies?` takes in a function of only one parameter, we need a helper function that takes one parameter.

```
; ok? : num -> boolean
; applies the comparison function to
; the parameter and the fixed number
```

But what are "the comparison function" and "the fixed number"? They're both parameters to `any-compares?`, so we can't possibly know what they are until `any-compares?` is called. However, we can write and test it by storing sample values of both in global variables:

```
(define num 17)
(define compare? >)
(check-expect (ok? 14) false)
(check-expect (ok? 17) false)
(check-expect (ok? 19) true)
(define (ok? num-from-list)
  ; num-from-list number
  ; num            number
  ; compare?       (number number -> boolean)
  (compare? num-from-list num))
```

Once this has passed its tests, *change* the definitions of `num` and `compare?`, *change* the test cases appropriately, and see if it still passes the tests. If so, we perhaps have enough confidence in it to *move it inside another function*:

```
(define (any-compares? compare? num nums)
  (local [(define (ok? num-from-list)
            (compare? num-from-list num)) ]
    (any-satisfies? ok? nums)))
```

Again, this helper function *could not* have been written to stand by itself at the top level, because it needs to know what `compare?` and `num` are. ▌

Looking closely at the definition of `any-satisfies?`, we notice that nothing in the code (except the variable names) actually mentions *numbers*. In fact, if we were to call `any-satisfies?` on a function from *string* to boolean and a list of *strings*, it would work just as well:

```
(define (contains-doll? toys)
  (local [(define (is-doll? toy) (string=? toy "doll"))]
    (any-satisfies? is-doll? toys)))
```

So what is the contract really? It wouldn't work with a function from string to boolean and a list of numbers, or *vice versa*; the input type of the function has to be the same type as the elements of the list. We often write this using a capital letter like X to represent "any type":

```
; any-satisfies?  (X -> boolean) list-of-X -> boolean
```

SIDEBAR:

The Java and C++ languages also allow you to write a function whose contract has a "type variable" in it, like the X above. C++ calls these "templates", and Java calls them "generics". Needless to say, the syntax is more complicated.

Exercise 28.2.3 *Use* `any-satisfies?` *to write a* `any-over-100K?` *function that takes in a list of* `employee` *structs (as in Exercise 21.2.1), and tells whether any of them earn over $100,000/year. Your* `any-over-100K?` *function should have no recursive calls.*

Exercise 28.2.4 *Develop a function* `count-if` *that takes in a function (from X to boolean) and a list of X's, and returns how many of the elements of the list have the property.*

Exercise 28.2.5 *Use* `count-if` *to write a* `count-evens` *function that takes a list of numbers and returns how many of them are even. Your* `count-evens` *function should have no recursive calls.*

Exercise 28.2.6 *Use* `count-if` *to write a* `count-dolls` *function that takes a list of strings and returns how many of them are* `"doll"`*. Your function should have no recursive calls.*

Exercise 28.2.7 *Use* `count-if` *to write a* `count-multiples` *function that takes a number and a list of numbers and returns how many of them are multiples of that number. Your function should have no recursive calls.*

Exercise 28.2.8 *Use* `count-if` *to write a* `count-earns-over-100K` *function that takes a list of* `employee` *structs and returns how many of them earn over $100,000/year. Your function should have no recursive calls.*

Exercise 28.2.9 *Use* `count-if` *to write a* `count-earns-over` *function that takes a list of* `employee` *structs and a number, and returns how many of the employees earn over that amount. Your function should have no recursive calls.*

Exercise 28.2.10 ***Develop*** *a function* `remove-if` *that takes in a function (from X to boolean) and a list of X's, and returns a list of the elements of the list for which the function returns false (i.e. it "removes" the ones for which the function returns true).*

(A function similar to `remove-if` is actually built into DrRacket: now that you've written your own version, look up the `filter` function in the Help system.)

Exercise 28.2.11 *Use* `remove-if` *to write a* `remove-over-5` *function that takes in a list of numbers and removes all the ones* > 5*. Your function should have no recursive calls.*

Exercise 28.2.12 *Use* `remove-if` *to write a* `remove-over` *function that takes in a number and a list of numbers and removes all the ones over that number. Your function should have no recursive calls.*

Exercise 28.2.13 *Use* `remove-if` *to write a* `fire-over` *function that takes in a number and a list of* `employee` *structs and removes all the ones that earn over that amount of money per year. Your function should have no recursive calls.*

Exercise 28.2.14 ***Develop a function*** `nth-satisfying` *that takes in a whole number n and a Boolean-valued function, and returns the n-th whole number that has the desired property. For example,*

```
(check-expect (nth-satisfying 3 even?)  4)
  ; even natural numbers 0, 2, 4
(check-expect (nth-satisfying 5 prime?)  11)
  ; prime numbers 2, 3, 5, 7, 11
(check-expect (nth-satisfying 5 over-10?)  15)
  ; 11, 12, 13, 14, 15
(check-expect (nth-satisfying 4 integer?)  3)
  ; 0, 1, 2, 3
```

Hint: You'll probably need a helper function that takes in an extra parameter.

28.3 Functions returning lists

Consider the function `cube-each`:

```
; cube-each :  list-of-numbers -> list-of-numbers
; returns a list of the cubes of the numbers, in the same order
(check-expect (cube-each empty) empty)
(check-expect (cube-each (list 2 6 -3)) (list 8 216 -27))
```

Defining this function should be straightforward by now. But what if you were then asked to write `sqrt-each` or `negate-each`? Obviously, these are all defined in essentially the same way, differing only in what function is applied to each element of the list. To avoid having to write each of these separately, we'll *parameterize* them with that function:

```
; do-to-each :  (X -> X) list-of-X -> list-of-X
(check-expect (do-to-each sqrt (list 0 1 4)) (list 0 1 2))
(define (cube y)
  (* y y y))
(check-expect (do-to-each cube (list 2 6 -3)) (list 8 216 -27))
```

Exercise 28.3.1 *Develop this* `do-to-each` *function.*

Exercise 28.3.2 *Use* `do-to-each` *to write* `sqrt-each` *with no recursive calls.*

Exercise 28.3.3 *There's a built-in function named* **identity** *which does nothing: it returns its argument unchanged. It's often useful as a simple test case for functions like* `do-to-each`.
     What should `(do-to-each identity ...)` *do? Try it.*

Exercise 28.3.4 *Use* `do-to-each` *to write* `add-3-to-each` *with no recursive calls.*

Exercise 28.3.5 *Use* `do-to-each` *to write a* `add-to-each` *function that takes in a number and a list of numbers and adds the number to each element of the list. No recursive calls.*

Exercise 28.3.6 *Use* `do-to-each` *to write a* `give-10%-raises` *function that takes in a list of* **employee** *structs and returns a list of the same employees, in the same order, but with each one earning 10% more than before. Your function should have no recursive calls.*

Now that you've written `do-to-each`, notice that not only is there nothing in the code that requires the elements of the list to be numbers; there is *also* nothing in the code that requires the input list to be the same type as the output type. For example,

```
(check-expect
  (do-to-each string-length (list "hello" "hi" "mazeltov"))
  (list 5 2 8))
```

works, even though it violates the contract as we stated it above. In fact, the contract should really be rewritten:

```
; do-to-each :  (X -> Y) list-of-X -> list-of-Y
```

which makes sense: if X and Y are *any* two types (possibly the same), it takes in a function from X to Y, applies it to each of a list of X's, and produces a list of Y's.

Exercise 28.3.7 *Use* `do-to-each` *to write a* **names** *function that takes a list of* **employee** *structs and returns a list of their names. Your function should have no recursive calls.*

Actually, there's a function similar to `do-to-each` built into DrRacket; now that you've written your own version, look up the `map` function in the Help system. (Just as `map-image` does something to each pixel of an image and produces an image the same size, `map` does something to each element of a list and produces a list the same size.) The biggest difference between `do-to-each` and `map` is that `do-to-each` always applies a one-parameter function, whereas `map` takes in a function of *any number* of parameters, and takes that number of lists. For example,

```
(check-expect (map + (list 1 2 3 4) (list 50 40 30 20))
              (list 51 42 33 24))
```

Exercise 28.3.8 *Rewrite exercise 23.4.1 using* `map` *or* `do-to-each` *wherever possible. Is the result significantly shorter or clearer?*

Exercise 28.3.9 *Develop a function* `do-to-each-whole` *that takes in a whole number n and a function f:* `whole -> X` *and produces a list of X's:* `(f 0)`, `(f 1)`, ... `(f (- n 1))`. *For example,*

```
(check-expect (do-to-each-whole 5 sqr) (list 0 1 4 9 16))
```

Again, there's actually a built-in function that does exactly this:

```
; build-list :  whole (whole -> X) -> list-of-X
```

As `build-image` builds an image of a specified size and shape by calling a function on the coordinates of each pixel, `build-list` builds a list of length N by calling a function on each of the numbers $0, 1, \ldots N - 1$. Now that you've written `do-to-each-whole`, feel free to use the predefined `build-list` instead.

Exercise 28.3.10 *The* `sort` *function from Section 23.6 sorts a list of numbers in increasing order. One could easily sort a list of numbers in* decreasing *order by replacing a* < *with a* > *in the function definition.* **Generalize** *the* `sort` *function so it takes in a function (call it* `precedes?`*) to tell whether one item in the list should come before another.*

Your function definition should no longer depend on the data in the list being numbers; generalize the contract as far as you can.

Exercise 28.3.11 *Develop a function* `sort-by-salary` *that takes in a list of* `employee` *structures and sorts them from highest-paid to lowest-paid. You should be able to do this in a few lines of code (not counting contracts, inventories, and test cases), without recursion, by using* `general-sort`.

Exercise 28.3.12 *Rewrite* `sort-candidates` *(from exercise 23.6.2) with the help of* `general-sort`. *It should take about four reasonably short lines, not counting contracts, inventories, and test cases.*

Exercise 28.3.13 *Develop a function* `ranked-election` *that takes in a list of strings (representing the votes cast by individual voters) and returns an ordered list of candidates, from most votes to fewest votes. It should take two or three reasonably short lines, not counting contracts, inventories, and test cases.*

28.4 Choosing a winner

The `smallest` and `largest` functions, finding the smallest and largest number (respectively) in a non-empty list, are of course very similar: where one has a <, the other has a >. The `highest-paid` function, taking in a list of `employee` structs and returning the one with the highest salary, is a little more complicated, but still does basically the same thing: it compares two objects, picks one of them as the "winner", then compares the winner of this bout with another object, and so on until you've reduced the whole list to one "champion".

Obviously, the difference between one of these functions and another is the comparison function, which we might call `beats?`. We can generalize all of these functions to a `champion` function that takes in the `beats?` function and a non-empty list (it doesn't make sense on an empty list), runs a single-elimination tournament, and returns the list element that "beats" all the rest.

Exercise 28.4.1 *Develop the function* `champion` *as described above.*

Hint: For efficiency, it's probably a good idea to adapt the technique from Section 27.1 so you don't call the function recursively twice.

Exercise 28.4.2 *Use* `champion` *to rewrite* `smallest` *with no recursive calls.*

Exercise 28.4.3 *Use* `champion` *to write* `highest-paid` *with no recursive calls.*

28.5   Accumulating over a list

Consider the functions `add-up` and `multiply-all` (Exercises 22.5.2 and 22.5.11). These functions are extremely similar: they both *combine* two objects to get a third object, which is then combined with another object to get a fourth, and so on. We should be able to generalize these. How do they differ, and how are they the same?

The `add-up` and `multiply-all` functions obviously differ in what function they apply (+ and * respectively). But they also differ in the answer to the base case: the right answer to (`add-up empty`) is 0, while the right answer to (`multiply-all empty`) is 1. So we'll need to add *two* parameters:

```
; combine :  X (X X->X) list-of-X -> X
...
(define (add-up nums) (combine 0 + nums))
(define (multiply-all nums) (combine 1 * nums))
(check-expect (add-up (list 1 2 3 4)) 10)
(check-expect (multiply-all (list 1 2 3 4)) 24)
```

Exercise 28.5.1 *Develop this* `combine` *function.*

You may notice that there's nothing in the function definition that requires the various types to be the same. On the other hand, not every possible combination of data types would make sense either.

Exercise 28.5.2 *Correct the contract for* `combine` *to reflect which things* must *be the same type. Allow as much generality as you can.*

Exercise 28.5.3 *Use* `combine` *to rewrite* `any-satisfies?` *with no recursive calls.*

Exercise 28.5.4 *Use* `combine` *to rewrite* `count-if` *with no recursive calls.*

Exercise 28.5.5 *Use* `combine` *to rewrite* `do-to-each` *with no recursive calls.*

Exercise 28.5.6 *Use* `combine` *to rewrite* `champion` *with no recursive calls.*

There are two different functions built into DrRacket that act like `combine`. Now that you've written your own version, look up `foldr` and `foldl` in the Help system.

28.6 Anonymous functions

In many of the above exercises, we needed to write a little function (either `locally` or standing on its own) for the sole purpose of passing it to a higher-order function like `any-satisfies?`, `count-if`, `remove-if`, `champion`, or `combine`. This feels silly and wasteful to me.

By way of analogy, suppose we wanted to compute $3 + (4 \cdot 5)$. We *could* do this in two steps:

```
(define temp (* 4 5))
(+ 3 temp)
```

but it's much shorter and simpler to just say

```
(+ 3 (* 4 5))
```

In other words, we don't need to give a *name* to the result of (* 4 5) if all we're going to do it pass it as an argument, once, to +.

If we're going to use something many times, it makes sense to give it a name and use that name each time. But if we're going to use it only once, it makes more sense to just use its value directly. Similarly, it seems silly to define a function with a name if we're only going to use it once, as an argument to another function.

Syntax Rule 9   (lambda (*parameter parameter* ...) *expression*)

is an expression whose value is a function that takes in the specified number of parameters. The parameter *names may appear in the* expression.

`lambda` can be thought of as just like **define**, except that it doesn't bother giving a *name* to the function, but just returns it instead. Any place that a function can appear — a "function" argument to a higher-order function, or even just after a left parenthesis — a `lambda` expression can appear too. For example,

```
((lambda (y) (* y y y)) 1234567890)
```

is equivalent to

```
(* 1234567890 1234567890 1234567890)
```

More usefully,

```
(do-to-each (lambda (y) (* y y y)) (list 1 2 5 -3))
```

is equivalent to

```
(local [(define (cube y) (* y y y))]
    (do-to-each cube (list 1 2 5 -3)))
```

which of course returns (list 1 8 125 -27).

Worked Exercise 28.6.1 *Recall Exercise 28.2.2, in which we re-wrote* `any-compares?` *using* `any-satisfies?`. **Re-do** *this exercise using* `lambda` *in place of* `local`.

Solution: Instead of defining the `ok?` function `locally`, we'll define it without a name using `lambda`:

```
(define (any-compares? compare? num nums)
  (any-satisfies? (lambda (x) (compare? x num))
                  nums))
```

∎

Exercise 28.6.2 *For each function you've defined in this chapter using* `local` *to create a function to pass to a higher-order function,* **rewrite** *it using* `lambda` *instead. Is the result longer or shorter than the* `local` *version?*

A list of lists can be thought of as a two-dimensional table: the i, j element of the table is simply the j'th element of the i'th list.

Exercise 28.6.3 *Define a function* `multiplication-table` *that takes in a list of numbers and produces a two-dimensional table of multiplication results on those numbers: for example,*

```
(check-expect (multiplication-table (list 1 2 3 5))
              (list (list 1 2 3 5)
                    (list 2 4 6 10)
                    (list 3 6 9 15)
                    (list 5 10 15 25)))
```

Hint: You can write this in two or three lines, with no `locals` or recursive calls, by using `lambda` and functions that you've already written.

Exercise 28.6.4 *Explain how any expression using* `local` *definitions can be rewritten to use* `lambda` *instead.*

Hint: In a sense, this exercise asks you to write a function that takes in Racket expressions and produces Racket expressions. We haven't discussed how to do that in Racket yet, however, so for this exercise you may simply describe, in English, what you would do to an expression containing `local` to convert it into an equivalent expression containing `lambda`.

Exercise 28.6.5 *Explain how any expression using* `lambda` *can be rewritten to use* `local` *instead.*

Hint: See previous problem.

```
┌────────────────────────────────────────────────────────────────────┐
│                            SIDEBAR:                                  │
│                                                                      │
│  Some programming languages, like C++, have nothing corresponding    │
│  to lambda: there's no way to define a function without giving it a   │
│  name. In Java, it can be done using something called an "anonymous   │
│  inner class". Needless to say, the syntax is more complicated.       │
└────────────────────────────────────────────────────────────────────┘
```

28.7   Functions in variables

If *function* is a data type, along with *number*, *string*, and so on, we should be able to store functions in variables. For example, following Syntax Rule 4, we could write

```
(define cube (lambda (y) (* y y y)))
```

Then, since the variable cube's value is a function, we should be able to use it anywhere that we could use a function, *e.g.*

```
(check-expect (cube 3) 27)
(check-expect (do-to-each cube (list 1 3 5)) (list 1 27 125))
```

In other words, such a variable would act exactly as though we had used Syntax Rule 5 to define a function by that name. In fact, deep down inside DrRacket,

```
(define (cube y) (* y y y))
```

is *just an abbreviation*[1] for

```
(define cube (lambda (y) (* y y y)))
```

Recall Section 27.3, in which we defined a smallest function

```
(define (smallest nums)
  (local [(define (smaller a b) (cond [(<= a b) a] [else b]))]
    (cond [(empty? (rest nums)) (first nums)]
          [(cons? (rest nums))
           (smaller (first nums) (smallest (rest nums)))])))
```

One might object to this definition that it re-defines the smaller function each time smallest is called, a small but annoying inefficiency. But now that we know that defining a function is just an abbreviation for defining a variable whose value is a lambda expression, we can rewrite this:

```
(define   smallest
  (local [(define (smaller a b) (cond [(<= a b) a] [else b]))]
    (lambda (nums)
      (cond [(empty? (rest nums)) (first nums)]
            [(cons? (rest nums))
             (smaller (first nums)
                      (smallest (rest nums)))]))))
```

Rather than defining smaller inside the smallest function, we've defined it once, locally, for just long enough to build an anonymous function, then (outside the local) give it the name smallest.

This isn't an essential, earth-shaking change to the function definition. Remember this technique, though, because it'll make a big difference in Chapter 30.

Exercise 28.7.1 *Rewrite the* sort *function from Section 27.3 in this style, with the* local *outside the function body.*

28.8   Functions returning functions

Just as a function can *take in* functions as parameters, a function can also *return* a function as its result. For a simple (and unrealistic) example, suppose we needed functions add-2-to-each and add-3-to-each, which could be defined easily by

```
(define (add-2-to-each nums)
  (do-to-each (lambda (x) (+ x 2)) nums))
(define (add-3-to-each nums)
  (do-to-each (lambda (x) (+ x 3)) nums))
```

---

[1] A well-known programming textbook using Scheme (Racket's immediate ancestor), Abelson & Sussman's *Structure and Interpretation of Computer Programs* [ASS96], uses the latter notation from the beginning.

We've written two extremely similar `lambda`-expressions, which we could generalize into a function that takes in the 2 or the 3 and returns the function that will be passed to `do-to-each`.

Worked Exercise 28.8.1 *Define a function `make-adder` that takes in a number, and returns a function that adds that number to its one argument.*

Solution: The contract looks like

```
; make-adder :  number -> (number -> number)
```

How would we test this? It turns out that `check-expect` doesn't work very well on functions — how do you test whether two functions are the same, short of calling them both on *every possible input*? So we'll have to *apply* the result of `make-adder` to a number and see what it produces.

```
(define add2 (make-adder 2))
(define add5 (make-adder 5))
(check-expect (add2 4) 6)
(check-expect (add2 27) 29)
(check-expect (add5 4) 9)
(check-expect (add5 27) 32)
(check-expect ((make-adder 3) 2) 5)
```

Defining the function, however, is easy:

```
(define (make-adder num)
  ; num       number
  (lambda (x) (+ x num)))
```

or, if you prefer `local`,

```
(define (make-adder num)
  ; num       number
  (local [(define (addnum x) (+ x num))]
    addnum))
```

∎

Exercise 28.8.2 *Define a function `make-range` that takes in two numbers and returns a function that takes in a number and tells whether it's between those two numbers (inclusive, i.e. it can equal either of them). For example,*

```
(define teen?  (make-range 13 19))
(define two-digit?  (make-range 10 99))
(check-expect (teen?  12) false)
(check-expect (teen?  13) true)
(check-expect (teen?  16) true)
(check-expect (teen?  19) true)
(check-expect (teen?  22) false)
(check-expect (two-digit?  8) false)
(check-expect (two-digit?  10) true)
(check-expect (two-digit?  73) true)
(check-expect (two-digit?  99) true)
(check-expect (two-digit?  100) false)
(check-expect ((make-range 39 45) 38) false)
(check-expect ((make-range 39 45) 42) true)
```

Exercise 28.8.3 *Define a function* twice *that takes in a function with contract $X \to X$, and returns another function with the same contract formed by calling the given function on its own result. For example,*

```
(define add2 (twice add1))
(define fourth-root (twice sqrt))
(check-expect (add2 5) 7)
(check-expect (fourth-root 256) 4)
```

If you did Exercise 9.2.8, recall the definition of the function digits, *which tells how many digits long the decimal representation of an integer is. What does* (twice digits) *do?*

What does (twice twice) *do?*

Exercise 28.8.4 *Define a function* iterate *that takes in a whole number and a function with contract $X \to X$, and returns a function that applies the specified function the specified number of times. For example,*

```
(define add5 (iterate 5 add1))
(check-expect (add5 17) 22)
(define eighth-root (iterate 3 sqrt))
(check-expect (eighth-root 256) 2)
```

Note that the twice *function above is a special case of* iterate:

```
(define (twice f) (iterate 2 f))
```

What does (iterate 3 twice) *do?*

In solving problems 28.8.3 and 28.8.4, you needed to define a new function as the *composition* of two existing functions (that is, one function applied to the result of another). This is such a common operation that Racket gives you a built-in function to do it:

```
; compose :  (Y -> Z) (X -> Y) -> (X -> Z)
```

For example,

```
(define f (compose sqr add1))
(check-expect (f 0) 1)
(check-expect (f 1) 4)
(check-expect (f 2) 9)
```

Exercise 28.8.5 *Rewrite the* `twice` *function of Exercise 28.8.3 using* `compose`.

Exercise 28.8.6 *Rewrite the* `iterate` *function of Exercise 28.8.4 using* `compose`.

SIDEBAR:

The Java language technically doesn't allow you to create, return, or pass functions
as values, but you can create, return, or pass "objects" that have functions associated
with them, which gives you the same power with more complicated syntax. However,
although you can create functions while the program is running, you have to specify
their *contracts* (which Java calls "interfaces") in advance, while writing the program;
you can't decide at run-time what contract the new function should have.

28.9   Sequences and series

Mathematicians often work with *sequences* of numbers. A *sequence* can be defined as a
function from whole numbers to numbers. For example, the sequence of even numbers can
be written $0, 2, 4, 6, 8, \ldots$ or, thinking of it as a function, as `(lambda (n) (* 2 n))`. Thus
one could write

```
(define evens (lambda (n) (* 2 n)))
```

Exercise 28.9.1 *Develop a function* `take` *which, given a whole number n and a sequence, produces a list of the first n values of that sequence. For example,*

```
(check-expect (take 5 evens) (list 0 2 4 6 8))
```

*This function will make it much easier to write test cases for functions that return se-
quences!*

Exercise 28.9.2 *Develop a function* `arithmetic-sequence` *which, given two numbers*
`initial` *and* `difference`, *produces the "arithmetic sequence" starting at* `initial` *and
increasing by* `difference` *at each step. For example,*

```
(define evens (arithmetic-sequence 0 2))
(define odds (arithmetic-sequence 1 2))
(define ends-in-3 (arithmetic-sequence 3 10))
(check-expect (take 5 evens) (list 0 2 4 6 8))
(check-expect (take 6 odds) (list 1 3 5 7 9 11))
(check-expect (take 5 ends-in-3) (list 3 13 23 33 43))
```

Exercise 28.9.3 *Develop a function* `geometric-sequence` *which, given two numbers*
`initial` *and* `ratio`, *produces the "geometric sequence" starting at* `initial` *and growing
by a factor of* `ratio` *at each step.*

Exercise 28.9.4 *Develop a function* `constant-sequence` *that takes in a number and
produces a sequence that always has that value.*

   (You can write this from scratch with `lambda`, *or by re-using a previously-written function.)*

Exercise 28.9.5 *Define a variable* whose value is the "harmonic sequence": 1, 1/2, 1/3, 1/4, 1/5, ...

Exercise 28.9.6 *Define a variable* `wholes` *whose value is the sequence of whole numbers.*

Hint: You can do this in three words, with no `local` and no `lambda`.

Exercise 28.9.7 *Develop a function* `scale-sequence` *which, given a number and a sequence, returns a sequence whose elements are that number times the corresponding element of the original sequence.*

Exercise 28.9.8 *Develop a function* `add-sequences` *which, given two sequences, returns a sequence whose n-th element is the n-th element of one sequence plus the n-th element of the other.*

Exercise 28.9.9 *Develop a function* `subtract-sequences` *which, given two sequences, returns a sequence whose n-th element is the n-th element of the first sequence minus the n-th element of the second.*

Exercise 28.9.10 *Develop a function* `mult-sequences` *which, given two sequences, returns a sequence whose n-th element is the product of the n-th elements of the two sequences.*

Exercise 28.9.11 *Develop a function* `div-sequences` *which, given two sequences, returns a sequence whose n-th element is the n-th element of the first sequence divided by the n-th element of the second.*

Note: If the second sequence is ever 0, the resulting "sequence" won't be defined on all whole numbers.

Exercise 28.9.12 *Develop a function* `shift-sequence` *which, given an integer number d and a sequence, returns a sequence whose n-th element is the n + d-th element of the given sequence. For example,*

```
(define positive-evens (shift-sequence 1 evens))
(check-expect (take 5 positive-evens) (list 2 4 6 8 10))
```

Note: If the integer is negative, the result may not technically qualify as a "sequence", because it may not be defined on all whole numbers.

Exercise 28.9.13 *Develop a function* `patch` *which, given two numbers n and x and a sequence, produces a sequence exactly like the given sequence except that it returns x on input n. (In other words, you've "patched" the sequence by changing its value at one particular input.)*

Exercise 28.9.14 *Develop a function* `differences` *which, given a sequence, returns its sequence of differences: element 1 minus element 0, element 2 minus element 1, element 3 minus element 2, . . .*

(You can write this from scratch, but try writing it by re-using some of the above functions instead.)

Exercise 28.9.15 *Develop a function* `partial-sum` *which, given a sequence, returns its sequence of partial sums. The n-th element of the sequence of partial sums is the sum of elements 0 through n − 1 of the original sequence. For example,*

```
(define sum-of-wholes (partial-sum wholes))
(check-expect (take 5 sum-of-wholes) (list 0 1 3 6 10))
(define sum-of-odds (partial-sum odds))
```

What does `sum-of-odds` *do? Why?*

Define a variable to hold the sequence of partial sums of (geometric-sequence 1 1/2), *and play with it. What can you say about its value?*

Exercise 28.9.16 *Define a variable* `fact` *to hold the sequence* $1, 1, 2, 6, 24, 120, \ldots$ *of factorials.*

(Obviously, you can do this from scratch using recursion. But try doing it by using operations on sequences, like the above.)

Many important mathematical functions can't be computed exactly by a few additions or multiplications, but are instead *approximated* by adding up the first entries of a particular sequence of numbers; the more entries you add up, the closer the approximation. These are called *Taylor series*. For example, e^x can be computed by the series

$$e^x = \sum_{n=0}^{\infty} \frac{x^n}{n!)}$$

where $n!$ is the usual mathematical notation for (`factorial n`) from exercise 24.1.8. In other words,

$$e^x = \frac{x^0}{1} + \frac{x^1}{1} + \frac{x^2}{2} + \frac{x^3}{6} + \frac{x^4}{24} + \ldots$$

Exercise 28.9.17 *Develop a function* `e-to-the` *that takes in a number x and returns the sequence of partial sums of this series.*

Theoretically, $e^x \cdot e^{-x}$ *should be exactly 1 for all values of x. So you can test an approximation's accuracy by multiplying these two and comparing with 1.* **Define** *a function* `exp-error` *that takes in the value of x and the number of terms of the series to use, multiplies the approximations of* e^x *and* e^{-x}, *and tells how far this is from 1.*

How many steps does it take to get within 0.1? Within 0.01? Within 0.001? Within 0.000001?

The built-in Racket function `exp` *computes* e^x. *Compare* (e-to-the x) *with* (exp x) *for various positive and negative values of x, looking in particular at how many steps it takes to get to various levels of accuracy.*

Exercise 28.9.18 *The trigonometric function* $\sin(x)$ *has the Taylor series*

$$\sin(x) = \sum_{n=0}^{\infty} (-1)^n \cdot \frac{x^{2n+1}}{(2n+1)!}$$

That is,

$$\sin(x) = \frac{x}{1} - \frac{x^3}{6} + \frac{x^5}{120} - \frac{x^7}{5040} + \ldots$$

Develop a function `taylor-sine` *that takes in a number* x *and returns the sequence of partial sums of this series. (Again, I did this by using previously-defined operations on sequences.)*

Compare `(taylor-sine x)` *with* `(sin x)` *for various positive and negative values of* x, *looking at how many steps it takes to get to various levels of accuracy.*

Exercise 28.9.19 *Did you ever wonder how people discovered that* π *was about 3.14159? There are various series that compute* π, *of which the simplest and best-known is*

$$\pi = \sum_{n=0}^{\infty} (-1)^n \cdot \frac{4}{2n+1}$$

In other words,

$$\pi = \frac{4}{1} - \frac{4}{3} + \frac{4}{5} - \frac{4}{7} + \ldots$$

Define the variable `my-pi` *to be the sequence of partial sums of this series. (You can do this from scratch, of course, but try doing it by using previously-defined sequences and operations on sequences.)*

Compare `my-pi` *with the built-in Racket variable* `pi`. *How many steps does it take to get to various levels of accuracy?*

28.10 Review of important words and concepts

Racket treats *function* as a data type, just like *number* or *string* or *list*. One can write a function that takes in, or returns, a function just as easily as one can write functions working on other data types (although it's a bit harder to write test cases). This technique allows a programmer to write, test, and debug a single *general* function that covers the functionality of many others, thus saving enormous amounts of programming time on re-inventing the wheel. Some other languages allow you to do this too — for example, some of this can be done in Java and C++ — but the syntax is usually more complicated and confusing.

Racket also allows a programmer to construct functions "on the fly", just in time to pass them as arguments to other functions, without bothering to name them. Again, some other languages allow this — including Java, but not C++ — but the syntax is more complicated and confusing.

28.11 Reference: higher-order and anonymous functions

This chapter introduced Syntax Rule 9, which constructs an anonymous function using **lambda** and returns it.

It also introduced several predefined (mostly) higher-order functions:

- `identity`
- `filter`
- `map`
- `build-list`
- `foldl`
- `foldr`

Chapter 29

Input, output, and sequence

For this chapter, **switch languages** in DrRacket to "Advanced Student Language".

In the real world, we don't usually give a computer *all* the information it needs, all at once, and then ask it to go off and produce an answer. More often, we start a program and engage in a *dialogue* with it. For example, a word-processing program shows us the current state of the document; we tell it to add, delete, or move some more words, the program shows us the result, we request some more changes, and so on. We've seen some ways to *interact* with a computer program through animations and event handlers, and in this chapter we'll see another (more old-fashioned, but still useful) approach to interaction.

In an animation, the program typically goes on running all the time, but responds whenever we move or click the mouse, type a key, *etc.* In some problems, however, the program *can't go on* until it gets some information from the user. A familiar (if unpleasant) example are the dialogue boxes that pop up on your screen saying basically "something went wrong; should I try again, or give up?"

Here's another example. Suppose you were a mathematician who wanted a list of prime numbers. Of course, there are infinitely many prime numbers, so if you wrote a program to produce a list of *all* of them, it would never finish and you would never see any results at all. A more useful approach would be for the program to show you a prime number, then another, then another, and so on until you told it to stop.

Even a program that will eventually stop may need to show you some information along the way, then do some more computation, show you some more information, and so on. Of course, you can do this with an animation, but that seems like overkill for information that's basically textual.

But first, we'll introduce another data type, which has actually been available to us all along, but we haven't needed it until this chapter.

29.1   The symbol data type

Racket has a built-in type called *symbol* which behaves, in some ways, like *string*. The most obvious difference is the spelling rules: a symbol literal starts with an apostrophe and does *not* end with an apostrophe, but rather at the next space, parenthesis, *etc*. As a result, a symbol literal *cannot contain* spaces, parentheses, and certain other punctuation marks. Indeed, the spelling rules for symbol literals are basically the same as those for variable names and function names, except for the apostrophe at the beginning. (You've actually seen these before: the first argument to `error` is normally the name of the function that found the problem, as a symbol.)

Like image literals, string literals, number literals, and boolean literals, a symbol literal evaluates to itself; it doesn't "stand for" anything else:

```
(check-expect 'blah 'blah)
(check-expect 'this-is-a-long-name 'this-is-a-long-name)
```

The most common operation on symbols is to test whether two of them are equal, using the `symbol=?` function, which works analogously to the `string=?` function:

```
(check-expect (symbol=?  'blah 'snark) false)
(check-expect (symbol=?  'blah 'blah) true)
(define author 'Bloch)
(check-expect (symbol=?  author 'Hemingway) false)
(check-expect (symbol=?  author 'Bloch) true)
```

And as with all the other types we've seen, there's a built-in function to test whether something *is* a symbol, named (not surprisingly) `symbol?`. It works exactly as you would expect, by analogy with `number?`, `image?`, `posn?`, *etc*.

Unlike strings, symbols are not thought of as made up of individual characters strung together. A symbol is *atomic*, in the original sense of that word as meaning "not made up of smaller parts". So there is no `symbol-length` or `symbol-append` function analogous to `string-length` and `string-append`. And symbols have no *ordering*, so there's nothing analogous to `string<?` and its friends: two symbols are either the same or different, and that's all you can say about them.

In exchange for these restrictions, computations on symbols are typically a little faster than those on strings. However, this by itself wouldn't be enough reason to introduce them in this course. I'm mentioning them here because the built-in input and output functions treat symbols a little differently from strings.

Exercise 29.1.1 *Modify the* `choose-picture` *function of Exercise 15.3.1 so it takes in a symbol rather than a string as its parameter, e.g.* `'baseball`, `'basketball`, `'Monopoly`.

Incidentally, the image functions that take in a color name (`circle`, `rectangle`, `triangle`, *etc*.) also accept the corresponding symbols: `'red`, `'orange`, `'purple`, `'black`, *etc*..

Exercise 29.1.2 *Develop a function named* `random-color` *that takes in a "dummy" argument and ignores it, but returns one of the symbols* `'red`, `'orange`, `'yellow`, `'green`, `'blue`, `'purple` *chosen at random.*

Exercise 29.1.3 *Develop a function named* `different-color` *that takes in a color name as a symbol, and returns a different color name, also as a symbol. Which input color goes with which output color is up to you, as long as the result is always different from the input.*

Hint: DrRacket knows a *lot* of color names. You could try to write a `cond` with dozens or hundreds of cases, but that would be horrible, and it would no longer work if somebody added one more color name to Racket. Instead, think about how you can satisfy the requirements of the problem without knowing all the possible colors.

Exercise 29.1.4 *Modify exercise 17.1.1 so it uses symbols rather than strings as the model.*

29.2 Console output

Racket has a built-in function named `display` that does simple textual output.

```
; display :  object -> nothing, but displays the object.
```

Practice Exercise 29.2.1 *Try typing each of the following lines in the Interactions pane:*

```
(display 5)
(display "this is a string")
(display 'this-is-a-symbol)
(display (make-posn 3 4))
(display (list "a" "b" "c"))
(display (triangle 20 "solid" "blue"))
```

SIDEBAR:

Another built-in function, `write`, acts like `display`, but shows strings with double-quotes around them, so you can easily tell the difference between a string and a symbol.

So far this doesn't look very exciting. If anything, it's *less* useful than what we've been doing up until now, because you can't use the result of `display` in another expression:

```
(+ 1 (display 2))
```

produces an error message because `display` doesn't return anything.

The `display` function becomes much more useful if we *build* something for it to display from smaller pieces. For example,

Worked Exercise 29.2.2 *Develop a function* `display-with-label` *that takes in a string (the "label") and an object, and prints the string followed by the object.*

Solution: The contract is

```
; display-with-label :  string object -> nothing
; Prints the string and the object.
```

A more-or-less realistic test case is

```
(define my-age 46)
(display-with-label "Age:   " my-age)
"should print" "Age:  46"
```

Make up some more test cases.

The skeleton and inventory are straightforward:

```
(define (display-with-label label thing)
  ; label     a string
  ; thing     an object of some kind
  ...
  )
```

We could easily display just the label, or just the thing (since display takes in *any* data type), but how can we combine them?

Recall the format function (first mentioned in Chapter 19), which is designed to build complex strings from a "template" with values filled in in various places, returning a string. Conveniently enough, each of the "values to fill in" can be of almost any data type. So we could try

```
(define (display-with-label label thing)
  ; label     a string
  ; thing     an object of some kind
  (display (format "~s~s" label thing))
  )
```

Try this on the example above, and it prints

```
"Age:   "46
```

Not bad, but the quotation marks are annoying. Fortunately, format has different "formatting codes": ~s shows strings *with* their quotation marks, and ~a shows strings *without* their quotation marks. (The main reason to use ~s is to allow the user to tell the difference between strings and symbols.) So

```
(define (display-with-label label thing)
  ; label     a string
  ; thing     an object of some kind
  (display (format   "~a~a" label thing))
  )
```

produces a better result:

```
Age:   46
```

This combination of format and display is common enough that Racket has a built-in function to do it: the printf function acts just like calling display on the result of format, so we could write the definition more briefly as

```
(define (display-with-label label thing)
  ; label     a string
  ; thing     an object of some kind
  (printf  "~a~a" label thing)
  )
```

■

> **SIDEBAR:**
>
> The `display` and `write` functions can indeed take in just about any data type, including images. However, `format`'s job is to build a string, and strings cannot contain images, so if you try `format` on an image, you'll get weird results.

Testing functions that use console output

How can we write test cases for a function like `display-with-label` that uses `display` or `write`? `check-expect` looks at the result *returned* by a function, but `display` and `write` don't return anything!

In Exercise 29.2.2, we used the "should be" approach. But as we already know, automated testing using `check-expect` is *much* more convenient. If only we could find out what the function printed, and compare it with a known right answer...

As it happens, there's a built-in function named `with-output-to-string` to do this: it evaluates an expression of your choice (presumably containing `display` or `write`), but *captures* whatever that expression tries to write, and puts it into a string instead; you can then check whether this string is what you expected with `check-expect`.

Its contract may seem a little strange at first:

```
; with-output-to-string :  (nothing -> anything) -> string
```

That is, you give it a *function of no parameters*; it calls this function, throws away any result it produces, and returns a string constructed from whatever the function `display`ed.

Worked Exercise 29.2.3 *Write automated test cases for Exercise 29.2.2.*

Solution: We need a function of no arguments to pass into `with-output-to-string`. We could write one for each test case:

```
(define age 46)
(define last-name "Bloch")
(define (test-case-1) (display-with-label "Age:  " age))
(define (test-case-2) (display-with-label "Name:  " last-name))
(check-expect (with-output-to-string test-case-1) "Age:  46")
(check-expect (with-output-to-string test-case-2) "Name:  Bloch")
```

This seems silly. We can define the functions more simply using `lambda`:

```
(define age 46)
(define last-name "Bloch")
(check-expect
  (with-output-to-string
    (lambda () (display-with-label "Age:" age)))
  "Age:  46")
(check-expect
  (with-output-to-string
    (lambda () (display-with-label "Name:  " last-name)))
  "Name:  Bloch")
```

Functions of no arguments can be thought of as a way to pass around expressions without evaluating them until later. They come up often enough in Racket that they have a special name: they're called **thunks**.

Exercise 29.2.4 *Recall the struct definition*

```
; An employee has a string (name) and two numbers (id and salary).
(define-struct employee [name id salary])
```

Develop a function `print-employee` *that takes in an employee and returns nothing, but prints out the information about the employee, nicely formatted. For example,*

```
(print-employee (make-employee "Joe" 17 54000))
"should print" "Joe, employee #17, earns $54000/year"
```

29.3   Sequential programming

When you evaluate an expression like `(+ (* 3 4) (* 5 6))`, Racket needs to compute both $3 \cdot 4$ and $5 \cdot 6$, then add them. It doesn't really matter which of the two multiplications it does *first*, as long as it knows both answers before it tries to add them.

But `display` and `write` don't produce "answers", they produce *side effects*, and it matters very much which of two `display` expressions happens first. Racket has a syntax rule to specify doing things in a particular order:

Syntax Rule 10 *(begin expr1 expr2 ...exprn) is an expression. To evaluate it, Dr-Racket evaluates each of the exprs in order, throwing away any results they produce except the last one, which it returns.*

For example, type the following into the Interactions pane:

```
(define result
  (begin
    (display (+ 12 5))
    (* 5 3)))
result
```

It prints out the number 17, but gives `result` the value 15.

Now let's try that in the opposite order:

```
(define other-result
  (begin
    (* 5 3))
    (display (+ 12 5))))
other-result
```

This still prints out the number 17, but `other-result` has *no value at all* (because `display` doesn't return anything). The result of `(* 5 3)` has been thrown away completely.

Worked Exercise 29.3.1 *Rewrite the function* `display-with-label` *to use* `begin` *instead of* `format`.

Solution: The contract, test cases, skeleton, and inventory are exactly as before.

In the function body, clearly, we need to `display` both the label and the object:

```
(define (display-with-label label thing)
  ...
  (display label)
  ...
  (display thing)
  ...)
```

More specifically, we want to display the label *first, followed* by the thing. To do this, we'll use begin:

```
(define (display-with-label label thing)
  (begin
    (display label)
    (display thing)
  ) )
```

∎

Controlling lines

Sometimes you need to specify that the output should be on more than one line. There are several ways to do this:

- Use the built-in function

  ```
  ; newline :  nothing -> nothing
  ; advances the display to the next line
  ```

  in between displays in a begin, *e.g.*

  ```
  > (begin (display "abc")
           (newline)
           (display "def"))
  abc
  def
  ```

- Hit ENTER in the middle of a quoted string, *e.g.*

  ```
  > (display "abc
  def")
  abc
  def
  ```

- Some languages don't allow you to do this, so they use a third approach instead: you can put the special character \n in the middle of a quoted string to indicate a "new line":

  ```
  > (display "abc\ndef")
  abc
  def
  ```

Notice that all three produced the exact same output; which one you use is largely a matter of personal taste.

Worked Exercise 29.3.2 *Modify* the `print-employee` *function to display its informa-tion on three separate lines,* e.g.

```
Joe
Employee #17
$54000/year
```

Solution: The contract, skeleton, and inventory are unchanged, but we'll need to modify the test cases. Here are two versions; either one should work.

```
(check-expect
  (with-output-to-string
    (lambda () (print-employee (make-employee "Joe" 17 54000))))
  "Joe\nEmployee #17\n$54000/year")

(check-expect
  (with-output-to-string
    (lambda () (print-employee (make-employee "Joe" 17 54000))))
  "Joe
Employee #17
$54000/year")
```

Next, we'll need to modify the function body. This can be done in any of several ways:

```
(begin
  (display (employee-name emp))
  (newline)
  (display "Employee #")
  (display (employee-id emp))
  (newline)
  (display "$")
  (display (employee-salary emp))
  (display "/year"))
```

```
(begin
  (display (employee-name emp))
  (display "
Employee #")
  (display (employee-id emp))
  (display "
$")
  (display (employee-salary emp))
  (display "/year"))
```

```
(begin
  (display (employee-name emp))
  (display "\nEmployee #")
  (display (employee-id emp))
  (display "\n$")
  (display (employee-salary emp))
  (display "/year"))
```

```
(printf "~a
Employee #~a
~a/year"
   (employee-name emp)
   (employee-id emp)
   (employee-salary emp))
```

```
(printf "~a\nEmployee #~a\n~a/year"
   (employee-name emp)
   (employee-id emp)
   (employee-salary emp))
```

Any of these five solutions should work; which one you use is largely a matter of personal taste. ∎

Exercise 29.3.3 *Develop a function* `try` *that takes in a string (function-name), a function of one argument, and a value for that argument. It should print that it is "about to call" the function name on the specified argument, then call the function, then print that it has "returned from " the function and what the result was, and finally return that result. For example,*

```
(try "cube" cube 5)
```

should print out

```
About to call (cube 5)
Returned from (cube 5) with result 125
```

and finally return the result 125. For another example,

```
(try "display" display "blah")
```

should print out

```
About to call (display "blah")
blah
Returned from (display "blah") with result
```

Exercise 29.3.4 *Develop a function* `count-down-display` *that takes in a whole number. It doesn't return anything, but displays the numbers from that number down to 0, one on each line, with "blastoff!" in place of the number 0. For example,*

```
> (count-down-display 5)
5
4
3
2
1
blastoff!
```

Exercise 29.3.5 *Modify exercise 21.7.10 by adding two buttons, labelled "save" and "load". If the user clicks the "save" button, the current image (not including the color palette, "save" and "load" buttons) will be stored in the file "current.png" with* save-image*; the image on the screen shouldn't change. If the user clicks the "load" button, the image on the screen should be replaced with the contents of "current.png" (although the color palette, "save" and "load" buttons should be unaffected).*

29.4 Console input

29.4.1 The read function

The opposite of `display`, in a sense, is the built-in function `read`.

```
; read :  nothing -> object
; waits for the user to type an expression, and returns it
```

Try typing `(read)` into the Interactions pane. You should see a box with a typing cursor in it. Type a number like 17 into the box, and hit ENTER; the `read` function will return 17.

Type `(read)` again, and type a quoted string like `"hello there"` (complete with the quotation marks) into the box; `read` will return that string.

What happens when you type `(read)` and type a couple of words like `this is a test` (*without* quotation marks) into the box?

What happens when you type `(read)` and type a parenthesized expression like `(+ 3 4)` into the box? What about `(+ 3 (* 4 5))`?

What happens when you type `(read)` and type a Boolean literal (`true` or `false`) into the box?

What happens when you type `(read)` and type a comment like `; this is a comment` into the box?

What happens when you type `(read)` and type a symbol like `'snark` (with its apostrophe) into the box?

SIDEBAR:

This last example should come out looking similar to a function call, but with the "function" being named `quote`. In fact, there *is* a `quote` function; play with it to find out what it does, then look it up in the Help Desk.

There's also a function `read-line` which reads a whole line of input as a single string, even if it has spaces, parentheses, *etc.* inside it. **Try it.**

29.4.2 Testing functions that use console input

It's harder to write test cases for a function that involves input: some information may be provided as arguments, but some will be provided as input. So we could write, essentially, an actor's script: I'll say this, the program should say that, I'll say something else, the program should reply with such-and-such.

But that's even more of a pain than using "should be". So there's a built-in function

```
; with-input-from-string :  string (nothing -> anything) -> anything
```

which calls the specified thunk, but any time it tries to read from the console, it actually gets input from the string instead. `with-input-from-string` returns whatever the thunk returns.

Worked Exercise 29.4.1 *Develop a function* ask *that takes in a string, prints it, waits for input, and returns that input.*

Solution: Contract:

```
; ask :  string -> object
; prints the string, waits for input, and returns it
```

Test cases, written as an "actor's script":

```
(ask "What is your name?)
; It prints "What is your name?".
; I type "Stephen" (without the quotation marks).
; It returns the symbol 'Stephen.
(define age (ask "How old are you?"))
; It prints "How old are you?".
; I type 46.
; It defines age to be 46.
```

Test cases, written using `check-expect` and `with-input-from-string`:

```
(check-expect
  (with-input-from-string "Stephen"
    (lambda () (ask "What is your name?")))
  'Stephen)
(define age
  (with-input-from-string "46"
    (lambda () (ask "How old are you?"))))
(check-expect age 46)
```

Definition:

```
(define (ask question)
  (begin
    (display question)
    (read)))
```

Remember that `begin` always returns the value of its *last* expression, which in this case is whatever `read` returns, which is whatever the user typed. ∎

Note: Even after your function has passed all its automated tests, it's probably a good idea to try a few tests in the Interactions pane, to make sure your program interacts with the user the way you want it to.

Worked Exercise 29.4.2 *Develop a function* greet-by-name *that takes no parameters, asks for your name, then displays "Hello, your-name-here!".*

Solution: Since this function takes keyboard input and *also* prints to the screen, we'll need *both* `with-input-from-string` and `with-output-to-string`:

```
(check-expect
  (with-output-to-string
    (lambda ()
      (with-input-from-string "Steve" greet-by-name)))
  "What's your name?Hello, Steve!")
```

This works, but it's a bit of a pain. The `with-io-strings` function combines the jobs of `with-input-from-string` and `with-output-to-string`; its contract is

```
; with-io-strings:  string thunk -> string
```

For example, the above test case could be rewritten as

```
(check-expect (with-io-strings "Steve" greet-by-name)
              "What's your name?Hello, Steve!")
```

I leave the rest of the definition as an exercise for the reader (and it's in the Help Desk documentation for `with-io-strings`). ∎

29.4.3   Exercises

Exercise 29.4.3 *Develop a function* `repeat-input` *that takes in a string (the "question"). It prints the question, waits for input, then prints the result twice, on separate lines, and returns nothing.*

Hint: You need to `read` only once, but use the result twice, so you'll need either a helper function or a `local`.

Exercise 29.4.4 *Develop a function* `ask-posn` *that takes in no arguments, asks the user for an x coordinate and a y coordinate, and creates and returns a* `posn` *with those coordinates.*

Hint: This one does *not* require `local`.

Exercise 29.4.5 *Modify exercise 29.3.5 so that when the user clicks the "load" or "save" button, the program asks you for a filename (using* `ask` *or something similar), then loads or saves that file rather than always using "current.png". You've now written a simple graphics editor.*

An optional nice feature would be to have "load", "save", "load from", and "save to" buttons: "load from" and "save to" should behave as above, but "load" and "save" will operate on the last filename you used.

Hint: You may want to use `read-line` rather than `read`, to avoid worrying about whether the input is treated as a symbol or a string, and to allow filenames to contain spaces.

29.5   Input streams

Many programs need to operate on a variable amount of information. We've seen how to do this with lists, but what if the information isn't provided in the form of a completed list?

Throughout this book, we've designed functions to correspond to the data type they take in. To handle a sequence of data coming from input, we'll need to describe it as a data type — an "input stream".

We've been using `read` to read information from the keyboard. But computer programs often read from files too: word processing documents, spreadsheets, image and music files, *etc.* Such files "feel" like lists: they're either empty or they have a sequence of finitely many objects. As you know, the end of a list is indicated by a special object named `empty`, which is recognized by the `empty?` function; similarly, the end of a file is indicated by a special object named `eof`, which is recognized by the `eof-object?` function.

While practicing with the `read` function, you may have noticed an `eof` button next to the input box. Clicking this button causes `read` to return an `eof` object, as though at the end of a file. (You'll also get an `eof` object if you read past the end of the string in `with-input-from-string`.)

The `read` function, in essence, returns the first object, or `eof`, from an input stream, and has the side effect of "advancing" the input stream so that the next call to `read` will return the next object in the stream. As a result, if we want to use the result more than once, we'll need to store it in a `local` variable.

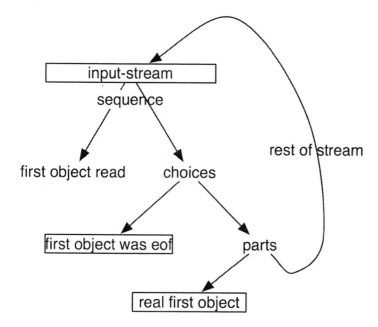

We can now write a function template for functions that operate on input streams.

```
#|
(define (function-on-input-stream)
  (local [(define obj (read))]
    (cond [(eof-object?  obj) ...]
          [else
            ; obj                    non-eof object
            ; (function-on-input-stream) whatever this returns
            ...
    )))
|#
```

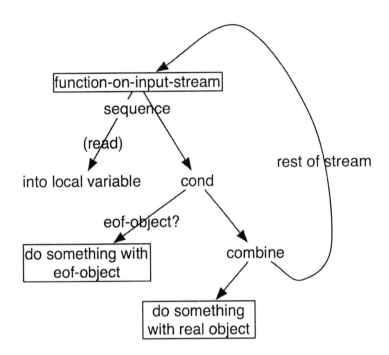

Worked Exercise 29.5.1 *Develop a function* add-from-input *which asks the user for a sequence of numbers, one at a time, terminated by* eof, *and returns their sum.*

Solution: The function takes no parameters, but reads from input and returns a number.

```
; add-from-input :   nothing -> number
; (reads zero or more numbers from input, terminated by eof)
```

We'll need several test cases. As with lists, we'll need an empty test case, and a one-element test case, and a more complicated test case. The function assumes that the inputs *are* numbers, so we don't need test cases with non-numbers.

First, I'll write them in the form of an "actor's script":

```
(add-from-input)
; It asks for a number.
; I hit the EOF button.
; It should return 0.
(add-from-input)
; It asks for a number.
; I type 7.
; It asks for a number.
; I hit the EOF.
; It should return 7.
(add-from-input)
; It asks for a number; I type 7.
; It asks for a number; I type -3.
; It asks for a number; I type 6.
; It asks for a number; I hit EOF.
; It should return 10.
```

But it's easier to run the test cases if we automate them with `check-expect`. Conveniently, `add-from-input` is *already* a thunk, so we don't need to wrap it up in a `lambda`:

```
(check-expect (with-input-from-string "" add-from-input)
              0)
(check-expect (with-input-from-string "7" add-from-input)
              7)
(check-expect (with-input-from-string "7 -3 6" add-from-input)
              10)
```

The template gives us a good deal of the definition:

```
(define (  add-from-input )
  (local [(define obj (read))]
    (cond [(eof-object?  obj)   0 ]
          [else
            ; obj                      number
            ; (add-from-input)         number
            ...
    )))
```

But this doesn't actually "ask" for numbers; to do this, let's replace the call to `read` with a call to `ask`. The only other thing left to do is add the two numbers:

```
(define (add-from-input)
  (local [(define obj  (ask "Next number?") )]
    (cond [(eof-object?  obj) 0]
          [else
            ; obj                      number
            ; (add-from-input)         number
            (+ obj (add-from-input))
    )))
```

If we want to make the function more "idiotproof", we can change the contract to read a sequence of *objects* rather than *numbers*, and have the function signal an error in that case.

```
(check-error (with-input-from-string "7 eight 9" add-from-input)
             "add-from-input:  That's not a number!")
...
(define (add-from-input)
  (local [(define obj  (ask "Next number?") )]
    (cond [(eof-object?  obj) 0]
          [(number?  obj)
            (+ obj (add-from-input))
          [else
            (error 'add-from-input "That's not a number!")
    )))
```

■

Exercise 29.5.2 *Develop a function* `read-objects` *which asks the user for a sequence of objects, terminated by* `eof`, *and returns a* list *of those objects, in the order that they were typed in.*

Exercise 29.5.3 *Develop a function* `read-objects-until` *which takes in an object (which we'll call the "terminator") and acts just like* `read-objects` *above except that it stops when it gets either the* `eof` *object or the "terminator".*

For example, suppose I type `(read-objects-until 'quit)`.
It asks me for an object; I type 3.
It asks me for an object; I type snark.
It asks me for an object; I type quit.
It returns the list `(list 3 snark)`.

Hint: Since you don't know what type the terminator object will be, you'll need `equal?`.

Exercise 29.5.4 *Develop a function* `echo` *which asks the user for a sequence of objects, terminated by* `eof`, *and displays each of them on a separate line, in the same order that they were typed in.*

Hint: You'll need `begin`.

29.6   Files

In the real world, programs read and write *files* at least as often as they read from the keyboard or write to the screen. There are predefined functions to make that easy:

```
; with-input-from-file :  string(filename) thunk -> anything
; Calls the thunk in such a way that if the thunk uses read or
; similar functions, it will read from the specified file instead
; of from the keyboard.
; Returns the result of the thunk.

; with-output-to-file :  string(filename) thunk -> anything
; Calls the thunk in such a way that if the thunk uses display,
; write, print, printf, etc., they will write to the specified file
; instead of to the screen.
```

Note: if you plan to write from a program into a file, and later read from the same file into a program, it's a good idea to use `write` rather than `display`; otherwise you may write out a string and read it in as a symbol. Also, `write` and `display` do a good job of showing images on the screen, but they don't know how to save an image to a file; if you need to store images in files, use `save-image` and `bitmap` instead.

Exercise 29.6.1 *Modify* *exercise 21.7.9 to add "save" and "load" buttons as in exercise 29.3.5, and optionally "save-to" and "load-from" buttons as in exercise 29.4.5. Note that when you save to a file and re-load later from the same file, the cursor position (as well as the contents) should be preserved. You've now written a very simple word processor.*

29.7 The World Wide Web

Another common source of information to programs is the World Wide Web. There's a predefined function that helps you get information from Web sites:

```
; with-input-from-url :  string thunk -> anything
; Calls the thunk in such a way that if it uses read or similar functions,
; they'll read from the specified Web page instead of from the keyboard.
```

For example,

```
(with-input-from-url "http://www.google.com" read-line)
```

will give you back the first line of the Google website (headers, HTML, Javascript, the whole works).

Of course, extracting really useful information from the Web requires recognizing the structure of an HTML or XML document. DrRacket comes with libraries to help with that, but they're beyond the scope of this book; look up "XML" in the Help Desk.

29.8 Review of important words and concepts

Historically, most programs have expected to "read" their input, either from a file or from the user's keyboard, and "write" their results, either to a file or in text form to the user's screen. In this chapter we've learned how to do that in (Advanced Student Language) Racket. These are our first examples of functions with *side effects* (almost: `define` and `define-struct` can be thought of as functions with side effects), and hence the first for which the *order of calling* functions makes a big difference. To tell Racket that we want to evaluate a series of expressions in order, not for their values but for their side effects, we use the `begin` form.

29.9   Reference: input, output, and sequence

In this chapter, we've seen the following new built-in functions:

- display

- write

- printf

- begin

- newline

- read

- read-line

- with-input-from-string

- with-output-to-string

- with-io-strings

- with-input-from-file

- with-output-to-file

- with-input-from-url

Chapter 30

Mutation

For this chapter, switch languages in DrRacket to "Advanced Student Language".

30.1 Remembering changes

Suppose you wanted to keep track of a grocery shopping list. You could easily define a variable to hold such a list:

```
> (define groceries (list "milk" "eggs" "chocolate" "cheese"))
```

And you know how to write functions that search the list, count elements in the list, do something to every element in the list ... but how do people *really* use shopping lists? At least in my house, there's a list stuck to the refrigerator. Every time I run out of an ingredient, or decide I need a particular ingredient for tomorrow's dinner, I add it to the list. The next time I go to the grocery store, I take the list with me, crossing things off the list as I put them in the cart. In other words, I'm *changing* the list all the time.

How would we do this in Racket? Well, we know how to add something to a list, sort of:

```
> (cons "broccoli" groceries)
(list "broccoli" "milk" "eggs" "chocolate" "cheese")
> groceries
(list "milk" "eggs" "chocolate" "cheese")
```

Notice that `cons` creates a new list one longer than the old one, but it doesn't change the old list.

For purposes of maintaining a shopping list, we'd really like a function that behaves like this:

```
> (add-grocery "broccoli")
> groceries
(list "broccoli" "milk" "eggs" "chocolate" "cheese")
> (add-grocery "cereal")
> groceries
(list "cereal" "broccoli" "milk" "eggs" "chocolate" "cheese")
```

In other words, we can find what's on the grocery list at any time by typing `groceries`, and we can *add* things to the list at any time by typing (add-grocery *ingredient*), which *changes the value* of the variable `groceries`.

So far, we haven't seen any way to do that in Racket. Here's how.

30.2 Mutating variable values

Syntax Rule 11   (set! *variable expression*)

is an expression with no value. It evaluates expression, *and then* changes *the already-defined variable* variable *to have that value. If* variable *isn't already defined, it's illegal.*

> SIDEBAR:
>
> The exclamation point is part of the function name; Racketeers usually pronounce it "bang", as in "I used set-bang to change the grocery list." Recall the convention that functions that return a boolean usually have names ending in a question mark ("?"). There's a similar convention that functions that *modify* one of their arguments have names that end in an exclamation point.

With this in mind, we can do things like
```
> (define groceries (list "milk" "eggs" "chocolate" "cheese"))
> groceries
(list "milk" "eggs" "chocolate" "cheese")
> (set! groceries (list "broccoli" "milk" "eggs" "chocolate" "cheese"))
> groceries
(list "broccoli" "milk" "eggs" "chocolate" "cheese")
```
Of course, re-typing the whole list just to add "broccoli" to the front is a pain. But here's the magic: set! evaluates the expression *before* changing the variable, and there's no rule against the expression containing the same variable. So realistically, we would probably write something like
```
> (define groceries (list "milk" "eggs" "chocolate" "cheese"))
> groceries
(list "milk" "eggs" "chocolate" "cheese")
> (set! groceries (cons "broccoli" groceries))
> groceries
(list "broccoli" "milk" "eggs" "chocolate" "cheese")
```
Even more realistically, we could write the **add-grocery** function as follows:

Worked Exercise 30.2.1 *Develop a function add-grocery that takes in a string and adds that string to the list groceries.*

Solution: The assignment doesn't say what the function should *return*, because we're really interested in it more for its side effects than for its return value. There are two reasonable choices: we could have it return nothing, or we could have it return the new list of groceries. Let's first try returning nothing.
```
; add-grocery : string -> nothing, but modifies groceries
```

How do we write test cases for such a function? Since it doesn't return anything, we can't use **check-expect** on the result of **add-grocery**. On the other hand, we need to be sure **add-grocery** is called *before* we look at **groceries**. This sounds like a job for **begin**:

```
(define groceries empty)
(check-expect (begin (add-grocery "cheese")
                     groceries)
              (list "cheese"))
(check-expect (begin (add-grocery "chocolate")
                     groceries)
              (list "chocolate" "cheese"))
(check-expect (begin (add-grocery "eggs")
                     groceries)
              (list "eggs" "chocolate" "cheese"))
```

The definition is easy, now that we know about set!:

```
(define (add-grocery item)
  (set! groceries (cons item groceries)))
```

∎

Worked Exercise 30.2.2 *Modify* the definition of **add-grocery** so it returns the new grocery list (as well as modifying **groceries**).

Solution: The contract changes to
; add-grocery : string -> list of strings, and modifies groceries

The test cases change too, since now codeadd-grocery is supposed to return something specific.

```
(define groceries empty)
(check-expect (add-grocery "cheese")
              (list "cheese"))
(check-expect groceries
              (list "cheese"))
(check-expect (add-grocery "chocolate")
              (list "chocolate" "cheese"))
(check-expect (add-grocery "eggs")
              (list "eggs" "chocolate" "cheese"))
(check-expect groceries
              (list "eggs" "chocolate" "cheese"))
```

The definition changes slightly:

```
(define (add-grocery item)
  (begin (set! groceries (cons item groceries))
         groceries))
```

∎

Exercise 30.2.3 *Define* the variable **age** to be your current age. *Develop* a function **birthday** that takes no arguments, increases **age** by 1, and returns your new age.

Exercise 30.2.4 *Develop* a function **buy-first** that takes no arguments, returns nothing, and removes the first element of **groceries** (as though you had bought it and crossed it off the list). If **groceries** is empty, it should throw an appropriate error message.

Exercise 30.2.5 *Develop a function* `lookup-grocery` *that takes in a string and tells whether that string appears in* `groceries`.

Write a bunch of test cases involving `add-grocery`, `buy-first`, *and* `lookup-grocery` *in various sequences. (For example, if you add a particular item, then look it up, you should get* `true`; *if you then buy the first item and look it up again, you should get* `false`.)

Hint: The function definition doesn't require `set!`.

Exercise 30.2.6 *Develop a function* `buy` *that takes in a string, returns nothing, and removes the specified string from* `groceries`. *If* `groceries` *is empty, or doesn't contain that string, it should throw an appropriate error message. If* `groceries` *contains more than one copy of the string, it should remove all of them.*

Write a bunch of test cases involving various combinations of `add-grocery`, `buy-first`, `buy`, *and* `lookup-grocery`.

Hint: The easiest way to write this function is to use non-mutating list functions to see whether the string appears in `groceries` and build the correct new grocery list, and then use `set!` to change the variable's value.

The functions `add-grocery`, `buy-first`, `lookup-grocery`, and `buy` illustrate a common situation in which we need mutation: when you want to provide *several functions* that share information (as well as needing to remember things from one call to the next).

Exercise 30.2.7 *Develop a function* `next` *that takes no arguments and returns how many times it has been called. For example,*

```
> (next)
1
> (next)
2
> (next)
3
```

Exercise 30.2.8 *Develop a function* `reset` *that resets the counter on* `next` *(see exercise 30.2.7) back to zero, and returns nothing. For example,*

```
> (next)
1
> (next)
2
> (next)
3
> (reset)
> (next)
1
```

Exercise 30.2.9 *Develop a function* `next-color` *that takes no arguments; each time you call it, it returns the next element in the list* (`list` `"red"` `"orange"` `"yellow"` `"green"` `"blue"` `"violet"`). *If you call it more than six times, it returns* `false`. *For example,*

```
> (next-color)
"red"
> (next-color)
"orange"
...
> (next-color)
"violet"
> (next-color)
false
```

30.3   Memoization

Recall Exercise 25.4.15, finding the longest sequence of characters that appear (in the same order) in two strings. In that exercise, you found a solution that works, but was probably fairly slow and inefficient. If you use the Stepper to watch what's going on in the execution of your function, you'll probably find that it's solving the exact same problem many times.

For another example of this, consider the Fibonacci function of Exercise 24.1.9. The "obvious" recursive definition works, but once n gets larger than about 20, it's surprisingly slow and inefficient. To illustrate this, let's change the test cases to use the `time` function, which displays how long it took to do something before returning the answer:

```
; fibonacci :  natural -> natural
(check-expect (time (fibonacci 0)) 1)
(check-expect (time (fibonacci 1)) 1)
(check-expect (time (fibonacci 2)) 2)
(check-expect (time (fibonacci 3)) 3)
(check-expect (time (fibonacci 4)) 5)
(check-expect (time (fibonacci 5)) 8)
(check-expect (time (fibonacci 6)) 13)
(check-expect (time (fibonacci 10)) 89)
(check-expect (time (fibonacci 15)) 987)
(check-expect (time (fibonacci 20)) 10946)
(check-expect (time (fibonacci 25)) 121393)
```

Exercise 30.3.1 *Tabulate how long the function takes on the above arguments.* **Predict** *approximately how long it will take on 30.* **Try it**.

To see what's going wrong, let's use the Stepper on a simple example like (`fibonacci 5`).

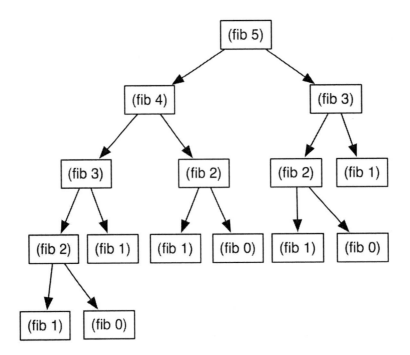

Notice that (fib 3) is called twice, (fib 2) three times, and (fib 1) five times. We're asking and answering the *exact same question* over and over.

We've seen something like this before: in Section 27.1 we had a function that called itself on the exact same question twice, and we made it much more efficient by using a local variable. Unfortunately, the fibonacci function doesn't call itself on the same question twice as "siblings" in the call tree, but rather as cousins, aunts, and more distant places in the call tree. So it's not clear how a local variable defined inside the function body could avoid this duplication. Instead, we'll need a more "global" solution.

Worked Exercise 30.3.2 *Modify the definition of* fibonacci *so it doesn't ask the same question over and over, and runs much faster.*

Solution: The contract and test cases are exactly the same as before; we're just trying to make things faster.

The idea of *memoization* is that once you answer a particular question, you *write down the answer* (a "memo to yourself") so the next time you are asked the same question, you can just return the same answer again rather than re-calculating it. Of course, this means every time you are asked a question, you first need to check whether you've been asked that question before. This calls for a mutable data structure to remember what we've been asked, and what the answer was last time.

One way to do this is to build up, in a global variable, a list of structures that each contain the question being asked and its answer.

```
; A pair has two natural numbers:  n and answer
(define-struct pair [n answer])
```

```
; *fibonacci-answers* is a list of pairs.
(define *fibonacci-answers* empty)
```

Every time `fibonacci` is called, it will start by looking in this global variable to see whether it already knows the answer; if so, it'll return it immediately. If not, it'll compute the answer as above, but before returning the answer, it will *record* the answer in the global variable.

```
(define (fibonacci n)
  (local [(define old-answer (lookup n *fibonacci-answers*))]
    (cond [(number? old-answer) old-answer]
          [(<= n 1) (record-and-return n 1)]
          [else (record-and-return n (+ (fibonacci (- n 1))
                                        (fibonacci (- n 2))))])))
```

This assumes we have two helper functions: a `lookup` function that looks in the table for a question and returns the answer, if known, or `false` if not; and a `record-and-return` function that takes in a question and its computed answer, adds that information to the table, and returns the answer. These are both easy:

```
; lookup :  nat-num(n) list-of-pairs -> nat-num or false
(check-expect (lookup 4 empty) false)
(check-expect (lookup 4 (list (make-pair 4 12))) 12)
(check-expect (lookup 4 (list (make-pair 3 12))) false)
(check-expect
  (lookup 4 (list (make-pair 5 3) (make-pair 4 12) (make-pair 3 2)))
  12)
(define (lookup n pairs)
  (cond [(empty? pairs) false]
        [(= n (pair-n (first pairs)))
         (pair-answer (first pairs))]
        [else (lookup n (rest pairs))]))
```

```
; record-and-return :  nat-num(n) nat-num(answer) -> nothing, but
;   modifies *fibonacci-answers*
(check-expect
  (begin (set! *fibonacci-answers*
               (list (make-pair 5 3) (make-pair 4 12) (make-pair 3 2)))
         (record-and-return 6 213))
  213)
(check-expect
  (begin (set! *fibonacci-answers*
               (list (make-pair 5 3) (make-pair 4 12) (make-pair 3 2)))
         (record-and-return 6 213)
         *fibonacci-answers*)
  (list (make-pair 6 213) (make-pair 5 3)
        (make-pair 4 12) (make-pair 3 2)))
(define (record-and-return n answer)
  (begin (set! *fibonacci-answers*
               (cons (make-pair n answer) *fibonacci-answers*))
         answer))
```

The resulting `fibonacci` function passes all the same tests as before, but much faster: on my old computer,

n	CPU time, simple version	CPU time, memoized version
10	4 ms	2 ms
15	40 ms	2 ms
20	366 ms	3 ms
25	4051 ms	4 ms

Exercise 30.3.3 *Let the mathematical function* fib3 *be as follows:*

- $fib3(0) = fib3(1) = fib3(2) = 1$

- $fib3(n) = fib3(n-1) + fib3(n-2) + fib3(n-3)$ *for* $n \geq 3$

Define a `fib3` *function in Racket, the obvious way without memoization.*
Define a `fib3-memo` *function in Racket, computing the same thing using memoization.*
Test that both functions produce the same answers on a variety of inputs.
Compare (e.g. using the `time` *function) the time it takes to compute each of the two. Try to predict how long it will take on a new input, and compare your prediction with the reality.*

Exercise 30.3.4 *Write a memoized version of the* `lcsubsequence` *function from Exercise 25.4.15. Run some timing tests: is it significantly faster?*

Hint: Since `lcsubsequence` takes *two* parameters rather than one, you'll need a table of structures that each have room for *both* parameters, as well as an answer.

Memoization and a closely-related technique called *dynamic programming* can sometimes turn an unacceptably-slow program into quite an efficient one; they're important techniques for professional programmers to know.

30.4   Static and dynamic scope

Recall the `add-grocery` function of Section 30.2. Suppose we called this inside a `local` definition of `groceries`:

```
(define groceries (list "milk" "eggs")) (define (add-grocery item)
  (begin (set!  groceries (cons item groceries))
         groceries))
...
(local [(define groceries (list "tuna"))]
       (add-grocery "chocolate"))
```

Here's a puzzle: without actually typing in the code and running it, try to predict what this expression returns.

The problem is that we have *two different variables* named `groceries`: the one defined at the top level, and the one defined in the `local`. This is perfectly legal: the one in the `local` temporarily hides the outer one, as we've seen before. But which one does `add-grocery` look at and change? Is it the variable that was in effect when `add-grocery` was *defined* (returning (list "chocolate" "milk" "eggs")), or the variable that's in effect when `add-grocery` is *called* (returning (list "chocolate" "tuna"))?

Different programming languages have made this subtle decision differently. The former (use the variable in effect at the time the function was *defined*) is called *static scope*, because it depends on where the function is defined in the program source code, which doesn't change while the program is running. The latter (use the variable in effect at the time the function was *used*) is called *dynamic scope*, because it depends on which function calls which as the program is running.

Racket uses static scope, as do most programming languages. But not all: some versions of the Lisp language, which is closely related to Racket, use dynamic scope. For purposes of this book, you only need to worry about static scope. **Functions use the variables in effect at the time they were defined.**

30.5 Encapsulating state

We've seen a number of functions that "remember" something from one call to the next by changing the value of a global variable. This is somewhat inelegant, and raises possible security issues: if some user mistakenly changed the value of that variable him/her-self, our function would no longer work correctly. It would be cleaner if the function had its own private variable that nobody else could see.

Fortunately, `local` is very good at creating private variables that can only be seen in one small part of the program.

Exercise 30.5.1 *Rewrite the* `next` *function of exercise 30.2.7 to not use a global variable.*

Hint: See section 28.7 for ideas.

Exercise 30.5.2 *Rewrite the* `next-color` *function of exercise 30.2.9 to not use a global variable.*

Exercise 30.5.3 *Rewrite the* `fibonacci` *function from exercise 30.3.2 to avoid using a global variable (or struct, for that matter).*

Hint: Remember that the `record-and-return` function refers to the table variable, so it needs to be defined inside the scope of that variable.

Exercise 30.5.4 *Rewrite the* `fib3` *function from exercise 30.3.3 to avoid using a global variable (or struct, for that matter).*

Exercise 30.5.5 *Develop a function* `make-lister` *that takes in a list, and returns a function like* `next-color`*: it takes no arguments, but each time you call it, it returns the next element in the list that was given to* `make-lister`*. If you run out of list elements, it returns* `false`*. For example,*

```
> (define next-bird (make-lister (list "robin" "bluejay" "crow")))
> (define next-day
  (make-lister (list "sun" "mon" "tues" "wed" "thurs" "fri" "sat")))
> (next-bird)
"robin"
> (next-day)
"sun"
> (next-day)
"mon"
> (next-bird)
"bluejay"
> (next-day)
"tues"
```

Note: Note that if make-lister is called several times, each of the resulting functions *must* have its own "memory"; you *can't* use a global variable, but *must* use the technique of section 28.7.

Exercise 30.5.6 *Rewrite the* lcsubsequence *function of exercise 30.3.4 to avoid using a global variable (or struct, for that matter).*

Note: This one *must* be done with its own private table, not a global variable, because the right answers to sub-problems would be different if somebody called the function again on different strings.

Exercise 30.5.7 *Develop a function* make-cyclic-lister *that takes in a list, and returns a function that lists its elements, but once it gets to the end, it starts over from the beginning rather than returning* false.

SIDEBAR:

The Java and C++ languages don't allow you to define a variable locally and then create a function that modifies it, but they give you another way to encapsulate state: a *class* with *private instance variables* and *public methods* that modify those instance variables.

Exercise 30.5.8 *Rewrite the definitions of* next *and* reset *so they don't use a global variable (but they still talk to one another).*

Hint: You've already rewritten next by itself, in exercise 30.5.1, but now there's a difficulty: you need to define *two* functions inside the scope of the local and give them both top-level names. One way to do this is to have the body of the local return a list of two functions, store this in a top-level variable, then define next as one element of this list and reset as the other element.

   The above solution has a couple of problems. First, it seems inelegant that we need to define a top-level variable in order to hold the list of two functions just so we can give them names. (One way around this is a Racket form named **define-values**, but that's not available in the Student languages.) Second, it's a fair amount of work just to build a resettable counter, and we'll have to do it all over again with different names if we want to build another.

Inspired by exercise 30.5.5, we might define a `make-counter` function that returns a two-element list of functions, the "next" and "reset" functions for this particular counter. That would solve the second problem, but not the first.

Another approach is to have `make-counter` return a function that serves both purposes. It takes in a string: if the string is `"next"`, it acts like `next`, and if it's `"reset"`, the function acts like `reset`. (If the string is anything else, it should produce an error message. And of course, if you'd prefer to use symbols rather than strings, that's fine, and slightly more efficient.) For example,

```
> (define count-a (make-counter))
> (define count-b (make-counter))
> (count-a "next")
1
> (count-a "next")
2
> (count-b "next")
1
> (count-a "next")
3
> (count-b "next")
2
> (count-a "reset")
> (count-a "next")
1
> (count-b "next")
3
```

SIDEBAR:

Languages such as Java and C++ have this technique built in; they call it "method dispatch". Now that you've seen how you could have done it by yourself, you may better appreciate having it built into the language.

Exercise 30.5.9 *Develop* this `make-counter` *function.*

Exercise 30.5.10 *Develop* a function `make-door` *that constructs a "door" object that represents whether a door is open or closed. A "door" object is a one-argument function:*

- *if the argument is "get-state", it returns the current state of the door, either "open" or "closed"*

- *if the argument is "open", it makes the state open, and returns nothing*

- *if the argument is "closed", it makes the state closed, and returns nothing*

- *if the argument is "toggle", it makes the state the opposite of what it was, and returns nothing.*

30.6   Mutating structures

When we learned about `define-struct` in chapter 21, we learned that certain functions "come for free": one constructor, one discriminator, and a getter for each field. In fact, another group of functions also "come for free": a *setter* for each field.

For example, you already know about `make-posn`, `posn?`, `posn-x`, and `posn-y`. There are also two other functions

```
; set-posn-x!  :  posn number -> nothing
; modifies the x coordinate of an existing posn
; set-posn-y!  :  posn number -> nothing
; modifies the y coordinate of an existing posn
```

Similarly, if you type

```
; An employee has a string (name) and two numbers (id and salary).
(define-struct employee [name id salary])
```

you get not only a constructor, a discriminator, and three getters, but also three setters:

```
; set-employee-name!  :  employee string -> nothing
; set-employee-id!  :  employee number -> nothing
; set-employee-salary!  :  employee number -> nothing
```

This has subtly different effects from `set!`. Consider

```
> (define joe (make-employee "joe" 386 80000))
> (define schmoe joe) ; two names for the same employee
> (define emps (list joe (make-employee "alice" 279 72000)))
> (set-employee-salary! joe 85000)
> (employee-salary joe) ; 85000
> (employee-salary schmoe) ; 85000
> (employee-salary (first emps)) ; 85000
```

By contrast, if we changed joe's salary with `set!`, the results would be different:

```
> (define joe (make-employee "joe" 386 80000))
> (define schmoe joe) ; two names for the same employee
> (define emps (list joe (make-employee "alice" 279 72000)))
> (set! joe (make-employee "joe" 386 85000))
> (employee-salary joe) ; 85000
> (employee-salary schmoe) ;  80000
> (employee-salary (first emps)) ;   80000
```

When we define `schmoe` to be `joe`, Racket now thinks of both variable names as referring to the same location in the computer's memory, so any change to the contents of that memory (as with `set-employee-salary!`) will be reflected in both. But (`set!` `joe` ...) tells Racket that the variable name `joe` should now refer to a different object in a different place in memory; `schmoe` still refers to the same thing it did before, and doesn't show a change.

Similarly, when we define `emps` to be a list containing `joe`, the list structure refers to the same location in memory that `joe` currently refers to. If `joe` is redefined to refer to something else, that doesn't change what the list refers to.

The phenomenon of two names referring to the same object in the computer's memory (rather than two objects with the same value) is called *aliasing*. We haven't had to worry about it until this chapter, because without setters and `set!`, there's no detectable difference between "two names for the same object" and "two objects with the same value". But professional programmers (in almost *any* language) have to worry about the difference.

Neither of these behaviors is inherently better than the other: sometimes you want one behavior and sometimes the other. The point is that before you write code that modifies things, you need to decide which of these behaviors you want.

Another interesting difference is that the first argument of `set!` *must* be a variable name:

```
(set!  (first emps) ...)
```

wouldn't make sense. However,

```
(set-employee-salary!  (first emps) ...)
```

makes perfectly good sense, and can be quite useful.

Worked Exercise 30.6.1 *Develop a function* `give-raise!` *that takes in an* `employee` *struct and a number (e.g. 0.10 for a 10% raise), and* modifies *the employee to earn that much more than before.*

Solution:

```
; give-raise!  :  employee number -> nothing, but modifies the employee
(define joe (make-employee "joe" 386 80000))
(define schmoe joe) ; two names for the same employee
(define emps (list joe (make-employee "alice" 279 72000)))
(give-raise!  joe 0.10)
(check-expect (employee-salary joe) 88000)
(check-expect (employee-salary schmoe) 88000)
(check-expect (employee-salary (first emps)) 88000)
(give-raise!  (second emps) 0.15)
(check-expect emps
              (list (make-employee "joe" 386 88000)
                    (make-employee "alice" 279 82800)))


(define (give-raise!  emp percentage)
    ; emp                     an employee
    ; percentage              a number
    ; (employee-name emp)     a string
    ; (employee-id emp)       a number
    ; (employee-salary emp)   a number
    (set-employee-salary!  emp
                        (* (+ 1 percentage) (employee-salary emp)))))
```

█

Exercise 30.6.2 *Develop a function* `change-name-to-match!` *that takes in two* `person` *structures and* modifies *the first one to have the same last name as the second. Any other variables or lists that already referred to the first person should now show the changed name.*

Exercise 30.6.3 *Develop a function* `flip-posn!` *that takes in a* `posn` *and* modifies *it by reversing its x and y coordinates.*

Hint: You may need a `local` for this.

Exercise 30.6.4 *Develop a function* `give-raises!` *that takes a list of* `employees` *and a number, and gives them all that percentage raise.*
    Develop a function `give-raises-up-to-100K!` *that takes a list of* `employees` *and a number, and gives that percentage raise to everybody who earns at most $100,000.*

Hint: It makes sense to do this with `map`, but `map` always returns a list of the same length as what it was given, even if the function it's calling doesn't return anything. So you may well get back a list of (`void`)'s: `void` is a built-in function that takes no arguments, does nothing with them, and returns nothing.
    If this bothers you, you could rewrite `give-raise!` so it returns the modified employee; then `give-raises!` will naturally return a list of all the modified employees. What will `give-raises-up-to-100K!` return? What do you *want* it to return?

Exercise 30.6.5 *Develop a function* `ask-and-give-raises` *that takes in a list of* `employees`. *For each one in turn, it prints the person's name and current salary, asks (via console I/O) how much percentage raise to give, and does so. It should return the list of all the employees with their new salaries.*

30.7 Review of important words and concepts

The `set!` form changes the value of a variable.

Some functions are terribly inefficient because they call themselves recursively more than once. In particular, functions that, in the course of a call tree, ask the exact same question several times can often be improved through a technique called *memoization*: maintain a table of known function answers, and start each function call by checking whether you've already computed the answer.

When a function needs to remember things in a variable (*e.g.* for memoization), it's often safer to define the variable locally, so that only that function can see them. We *encapsulate* the state of the program in this hidden variable. In some cases (*e.g.* `make-lister` and `lcsubsequence`) it's not just a matter of safety. In addition, when several different functions need to share the same state variable, sometimes the best solution is to encapsulate the information into a single function that performs several different tasks.

The `set!` form modifies a variable definition, but sometimes it's more useful to modify *part* of a data structure, leaving it in place so that all existing references to it show the change. This can be done using *setters*, functions that "come for free" with `define-struct`.

30.8 Reference: Built-in functions for mutation and assignment

This chapter introduced one new function (technically a special form): `set!` . It also introduced the family of *setter* functions: when you do a `define-struct`, you get not only a constructor, a discriminator, and a getter for each field, but also a setter for each field. These have names like `set-posn-x!`, `set-employee-salary!`, *etc.*

Chapter 31

Next Steps

There are lots of other things I'd like to discuss in this book, but I don't want it to get too long and expensive. So now that you've gotten this far, I'll suggest some other books to read next.

As I've mentioned before, much of this book is based on *How to Design Programs* [FFFK01]. I recommend getting that book (it's available on the Web for free at http://www.htdp.org) and reading the following chapters:

- 14-16 about binary and *n*-ary trees,

- 25-32 about "generative recursion" and "accumulative recursion", which enable you to do a number of things more easily than you could with the "structural recursion" we've used in this book

- 39-43 about object-oriented programming and how it works.

(Some of these chapters refer to an old "draw.ss" teachpack, which has since been replaced by the picturing-programs teachpack. Ignore the graphics parts of the book.)

As I write this, the authors of *How to Design Programs* are working on a second edition. It's not finished yet, but it should be good. Do a Web search on "htdp2e" and you'll find it.

If you want more exercises involving animation, see *How to Design Worlds* [FFF+08a], on the Web for free at http://world.cs.brown.edu.

If you want to learn Java, there are lots of good (and not-so-good) books on the market, but there's one that builds on what you've learned in this book: *How to Design Classes* [FFF+08b]. As I write this, *How to Design Classes* isn't finished, but you can find out about it and request a draft copy at http://www.ccs.neu.edu/home/vkp/HtDCH .

Racket comes with lots of powerful tools we haven't discussed. Most of these are documented in the Help Desk. Here are some that might interest you:

- The picturing-programs library allows you to write programs that run on several computers at once, communicating over a network. It takes a *client/server* approach: one computer (the "server") keeps track of information that all the computers share, and each "client" computer shows its own view of that shared information. This could be used, for example, to develop a multi-player game. To find out more about this, look up the 2htdp/universe module in the Help Desk, then look for the section entitled "The World is not Enough".

- Racket comes with a built-in Web server, with which you can easily write powerful, interactive Web applications. A Racket feature called *continuations*, which most languages don't have, makes it *much* easier to write Web programs. Open the Help Desk and follow the link "Continue: Web Applications in Racket".

- In this book, we've written "contracts" in comments. In fact, Racket allows you to write contracts as part of the code, and will automatically enforce them for you: look in the Help Desk for `define/contract` and `define-struct/contract`. Or open the Help Desk, follow the link "Guide: Racket" and look for the chapter on "Contracts".

- Modules allow you to break a large program into separate source files, each with a well-defined interface (in the same way that each individual function has a well-defined interface). Open the Help Desk, follow the link "Guide: Racket", and look for the chapter on "Modules".

- Racket supports class-based object-oriented programming, similar to classes in Java and C++ but more flexible. Open the Help Desk, follow the link "Guide: Racket", and look for the chapters on "Classes and Objects" and "Units".

- One of Racket's most powerful features is called "macros": they're basically functions which, rather than taking in and returning values, instead take in and return Racket code. They allow you to write functions that don't pre-evaluate their arguments (like `or`, `and`, `define`, and `define-struct`), and even completely change the syntax of the language. Most programming languages don't offer anything similar, so if you're trying to solve a problem that lends itself to macros, it may be *much* easier and simpler to solve in Racket than in most other languages. Open the Help Desk, follow the link "Guide: Racket", and look for the chapter on "Macros".

- If you want to write Racket programs that run on their own, without the user needing to know about DrRacket, open the "Guide: Racket"; first read the chapter on "Modules" (above) and then read the chapter on "Running and Creating Executables".

- The graphics and GUI programming we've been doing in this book are pretty simple: great for a beginning programming course, but if you want to do industrial-strength graphics programming, especially 3-D graphics, you'll need more flexibility. Open the Help Desk and look for the section on "GUI and Graphics Libraries".

Index

Bibliography

[ASS96]   Harold Abelson, Gerald Jay Sussman, and Julie Sussman. *Structure and Interpretation of Computer Programs.* McGraw-Hill, 1996.

[Bro95]   Frederick Brooks. *The Mythical Man-Month: Essays on Software Engineering, Anniversary Edition.* Addison-Wesley, 1995.

[FFF+08a]   Matthias Felleisen, Robert Bruce Findler, Kathi Fisler, Matthew Flatt, and Shriram Krishnamurthi. *How to Design Worlds: Imaginative Programming in DrScheme.* self-published on Web, http://world.cs.brown.edu, 2008.

[FFF+08b]   Matthias Felleisen, Robert Bruce Findler, Matthew Flatt, Kathryn Gray, Shriram Krishnamurthi, and Viera K. Proulx. How to design class hierarchies. In preparation, 2008.

[FFFK01]   Matthias Felleisen, Robert Bruce Findler, Matthew Flatt, and Shriram Krishnamurthi. *How to Design Programs: an Introduction to Programming and Computing.* MIT Press, 2001. See http://www.htdp.org.

[Mil56]   George A. Miller. The magical number seven, plus or minus two: Some limits on our capacity for processing information. *The Psychological Review*, 63:81–97, 1956.

[Par72]   D. L. Parnas. On the criteria to be used in decomposing systems into modules. *Communications of the Association for Computing Machinery*, 15(12):1053–1058, Dec 1972.

CPSIA information can be obtained at www.ICGtesting.com
Printed in the USA
241380LV00001B/78/P

9 781848 900158